Pyrosketchology: An Illustrated Guide to Nature Journaling about the Fire Environment

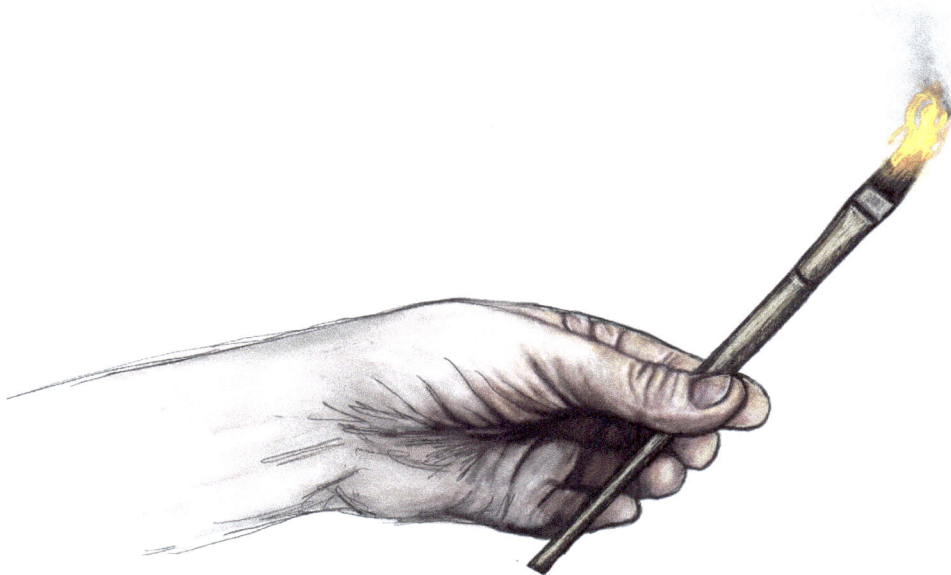

Written and Illustrated by
Miriam H Morrill

Cover Art and Book Illustrations by Miriam Morrill

Published by Morrill Intentions Press

979-8-9901071-0-6

Table of Contents

Chapter 8: Fire & Smoke

Chapter 9: Fire Severity & Effects

Chapter 10: Fire Regimes

Chapter 11: Getting Started

References

Acknowledgements

About the Author

Chapter 1: Pyrosketchology Introduction

Pyrosketchology Guide

Pyrosketchology is an approach aimed at building awareness of the fire environment through observations, sketching, and nature journaling practices. You do not need artistic skills or knowledge of fire to use this guide. Whether you're an educator seeking creative outdoor exercises, a nature enthusiast interested in the fire environment, a property owner evaluating fire hazards, or a firefighter/practitioner aiming to enhance situational awareness, this guide will serve many purposes grounded in personal observation practices.

In pyrosketchology, journaling practices prioritize capturing field observations over creating realistic and artistic sketches. Given the limited time in the field, more artistic details can be omitted or added later, ensuring simplicity in field notes and sketches. I do share a number of techniques to help enhance some sketching and painting techniques for those interested in expanding their visualization skills.

The technical information presented has been synthesized and distilled for a general audience, with visuals stylized or simplified to support sensory observations and creative journaling practices. While the majority of observations and practices are intended for the outdoors, references to online resources and technologies are provided for expanded observation scales.

Nature Journaling

Nature journaling, the personal practice of documenting nature observations, is not a new approach but a method employed by scientists, explorers, naturalists, and artists throughout history. Despite advancements in technology, in-nature and hands-on practices remain superior for building connection and learning about nature. John Muir Laws, an artist, educator, and naturalist, advocates for using a mix of pictures, numbers, and words to describe observations, along with journaling prompts like "I notice...," "I wonder...," and "It reminds me of..." to develop deeper observation and journaling skills.

Laws has published a number of exceptional books with tips and techniques for learning and teaching about the practice of nature journaling that would be a great reference to accompany this guide.

Sensory Engagement

One of the reasons nature journaling is so effective as a learning tool is that it engages multiple sensory inputs, leveraging more regions of the brain. I believe it's critical to involve all of our senses when making observations around the fire environment and tuning into changing conditions.

Many of these cues are invisible to the eye, such as the smell of plant compounds that can indicate the different phases and conditions of living plants or the influence of air moisture on dead vegetation. Utilizing multiple senses, like touching, smelling, and listening, will help transform these invisible cues into valuable observations. Sensory observation skills require practice, and when framed around the fire environment, they can create a multilayered sense and awareness of the fire surroundings.

See
Smell
Feel
Hear
Touch
Move

Fire Environment

The fire environment is defined as the mix of elements and conditions influencing fire ignition, combustion, and spread. Weather, topography, and fuels (vegetation) constitute the primary elements of the fire behavior triangle and the interactions between those are used to frame observations of the fire environment. Some pyrosketchology practices will focus only on individual elements within the fire behavior triangle, to enhance specific observation or journaling skills, while other observations require combined observations to build an overall sense of fire. All pyrosketchology observations should relate to at least one of the fire behavior triangle elements. Additionally, the guide includes broader topics such as fire seasons and regimes that are intended to help unravel the complexities of the fire environment and foster a deeper understanding of fire as a part of the earth systems.

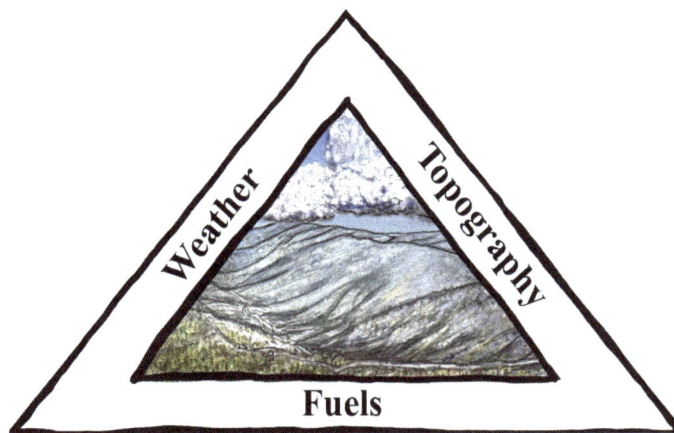

Journaling, as a tool for building awareness of the fire environment, is most effective when centered around observations before, during, and after a fire. However, the pyrosketchology emphasis extends to the overall environment and cues that indicate changing conditions leading to and influencing fire.

Ecological Sensemaking

Sensemaking is our understanding or "sense" of a place that evolves through our personal perspectives and experiences with that place. It can be a deeply personal way of knowing but can also be limited and biased through our personal lenses. To enhance our sense of place, we need a broader socio-ecological perspective. This means developing a journaling practice that takes a systems-thinking approach. When I started exploring pyrosketchology approaches, I struggled with what elements to observe and how to journal about them. It did not become clear until I realized the different spatial and temporal scales of observation needed to tease out and intertwine the complexities of the fire environment and socio-ecological interactions. Throughout the guide, you will notice different scales of observation and how to use certain types of visuals for each of these scales. I will summarize the primary scales of observation over the next couple of pages.

Situational Awareness

The guide also emphasizes the development of situational awareness (SA) skills to enhance awareness of threats, hazards, and risks within the fire environment. SA is cultivated through keen awareness, attention to environmental cues, and the analysis of trends to predict and respond to threats. Learning the environmental cues, or what I refer to as fire behavior indicators, is key to building SA. I have outlined some ways to frame these observations in the illustration on the next page. A table on page 11 provides a summary of fire behavior indicators from the National Wildfire Coordinating Group's *Fire Behavior Field Reference Guide*. More detailed fire behavior indicators are outlined in each chapter.

Situational Awareness Observations & Journaling

What has happened

- Knowledge of the baseline environmental conditions (climate and fire history), fire environment indicators, and the thresholds for changing fire hazard and risk levels.

- Observations of the past fire environment/fire events, such as post-fire pattern indicators (char height and ash color), and high wind effects (wind-flagged and felled trees).

- Analysis of your knowledge confidence, response to observations, and your overall relationships with the fire environment.

What is happening

- Awareness of the current fire environment indicators around you using mixed sensory inputs (sight, sound, scent, touch).

- Observations of the current fire environment and fire behaviors using narrative descriptions, visuals, and measurements.

- Comparisons between observed and assumed, or referenced, fire environment indicators to assess fire hazard/risk levels, to evaluate uncertainties, and to enhance observation focus and accuracy.

What may happen

- Predicting the potential fire weather (cloud types, atmospheric conditions) and fire environment conditions (fuels curing) within the coming hours, days, and/or months.

- Comparisons between past and present observations and the current or proposed fire mitigation, readiness, and prevention trends and activities to assess positive or negative changes in the fire environment.

- Comparisons between your past and present state of mind, abilities, and support to respond to the fire environment conditions.

Insight & Situational Awareness

- Activating the brain and body through multiple-sensory, targeted, and place-based observations.

- Engaging in ongoing journaling activities that include narrative, visual, and mathematical (measurements) descriptions to enhance observation skills, learning, and memory.

- Integrating observations about your external and internal environment to become more aware and adapted to the fire environment.

Generalized Fire Behavior Indicators

	Low Intensity FB	Moderate Intensity FB	High Intensity FB
Air Temperature	<60°F	60-80°F	>90°F
Relative Humidity	>40%	30-40%	<15%
Wind Speed	0-4 mph	5-10 mph	10-20+ mph
Cloud Type	Stratus	Cumulus	Cumulonimbus
Percent Slope	<10%	10-20%	>20%
Percent Cured Grass	<25% (Green)	25-50%	>75%
Leaf/Grass Concentration	Sparse	Patchy/Continuous	Continuous/Concentrated

Fire Behavior	Creeping/Backing	Advancing/Torching	Crowning/Eruptions/Erratic
Flame Length (feet)	<4 feet	4-8 feet	>8 feet
Rate of Spread (speed)	<.03-.06 mph	1-2 mph	>2-6 mph
Smoke	Light/Thin/Drifting	Heavy Plume	Heavy/Pyrocumulonimus

Ash Color	Black	Black/White	White
Tree Trunk Char	<4 ft	4-8 ft	>8 ft
Burn Severity:			
Grass	<50% Consumed	50-80% Consumed	>80% Consumed
Shrubs	5-30% Consumed	30-100% Consumed	90-100% Consumed
Trees	5-10% Consumed	10-80% Consumed	>80%

Meaningful Metadata

It is important to use familiar measurements and meaningful metadata when journaling about the fire environment and building your SA. You want data and information cues to come quickly without spending too much time on converting, translating, and understanding observations and data. Metadata is data about data that can be used to analyze, organize, and provide meaning, such as using numbers to prioritize order or rank hazards. An example I use in pyrosketchology is organizing temperature observations into color-coded categories relevant to environmental conditions. I apply those colors to visuals that are meaningful to my sense of temperature. In Chapter 2: Fire Weather and Chapter 5: Fire Seasons, you'll see examples of how I've grouped and organized temperatures, relative humidity levels, and wind speeds into meaningful metadata.

Observation Scales

As mentioned earlier, it is important to consider the scale of observation when making observations and journaling about the fire environment. Feel free to explore your own naming convention and scales of observation, but here is what I use.

Spatial Scales:

Close-up Observations

These are observations of an individual element, such as a single plant or leaf. I typically use simple sketches that focus on key physical and chemical features, such as shape, size, texture, and chemical composition. Even when focusing on a single object, observations should try to relate to one or all elements of the fire behavior triangle. For instance, how temperature and moisture influence the plant and how landscape aspect and slope influence plant conditions. These observations often relate most strongly to fire ignition and combustion.

Scene Observations

Scene observations are focused on a collection of things within the viewable area, like the concentration of trees, shrubs, and grasses in the area. I typically use two types of diagrams: a cross-section view (vertical arrangement) and a bird's-eye view (horizontal arrangement).

I sometimes use symbols or simplified sketches to represent elements in these diagrams. These observations often relate to the vertical and horizontal fire spread through vegetation.

Landscape Observations

These are observations of larger landscape elements, such as valleys, mountains, aspects, slopes, and elevations, as well as the combined fire behavior elements of weather, topography, and fuels. I typically use a landscape sketch that differentiates observations between the foreground, mid-ground, and background or 3D block landscape diagrams or sketches.

In the landscape sketch, the background portion includes the sky and larger landscape shapes, but not details. I use this to assess things like the steepness of the slope. I use the mid-ground portion of the sketch to look at horizontal patterns in vegetation, like patches and gaps. I use the foreground area of the sketch to look at the composition of key elements of vegetation, like the mix of trees, shrubs, and grass within the landscape. These observations can provide a different scale of observation on fire spread that includes the interactions between weather, topography, and fuels.

Temporal Scales:

Event Observations

These observations are over short periods of time and may occur within hours, days, or weeks. Temporal observations can also include a mix of past, present, and predicted (future scenarios), like the example below. These observations may include a mix of spatial scales as well but are organized in a manner to help convey time.

I often use lists, tables, graphs, or a series of sketches to convey these observations. I also like to use arrows to help indicate the flow of time.

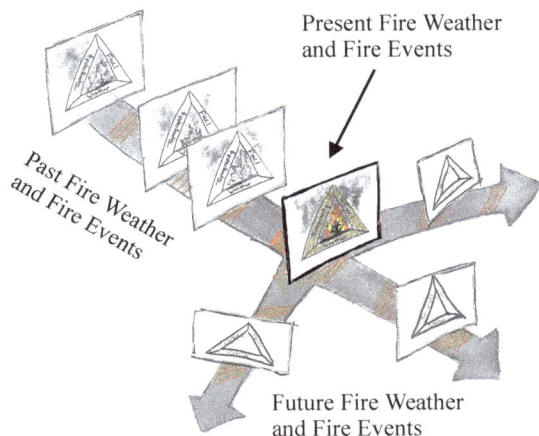

Present Fire Weather and Fire Events

Past Fire Weather and Fire Events

Future Fire Weather and Fire Events

These observations often relate to things like fire weather events, wildfires, or prescribed fires, as well as fire mitigation activities, like the stages of a fuel treatment. In many of my temporal observations, I emphasize metadata elements, which typically include weather conditions and fire or project metrics like acres burned or treated.

Season Observations

These observations often occur over several months and consider things like seasonal weather trends, plant phenology, and grass curing stages, which influence fire ignition and spread.

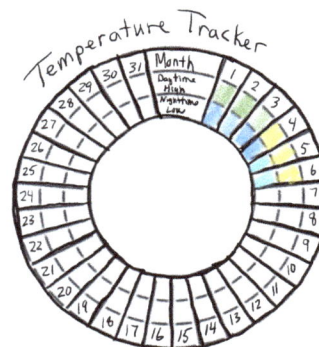

I like to use circular graphs and diagrams that may include colors and symbols to help convey the meaning of metadata. I also include a mix of spatial scale observations but frame the discussion around seasonal trends.

Regime Observations

These observations consider the long-term trends of the fire environment over years and decades and may include a mix of spatial scales. For example, close-up observations of a plant or leaf use the lens of plant adaptations to fire, while scene observations focus on ecosystem functions associated with fire. To help frame these observations, I may use visuals and designs like spirals or mechanical gears with layers of sketches, including key plants or ecosystem features associated with fire.

13

Journaling Emotion

I would be remiss if I did not mention how discussions and observations about fire can trigger emotions, stress, and trauma responses. These emotions can limit and alter observations and situational awareness, so taking time to evaluate your emotional response is important. A valuable reference for understanding how trauma and emotions can influence fire and science communications is Faith Kearn's book titled "*Getting to the Heart of Science Communication.*"

I highly recommend taking time to find ways to integrate your feelings into your journal. If you struggle with describing thoughts and emotions, consider an exercise where you describe how you physically feel in different parts of your body while experiencing different emotions. This can help you describe and evaluate feelings and potentially identify approaches to reducing stress. You can also use an x and y graph to track your observation and prediction accuracy under different situations and emotional moods to evaluate how emotions influence your skills.

Simplified Emotions

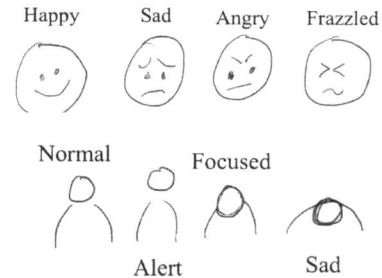

Happy   Sad   Angry   Frazzled

Normal   Focused

Alert   Sad

Connecting to Feelings

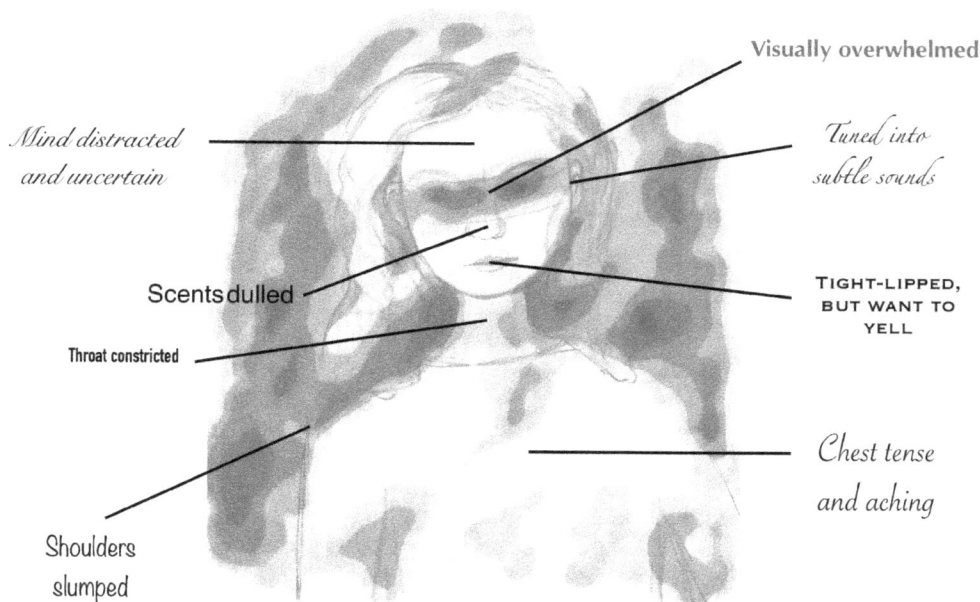

Visually overwhelmed

Mind distracted and uncertain

Tuned into subtle sounds

Scents dulled

TIGHT-LIPPED, BUT WANT TO YELL

Throat constricted

Chest tense and aching

Shoulders slumped

To journal about feelings, you can also use colors, patterns, fonts, cartoons, and impressionist images to help express emotions. An interesting study in Finland asked people to map where they felt different emotions on their bodies. The results were fairly consistent across cultures (Nummenmaa 2014), and colors were used to indicate feelings like sadness, love, and anxiety across the body. There are several online illustrations of the emotional color maps that could be a fun reference.

I was inspired by this study, and a number of years ago, I created some fantasy characters that personified emotions by using a combination of facial expressions and color schemes associated with certain emotions. You can also use simple emojis if detailed sketches feel intimidating. The point of this exercise is to deeply evaluate emotions and consider how they can influence the body and your observational abilities.

Analyzing Reactions

It's also important to recognize and evaluate your state of mind and physical abilities while journaling to enhance your situational awareness (SA). The Central Intelligence Agency's "*Psychology of Intelligence Analysis*" document (Heuer, 1999) offers some interesting insights into the strengths and weaknesses of human information analysis. Heuer mentions that it is fairly common for people to notice and interpret what they expected to see, focusing on belief-confirming observations and information. This means that some information and observations may be missed or disregarded, leading to poor analysis and potentially false clues.

Colors & Expression of Emotions

Sad, sick, hopeless

Shocked, fearful, confused

Happy, relaxed, curious

Angry, frustrated, overwhelmed

Here are a few recommendations for information analysis, which I have framed around the fire environment:

- Clearly delineate your assumptions and emotions about the fire environment indicators, fire hazard/risk levels, and interpretations of your observations.

- Specify your confidence, uncertainty, and feelings about the information sources, observations, indicators, and predictions.

- Elaborate on potential alternatives to the cause and meaning of observations.

- Periodically re-examine your information, observations, and fire behavior indicators.

- Emphasize the process of observation, journaling, and analysis over making determinations and polished journal pages.

Chapter 2: Fire Weather

Fire Weather

Heat & Humidity

Sensing Air Temperature

Insect Thermometers

Humidity in Shades of Blue

Heat Transfer—Dark & Light Landscapes

Global Temperatures & Jet Streams

Cloud Families, Levels & Movements

Wind Shear

Cloud & Wind Journaling Exercise Journaling

Clouds at a Distance

Temperatures & Air Pressure

Troughs & Ridges

High Ridge Breakdown

Weather Fronts

Journaling Weather Fronts- A Time Series Weather

Thunderstorms

Lightning

Key Thunderstorm Observations Journaling

Thunderstorms

Atmospheric Stability & Instability

Orographic Clouds & Winds

Diurnal Terrain Winds

Land & Sea Breezes

Open & Filtered Winds

Funneled Winds—Forest Chimneys

Formed by Winds—Past Winds

Griggs-Putnam Wind Deformation Index

Felt Winds—Beaufort Wind Force Scale

Wind Types Table

Journaling Wind Force Observations

Wind Metadata, Maps & Graphs

Fire Weather

Fire weather refers to "the range of weather conditions, over short periods of time, that promote the ignition, motion, and growth of fire" (Sugihara et al., 2006). In the United States, fire weather criteria are defined within different vegetation communities and geographic areas. Fire weather watches are issued by the National Weather Service in advance of probable fire weather conditions. Red flag warnings are issued when fire weather conditions are imminent or occurring. In this chapter, I discuss more than the official definitions of fire weather. I want to build context around weather conditions (temperature, relative humidity, and wind speed) that help influence the general and changing fire environment. The majority of weather information in this chapter was synthesized from the National Weather Service and the National Wildfire Coordinating Group's (NWCG) fire behavior training resources unless otherwise referenced.

Sensing Heat & Humidity

There are different metrics used to define and describe temperature. I use degrees Fahrenheit (F°) in this book. The exchange and movement of heat and moisture between the sun and the earth drive cloud development and wind flow, which I'll discuss further. I want to start this chapter with framing air temperature and humidity around observations and awareness of conditions relevant to fire weather. Air temperature has a strong influence on the ignition, flammability, and spread of fire in vegetation.

The warmer the temperature, the less heat is needed for the ignition source, and the faster a fire can spread. Under lower temperatures, and even in freezing conditions, you can ignite and burn a campfire or debris pile, but a vegetation fire is less likely to ignite and spread. The temperatures targeted for many prescribed burns are often between 60°F and 80°F, depending on the season and burning objectives (USDA 2012 and Fast et al.). These are air temperatures when a fire can be more easily ignited and spread at low to high rates of speed but are more easily managed. When temperatures start to reach 80° to 90°F or higher, you may observe more extreme and erratic fire behaviors. It's helpful to observe and journal temperatures at low, moderate, and higher ranges to become aware of those changing conditions.

Heat influences weather in various ways. Fire weather conditions are generally hot, dry, and windy, but there are many other obvious and subtle sensory observations we can make about fire weather. Using weather data is a crucial component for journaling about the fire environment. There is a journaling exercise in a couple of pages that may help you tune into the important temperature ranges in the fire environment.

The warmer the air is, the more water vapor it can hold. Water vapor is the gaseous form of water, which transforms into water droplets or snow at cooler temperatures. Relative humidity is the percentage of water vapor in the air compared to the maximum amount it can hold at various temperatures. Relative humidity is abbreviated as RH. At 100% RH, the air is fully saturated.

The National Weather Service (NWS) and various fire management agencies use low relative humidity (RH) levels as one of the criteria for defining red flag and fire weather conditions. Another factor associated with RH is tied to the ability of vegetation to recover overnight when moisture typically rises. When there is a strong high-pressure area dominating an area, plant recovery may not occur, making them more flammable.

General weather conditions for high fire danger periods include temperatures over 80°F, relative humidity below 20%, and wind speeds over 20 miles per hour.

Wind is another factor used for determining red flag conditions and will be discussed later in the chapter. Red flag conditions identify periods of potentially high fire danger for specific climates and vegetation communities. You can look up fire weather information for your local area by going to the NWS Fire Weather website. You can also use some generalized RH criteria to help build a sense of fire weather conditions.

In the fire environment, we are looking at the RH levels that influence the ignition, flammability, and spread of fire in vegetation. A high fire danger factor for many environments is RH levels below 15%, lasting several hours or more. Other vegetation communities may experience fire hazard conditions when RH levels are below 20%, 30%, or 50%. Some people use the general rule of temperatures over 90°F, RH below 20%, and wind speeds over 20 miles per hour to estimate high fire danger periods. RH is also used to define the timing and objectives of prescribed burns, which can tell us when fires can burn, but typically at a lower intensity level than compared to wildfires burning during red flag fire weather conditions. Some prescribed burns have objectives that require a lower RH, while others require a higher one, but as a rule, burning prescriptions avoid high fire danger periods. Many prescribed burn managers around the United States recommend burning prescriptions with RH levels above 25%, 30%, and 40%, depending on the ecosystem and objectives.

Sensing Air Temperature & Moisture

Before we move deeper into fire weather observations, let's do a warm-up exercise to build our sense of temperature and humidity levels associated with fire weather conditions. Many weather specialists are now using what is called the Vapor Pressure Deficit (VPD) as an indicator of dryness instead of RH, but I prefer to use RH to simplify the information, observations, and calculations used for journaling. I'll share more about the VPD in Chapter 4: Fire Fuels and Chapter 5: Fire Seasons.

The World Health Organization suggests that a minimum air temperature of around 64°F is the most comfortable level for healthy and appropriately dressed individuals. Using the low 60s as our cool yet comfortable range, we can associate our sense of weather conditions typical of lower intensity fire behaviors. According to Jeffrey Walker, a physiology professor at the University of Arizona, the human body functions and feels most comfortable when the ambient temperature is around 70°F to 72°F. We can use the low 70s temperature range as our optimal comfort level, which can be associated with more moderate intensity fire behaviors. A number of sources identify air temperatures between 80°F to 90°F as feeling hot to most people, and this is also when fire behavior can pick up and move from moderate to high-intensity fire behaviors. When the air temperature equals our body temperature, the mechanisms for dispersing heat become overcharged, especially when humidity is high and interferes with our evaporative cooling process. This temperature range can be used to associate with high to extreme intensity fire behaviors.

Everyone has different comfort levels and feelings about them, and these will change based on health and other things, so you'll want to experiment with your sense of temperature and see how you can frame them around the relevant fire environment and fire weather temperature ranges. A study by Yujin Sunwoo on the physiological and subjective responses to low relative humidity offers an interesting approach to sensing lower levels of RH when fire conditions are more extreme. Results of the study showed that at a temperature of 77°F, a 30% or less RH would cause human skin and eyes to become dry. Below a 10% RH, the nasal mucosa tissue is more likely to become dry (Sunwoo 2006). The NWS uses the dew point to calculate comfort levels, which can be calculated using temperature and RH. A dew point below 55 is considered comfortable, while 55 to 65 will make us feel sticky and muggy. I prefer to use relative humidity as my air moisture metric, so rarely use dew point. But I like the sensory description for sensing dry to moist conditions. Using the same 77°F temperature in the study, and the dew point of 55, I calculated that a 47% RH would make us feel sticky. We all have different comfort levels and many people and situations will alter our abilities to sense the differences in temperature and humidity. The following information and exercise are intended to help you develop a deeper sense of temperature and humidity.

Sensed Air Temperature Color Code

☐ **Cool & Comfortable** (68°F to 73°F)

☐ **Warm & Comfortable** (74°F to 79°F)

☐ **Hot** (80°F to 90°F)

☐ **Very Hot** (Over 90°F)

Sensed Air Moisture Description

- **Comfortable**—RH 31% to 47%, with cool and warm temperatures, should have no noticeable effects from moisture.

- **Dry**—RH 15% to 30%, with cool to hot temperatures should make your eyes, lips, and skin feel dry.

- **Very dry**—RH 15% or less, with cool to hot temperatures, can make your eyes, lips, nasal passages, and skin feel very dry.

In the graphic on the next page, I have attempted to visualize the sense of temperature and humidity levels that are important to the fire environment and red flag fire weather conditions using colors and sketching expressions. Journaling these observations over time can help develop and refine your physical sense of changing fire weather conditions.

Warm-Up Journaling Exercise

Step 1: Track your local weather forecast for temperatures between 68°F and 90°F as triggers for observation. We want to tune into the moderate temperature ranges, where there is a transition to higher fire danger.

Step 2: Find a location outdoors or open to outdoor temperatures that is blocked from direct sunlight and the wind for the targeted temperature and humidity observations. You may want to start this exercise before weather conditions are ideal for outdoor observations. You will have more control over temperatures indoors and can start by setting your cooling or heating system to 60°F and working up to 68°F to find your comfortably cool temperature zone and work your way up to higher temperatures.

Step 3: Expose as much bare skin to the air as possible and stand or sit still for a few minutes, contemplating your sense of temperature and humidity.

Step 4: Create a temperature and RH legend similar to the example on the next page.

Step 5: In your journal, create a modified happy face or personal caricature or avatar. I replicated my

Facebook avatar for the example, but a happy face would be quicker and easier. Add visual indicators for your sense of humidity. I have used pencil strokes on the face to indicate dry skin and red lines around the eyes and nose (nasal passage). Visualize your sense of temperature with temperature-associated colors that you can fill in around your symbolized face. Feel free to explore other approaches to visualizing your sense of humidity, but try to eventually settle on a consistent visualization so that you can track these observations over time.

Step 6: Add the actual temperature and humidity levels near your sketch.

Step 7: Describe how the temperature and humidity feel to you. The ideal nature journaling approach includes a mix of pictures, numbers, and words. You may also want to use a thesaurus to explore more descriptive words to help develop a range of descriptions.

Lower Fire Danger

70°F & 35% RH

I feel a little cool, but comfortable in a light jacket.

Growing Fire Danger

76°F & 22% RH

I am comfortable in a t-shirt, but my eyes are dry.

High Fire Danger

86°F & 10% RH

I feel hot and uncomfortable, with dry eyes, skin, and nasal passages.

A couple of examples from my journal pages.

Insect Thermometers

Insect observations are fun tools for gauging temperatures and building a deeper sense of temperature changes in the environment. These observations are often tied to seasonal changes and can be added or summarized in fire season observations. I recommend you review information on the National Phenology Network's Nature Notebook website. A few examples of insects that you can use for temperature observations are butterflies, bees, crickets, cicadas, katydids, and flies.

Butterflies and bees emerge at lower springtime temperatures, reaching their optimal flying performance at moderate temperatures similar to those used in the previous journaling exercise. At temperatures above 100°F, some butterfly species reduce or end their flight activity (Mattila et al., 2015), and many cricket species stop calling (Nebraska Dept. of Entomology). The Farmer's Almanac has used cricket calls as an approach to calculate temperatures for many decades. As the temperature increases, the pitch and pace increase until the temperature is too hot.

To calculate the temperature in Fahrenheit (F) using cricket calls:

- Count the number of cricket chirps heard within a 14-second period.

- Add 40 to the number of chirps counted.

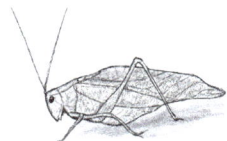

Katydids can be used to gauge temperature; their calls sound different as the temperature increases (Living Earth Public Radio —Insect Thermometers).

I have added the cricket and katydid calls associated with different temperature ranges to a temperature color code for journaling purposes. These same temperature-associated colors can be used to accentuate a wide range of visuals, like in the previous temperature and humidity exercise. When journaling about temperature and fire weather, it is crucial to note instances when temperatures deviate from the normal range for that specific time of year. Further information and examples on how to document these anomalies can be found in Chapter 5: Fire Seasons.

Temperature Color Codes

>100°F many insects (bees, butterflies, and crickets) reduce or stop activities and calls.

91°F to 100°F some larger insects (e.g. butterflies and bumblebees) reduce their actives.

80°F to 90°F katydid calls sound like "katy-did-it."

74°F to 79°F katydid calls sound like "katy-didn't."

68°F to 73°F katydid calls sound like "katy-did" or "she-didn't."

62°F to 67°F katydid calls sound like "katy." Some butterflies slow their activities.

55°F to 61°F katydid calls sound like "Kate." some butterflies cannot fly.

33°F to 54°F katydids and crickets typically stop their calls. Some insects die.

32°F or less freezing temperatures and many insects die.

Humidity in Shades of Blue

The color of the sky can inform us about general temperature, humidity, and other atmospheric conditions. Water vapor, water droplets, and other particles, like dust, in the sky will absorb and reflect sunlight, creating different shades of blue. On NASA's GLOBE program website, a range of fun sky observations is outlined. You can use these color indicators to focus observations around temperatures, humidity levels, and fire weather journaling practices.

One tool for determining the shade of blue in the sky is called a cyanometer. This is a simple product, a circular band of blue shades, that can be held up to the sky for comparison. The cyanometer is attributed to Horace-Bénédict de Saussure and Alexander von Humboldt and has been used by artists, students, and nature journalers to describe and paint sky observations.

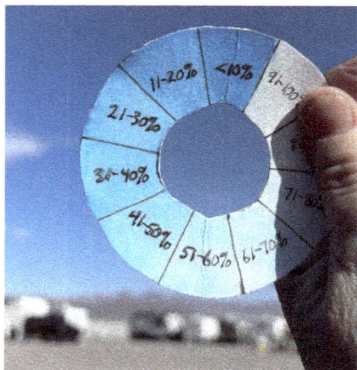

This is an image of my personalized cyanometer, which I have broken into color values associated with RH levels. Through ongoing observations, your colors and RH levels will become more accurate.

Relative Humidity Color Codes

Matching your sketch or painting to the exact hue of color in the sky can be very challenging. For my journaling purposes, I am more concerned with how light or dark the blue is. I am also more interested in building my skills around estimating the relative humidity level based on sky color than creating the perfect work of art. This will take practice and should be refined to your local area and around your observation goals. For example, I have organized the relative humidity (RH) categories based on the moisture levels that influence fire behavior, but you may be more interested in which RH levels influence plant phenology or your garden. The blue color hues I have used for my personalized cyanometers are evolving as I continue my observations and comparisons of sky color and RH.

Dark Blue Skies

Skies appear darker blue when there are low levels of water vapor in the air, colder temperatures, and/or when viewing from higher altitudes. The higher portions of the sky appear darker than closer to the ground. The sky can appear darker blue when the atmosphere is unstable and/or when the sun's angle is low (late fall to early spring). In my journaling practice, I am trying to find the sky shades of blue that most commonly associates with RH levels below 30%. I would like to narrow that range to several smaller breakdowns in RH to better associate with fire weather conditions (below 15%), but need to make numerous observations over different seasons before I feel confident about the color value for this range.

Light to Medium Blue Skies

Skies appear light to medium blue when there are moderate levels of water vapor in the air, moderate temperatures, and/or when there is an unstable, stable, or partially stable atmosphere. The middle portion of the sky often appears a light to medium blue. In my journaling practice, I have been noticing RH levels between 31% and 60% falling within this color range, but other conditions like high winds and particles in the sky make the sky look lighter than I would estimate with my associated color value.

Very Light Blue Skies

Skies appear a very light blue when there are high levels of water vapor in the air, warmer temperatures, and when there is a stable atmosphere. The portion of the sky closest to the horizon is typically a very light blue or brown color. When the sun's angle is high, like during the summer, the sky typically appears lighter in color. I am currently estimating the RH levels for the very light blue skies as above 60%.

Other Colors of the Sky

The sky can appear gray, tan, pink, orange, and/or red, especially when there are large particles like smoke, dust, and salts in the air. This usually occurs in the lower portions of the sky and is most apparent during sunrise and sunset.

I have been using a dot journal for tracking the bulk of my weather observations. I tape in small squares of drawing paper to use more colors and provide more page area to work with (top and bottom side of the insert). In the example below, I have broad relative humidity (RH) categories where I use a colored pencil to add a small circle of blue color based on my actual observation and the actual RH. Over time, I will be able to organize a narrower range of RH categories and color values that are more accurate to the place where I am making observations.

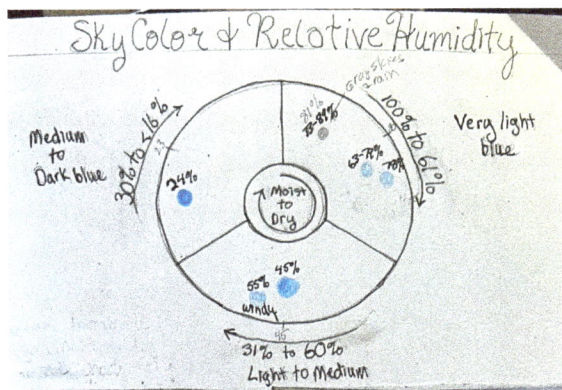

When I have an RH and sky color code, I use the relevant color along with the RH data for other journal pages to help accentuate the actual sky color observations. I like to include more than the RH for the moment I am making observations, but the daily high and low to add broader context to the setting.

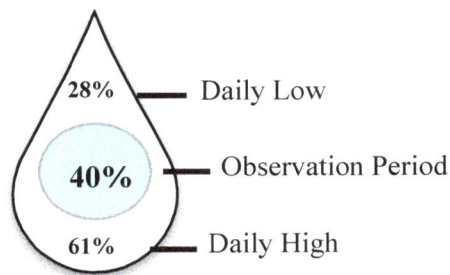

The two cyanometer examples below, are experimental approaches to using color bands and RH levels in broad categories and more narrowed categories.

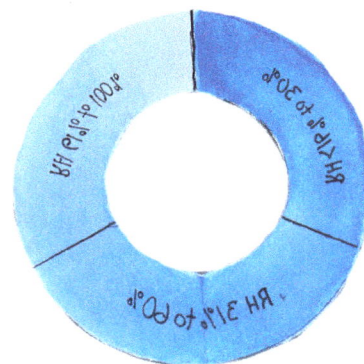

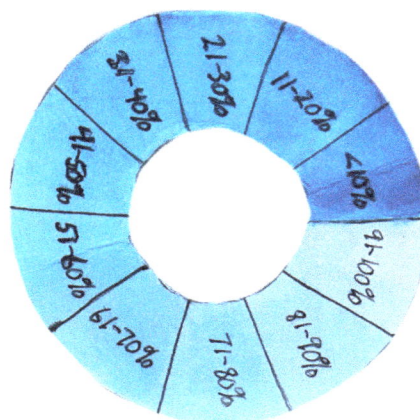

Sky Color Exercise

Step 1: Create a small rectangle on your page for a sketch of the sky colors. Leave enough space to differentiate the shades of blue from high to low areas of the sky.

Step 2: Sketch or paint the various shades of blue in the sky, starting at the top and working your way down. Include notes and questions that relate to temperature and moisture levels indicated by your observations. You may want to use a cyanometer to help differentiate the values of blue. I recommend utilizing the blue values found within a 30° to 45° angle from the horizon or the lower 1/3 of the sketch. I will discuss how to estimate this angle for cloud observations further in this chapter.

The high portion of the sky is a darker blue color. Is this a result of colder and drier air? Estimating that the RH is under 16%

The sky transitions to lighter blue and white colors as it gets closer to the horizon. Is this an indicator of warmer moister air or more particles of dust etc? Estimating the RH is under 20%.

The forecasted RH ranges 15-25% through the day and night

Step 3: Add the forecasted relative humidity (RH) for the time of your observation data and consider how the shades and values of blue may differ throughout different heights of the sky. Also, add notes about wind speeds, air quality, time of day, and time of year, and consider what that could mean for the blue values in the sky.

Step 4: Continue these observations over time and review your notes to better adapt blue color values and/or create your own cyanometer.

Heat Transfer

Dark & Light Landscapes

In this section, we will explore how the sun's heat is transferred between the Earth's surfaces and the air, influencing weather. Three heat transfer processes—conductive, convective, and radiative heating—play a role. Conductive heat moves through solids, while convective heat moves through fluids like water and air. Radiant heat, such as sunlight, requires no substance to travel through.

When the sun warms water, soil, and plants, their surfaces absorb and reflect heat at varying rates based on their conductivity. Dark surfaces absorb more heat, while light surfaces tend to reflect it. Examining dark and light areas in a landscape allows us to observe how heat is exchanged in the environment. As these surfaces warm, some heat is released convectively, creating temperature layers and influencing cloud and wind formation. After surveying the landscape, observe the sky for clouds that may have formed over darker areas.

Consider creating a black and white sketch or painting to focus on shades and values rather than colors. A simple representation, like dark and light blobs, can effectively convey the landscape. Add notes to the sky area regarding your observations on heat transfer across the landscape and sky.

Global Temperatures & Jet Streams

Now, stepping back, contemplate the colder and warmer continents globally and how temperatures and wind patterns impact large-scale conditions. Visualize the jet stream's location and movement, influenced by temperature fluctuations.

Jet streams, created by the Earth's spin, traverse the globe from west to east, their paths affected by pockets and regions of warm and cold air. Continental areas with different air temperatures generate general wind patterns, with warmer regions experiencing west-to-east winds and cooler areas having east-to-west winds. Over the United States, these winds are known as the prevailing westerlies. There are other types of winds, which I'll discuss further along in the chapter.

Throughout this chapter, we focus on key weather elements influencing fire behavior—temperature, humidity, air pressure, atmospheric stability, and winds. Clouds and winds serve as indicators for observing many of these weather conditions, which I'll discuss after a brief introduction to cloud types. Try to keep in mind these larger global temperature and wind influences.

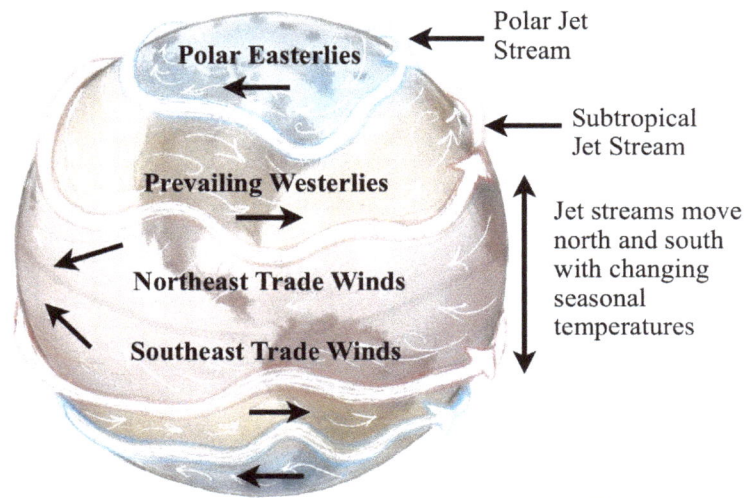

Cloud Families, Levels & Movements

Cloud Characteristics

In this section, our focus is on observing cloud families, levels, and movements, particularly when they indicate and forecast winds and humidity levels. Clouds form when water vapor cools, condenses, and transforms into liquid water molecules in the air. Clouds exhibit distinct characteristics based on their location in the high, middle, or low levels of the sky. Three main cloud families—Cirrus, Cumulus, and Stratus—each have unique visual characteristics.

Estimating Cloud & Wind Levels

The height or level of clouds in the sky can be used to predict incoming weather changes, with high-level clouds providing a 12-24 hour heads-up (Gooley 2021). To estimate cloud levels, hold your arm straight out at a 30° to 45° angle from the horizon (your eye level) when observing clouds at a distance. Reference books and online resources, including a flowchart poster by the World Meteorological Organization (WMO), can aid in identifying cloud families and estimating cloud levels using hand and finger measurements. An illustration in Chapter 3: Topography also offers some options for estimating angles which can be used for cloud observations..

Common Cloud Types & Levels

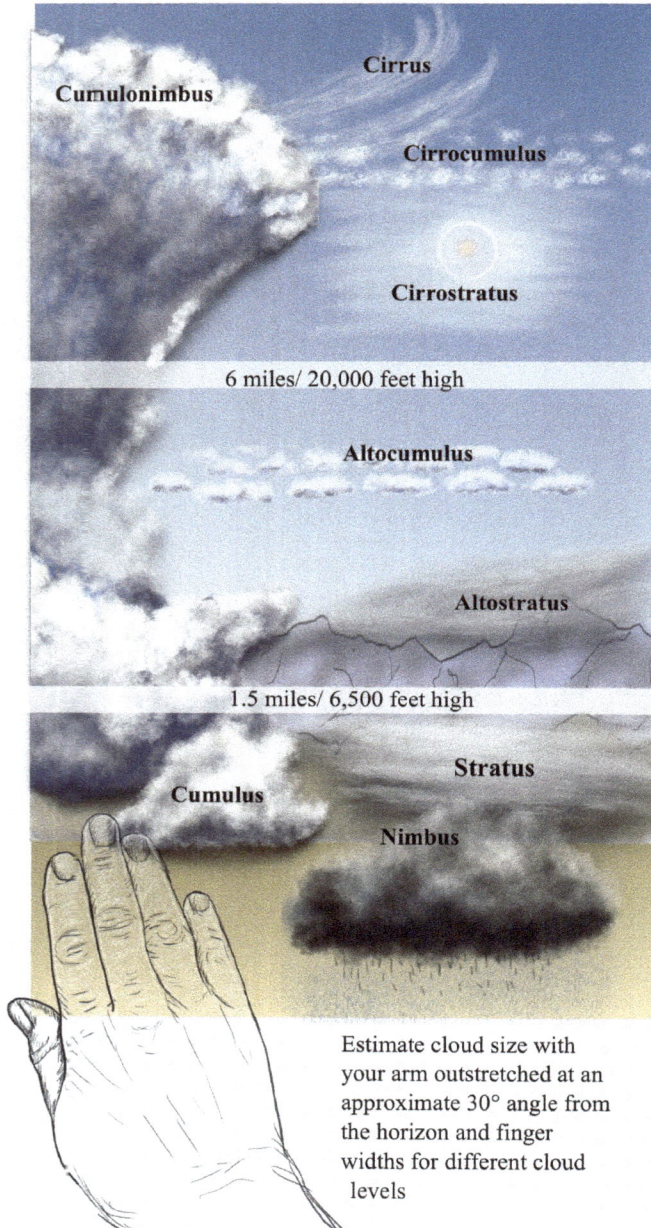

Cumulonimbus

Cirrus

Cirrocumulus

Cirrostratus

6 miles/ 20,000 feet high

Altocumulus

Altostratus

1.5 miles/ 6,500 feet high

Stratus

Cumulus

Nimbus

Estimate cloud size with your arm outstretched at an approximate 30° angle from the horizon and finger widths for different cloud levels

It's helpful to remember that clouds change quickly and can transform from one cloud type into another or rise and fall to different levels, depending on temperature and moisture interactions in the atmosphere. I'd recommend journaling cloud movements throughout the day and over different seasons.

High-Level Clouds & Winds

- Clouds at altitudes around 20,000 feet or 3.7 miles above the ground, matching the cruising altitude of commercial airplanes. Individual cloudlets measure approximately one finger width.

- Cirrus clouds, composed of ice crystals, can manifest as delicate white strands, rows of cotton-like puffs, or a transparent filmy layer often accompanied by iridescence.

- The presence of halos around the sun and moon or reduced visibility due to lower-level clouds can occur. Clear visibility indicates lower relative humidity (RH) levels.

- Aircraft condensation trails may be observed at the lower part of this level, their appearance influenced by moisture levels and wind conditions.

- Cirrus clouds serve as a weather forecaster, predicting changes 12 to 24 hours ahead. They can signify high winds aloft, hinting at potential weather alterations, including shifts in wind direction and speed.

- Cumulonimbus clouds may develop into this level, forecasting potential thunderstorms, increased winds, and possible lightning.

- Winds at this level are generally laminar (smooth) and less turbulent than winds interacting with terrain, encompassing jet streams and prevailing winds.

Cirrus clouds, with falling ice crystals, appearing as wispy tails

Altocumulus clouds appearing as rows.

Asymmetric clouds shaped by the wind

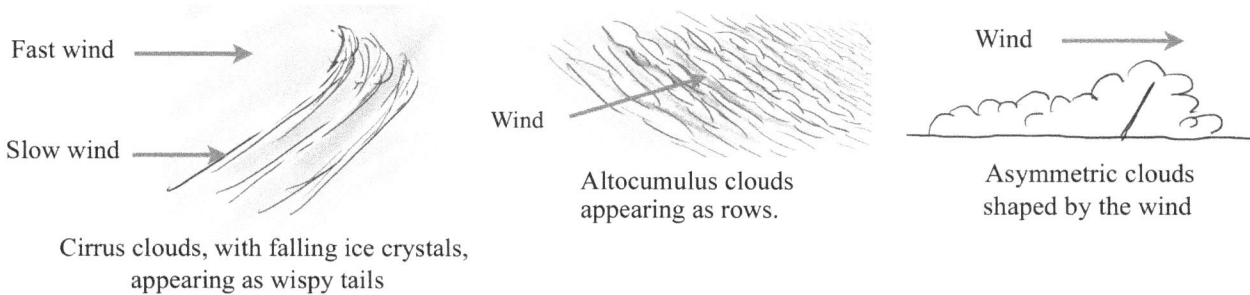

Middle-Level Clouds & Winds

- Clouds forming between 6,500 and 20,000 feet or 1.2 to 3.7 miles above the ground, with individual cloudlets typically measuring two to three finger widths.

- Clouds may consist of ice crystals or water droplets, presenting as translucent white or gray layers with some shading at the base.

- Partial obscuring of the sun and moon is possible, and clear skies suggest lower RH levels.

- These clouds aid in predicting weather changes up to 12 hours ahead and indicate atmospheric instability.

- Cumulonimbus clouds at this level may lead to lightning and severe wind downbursts, significantly influencing fire behavior.

- Lenticular clouds can signal foehn and terrain winds, exerting strong influences on fire behavior.

- Winds at this level can be either laminar or turbulent, influenced by interactions with higher-level winds and the terrain.

Low-Level Clouds & Winds

- Clouds developing below 6,500 feet or 1.2 miles from the ground, with cumulus cloudlets measuring about three to five finger widths.

- Opaque white, gray, or bluish low-level clouds, with cumulus clouds displaying flat bottoms and shadows, while stratus clouds appear as a widespread layer.

- Sun and moon visibility can be entirely obscured by clouds at this level and above.

- These clouds provide real-time indications of current or imminent weather conditions and winds.

- Cloud movements in variable directions are associated with weather systems, and heavy moisture-laden clouds sinking to lower levels indicate higher RH levels.

- Cumulus clouds, formed through convective heating from the Earth's surfaces, may evolve into cumulonimbus clouds, contributing to gusting winds and escalating fire behavior with increased wind speeds.

27

Wind Shear

Wind shear refers to a sudden, short-distance change in wind speed and/or direction, resulting in a tearing and/or shearing effect on clouds. These cloud observations act as indicators of turbulence (wind shear), showcasing strong wind updrafts and downdrafts that can critically affect fire behavior. Microbursts, often referred to as small-sized downdrafts, can have effects similar to tornadoes. Wind shear can result from temperature inversions, interactions between low and high-pressure air masses (weather fronts), thunderstorm updrafts and downdrafts, and surface obstructions like mountain ranges. The illustrations on the next page are examples of wind shear observations for heightened situational awareness.

Whirlwinds

Whirlwinds and dust devils are triggered by wind shear at ground level, signifying an unstable atmosphere. These vortexes can reach spinning winds of up to 120 mph. They typically occur in open and flat areas, particularly on the leeward side of topographic features, where there is a significant variance in surface temperatures and low-level winds. Super cell thunderstorms can also trigger spinning.

Cloud & Wind Journaling Exercise

This sketch, emphasizing basic cloud families, cloud levels, and cloud movements, should be small and quick, with limited detail. The exercise aims to enhance awareness of wind movements.

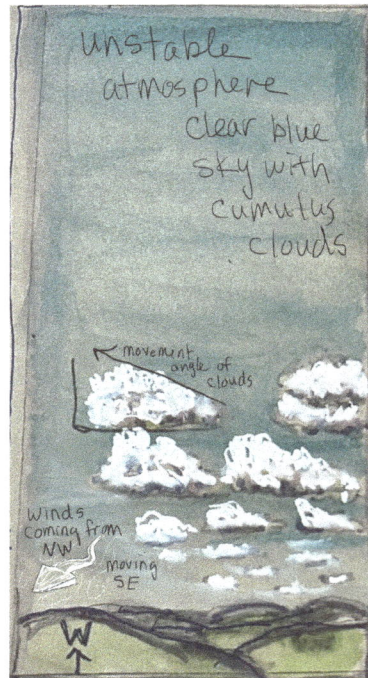

Step 1: Estimate cloud levels using finger widths and create a small rectangle box for a sketch with three levels of sky and terrain below.

Step 2: Determine cloud movement direction and note variations at different levels.

Step 3: Use light pencil lines to outline basic cloud shapes - puffy tops for cumulus clouds, and flattened, rounded shapes for stratus clouds. Add shading for depth.

Step 4: Correct asymmetry and add details to cloud outlines. Include shadows and highlights to convey sunlight effects.

Step 5: Add arrows or swirly lines to indicate cloud movements and wind direction. Use colored arrows for various sky processes.

Step 6: Sketch an outline of hills, valleys, or mountains below the cloud observations, adding shadows or color.

Cirrus Clouds & Wind Shear
with temperature differences and a
change in wind speed

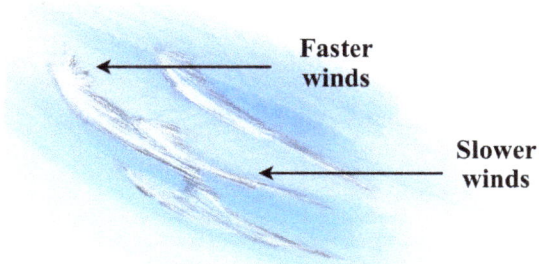

**Faster
winds**

**Slower
winds**

Altocumulus Clouds & Wind Shear
with converging air masses (weather front)

**Warm air mass
winds**

Cold air mass winds

Cumulonimbus Cloud & Wind Shear
with dry and wet microbursts

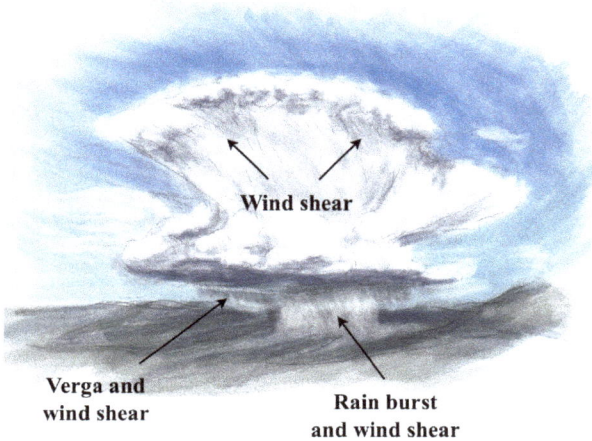

Wind shear

**Verga and
wind shear**

**Rain burst
and wind shear**

Cumulonimbus Cloud & Wind Shear
with dry microbursts and a dust vortex

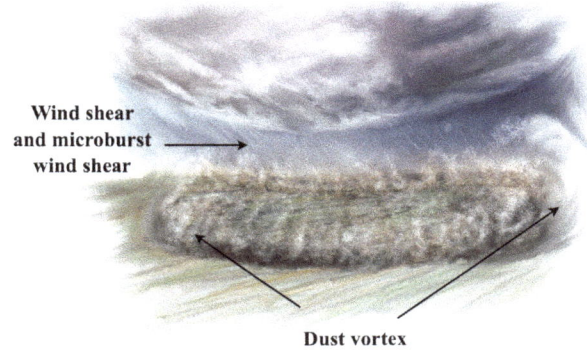

**Wind shear
and microburst
wind shear**

Dust vortex

Mountain Wave Clouds & Wind Shear with Changes in Wind Direction

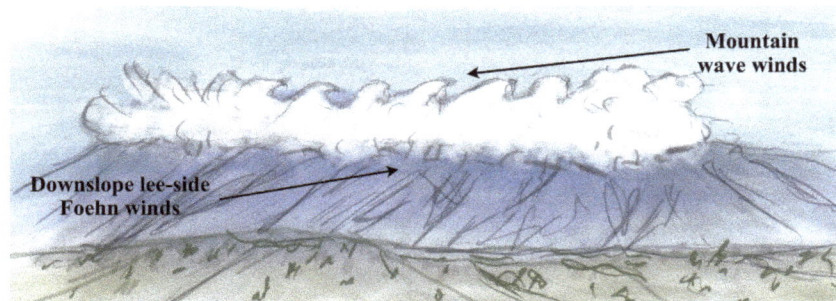

**Mountain
wave winds**

**Downslope lee-side
Foehn winds**

Journaling Clouds at a Distance

Create a 3-dimensional bird's-eye view landscape to visualize clouds and wind movements across a large landscape.

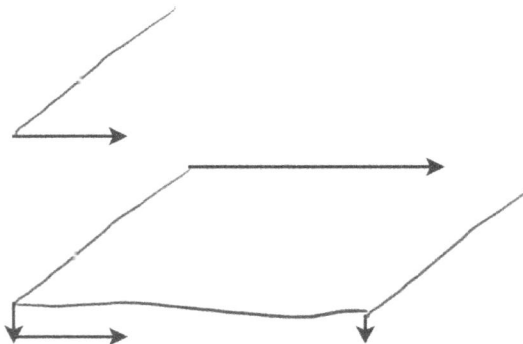

Step 1: Create a flattened square with a 30° angle on the left and right sides.

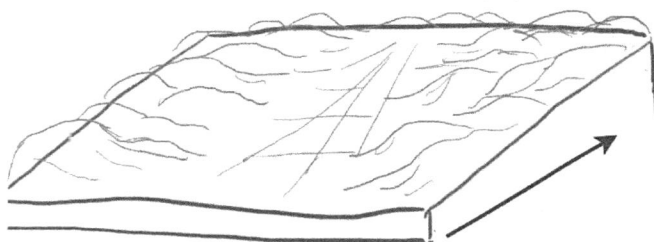

Step 2: Add landscape outlines over the angled square, depicting mountains and valleys.

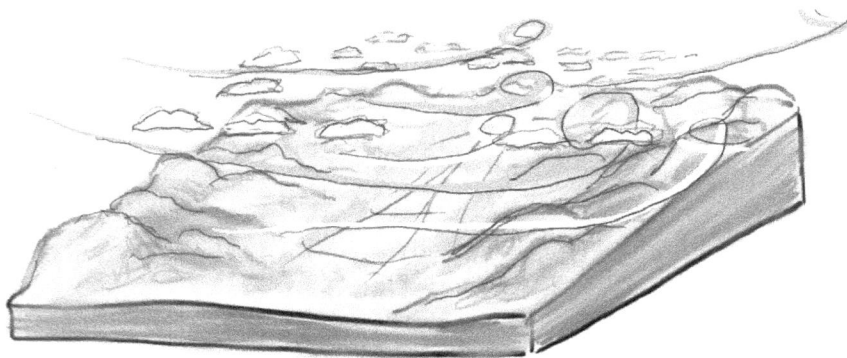

Step 3: Overlay clouds and winds, capturing overall shapes and movements.

Step 4: Add shadows or color to the landscape and clouds.

Perspective Drawing for Cloud Journaling

Use perspective drawing to convey the direction of cloud and wind movement toward and away from you. Clouds in the distance will appear squished and close together, while closer clouds will seem taller and more widely spaced.

Sketching Cloud Perspectives

3. In the foreground (area closer to you), sketch larger full-shaped clouds. Sketch smaller, more flattened, and squished clouds the further away and nearer to the horizon.

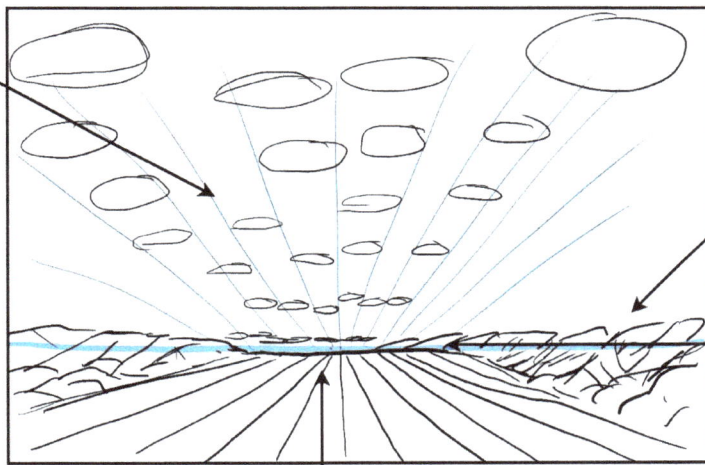

1. Use a faint line to create the horizon level, which should be at eye-level. Sketch in the basic shapes of the landscape along the horizon.

2. Use faint lines pointing to the horizon and getting wider as the lines move closer to the foreground to create perspective. Add the landscape features along these lines, growing larger the closer they to the foreground.

4. If you aim to depict more realistic clouds, consider reshaping them to showcase details, shadows, and colors that align with your observations. In this elementary journaling exercise, feel free to maintain simplified diagrams and sketches, following the example I've provided.

Temperature & Air Pressure

Now that we've delved into cloud types and levels, let's apply that knowledge to more intricate atmospheric conditions such as air pressure, weather fronts, and atmospheric stability. These are crucial observations for understanding and evaluating fire behavior. The heat transfer across local, regional, and global environments induces varying air temperatures. These warm and cool temperature areas in the atmosphere have different weights and pressure levels (pounds per square inch), causing the air to either rise or sink. These areas can be as small as a low-pressure zone on one side of a mountain or as extensive as covering a large region the size of several states. These pressure areas can change throughout a day or persist for many weeks to months, as seen in seasonal weather patterns and monsoon systems, discussed in Chapter 5: Fire Seasons. Different cloud types and weather conditions are associated with these air pressure systems, aiding in observations of changing weather systems.

Low & High Air Pressure

A low-pressure area emerges when warm air expands and rises above the cooler air surrounding it. Conversely, a high-pressure area forms when cooler air condenses into liquid water molecules and descends below the surrounding warm air. Visualizing a high-pressure area as a blue stick surrounded by pink cotton candy helps: as the stick (representing the sinking cold air center) is twisted down, the cotton candy rises higher above the stick. In a low-pressure area, the red stick is twisted upward, and the pink cotton candy rises around it. These low and high-pressure areas are typically depicted on weather maps as a capital "H" or "L," sometimes encircled. The interaction of cold and high-pressure areas creates weather systems known as warm fronts and cold

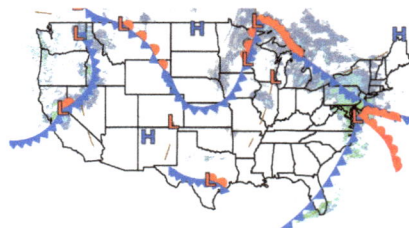

fronts, marked on weather maps by dark blue lines with small triangles for cold fronts and red lines with small half-circles for warm fronts.

Air Pressure Areas & Wind Direction

Observing the wind direction provides insights into the origin of low and high air pressure areas. A low-pressure air parcel spins in an upward counterclockwise spiral, while a high-pressure air parcel spins in a downward clockwise spiral. Facing the wind, the high-pressure area will be on your right, and the low-pressure area will be on your left. Winds from the high-pressure area move downward toward the low-pressure area, filling in behind the rising air.

Low & High Pressure Air Parcels

Troughs & Ridges

The cold air encircling a low-pressure center creates sunken airwaves known as troughs, varying in size and shape. Conversely, the warm air around a high-pressure center forms raised airwaves termed ridges. Ridges typically bring sunny conditions, while troughs often bring cloudy weather.

High Ridge Breakdown

As the jet stream propels weather systems like warm and cold fronts across the landscape, the cool air troughs surrounding the low-pressure area are pushed east and sink under the warm air ridges surrounding the high-pressure area. This situation, called a high-pressure ridge breakdown, can lead to critical fire behavior conditions. Observations linked to a high ridge breakdown resemble those of a cold front, to be discussed in the following pages. Wind speeds intensify under the ridge areas in a southwesterly direction. As the low-pressure center approaches the high-pressure center, temperatures drop, and wind direction shifts in a west-northwesterly direction as the cold front advances into the area.

Weather Fronts

A weather front marks the boundary between an existing pressure system and the one replacing it. These pressure systems or areas move within the high and middle levels of the atmosphere, and the type of front is defined by the pressure system that takes over. As mentioned earlier, low-pressure areas (warm fronts) move in a counterclockwise direction, and high-pressure cold fronts move in a clockwise pattern. When these two air masses approach each other, the wind shifts in directions. Typically, warm fronts are slower moving, bringing moist weather (troughs), while cold fronts are fast-moving, bringing dry weather (ridges).

Several observations can help predict an oncoming warm front due to its slower pace (Gooley 2021).

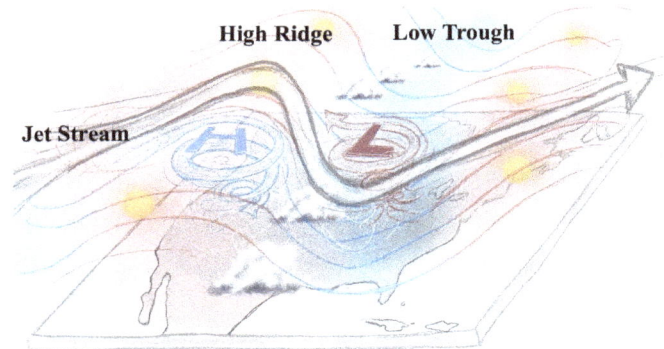

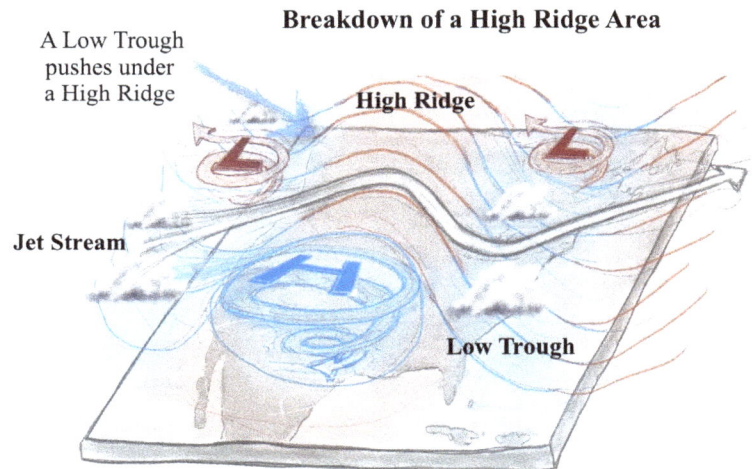

Warm Front

Warm air replacing cold air →

Warm Front Observations

- Cirrus and cirrostratus clouds serve as early indicators of changing weather and an impending warm front.

- Altocumulus clouds may be observed before the arrival of a warm front.

- Winds intensify from an easterly to a southeasterly direction, 10-20 mph, as the warm air mass merges and replaces the cold one, with speeds typically ranging from 10-20 mph.

- Altocumulus, cumulonimbus, and stratus clouds may be present with areas of rain as the warm front moves into the area.

- Relatively warm air and mixed cloud types become apparent as the warm front settles into the area.

- Reduced fire behavior hazards but increased smoke congestion and air quality concerns.

Cold Front Observations

There are both fast and slow cold fronts, each with common and different observations to note. A fast cold front poses a higher fire danger with more air lifting and unstable atmospheric conditions. Common cold front observations include:

- Clouds appearing in the direction the front is coming from and lowering in the atmosphere over time.

- Winds sharply shifting from a westerly to a northwesterly direction, 15-30 mph, as the cold front moves into the area.

- A relative drop in temperature, sometimes with scattered rain when the cold front arrives. In the western United States, cloud bases are often too high for rain to reach the ground during a cold front, resulting in virga – rain that dissipates before reaching the ground – appearing as hanging dark striations below a cloud.

- Increased fire dangers, especially with a fast cold front, and typically reduced air quality concerns.

- If a second cold front follows the weather system, it usually brings lower humidity levels and higher fire danger conditions.

Stable/Slow Cold Front

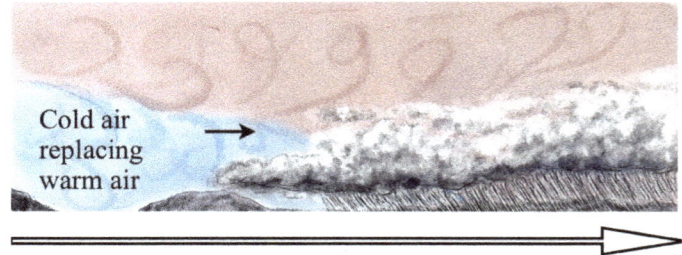

Cold air replacing warm air →

Unstable/Fast Cold Front

Cold air replacing warm air →

Journaling Weather Fronts

Recording weather fronts and dynamic weather changes proves valuable when documented as a time series. In this short series, I have encapsulated some fire weather observations related to cold fronts. While I delve further into this journaling approach in Chapter 7: Fire Mitigation & Readiness, it essentially serves as a storytelling technique. This involves incorporating visuals and information that effectively convey the timeline, setting, characters, elements, and the evolving experience.

Fast, Cold, and Unstable - Cold Front Observations in Chico, California

On an autumn day in the flat valley lands of Chico, California, I noticed the onset of southwesterly winds gaining speed, ranging from 20 to 30 mph. Altocumulus clouds began forming in the distance, prompting me to engage my situational awareness and monitor the approaching cold front.

As the day progressed, a noticeable chill set in, accompanied by a drop in temperature and intensified winds reaching 25-35 mph from the west-northwest. A powerful gust, nearly 60 mph, caught me off guard, sending my hat flying and nearly pushing me off balance. Observing cumulonimbus clouds forming over the nearby mountains and valley, I decided it was time to head home, preparing for my next round of observations.

Throughout the late afternoon, the northwesterly winds persisted, but the majority of clouds dissipated. Despite my skin feeling as dry as the crumbling grasses in my hand, the sky transformed into a beautiful, bright blue canvas. Notably, small saucer-shaped clouds appeared over the eastern mountains, indicating lenticular clouds and suggesting the presence of 20-60 mph foehn winds pushing from the east. With this observation, I concluded my observations.

Weather Front Mapping & Tracking

Observing and journaling large-scale weather fronts and patterns can be challenging. You can express your thoughts on weather observations or create an observational time series, as discussed on the previous page. Sometimes, a simple geographic map can provide the easiest approach. I've purchased a stencil of the United States to assist in sketching individual state boundaries, multiple states, or the entire country. Typically, I keep this sketch small, using black and white pencil or a light-colored pen. I incorporate a few symbolic elements to denote major landscape features, such as mountain ranges, and add symbols for low and high-pressure areas based on my observations. This sketch also serves as a visual location map, which is a valuable addition to your journal. I often include additional location details, like the names of nearby mountain ranges, waterways, and major highways, in the blank space on the sketch.

In my journal, I create a monthly template with a taped piece of paper where I sketch typical clouds observed during that week on the top side and a map featuring forecasted weather patterns on the bottom. I include notes comparing the forecast with actual observations, using this practice to develop a better understanding of cloud observations and changing weather patterns.

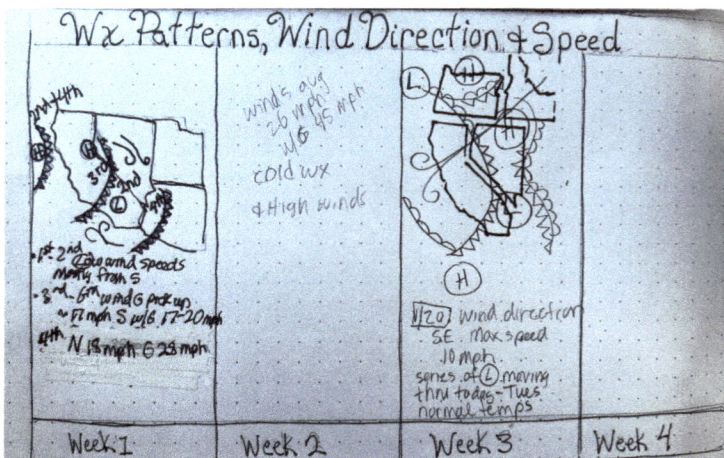

Thunderstorms

Observing thunderstorms is crucial for enhancing situational awareness and assessing fire risks and behavior, especially when associated with cold fronts. Thunderstorms, also known as cumulonimbus clouds, are often linked to high-moisture weather fronts, whether warm or cold, but they can also occur with minimal precipitation. Thunderstorms can take various forms, from a single cumulonimbus cloud cell to multiple cloud clusters, multi-cell lines (e.g., squall lines), or even supercells that can lead to tornadoes. The classification of thunderstorms as wet or dry depends on the minimum precipitation required to saturate surface vegetation, influenced by factors like the type of vegetation in the area (e.g., forests versus grasslands). Making simple observations of rain and virga (precipitation that doesn't reach the ground) from the cloud is essential. Some cumulonimbus clouds may exhibit no observable precipitation or virga, while others may feature a mix of rain and virga, and some may unleash heavy rain downpours. Understanding the phase of cumulonimbus development is crucial for observing wind and moisture indicators, which will be discussed after the section on lightning below.

Lightning

Lightning results from the energy exchange within developing cumulonimbus clouds. While lightning can occur within clouds or between clouds, the focus here is on the two types that strike the ground and can cause wildfires. Negative lightning bolts, emanating from the lower portions of the cloud, are the most common. They often display branching and forking streaks called leaders. Positive lightning bolts, less common and stronger, originate in the upper portions of the cloud and appear wider and brighter. Positive lightning strikes, having more energy, can ignite potentially moistened vegetation.

Positive & Negative Lightning

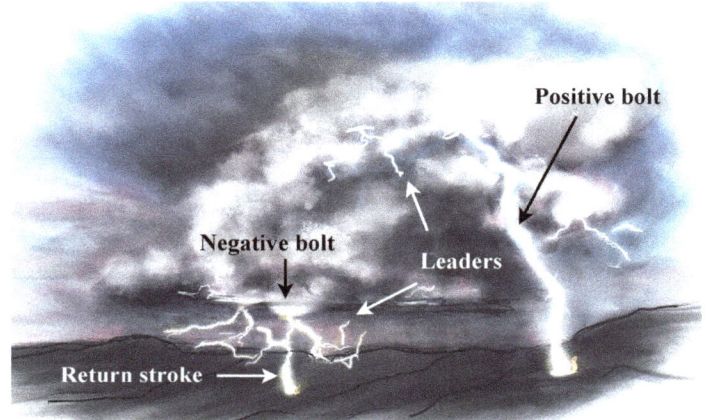

The color of lightning can also provide insights into wet or dry conditions. White lightning suggests fairly dry air, yellow-tinged lightning indicates dry air with dust, red-tinged lightning signifies rain, and blue-tinged lightning suggests hail.

Lightning Color Indicators

White indicates dry air

Yellow indicates dust in the air

Red indicates rain

Blue indicates hail

While color nuances might be challenging to discern, many websites display active lightning, providing additional or alternative ways to observe lightning in an area. Safety is paramount during lightning observations; it is recommended to stay indoors or in a vehicle. If outdoors, avoid high places and tall trees.

There are several websites that display live lightning activity, and various agencies develop lightning strike maps, such as the example from the US Forest Service on this page.

Journaling Lightning Observations

A variety of drawing materials can be used for journaling lightning observations, such as white or black paper, pencils, pens, or watercolors. Visualization approaches can range from using circles, as shown in the lightning color graphic, to sketching the lightning bolt alone or combining it with cumulonimbus cloud and landscape sketches for a more comprehensive depiction. Including lightning maps is also helpful to add context to where lightning is occur and moving across a landscape. Combining visuals and notes of cumulonimbus clouds and lightning is recommended, as the interplay of these elements indicates winds and ignition potential, whether wet, dry, or involving lightning ground strikes. Tips for journaling will be shared after the section on thunderstorm phases.

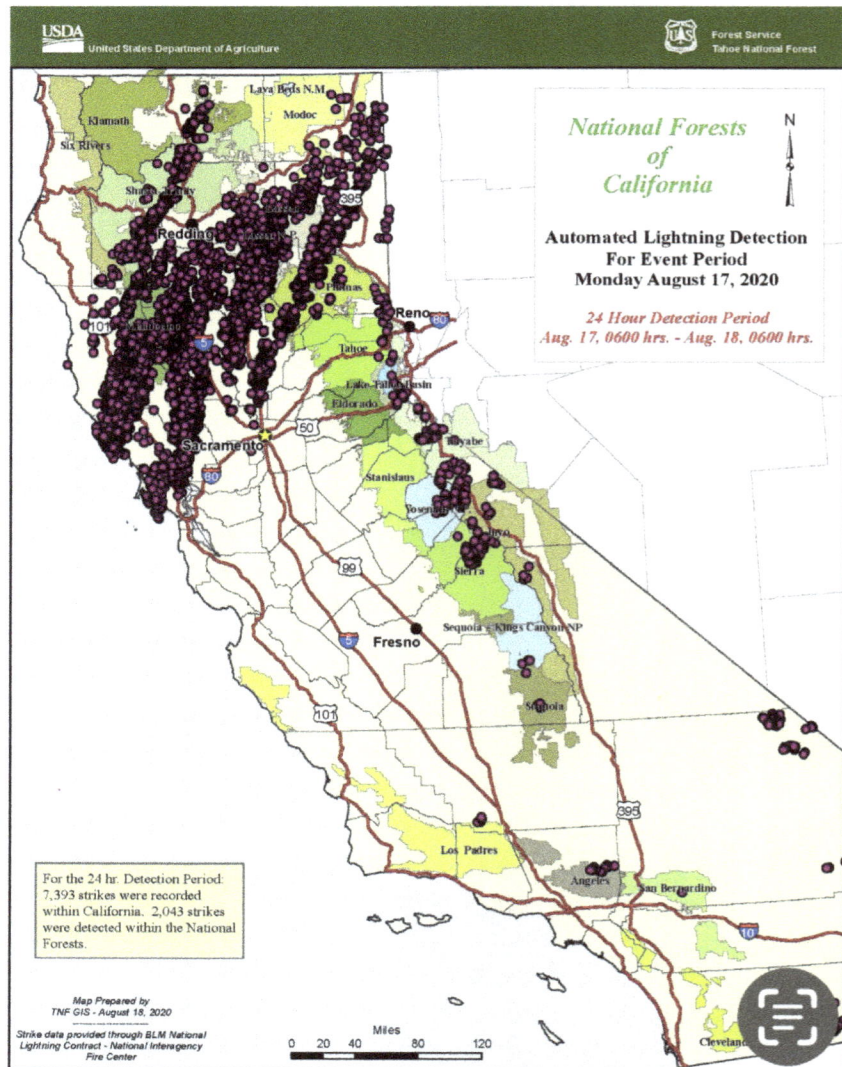

Thunderstorm Phases

A thunderstorm initiates with low to middle-level cumulus clouds transforming into cumulonimbus clouds over time. These phases present varying levels of fire risk, influenced by lightning strikes and changing winds, particularly the wind shear effects from convective updrafts and downdrafts. Dry lightning poses an evident fire risk, and as cumulonimbus clouds build and collapse, swift and erratic downdraft winds can lead to unpredictable fire behavior. The illustration outlines the evolving clouds during thunderstorm development. Yellow arrows signify rising convective heat with wind updrafts, while purple arrows indicate sinking and cooling air with wind downdrafts.

Altocumulus clouds growing tall and billowy signal an early warning sign of potential thunderstorm development. These turret-shaped clouds are known as altocumulus castellanus. Additional cloud types, not depicted in the illustration, associated with thunderstorms, help identify development phases and winds. Shelf clouds, with a wide-wedge shape, may precede cumulonimbus clouds, indicating updraft winds. Bulbous hanging mammatus clouds and funnel-shaped clouds bulging from the bottom of cumulonimbus clouds suggest downdrafts.

Estimating the distance of the thunderstorm is possible by holding your hand out toward the cumulonimbus cloud. If the cloud's height matches all four fingers or your fist, it is approximately 30 miles away (Gooley 2021).

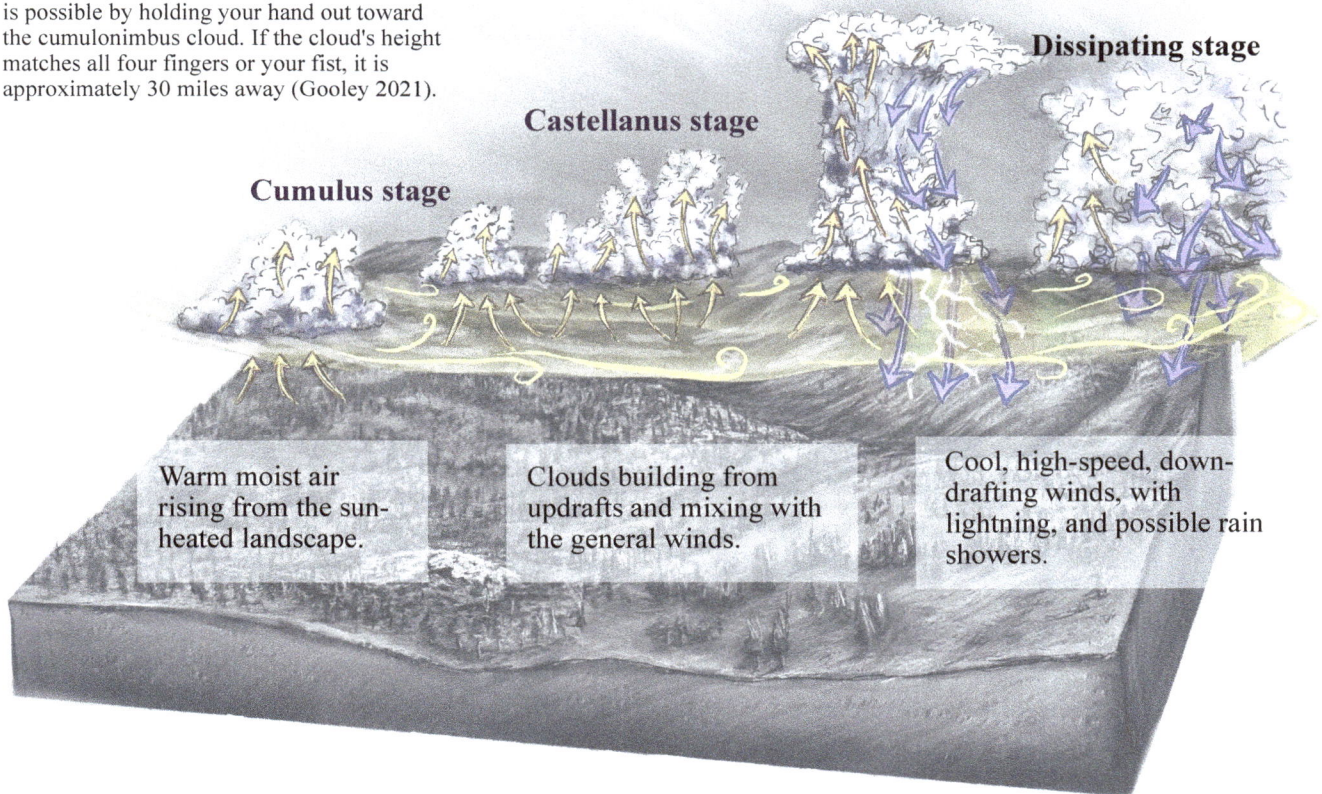

Mature cumulonimbus stage

Dissipating stage

Castellanus stage

Cumulus stage

Warm moist air rising from the sun-heated landscape.

Clouds building from updrafts and mixing with the general winds.

Cool, high-speed, down-drafting winds, with lightning, and possible rain showers.

As altocumulus castellanus clouds evolve into the distinctive cumulonimbus anvil shape, they can extend into the high levels of the atmosphere. The uneven anvil shape reveals the direction of the prevailing wind. Thunderstorms usually develop in the late afternoon after periods of convective heating from the surface. Cold, robust wind gusts can be experienced from miles away, featuring 30 mph updrafts and 100 mph downdrafts. Dark portions of the cloud indicate updraft areas, while lighter areas suggest downdrafts and rain.

Key Thunderstorm Observations & Journaling Approach:

- The shape of mature cumulonimbus clouds, with a large anvil and tilted cloud shapes from wind shear, informs about strong updrafts and downdrafts.

- Observing the shape of the dissipating cumulonimbus cloud stage reveals strong wind shear and downdraft winds.

- Signs of virga indicate strong wind shear and downdraft/microburst winds without saturating precipitation.

- Dust clouds or dust vortices on the ground below the cumulonimbus cloud indicate wind shear from microburst winds.

- White and yellow-colored lightning bolts may indicate dry air.

- The position and shape of lightning help determine the type of lightning occurring (negative or positive) and the likelihood of igniting a wildfire.

There are various approaches to journaling about thunderstorms, but to link them with fire risks and hazards, I recommend focusing on observations over time to help identify dry and wet thunderstorms and lightning ground strikes. A simple approach is to sketch a horizontal line to represent the ground. You can add mountain shapes over the line or leave it straight, similar to my example. Sketch the shape of the cumulonimbus cloud, emphasizing any wind shear influences. Also try to sketch signs of rain and or virga for each cloud or cluster. You should always add the date next to each observation and may also want to add the time of day. I would also recommend adding the forecasted or measured precipitation for the day. Add any lightning observations emphasizing the location (high or low) to indicate negative or positive lightning bolts and any observed ground strikes. Try to label the observation as a wet or dry thunderstorm or write as a question. If you want to create a more detailed sketch, I have some sketching and painting tips below.

Wet Cumulonimbus
(Rain)

March 20, 2022
precipitation
0.5 inches

Mixed Cumulonimbus
(Virga & Rain)

May 15, 2022
precipitation
0.1 inches

Dry Cumulonimbus
(Virga)

Sept 8, 2022
precipitation
0 inches

Negative lightning bolt with a dry strike

Pencil & Watercolor Sketch of a Cumulonimbus Cloud

Step 1. Start with a light pencil sketch, including an outline of the cloud shape, any lightning bolts, virga and or rain, and some of the landscape below.

Step 2. Use watercolor or colored pencil to add color around the cloud and over the landscape. Also add some light watercolor or colored pencil over dark areas of the cloud. I have used a purple color for the shaded areas of the cloud to help differentiate those areas from the sky.

Step 3. Use more color over the sky, landscape, and clouds until you feel the cloud has enough shadow and definition to accentuate billowing cloudlets and the wind shear. Also add some darker gray below the cloud where the rain or virga is observed. I like to use vertical pencil lines to help differentiate the rain from the cloud.

Step 4. Use some white gauche paint and or white gel pen over the virga or rain areas, if you want to accentuate sunlight. If you have any lightning bolts, use white gel pen to fill in the center of the bolt and use a fine point colored pencil to add any color around the edges or just add notes about the color.

Atmospheric Stability & Instability

The high and low-pressure areas influence the atmosphere, rendering it stable, partially stable, or unstable, with significant implications for assessing potential fire behavior. The following observations are associated with generally stable or unstable conditions and do not delve into the various partially stable conditions.

Stable atmosphere with sinking clouds

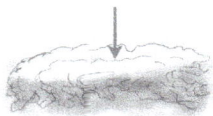

Unstable atmosphere with rising clouds

Stable Atmosphere

In a stable or partially stable atmosphere, rising warm air from the earth is impeded or capped off at lower altitudes due to high winds or a layer of cool air above the warm air. This can lead to issues with smoke dispersal, discussed further in Chapter 8: Fire & Smoke, causing more smoke and air quality problems by holding air close to the surface.

Several observations indicate a stable atmosphere, such as flattened low-hanging clouds, lack of surface winds, lingering temperature inversions, and low-drifting smoke and fog. Additional indicators include high-level clouds like cirrus clouds, stretched and pulled by high winds, contributing to a partially stable atmosphere. It's worth noting that atmospheric stability can change within a few hours or weeks, often stabilizing overnight and becoming unstable later in the morning as temperature inversions lift and warm air rises throughout the day.

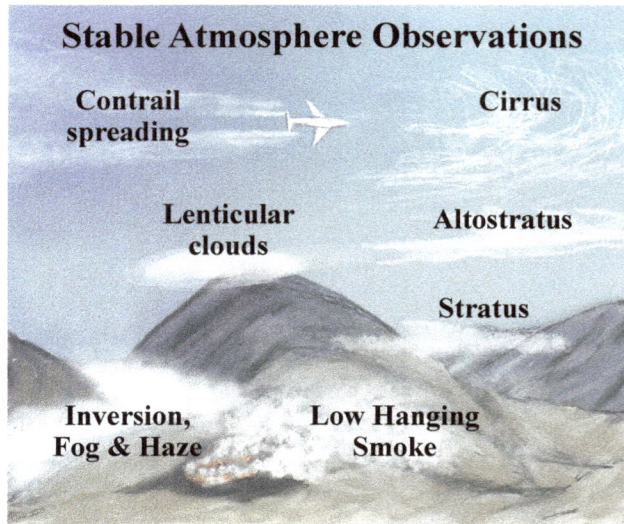

Stable Atmosphere Observations

Contrail spreading

Cirrus

Lenticular clouds

Altostratus

Stratus

Inversion, Fog & Haze

Low Hanging Smoke

On a clear day, indicators of a stable atmosphere include phenomena like a squished-looking sun and objects on land or water appearing to float (a Fat Morgana). The sky may also appear more brown or tan, especially close to the horizon and at sunrise and sunset.

Stable Atmosphere Summary

High-level

- Cirrus clouds with a filmy appearance against the sun or moon

Mid-level

- Altostratus clouds stretched by the wind or sinking from high moisture levels in a warm front
- Lenticular and mountain cap clouds formed by high winds

Low-level

- Stratus clouds
- Poor visibility, haze, and a lighter milky-colored sky

- Limited rise of smoke columns with low-drifting smoke
- Temperature inversions and/or fog, typical in the early morning
- Lower surface wind speeds, except in the case of terrain winds
- Lower intensity fire behavior unless increased surface winds (foehn) occur.

Unstable Atmosphere

In an unstable or partially unstable atmosphere, warm air is always beneath cool air, often caused by convective heating from the earth. This accelerates rising air movement and creates a lifting effect, observed in small-scale low-pressure systems like fires, fire whirls, and thunderstorms. Rising air in an unstable atmosphere can contribute to more intense fire behavior and higher flame lengths.

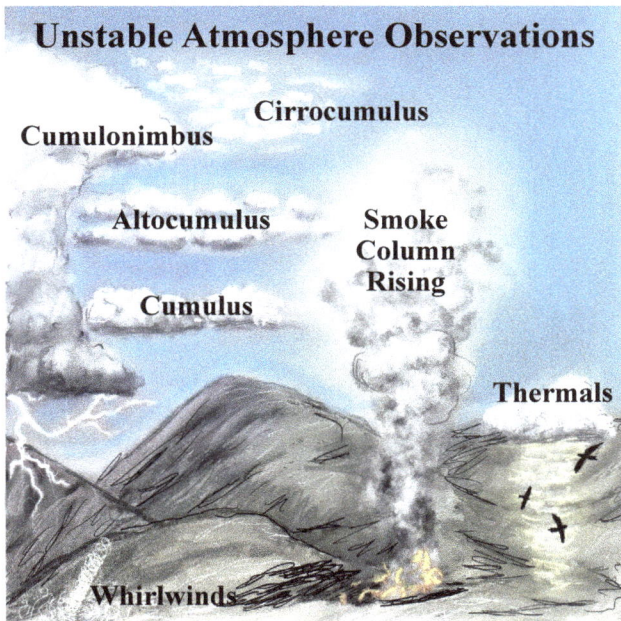

Unstable Atmosphere Observations

Key indicators of an unstable atmosphere include vertical movements of clouds, such as building cumulus becoming castellanus and cumulonimbus clouds. When clouds grow taller than they are wide, it signifies a very unstable atmosphere.

Without clouds, the sky in an unstable atmosphere appears clear and bright blue, with clean white colors near the horizon. Convective influences in the lower atmosphere can be observed through large birds soaring in a circular pattern to gain lift or the presence of whirlwinds or dust devils.

Unstable Atmosphere Summary

High-level
- Numerous cirrocumulus clouds appearing as a row
- Sky typically appears darker blue if not obscured by cloud layers or lower-level particles and pollution, which can give the sky a milky color.

Mid-level
- Altocumulus and cumulonimbus clouds
- Sky color transitions between a darker blue at the upper level and a medium blue.

Low-level
- Inversion lifting or weak inversion
- Good visibility
- Increasing surface wind speeds
- Cumulus clouds
- Smoke plumes rising straight up
- Whirlwinds and air thermals
- Higher surface wind speeds

Orographic Clouds & Winds

Orographic clouds and winds emerge when higher-level general winds interact with lower local winds, and the rising convective heat and moisture coalesce into clouds along mountain tops. The positioning of these clouds serves as an indicator of potential terrain-driven winds.

Initiate your observations by examining terrain features and noting the locations of altocumulus clouds. Mountain-cap clouds, stationary atop peaks, reveal convective heating and cooling along elevational transitions. Altocumulus lenticularis, flat disc-shaped clouds on the lee side of mountains, moving downwind for miles, signal mountain waves and potential downslope winds. The dry lee side and downslope winds, reaching speeds of up to 90 mph and

accelerating through steep terrain (foehn winds), can lead to extreme fire behaviors. Examples include the Santa Ana winds in Southern California and the Chinook winds on the eastern slopes of the Rocky Mountain Front.

Altocumulus clouds along the lee side of mountains can indicate areas where general winds converge into high-speed turbulent zones, contributing to extreme fire behaviors. Altocumulus clouds forming in mountain gaps and between steep canyons are indicators of high-speed channel and gap winds, leading to extreme fire behaviors.

An additional high-speed wind, not depicted in the illustration, is the glacier winds. These winds result from variable heating and cooling along steep icy surfaces, sinking downslope at speeds typically ranging between 30-50 mph.

Orographic Clouds & Winds

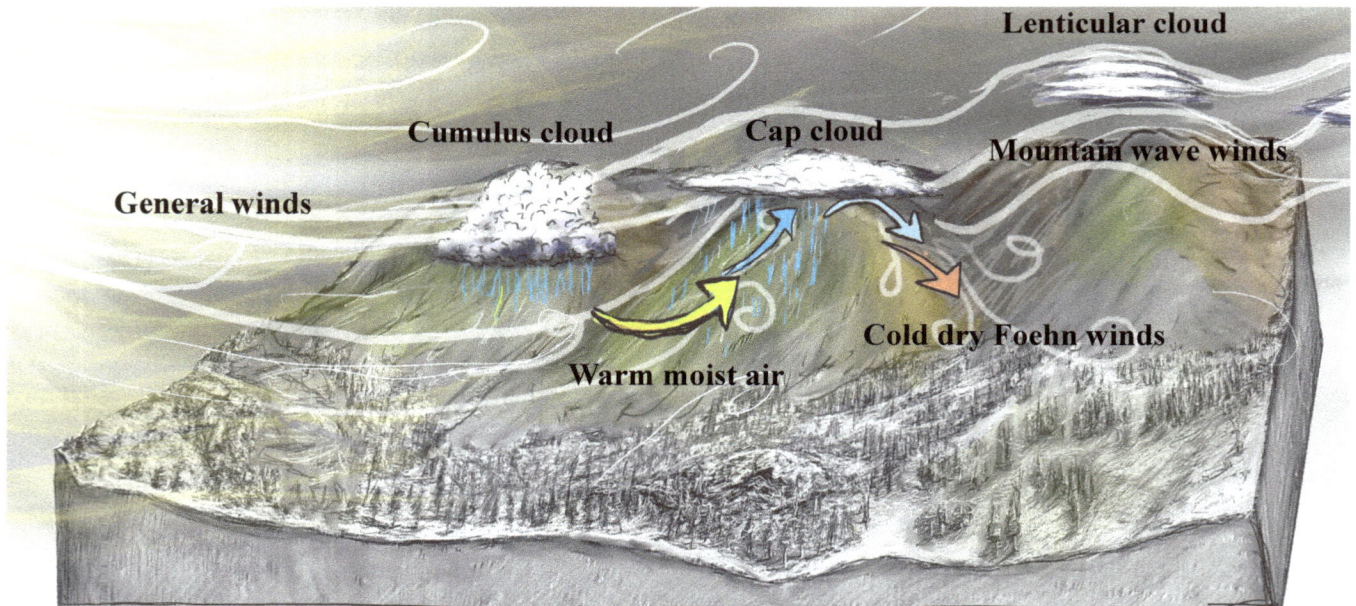

Lenticular cloud

Cumulus cloud

Cap cloud

Mountain wave winds

General winds

Warm moist air

Cold dry Foehn winds

Diurnal Terrain Winds

Understanding the diurnal nature of many convective and orographic winds is crucial for situational awareness. Various NWCG fire behavior guides highlight significant diurnal winds, including upslope, downslope, upvalley, downvalley, sea breeze, and land breeze.

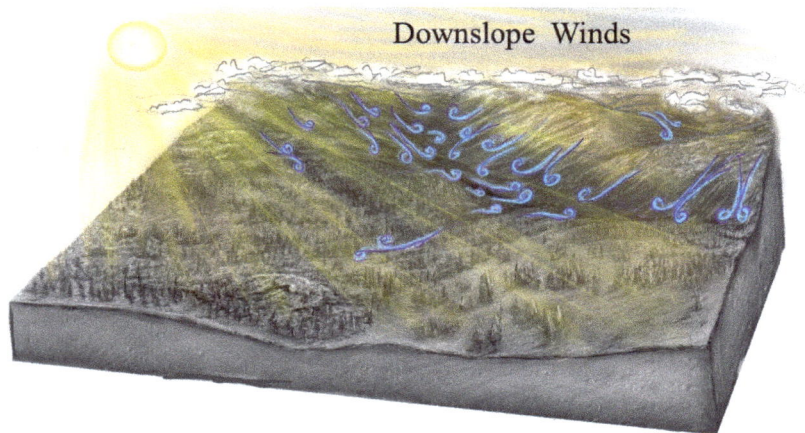

Downslope winds manifest in the evening after sunset as slopes cool, and air descends downslope. Wind speeds generally range between 2-5 mph.

Upslope winds typically occur in late morning and afternoon, as the sun warms mountain slopes, causing warm air to rise upslope. Speeds typically range between 3-8 mph.

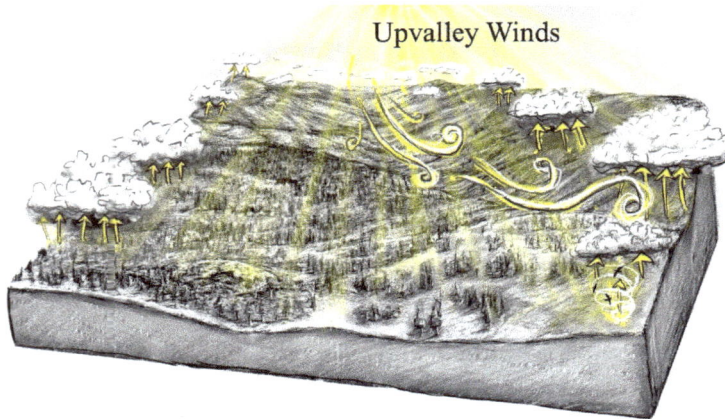

Upvalley Winds

Upvalley winds appear in the late afternoon after upslope winds have ceased, valley areas have warmed, and warm air rises, flowing through the valley. Wind speeds typically range between 10-15 mph.

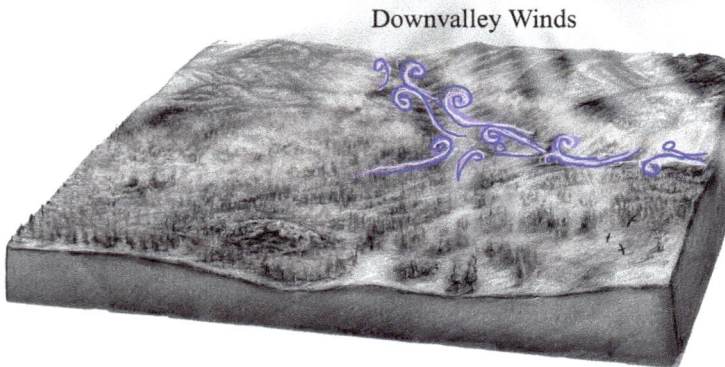

Downvalley Winds

Downvalley winds occur late at night after downslope winds have ceased, and cool air pools and sinks through the valley. These winds typically range between 5-10 mph.

Land & Sea Breezes

Sea and land breezes are linked to temperature and moisture exchanges between the ocean and land at different times of the day.

A sea breeze develops in late morning and afternoon as warm air rises over the land, pulling cool air from the ocean inland beneath it. Cumulus clouds a few miles or more inland during late morning and afternoon are indicative of a sea breeze. Sea breeze speeds usually range between 10-20 mph, unless other high and local winds interact or replace them.

Sea Breeze

A land breeze occurs at night when warmer air over the ocean, which takes longer to gain and lose heat, rises. Meanwhile, cool air over the land sinks down to replace the lifted air over the ocean. Low cumulus and stratus clouds over the ocean at night and in the early morning can be indicative of the land breeze. These winds typically range between 3-10 mph.

Land Breeze

Open & Filtered Winds

General and local winds not only traverse the terrain but are also filtered through vegetation. In fire management definitions, these winds are categorized into open surface winds, measured at 20 to 30 feet above the dominant vegetation, and mid-flame winds. The speed of these winds varies based on general and local wind influences. Mid-flame winds, measured at the mid-height of flames, can be sheltered or filtered by vegetation.

You can estimate mid-flame winds by dividing the forecasted general wind speed by slope and forest sheltering calculations, as illustrated. Various data calculations determine a fire's rate of spread. For a general estimate in forest and shrubland ecosystems, use the 10% wind speed rule, and 20% of the wind speed in grassland ecosystems under dry conditions— Rule: 10% to 20% of the 20-30 foot average wind speed (Cruz 2019). Compare your calculations for mid-flame wind speeds and fire rate of spread based on the 10% rule. Further details about evaluating the fire's rate of spread are covered in Chapter 4: Fire Fuels and Chapter 8: Fire & Smoke.

Mid-flame winds in a thick forest, on flat ground, are less than 1/5 of the 20-foot wind speed

Mid-flame winds in an open forest, on flat ground, are about 1/3 of the 20-foot wind speed

Mid-flame winds in the open, on flat ground, are about 1/2 of the 20-foot wind speed

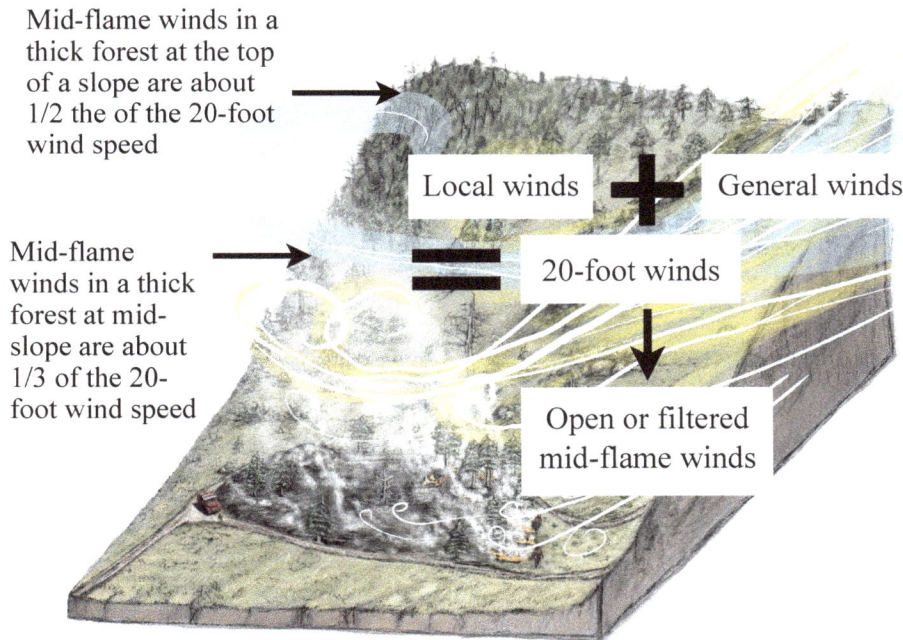

Mid-flame winds in a thick forest at the top of a slope are about 1/2 the of the 20-foot wind speed

Mid-flame winds in a thick forest at mid-slope are about 1/3 of the 20-foot wind speed

Local winds **+** General winds

= 20-foot winds

Open or filtered mid-flame winds

Funneled Winds—Forest Chimneys

A small-scale wind crucial for assessing potential fire behavior is found in forest openings. These winds develop when warm air in a forest opening rises, pulling cooler air from the surrounding forest and acting as a chimney. The same forest opening will be colder at night, causing air to sink into the opening, with winds flowing into the thicker forest area. These breezes may be subtle, but standing inside a forest opening and then deeper within the forest should reveal noticeable differences. These winds can influence fire behavior within a forest. A useful way to sketch this effect is by emphasizing sunlit areas and shadows. Refer to page 81 of Chapter 3: Fire Fuels for tips on sketching a forest opening.

Formed by Winds—Past Winds

Observing landscapes shaped by the wind, such as rolling sand dunes and carved snowdrifts, provides insights into past prevailing wind influences on the land and vegetation. Known as mean wind speed, this occurs over different seasons and has a cumulative effect. The structure and form of tree or shrub species, along with their location within the terrain, influence the level of wind effects. Individual or clumped trees in the open and trees along the forest edge offer the best indicators for these wind effects.

Wind-Flagged

Wind-flagged trees indicate wind direction and a range of wind speeds. The Griggs-Putnam Index is one tool to estimate wind speed and direction from mean or historic wind effects on trees. Further information on this index will be shared later in this section.

Wind-Felled

Wind-felled trees and branches signal high and extreme wind speeds, but can also indicate tree disease and soil issues. In many cases, these signs may point to storm winds and strong downdrafts. Estimate past wind direction by observing the fallen tree canopy.

Wind-Sheltered

In some ecosystems where vegetation is sparse and growth forms are less easily altered by the wind, look for wind-sheltered effects. Grass and vegetation may accumulate on the lee side of shrubs and trees.

This effect is observable in various vegetation communities, revealing subtle differences in habitat use and animal activities. For instance, notice small burrows or mammal scat on the lee side of shrubs, where rabbits and mice find shelter from the wind.

Griggs-Putnam Wind Deformation Index

Developed for wind energy projects, the Griggs-Putnam Wind Deformation Index estimates wind speeds based on the mean prevailing wind. Originally calibrated for Douglas-fir and ponderosa pine, it includes a scale for broadleaf deciduous trees. The triangular and conical shape of evergreen tree crowns displays different wind deformations than the circular, oblong, and spreading shapes of deciduous tree crowns. Wind flagging effects are commonly associated with strong winds, but there are also observations for lower wind speeds. Deformation effects vary based on the timing, seasonal nature of prevailing winds, or winds with high salt levels. Coastal trees exhibit stronger deformation in similar wind speeds compared to inland trees.

Seasonal Wind-Flagging & Griggs-Putnam Index Observations
(Lawrence 1939 & Putnam 1948)

Strong Prevailing Winds Only in the Fall to Early Spring (Non Growing Season)

Strong Prevailing Winds Only in the Spring to Late Summer (Growing Season)

Strong Prevailing Winds All Seasons

Prevailing wind direction

Winter-flagged trees display a tattered appearance, characterized by small early-growth branches on the windward side and long branches on the leeward side of the tree. The long branch tips seem clipped and angled, giving the tree profile a chevron shape.

During spring to summer, flagged trees lack branches on the windward side and exhibit long, bushy branches on the leeward side. Branches closer to the windward side are swept toward the leeward side. The tree profile appears jagged, with shorter branches intermixed along the leeward side.

All-season flagged trees have no branches on the windward side and very bushy branches on the leeward side. The tree profile can vary depending on the prevailing seasonal winds. If the seasonal winds come from the same direction, the windward side will appear smooth and rounded, while the tree profile will have an angled and wedge shape.

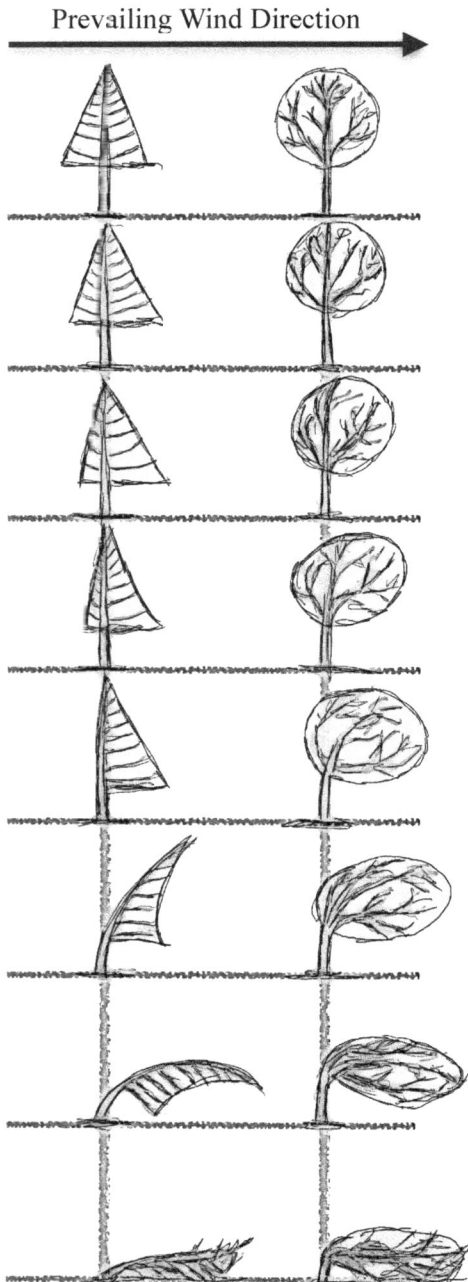

Prevailing Wind Direction

The effects listed below are standard for trees and do not include the effects of salt, ice, or snow that would exacerbate the appearance..

No Effect (0-6 mph mean wind speeds). No observable deformation to the tree

Brushing (7-9 mph winds). Needles, leaves, and small branches on the windward side appear bent (brushed) away from the prevailing wind. Potentially subtle tree crown deformation.

Slight Flagging (9-11 mph winds). Brushed effects with small branches on the windward side appearing bent away from the prevailing wind. An asymmetric appearance with shorter branches on the windward side and longer branches on the lee-side.

Moderate Flagging (11-13 mph winds). Brushed effects and larger branches on the windward side bent away from the prevailing winds. A growing asymmetric appearance to the tree crown.

Strong Flagging (13-16 mph winds)
Brushing effects and all tree branches bent away from the prevailing winds. A strong asymmetric appearance to tree crowns, like a flag.

Partial Throwing (16-18 mph winds). Strong brushing and flagging with the upper tree trunk bent away from the prevailing winds. A lopsided and asymmetric appearance to the tree.

Complete Throwing (18-21 mph winds). The entire tree trunk is bent away from the prevailing winds. A strongly lopsided and leaning tree.

Carpeting (Over 21 mph winds). The tree is leaning against the ground and growing in a creeping and shrublike form.

When observing wind effects, walk around a tree, observe branch lengths for a good viewpoint of the tree profile, and consider sketching a tree cross-section. Include estimated wind speeds and directions, comparing them with calculated mean wind speeds based on local climate. Keep in mind the seasonal influences and potential deformation differences between basic tree shapes as you reference the illustrated index on the previous page. Tips for drawing different tree shapes are available in Chapter 4: Fire Fuels.

Felt Winds — Beaufort Wind Force Scale

One of my favorite tools for estimating wind speed is the Beaufort Wind Force Scale. In 1805, British Admiral Sir Francis Beaufort created this scale to help sailors navigate using consistent visual cues. The scale has evolved for wind observations on land and has been modified for firefighter wind observations.

On the next two pages, I have adapted the wind force scale by merging firefighter terminology, other relevant terms, and observations more suitable for journaling about the fire environment. I omitted the wind force scale numbers to avoid memorizing another index or numbering system. I am more interested in the observational cues and associated wind speeds. The wind speed categories in my scale are the same as the original, with additional observations engaging multiple senses and deepening observations for breezes. I have also included some potential observations based on 2018 research by Loïc Tadrist et al. on foliage motion under wind influences. These observations encompass leaf flutters to branch buffeting, associated with specific wind speeds and movements of large-lobed leaves. Small illustrations and descriptions for closer observations are added to the side of my modified Beaufort Wind Force Scale.

When using scales, indexes, and protocols for specific surveys, I recommend following official guidance. However, when connecting with your personal sense of something, I recommend adapting labels and descriptive terms that resonate more strongly with your understanding and experience. Keep the original and general wind force descriptions within the same wind speed categories as a baseline and add notes on personal observations that may relate better to your local area.

The key to these observations is discerning subtle differences in vegetation movements based on wind speed categories. For example, a light breeze may only lift and slightly shake leaves, while higher wind speeds may cause trees to wave. Gale or storm-level winds may break and fell trees and tear roofing materials from houses. The included observations and descriptions are generalized and should work in many different environments.

I recommend using the same tree in an open area and/or along a forest edge close to home for regular wind observations. This is a practice you'll want to do throughout the year and expand to different vegetation communities once you've developed your observation skills. Consider purchasing or creating a see-through grid and using the vertical grid lines to estimate the profile and posture of the vegetation (non-wind shape) and the horizontal grid lines to compare the angle of movement. A great journaling exercise for these observations is to explore different descriptive terms and metaphors for your experiences and observations at different wind speed categories. You may want to describe light winds as whispering, dulcet, or lilting, and growing wind speeds as rich and clear, or strong winds as howling, explosive, or deafening. Other terms may describe the pattern and pulse of winds, such as staccato, cascading, or rolling waves. You may even want to pull out a thesaurus at home and create a table of descriptive terms to explore and learn what resonates for you.

I have included a table with the different wind types discussed in this chapter on the next two pages. As you practice your wind force observations, try to include the potential wind types that may be associated with them. Also, refer back to the wind deformation observations of the mean winds and use those as comparisons to the different trends in wind directions and speeds in your area.

Modified Beaufort Wind Force Scale

Hurricane Force Wind (74+ mph): Violent and destructive winds.

Storm Wind (55-72 mph): Rarely experienced winds. Considerable damage to buildings.

Gale Wind (47-54 mph): Seldom experienced winds. Trees are broken. Signs blown down, and damage to buildings.

Dangerous Wind (39-46 mph): Winds cause some structural damage. Extreme fire behavior.

Severe Wind (32-38 mph): that cause extreme stress on objects. Extreme fire behavior. Tree canopy and buildings offer no protection.

Very Strong Wind (25-31 mph): Winds damage tree tops. Very difficult to walk.

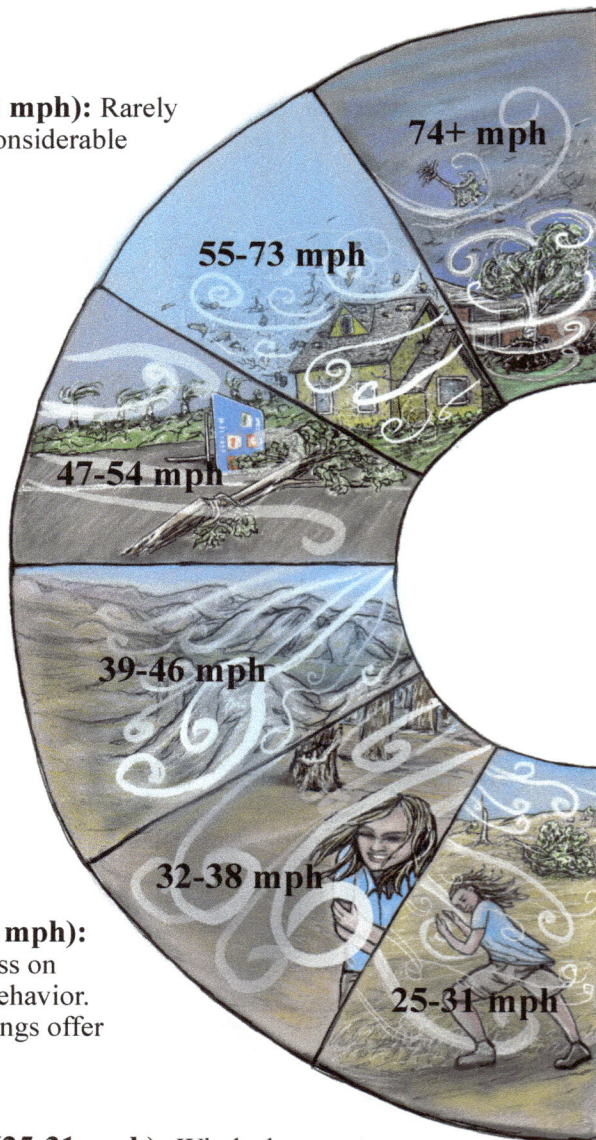

Calm (0 mph): A feeling of stillness. Smoke rises strait up (unstable atmosphere) or fans out in layers (stable atmosphere).

Subtle Breeze (1-3 mph): Smoke plume bends with the wind. Thermals with clouds and soaring birds. The tops of grasses sway.

Large leaves gently lift on the windward side of trees with light rattling sounds.

Light Breeze (4-7 mph): Winds noticeable on the face. In the open, high tree branches and the small branches on pole-sized trees gently sway.

Large leaves fold and flap with brisk rattling sounds.

Strong Breeze/Light Wind (8-10 mph): Grasses billow and wave. Small branches are in constant motion throughout the tree canopy. Tree tops, in dense forests, briskly sway.

Large leaves fold, wrap, and rotate with raucous rattling sounds.

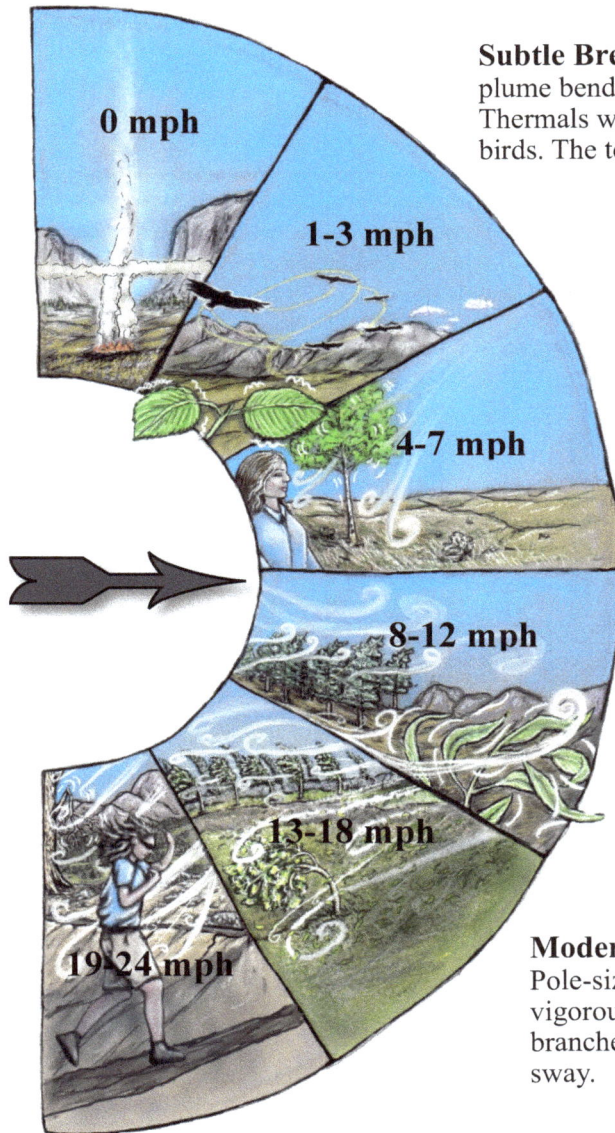

Moderate Wind (13-18 mph): Pole-sized trees, in the open, vigorously sway with clacking branches. Entire trees in the forests sway.

Difficult to discern individual leaf or tree sounds from the terrain and cumulative wind sounds.

0 mph

1-3 mph

4-7 mph

8-12 mph

13-18 mph

19-24 mph

Strong Wind (19-24 mph): Trees vigorously shaken. Branches break. Resistance felt when walking. Power lines thrum.

Wind Types Table

Wind Type	Speed	Wind Force	Timing	Direction	Description
Downslope winds	2-5 mph	Subtle to light breeze	In the evening after sunset and when the daytime winds end	Downhill	Steeper hillsides where cooling air on a hillside sinks downhill.
Upslope winds	3-8 mph	Subtle to strong breeze	In the late morning	Uphill	Occurs when the tops and sides of steep slopes heat-up from the sun and the warm air rises pulling the airflow uphill.
Land breeze	3-10 mph	Subtle to strong breeze	During the night	Offshore	Occurs when warm air over the ocean rises and cool air over the land sinks pulling winds out to the ocean/sea (land to sea).
Downvalley winds	5-10	Light to strong breeze	Occurs late at night after the downslope winds have ended	Down-valley	Cooled air and winds push downvalley.
Upvalley winds	10-15 mph	Light to strong breeze	Occurs in the late afternoons after upslope winds have ended	Upvalley	Valley lands heated up by the sun and upvalley/cross-slope winds are created.
Sea breeze	10-20 mph	Strong breeze to moderate wind	Occurs late in the mornings throughout the afternoon	Onshore	Warming air rises over the landscape and the cooler air over the ocean is pulled in behind (sea to land). Stronger on sunny days.
Warm front winds	10-20 mph	Strong breeze to moderate wind	Southeasterly direction in the Northern hemisphere. Variable and seasonal	From the southeast	An air mass/weather systems that are slow moving with warm moist air moving in a counterclockwise pattern. Expect wind shifts as the front moves in.

Wind Type	Speed	Wind Force	Timing	Direction	Description
Cold front winds	15-30 mph	Strong to very strong winds	When a cold high pressure system replaces a warm low pressure system	Northwesterly winds in the Northern hemisphere. Variable and seasonal	Occurs when a cold high pressure area replaces a warm low pressure area. Seasonally influenced patterns.
Low level jets	25-45 mph	Very strong tdamaging winds	Strongest in the early morning. Can be enhanced by cold fronts.	High above the ground and typically blow in a southerly direction parallel to a cold front boundary	Typical in the Rocky Mountains and high plains. Created by temperature gradients of high elevation mountains and by cold and adjacent warm air mass interactions.
Glacier winds	30-50 mph	Dangerous to gale force winds	Variable with warming temperature changes	Downslope from icy mountains with glacier flows	A shallow gravity wind along icy surfaces of a glacier. Caused by the temperature differences between the air in contact with cold surfaces and in adjacent free air.
Thunderst orm winds	25-60 mph	Very strong to storm winds	Often occurs in the late-afternoon	Radiate from the center of the storm in updrafts & downdrafts	Typical with warm fronts and cold fronts with high moisture levels.
Foehn/ Chinook and Gap winds	20-90 mph	Strong to hurricane level winds. Lenticular clouds	When general/ frontal winds pass over mountains. Seasonally influenced	Downhill on steep leeward slopes	General/ frontal winds cascade over the leeward side of high elevation mountains. Winds become warm and dry as they move downslope.
Vortex winds	50-120 mph	Gale force to hurricane wind levels	During unstable atmospheric conditions and local heating	Vortex spinning	Can be caused by small whirlwinds triggered by local winds on the lee-side of topographic features or by large whirlwinds triggered by supercell thunderstorms.

Wind Metadata, Maps & Graphs

One challenge in journaling about wind types is the highly variable weather data on different websites. You may find that historic and weather trend websites report data from a nearby weather station rather than your exact local area. Many weather stations use a meter positioned somewhat higher, closer to monitoring the 20-foot wind level. This data might be more suitable for assessing larger weather system winds, such as cold fronts and warm fronts. Consider what wind speed and direction trends may tell you about common wind types in the overall area. A regular observance and journaling practice of your local winds may help you interpret weather station data and understand terrain and diurnal winds.

Keep in mind that there will be significant differences between seasons, with stronger indications of terrain and diurnal winds during warmer periods.

Remember that weather system winds can dominate local terrain winds, so compare your large weather system map with your local wind direction data. This is a thinking process, so don't worry about guessing wrong.

While you can print and paste wind graphs from your favorite weather website into your journal, recreating a graph can help you remember and

evaluate the winds better than just referencing a website. When creating your wind graph, consider organizing it with broad time periods where wind directions are most similar (northerly, westerly, southerly, easterly directions). Note whether these

Puget Sound Ecoregion
Cascade mtns.
Ridgefield, WA
Olympic mtns

Present Winds
High pressure system over Pacific ocean with prevailing winds from NNW and or Seabreeze through the sound and river drainage.

Unstable Atmosphere

Sky has cumulus clouds which appear to be building up along the hills to the west and along the Columbia River toward the coastline. May also be altocumulus. Clouds taller than wide.

Hillsides with gentle to moderate slopes (<30%). Aligned N to S.

Past Wind Signs
Subtle bend in around 10% of trees at the uppermost tip and lower tree branches

Leaning NNW & NE. This is a different direction from current/present winds. Prevailing winds in the winter are from the south SBW.

Estimate 5 mph at eye level winds.

Soft rattle of leaves & small branches

Sheltered eye level winds along trail.

Forecasted Winds

Time	8am	9am	10am	11am	12pm	1pm	2pm	3pm	4pm	5pm
Speed	5 mph	5 mph	8 mph	6 mph	9	6	9	10	8	6
Direction	N	NNW	NW	N	W	N	NW	WNW	NW	NW

wind directions and speeds best associate with a particular wind type, as described in the table on the previous page. I recommend creating a map or 3D landscape sketch, as shown earlier in the chapter, to compare with forecasted wind directions and assess if wind timing and direction relate to weather system and terrain winds. In this process, a mix of data sources, visuals, and observations can help you develop a better sense of wind types in your area.

Past & Present Winds Prior to Fire

Present Winds During Fire

Past Winds Post Fire

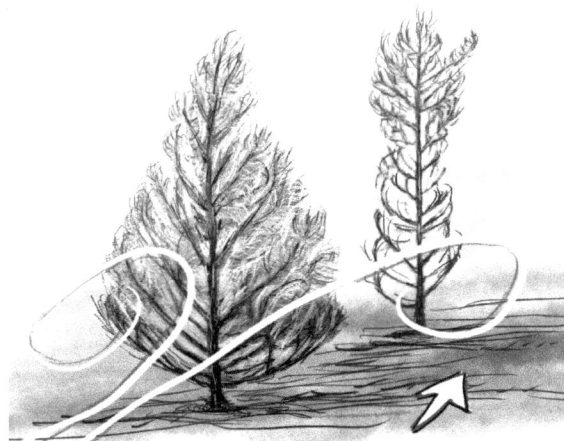

Wind Situational Awareness

Journaling for situational awareness involves building an ongoing observation practice to stay attuned to changing levels of risk, such as potential, current, and past fire behavior. It's crucial to make this a regular practice, with sketches being a supplementary aspect rather than the primary focus. I've used daily planners, small notebooks, and affordable sketchpads, primarily filled with written notes and metadata about the weather.

Consider giving yourself wind observation prompts for past, present, and predicted winds. Label the weather data from meteorological sources as "forecasted" and include both forecasted and observed weather information for comparisons. Utilize different visual scales and multiple sensory observations— visual cues, sounds, scents, and skin—to better associate weather systems and terrain-driven winds.

A journaling technique is to use different colored ink for titles of past, present, and predicted. You can also tape vellum paper into your journal for predicted winds and use actual journal pages for past and present winds. Create a perpetual journal with small sketches and notes about wind speed categories or wind types over time. Dedicate pages in your journal for seasonal or monthly wind observations, adding small diagrams or sketches with dates, times, wind speeds, and wind directions.

Estimating Potential Wildfire Risk & Fire Movements

Focus observations around increasing fire risk. Fire danger and red flag wind conditions vary, so research local red flag wind speeds to refine your observations. A good starting point for comparisons is several hours to several days of winds at around 10 mph. Prescribed fires in the United States often recommend winds under 10 mph. Wind speeds over 10 mph, gusty winds, and shifting wind directions during the dry season pose a higher fire risk in many ecosystems.

Estimate a wildfire's average forward rate of spread by multiplying 10-20% with the average open/ unsheltered wind speeds. For nature journaling, use wind speeds and directions as generalized fire behavior indicators. Compare wind speed/fire spread rules for forecasted, measured, or wind speed indicators (Griggs-Putnam & Beaufort). Include observations on when and where wind directions change to estimate the potential path and speed of the fire.

- 10% of the average wind speed in shrub and forest ecosystems

- 20% of the average wind speed in grassland ecosystems

- Use wind direction to estimate the fire's potential movement

Positional Awareness

Develop positional awareness while journaling about weather. Your wind, temperature, and humidity observations will change as you move. Include a location or route map and a table with forecasted winds during your time outdoors. You can visualize how you experience the wind as you move through a landscape by using something as simple as a stick figure, with hair or clothing movements, to indicate the wind speed and direction.

Include notes on how the wind felt at different times and locations. Ensure to incorporate predictions, but don't solely rely on forecasts—develop your observation skills through on-the-ground experiences. I have an example of my wind and positional awareness observations on the next page.

Desert Walk and Wind Observations
Desert Hot Springs, CA
9 am and 11 am on April 16, 2021

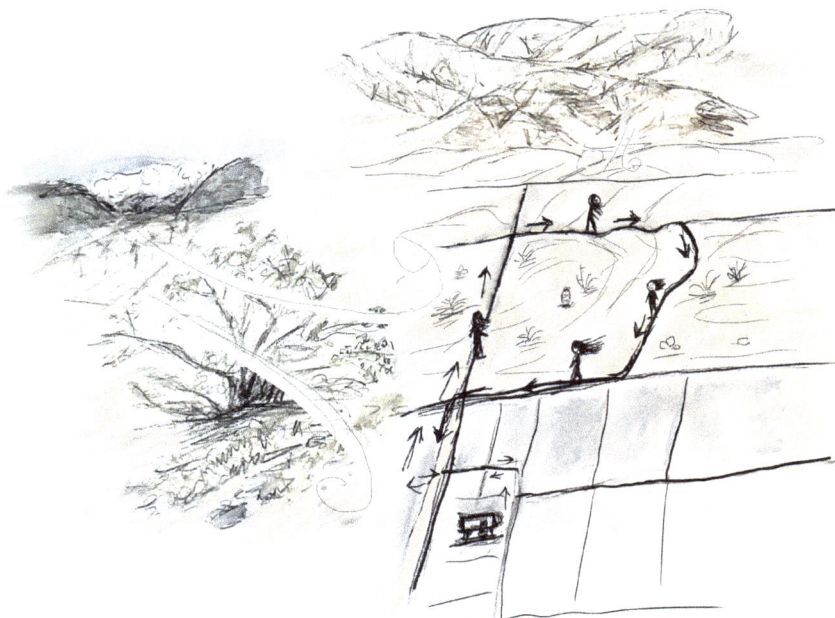

I observed a gap in the clouds to the northwest, beyond the mountains in the valley of windmills. A strong breeze blew from the west-northwest, brushing against the left side of my face and tousling my hair. The scent of desert shrubs mingled with moisture lingered in the air.

As I walked, I noticed grasses, vegetation debris, and small animal burrows on the east-southeast side of most bushes. Upon turning east onto the desert road, the wind picked up, tousling my hair and occasionally blowing it into my face. Additional gusts came from the north and descended from the nearby mountains, about a quarter-mile to the north.

The winds grew stronger as I headed south, causing the desert shrubs to whip dramatically and sand to sting my eyes. The sound of the wind became loud and haunting. Returning to the trailer, the winds whipped the nearby palm trees, creating a sound reminiscent of heavy rain. The trailer rocked and shook with each heavy gust.

Forecast Weather During Potential Walk

Time	9:00 am	10:00 am	11:00 am	12:00 pm	1:00 pm	2:00 pm	3:00 pm
Wind Speed & Direction	11 mph westerly	13 mph westerly	17 mph westerly	19 mph westerly	20 mph westerly	22 mph westerly	23 mph westerly
Temperature	68° F	71° F	79° F	76° F	78° F	79° F	79° F
Relative Humidity	45%	38%	33%	30%	28%	27%	27%

Chapter 3: Topography

Topography

Topography, one of the three main elements of the fire behavior triangle, has a few key elements we want to focus on for fire environment observations. The NWCG categorizes these as topographic characteristics and topographic features. To observe and journal these elements as part of the fire behavior triangle, we need to think about our perceptions of scale. In Almo Farina's book on Ecosemiotic Landscapes, there are three perceptual landscapes: latent, sensed, and interpreted. The latent landscape is one that is not perceived due to sensory limitations. Animals have different sensory systems and perceive the environment differently. A sensed landscape has different gradients based on the animal's sensory abilities to perceive the landscape. An interpreted landscape is assigned meaning based on their use of the landscape.

I think our landscape perceptions are often like that of being a flea on a dog's back; we don't get a full sense of the bigger picture due to our perceptions and perspectives of the land.

To expand our sense of the fire environment, we need to utilize different tools like maps, illustrations, satellite images, and web cameras. I like to use Google Earth, live webcams, like AlertWildfire.org, and also GIS maps where I scale my perspective. You can use these tools to help diagram or sketch your landscape and or print and paste these into your journal. Of course, you can also find good lookout points to make some of these observations. Topography elements are integrated throughout the book, but this chapter emphasizes the topographic features of elevation, slope aspect, and slope angle, and some key topographic features.

Elevation

The Oxford Dictionary defines elevation as a measurement for lands that are located at different heights or altitudes above sea level. Something to keep in mind for elevation is that the higher the elevation, the cooler and drier the air. This means that there is more moisture on the surface (snow) or in the ground (water), while the air is dry. Lower elevations generally have warmer temperatures and higher moisture levels in the air. There is still water on the surface and in the ground, with some of the surface and groundwater coming from higher elevations.

Vegetation Zones

Different elevations have different climate zones and vegetation communities. I created the Butte County block landscape illustration and added small sketches of the different vegetation groups to accentuate key elevational zones and vegetation communities. These same zones have unique fire regimes and are used to guide fire mitigation activities. You'll learn more about fire regimes and fire mitigation in the other chapters. I would recommend you start journaling elevation observations using simple visualizations. Another visualization option is to create a large-layered wedge of the elevational zones, like I created for Chapter 10 Fire Regimes.

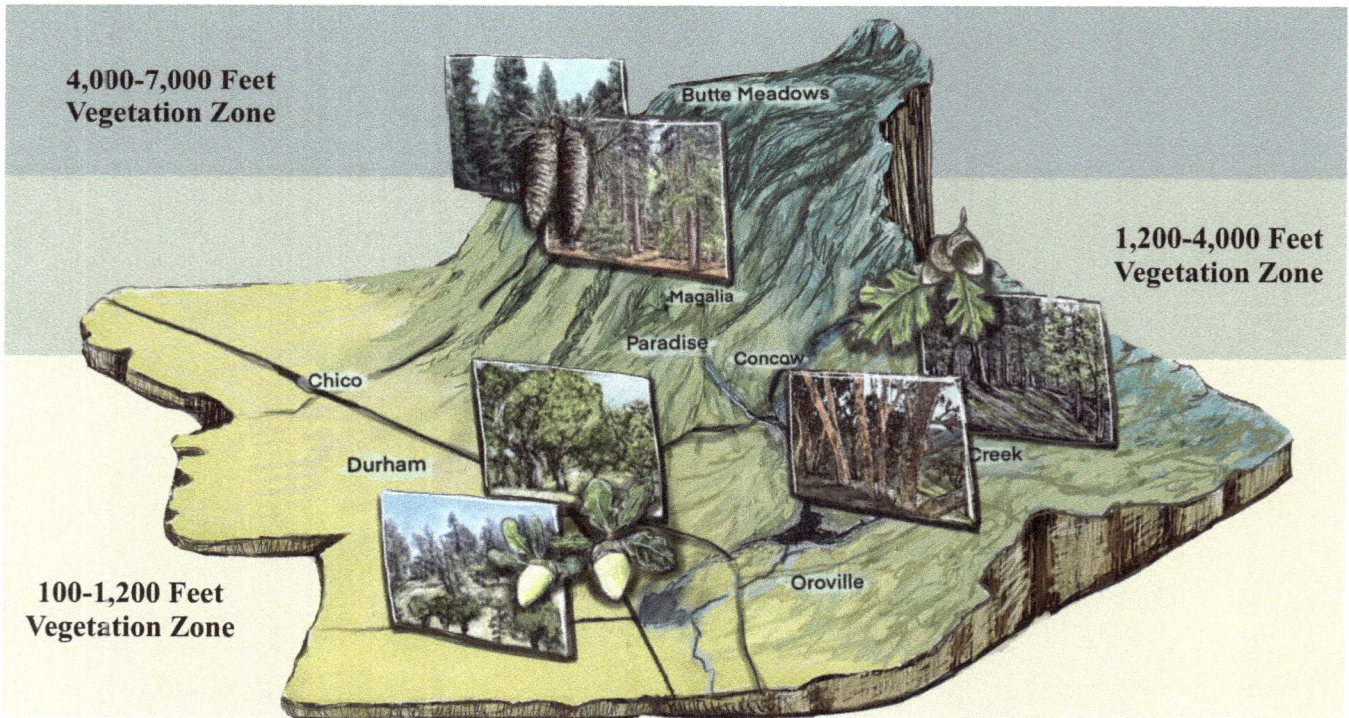

4,000-7,000 Feet
Vegetation Zone

Butte Meadows

1,200-4,000 Feet
Vegetation Zone

Magalia

Paradise

Concow

Chico

Durham

Creek

100-1,200 Feet
Vegetation Zone

Oroville

As mentioned earlier, higher elevation zones have lower humidity levels, which can result in drier conditions for vegetation. Higher elevations tend to have more columnar-shaped trees, with needles, like fir trees, which are more adapted to cold weather and high winds. In general, the higher the elevation, the shorter and sparser the trees become. Lower elevations tend to have trees with forking and wide-spreading branches and large leaves, unless located in hot and dry landscapes, like a desert, where the tree and shrub leaves are typically tiny and thick.

Dimensional Landscapes

The 3-dimensional landscape is one of my preferred visualizations for communicating elevation and aspect. 3D visuals convey information in a way that is closer to what we observe. These can be challenging to draw, but there are simplified approaches that can still accentuate important visual attributes, like using a triangle or simple mountain shape for elevational heights. It's also important to associate your weather and other metadata with elevation and other topographic characteristics. I always add elevation to my journal page no matter what I am journaling about. When you return back to your journal pages, you may start to notice trends and build a deeper sense of the environment.

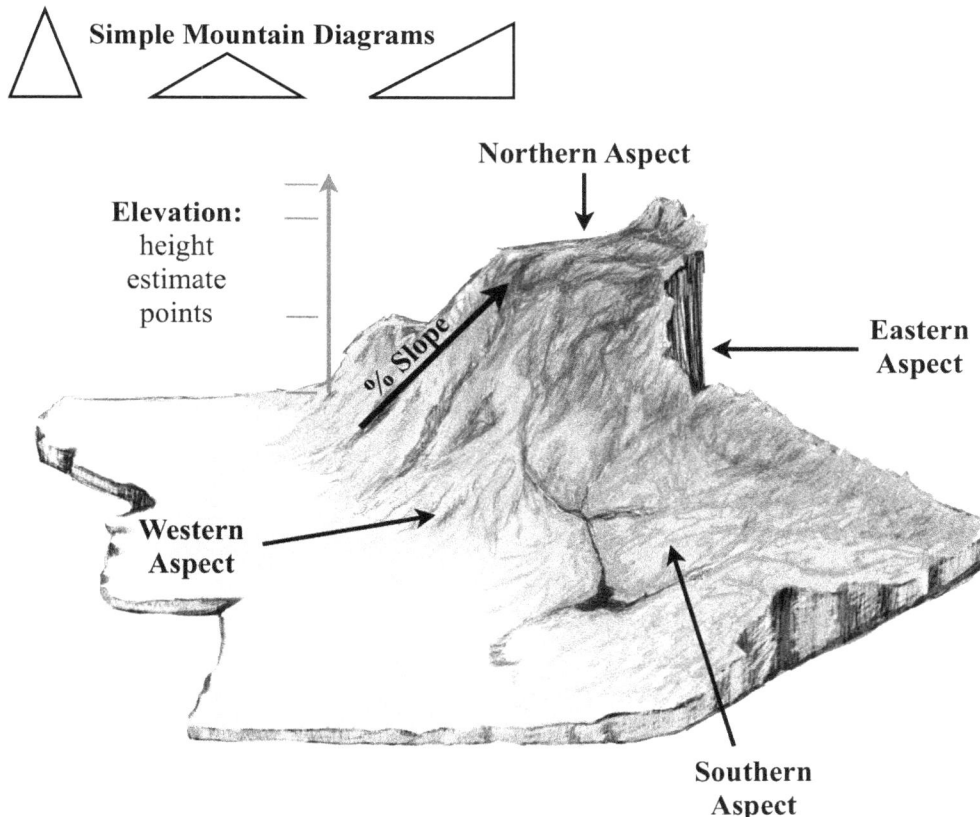

Simple Mountain Diagrams

Elevation:
height
estimate
points

Northern Aspect

% Slope

Eastern Aspect

Western Aspect

Southern Aspect

Slope Aspect

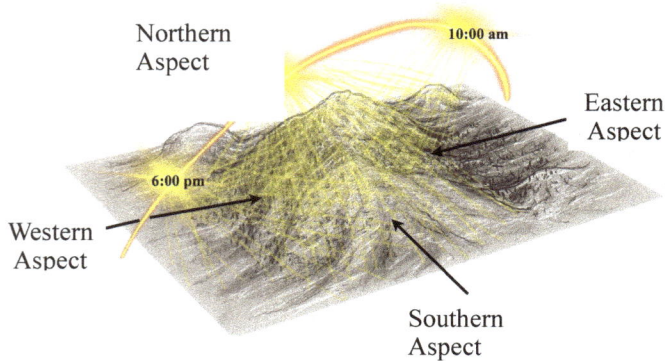

The slope aspect is the direction a mountain or hill is facing (north, east, south, or west). Journaling about the aspect of a slope is important because each direction receives different levels of sun exposure. As you know, the earth sits at an angle, and as it rotates, the sun will have different levels of heating throughout the day and over seasons. The slope aspect and angle of sun exposure illustration show the summer angle of the sun during the summer and fire season. The curving line does not necessarily represent the exact path of the sun, but you can get a sense of the sun's arc throughout the day. The line represents the top of the arc (degree of angle), while the bottom of the landscape is the zero-degree angle. Thus, the summer sun has a wider arc, creating more sun exposure than in the winter. There is another version of this illustration with both the summer and winter angles of the sun in the chapter on fire seasons.

The exposure of the sun influences the local climate and has a strong influence on vegetation conditions and fire risk. The Campbell Prediction System has a helpful graphic of how the vegetation flammability changes throughout the day based on the slope aspect. I have made some slight modifications to the graph adding a thermometer and vegetation elements. I'll discuss vegetation flammability more in Chapter 4: Fire Fuels and Chapter 5: Fire ignitions and Prevention.

A few general points to remember about the slope aspect in the northern hemisphere:

- Northern aspects generally have lower temperatures throughout the day and, depending on elevation, may have higher ground moisture levels, with snow lasting later into the season.

- Eastern aspects have the earliest solar heating (mid-morning) and earliest cooling times (early evening).

- Southern aspects have the highest amount of heating from sun exposure, starting late morning and ending in the early evening.

- Western aspects have the next highest amount of solar heating, starting in the late morning and ending in the late evening.

Fuel Bed Flammability by Aspect & Time
(Campbell Prediction System)

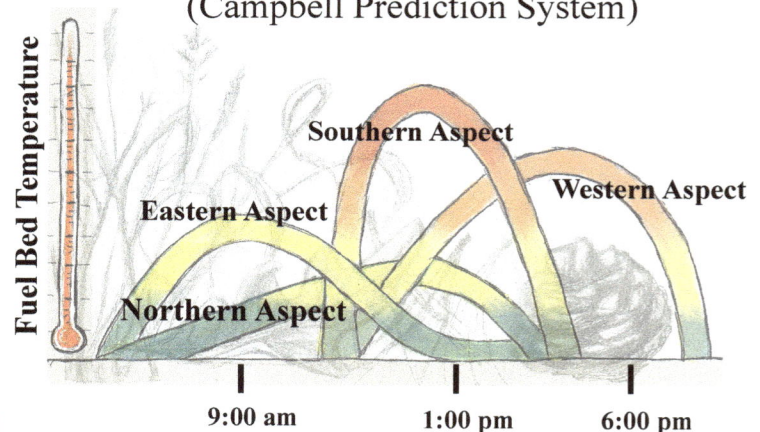

Peak Fuel Flammability by Time

Journaling Elevation & Aspect

One exercise for observing and journaling about elevation and aspect is to hike a trail or drive up and down a mountain. Stop along the way and take notice of the differences in temperature, moisture, and vegetation. Include metadata about the elevation and aspect for your observation points.

You can sketch or diagram the overall elevation and aspects from a good viewpoint or by using the 3-dimensional features in web maps, like Google Earth. I like to use the bird's-eye view of a landscape, where I can see more depth of the topography. Make sure to add arrows and labels for the different aspects from your viewing perspective. Sometimes your sketch will not have north facing the top of your page, so make sure to label the direction the scene is facing.

Slope Aspect Sketching Tips:

Step 1: Create a flattened and angled square as a landscape base for your sketch.

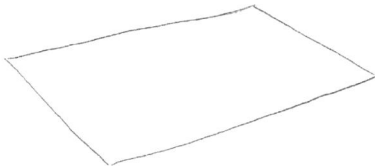

Step 2: Draw the outline of the mountain(s) with the top portion of the mountain rising above the base. Add a few lines for the prominent ridges, canyons, and valleys.

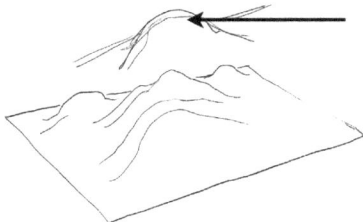

Step 3: Add pencil lines in crossover directions to help accentuate different aspects of the mountain. Additional pencil lines can be added and or smudged to create darker values and shadows. You can also erase some of the shadows or add a white gel pen to accent the sunlit areas of the mountain.

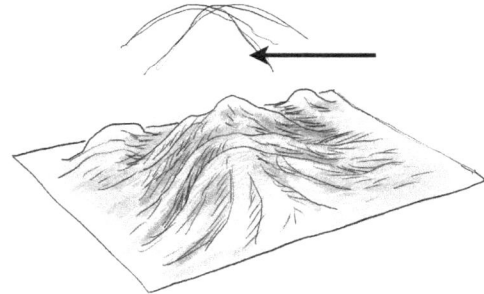

Step 4: Continue adding more shadows and highlights, as desired. Add short vertical pencil or pen marks into areas where trees and concentrated vegetation are located.

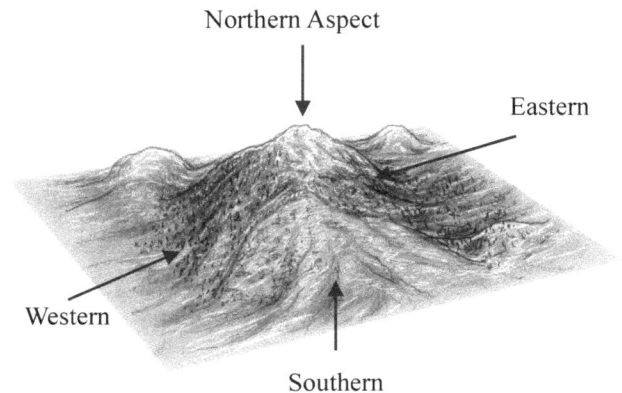

Slope Angle

A slope angle measures the steepness of a mountain, hill, or valley, typically denoted as a percentage. The slope is measured by the rise in elevation over the run in horizontal distance of the slope.

Percent Slope

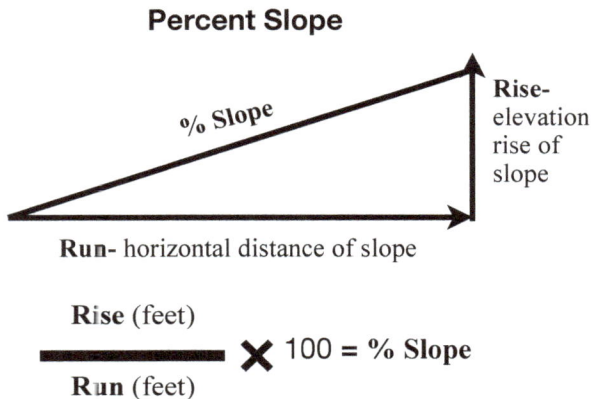

$$\frac{\text{Rise (feet)}}{\text{Run (feet)}} \times 100 = \% \text{ Slope}$$

In general, the steeper a slope, the faster and often more intense a fire may burn. This change in fire behavior is due to the heat transfer processes of a fire. The radiant and convective heat waves from a fire are compounded when they hit a steep angle, and the uphill vegetation preheats, dries, and ignites, spreading the fire at a faster rate. A number of NWCG fire behavior guides use a 30% or more angle as the point at which more solar radiation will have a significant effect on the drying of vegetation. Several studies have also shown that a 10° slope (20% slope) can double the fire rate of spread, and a 40° angle slope can have four times the rate of spread (Butler 2007). Another concern with slope as it relates to fire is the rolling materials that can be carried downhill, igniting new areas below the fire area.

General Slope Angles and Percentages

- A flat or gentle slope is less than 10%.

- A moderate slope is between 10% and 15%.

- A steep slope is over 15%.

- Critical fire behavior slopes are over 20%.

- A 10° angle is about the same as a 20% slope.

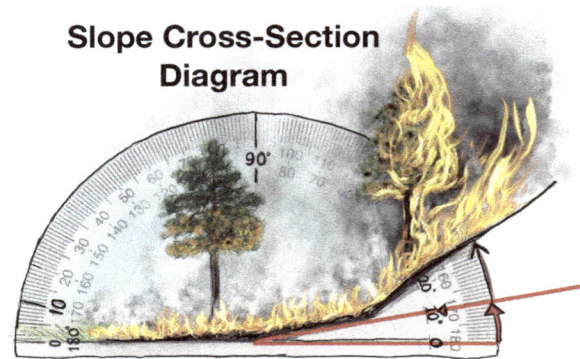

Slope Cross-Section Diagram

Biometric Slope Estimates

There are several tools for measuring the angle or percentage of slope, but I recommend approaches that engage more of the brain and body. If you didn't know, we have more than the five senses. We also have unique neural pathways in the body that are connected to balance and movement. Using biometric measurements is not necessarily accurate but engages your body and senses more than technological and mechanical tools.

Try to integrate slope observations with your information and observations about elevation and aspect for a more complete sense of how topography influences the fire environment. I like to focus my slope observations on whether the slope is higher or lower than 30% and/or 20%. This helps build a sense of the changing fire hazard levels.

To use these biometric estimates, you should be viewing the slope from a distance and have your arm stretched out in front of you. Hold one of your hands within your view of the slope. You can use one hand, with the gap between your fingers to estimate the angle, as shown in the illustration on the next page.

You can also use two hands, with four fingers or your pointer finger held over the top angle of the slope, and your thumb held as the zero percent angle. Hold your other hand up, at the same distance as the other hand, and see how many fingers can fit within the opening or arc you've created with the hand formed over the slope. If you can fit four fingers, you have about a 10° angle or 20% slope. If you can fit your fist, you have close to a 30% slope.

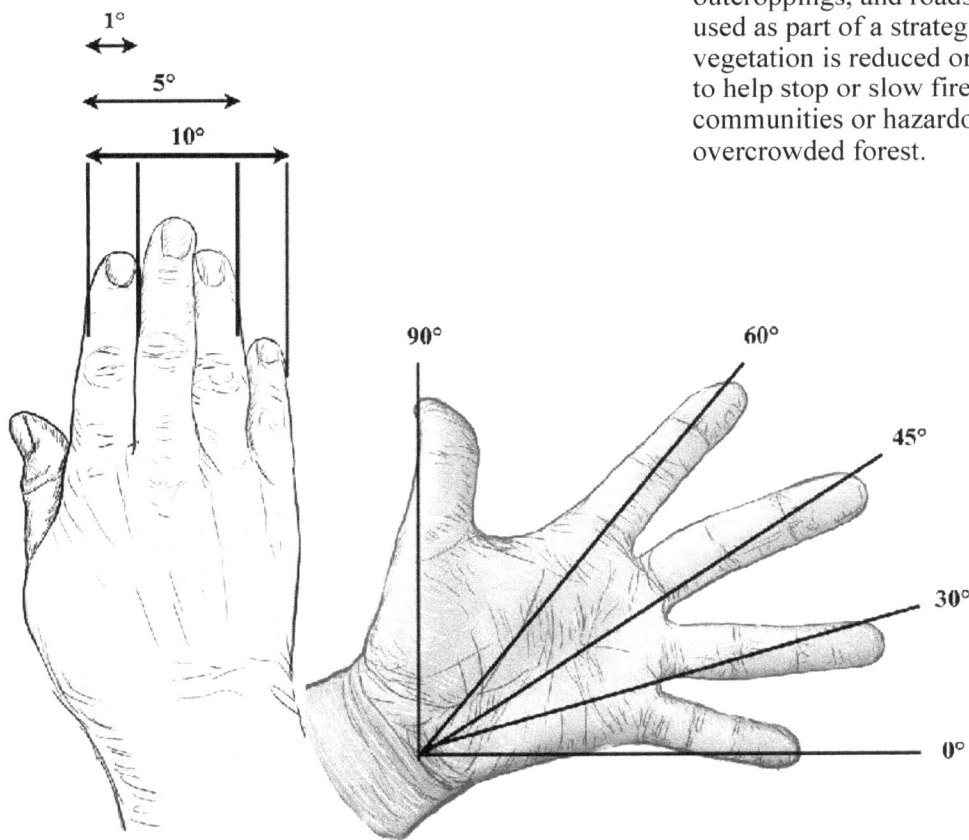

Terrain Features

When observing a landscape, there are terrain features that influence fire behavior, especially terrain-driven winds, as discussed in Chapter 2: Fire Weather. There is an illustration on the next page with key terrain features in the fire environment. Canyons and valleys can funnel winds and fire at high speeds. Ridge tops and saddles can have winds from different directions causing erratic fire behavior. Narrow canyons with steep sides are of high concern. These features are often broken into two categories, slot or box canyons. Slot canyons are open on both ends, while box canyons are closed on one end. Other terrain features to look for are things that act as obstacles to fire movement. These can be rivers, lakes, wetlands, rock outcroppings, and roads. These obstacles are often used as part of a strategic fuel break, where vegetation is reduced or removed within a certain area to help stop or slow fire spread into other communities or hazardous vegetation areas, like an overcrowded forest.

In your topography journaling, aim to convey some of the terrain features, elevation, aspect, slope, and notes about current or potential wind and fire behavior. Another approach for diagramming or sketching mountain ranges is shared in the next couple of pages.

You could also represent angles in your journal by sketching around your hand to create the desired shape and angle.

Terrain Features

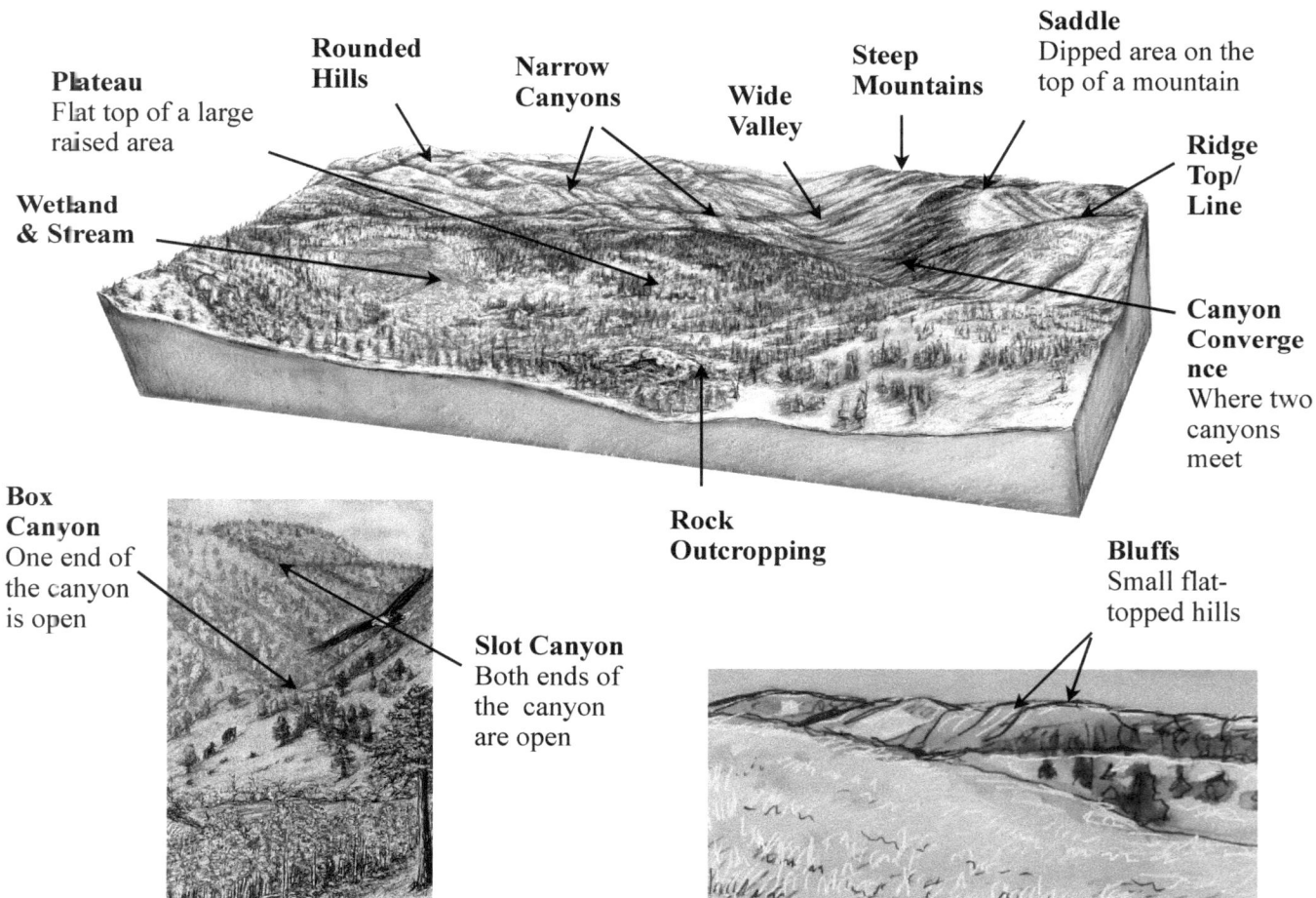

Plateau
Flat top of a large raised area

Rounded Hills

Narrow Canyons

Wide Valley

Steep Mountains

Saddle
Dipped area on the top of a mountain

Ridge Top/ Line

Wetland & Stream

Canyon Convergence
Where two canyons meet

Rock Outcropping

Box Canyon
One end of the canyon is open

Slot Canyon
Both ends of the canyon are open

Bluffs
Small flat-topped hills

Landscape Depth

There are other observations and journaling approaches to deepen your sense of the landscape. One of my typical approaches is to sketch a landscape from a high viewpoint and use some basic art principles to help convey distance and depth. In this sketch, you split your landscape into three portions: background, middle ground, and foreground. The proportions for these areas will vary based on the landscape and your perspective. In some cases, you may only have a foreground and background.

The distance estimates are based on general principles about how our eyes and brains perceive the details, colors, and light as sunlight filters through the atmosphere under different conditions. The distance scales are based on clear air quality conditions when most people can see 80 to 100 miles into the distance. The background portion of your sketch should include the distant landscape elements, where we see faded shapes in the colors of blue or purple. The middle ground includes landscape elements with basic shapes and patterns, and the muted colors of green and brown. These patterns can be things like rounded forest edges, wavy treetops, or the rolling hills of a grassland. The foreground will have a full range of colors and details, with individual plants that can be observed. You will also want to include more distinct highlights (sunlit areas) and shadows in the foreground.

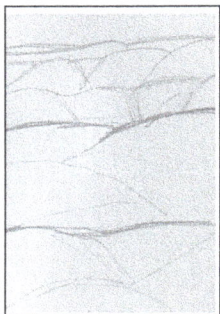

Sketching Exercise

Step 1: Choose a landscape view where you can see at least 40 miles away. Determine which parts of the landscape are in the foreground (within 1-5 miles), middle ground (5-20 miles away), and the background (20-80 miles away). Sketch a small rectangle frame with light pencil lines. Create tick marks on the edge of your sketch box or create horizontal lines to differentiate and organize the three distance areas. You can use a hilltop or a flat area as the borders between distances and differentiate those areas later with colors and details.

Step 2: Sketch minimal details into the background area of your scene. You may just have mountain outlines that will be colored in or you may want some vertical lines to convey the slope. Sketch the outlines of the general landscape patterns and shapes in the middle-ground. This can be accomplished with zigzag lines or scribbled patches for treetops and vegetation groupings.

Step 3: Sketch more detailed landscape elements, like small slopes and dips on a hill, individual features like rock outcrops, and the groups or individual plants in the foreground. The trees should not be detailed, but basic shapes, shadows, and highlights. Use colored pencils and/or watercolors with light blue and purple colors for the background mountains or landscape.

Color in the sky, starting at the top and working your way down to the horizon, where the sky is nearly white or tan. Use muted or medium-colored greens and browns in the middle ground, without too many details. Use a full range of bright colors in the foreground, with more details. Include some shadows and highlights to accentuate individual elements, depressions, and elevated areas in the landscape.

Gridded Landscape Sketches

If you need help sketching a landscape, a good approach is to use a gridded viewfinder. You can buy or make the gridded viewfinder or even use the grid feature on your camera viewfinder. Roseann Hanson's book "Nature Journaling For A Wild Life" includes detailed instructions for grid drawing, along with other journaling guidance. The book also includes sketching paper and a clear plastic gridded viewfinder that can be taken out and used in the field. Here are some basic tips to help you explore this technique.

Step 2: In your journal, use a pencil and ruler to create a small rectangle in the same proportional ratio (height and width) as the viewfinder. Create two pencil tick marks along the top, sides, and bottom of the rectangle at equal distances. You may also want to pencil in lines for the viewfinder within your sketch area.

Step 1: Hold up a viewfinder to help frame the scene. If you can line up the horizontal and/or vertical grid-lines with major landscape features, you will have an easier time re-finding the same scene if you put your viewfinder down.

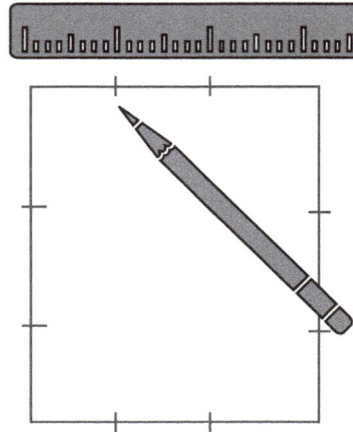

Step 3: Sketch with light pencil lines the basic landscape shapes, including mountains, slopes, roads, and large vegetation areas you observe within your viewfinder scene.

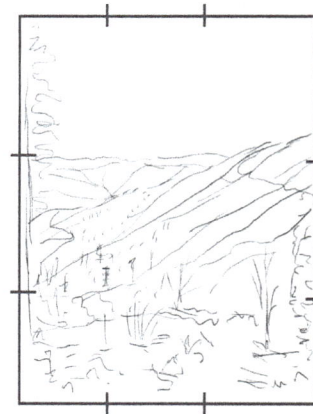

You may want to line up key landscape elements to the horizontal and vertical lines of the viewfinder. Once you have your outlines, use the viewfinder rectangles to help assess proportions of where things are located and add more details, one area at a time.

Landscape Journaling Warm-Up

A warm-up exercise you might try before starting
your topography journaling is blind contour drawing.
This exercise is employed by many artists to loosen
hands and improve hand-eye coordination. In this
practice, you look out at an object and draw the shape
outlines without looking at the page. This exercise is
excellent for creating a simplified and generalized
landscape scene, especially when you're feeling
overwhelmed by details. It's also helpful when you
feel hesitant to start a new drawing on a blank page.
Let your sketch be sloppy, and remember it's an
exercise.

I prefer using a pencil or a light-colored brush pen for
blind contour drawing, followed by adding a small
frame around the main area of the drawing.
Additionally, I enjoy adding a touch of color to
enhance the initial sketch. Sometimes, the blind
contour drawing turns out quite differently from what
I intended, and with those sketches, I like to
experiment with color swatches. It allows me to try
out colors I plan to use in other sketches, but I like to
see how they look on paper first.

Chapter 4: Fire Fuels

Fuel Groups—Fire Carrying Fuels
Fire Behavior Based on Surface Fuel Loading
Sketching Fuel Groups
Sketching & Describing Tree Shapes
Horizontal & Vertical Fuel Arrangements
Forestry Biometric Measurements
Tree Canopy Cover
Fuel Beds
Fine Fuels
Dead Fuel Moisture
Estimating Dead Fuel Moisture
Dead Fuel Moisture Snap Test
Pine Cone Indicators
Leaf Shape & Fuel Bed Flammability
Leaf & Fuel Bed Sketch & Diagram
Fuel Moisture Perpetual Journaling
Live Fuel Moisture & Vapor Pressure Deficit
Multi-Sensory Observations
Descriptive Words
Detailed Fuels Observations
Combining Fire Environment Observations
Leaf Flammability Burn Test

Fire Fuels

Fuels encompass any combustible material, but in the natural fire environment, our focus is on vegetation. I've shared some fuel-related information in previous chapters and will delve into other aspects in subsequent chapters. This chapter will concentrate on some basic fuel characteristics that influence fire behavior. While there are numerous guides to evaluating fuels and fire behavior on the internet, I've simplified some information for journaling purposes to foster a general understanding of the fire environment.

Fuel Groups—Fire Carrying Fuels

I prefer to commence my fuels journaling by observing the landscape broadly, then narrowing down to specific observations and measurements. For scene scale observations, I focus on fuel groups, which are general classifications of vegetation communities exhibiting similar surface fire behaviors. I'll discuss different fire types and behaviors inC Chapter 8: Fire & Smoke, but in essence, surface fuels are the primary carriers of fire in the landscape. Four general fuel groups include grasses, brush, timber, and slash (heavy fallen logs and woody debris), further categorized based on fuel concentration and accumulation.

When observing a landscape from a fuel group and surface fire perspective, we examine low-lying vegetation like grasses, small shrubs, fallen trees, and associated debris such as leaves, cones, seeds, and branches. With fuel group observations, it's essential not to dwell on the minutiae of each tree or bush but rather envision how fire could traverse the landscape.

Fuel Group Associated Fire Behavior

In the Standard Fire Behavior Fuel Models (Scott 2005), flame length and fire rate of spread (ROS) are estimated for each fuel group. The ROS, measured in miles per hour for ease of journaling, represents the speed at which fire moves away from the ignition point. These estimates are influenced by standardized climate conditions, particularly for grasses, assuming two-thirds of the surface vegetation is cured or dried, winds are less than five miles per hour, and slope is zero percent.

The graphic on page 75 illustrates standard fuel group fire behavior ratings and visualizes increased fire behavior with higher surface fuel accumulation. Flame lengths and fire rate of spread determine the fire behavior rating.

Before sketching fuel groups, simply observe and consider vegetation conditions and potential fire behavior based on the graphic. Walk around, closely examine ground vegetation and debris, take notes, and contemplate how they contribute to surface fuels influencing fire behavior. A section later in this chapter covers observing and journaling these smaller vegetation elements.

While imagining fire on the landscape may be stressful for some, remember that many conditions must align for a fire to ignite and spread.

Example Fuel Groups

Closed canopy forests (tree tops close together) have fallen leaves, branches, and logs as the primary surface fire carrier. Fires can move into the canopy and burns independently from the surface fire.

Open canopy forest fuel groups have some fallen leaves and branches, but grasses are the primary fire carrier. Individual or clumps of trees can burn, but do not spread as an independent crown fire.

Woodland savanna fuel groups are typically categorized as a grass fuel group, with mostly grass as the primary fire carrier.

Brush/Chaparral fuel groups have fallen leaves, flower-heads, branches, seeds, and some grasses as the primary fire carrier.

Shrub fuel groups, like sage brush, have small shrubs, shrub little, and grasses as the primary fire carrier.

Patchy and sparse shrub fuel groups, with mostly barren land, are not much of a fire carrier, unless invasive grasses fill in the area.

Tall grass fuel groups have thick grass and duff layers as the primary fire carrier.

Short grass fuel groups have shorter and lighter grass levels as the primary fire carrier.

Sparse and patchy grass fuel groups, have a minimal fire carrier, unless invasive grasses fill in to the area.

Fire Behavior Based on Surface Fuel Loading

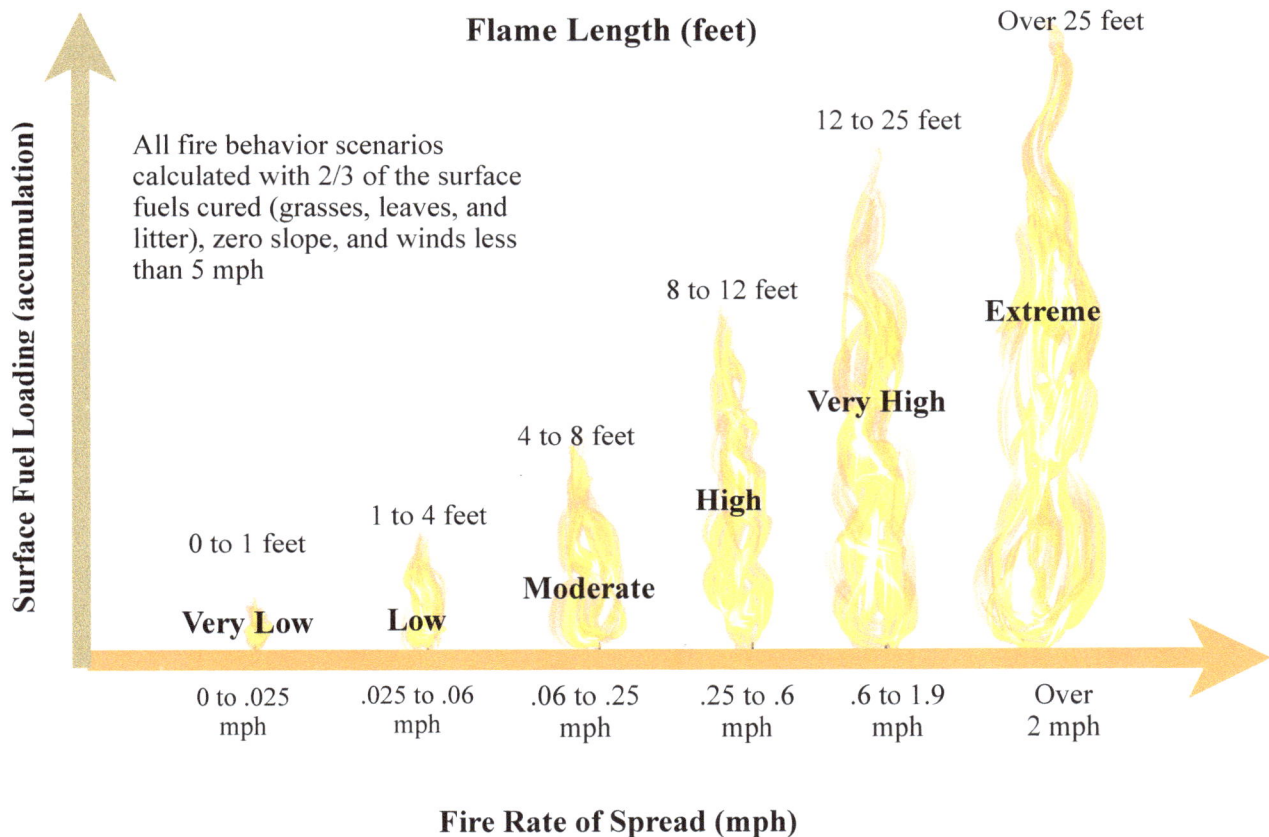

Flame Length (feet)

Surface Fuel Loading (accumulation) →

All fire behavior scenarios calculated with 2/3 of the surface fuels cured (grasses, leaves, and litter), zero slope, and winds less than 5 mph

Over 25 feet

12 to 25 feet

8 to 12 feet

Extreme

4 to 8 feet

Very High

1 to 4 feet

High

0 to 1 feet

Moderate

Very Low

Low

| 0 to .025 mph | .025 to .06 mph | .06 to .25 mph | .25 to .6 mph | .6 to 1.9 mph | Over 2 mph |

Fire Rate of Spread (mph)

Fuel Groups and Typical Fire Behaviors:

- **Forest fuel groups** can exhibit low to high fire behavior ratings depending on tree density and slash accumulation.

- **Shrub fuel groups** may range from low to high fire behavior, contingent on grass concentration.

- **Grass fuel groups** can vary from very low to very high fire behavior based on grass size, accumulation, and continuity.

Sketching Fuel Groups

Now let's look at sketching a fuel group scene. Follow the descriptions of how to observe the fuel groups at the beginning of the chapter and use the following visual as a reference. I like to combine this fuel group sketch with both a horizontal and vertical diagram in my journal. See the examples on the page 78. I also add estimates of the fire behaviors based on fuel group.

Use a pencil or pen to sketch a rectangular frame and the landscape outlines.	Sketch the general shapes of larger vegetation and use small penal marks to create broken lines for vegetation patches.	Use watercolor paint or colored pencil to accentuate the plant types and conditions.

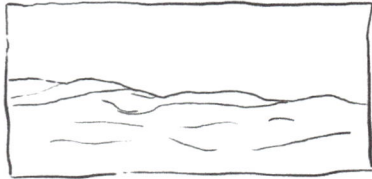

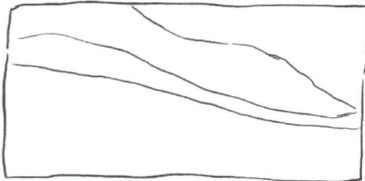

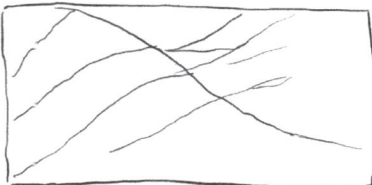

If you need help drawing trees or want some simplified approaches to save time while drawing in the field, consider using simplified tree shapes. As you expand your journaling practice, you may learn to define or identify tree species by their shape. In your sketches, pay attention to the distance from the ground up to the bottom of the tree canopy and if there are ladder fuels.

Sketching Tips:

• Sketch the basic shape of the tree canopy.

• Outline the basic shape of the tree trunk and add a few lines to represent the spread of the tree branches in the canopy.

• Sketch along the edge of the canopy shape with varied waves and squiggles that best represent the grouping and spacing of leaves.

• With graphite or colored pencil, add dark values to the base of the canopy and shaded areas.

• If using watercolor, go over the pencil sketch with light green and then dab darker green blotches into shaded areas of the canopy.

• Add black and brown colors to the tree trunk and branches, and use a white gel pen to accentuate sunlit leaves, branches, and the tree trunk.

Sketching & Describing Tree Shapes

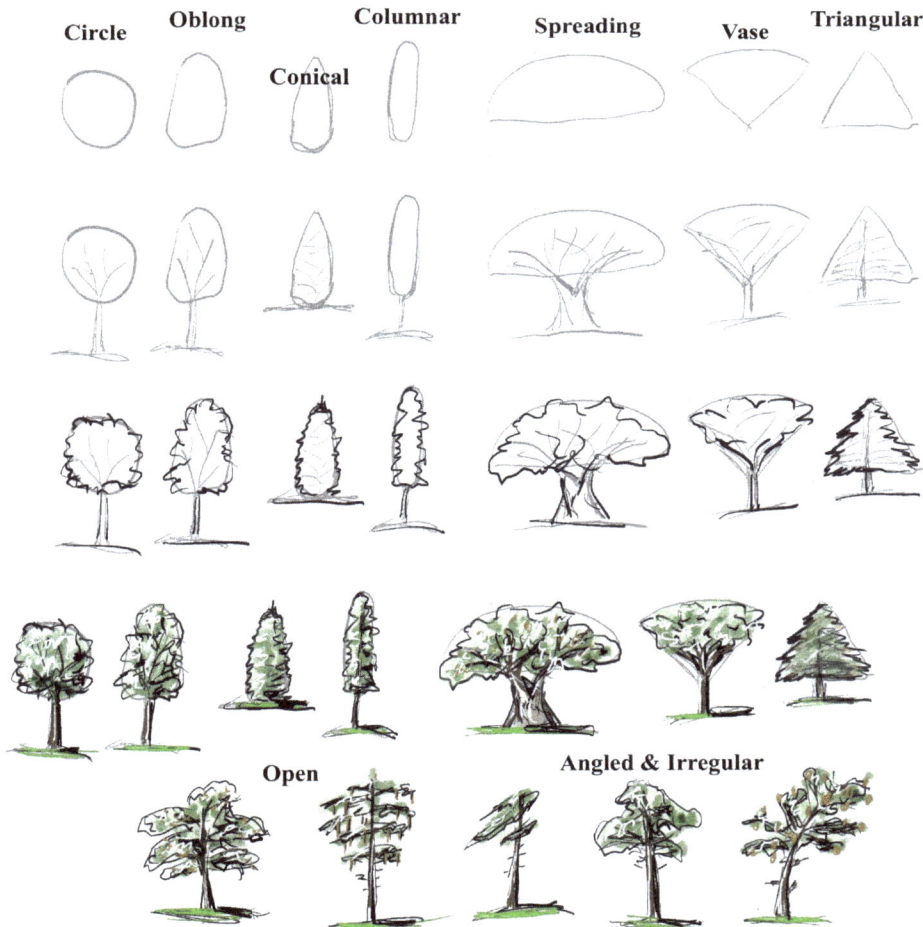

Circle   Oblong   Columnar   Spreading   Vase   Triangular
Conical

Open   Angled & Irregular

Horizontal & Vertical Fuel Arrangements

A fuel group can be visualized in different ways, but two of my favorites are the horizontal and vertical fuels arrangement diagrams. This approach is an interpretation of the fuel arrangement and does not need to be exact. Look for an area that has a good representation of the overall fuel group for the horizontal fuels sketch. I recommend creating a small square in your journal to limit the time and effort. I prefer to represent trees and shrubs with symbols and fill in the areas covered by grass with colors. Make sure to create a legend since you may mix and match symbols for different scenes and sketches. Also, consider changing the size of symbols to give a sense of the size and space between trees and/or shrubs.

In the vertical fuels arrangement diagram, you are creating a cross-section of the scene. One important observation is focused on ladder fuels. Ladder fuels are those grasses, shrubs, and trees that are close enough together to carry fire vertically from the ground into the tree canopies. One way to estimate if the flames from grasses and shrubs can reach the lower branches of a tree is to multiply 1.5 times the surface fuel height. I like to use 2 to 4 times the fuel

height for a broader possible range of flame height. I'd recommend using the same observation area for the horizontal diagram, with a cross-section line that includes a range of vegetation heights and topographic changes (slope). I like to add little simplified figures into the vertical diagram to help convey a sense of size and add biometric measurements. There is information on biometric measurements on the following page.

Horizontal Arrangement

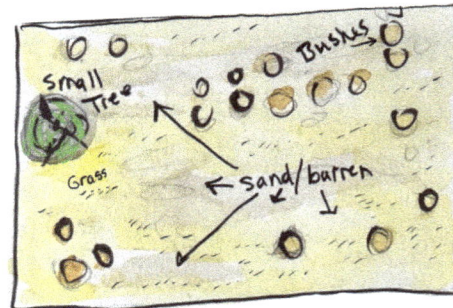

Measuring the horizontal distance between shrubs and trees, and estimating the continuity of surface vegetation.

Vertical Arrangement
Ladder fuels

Vertical dots represent the height of trees or shrubs or the distance between the surface vegetation and the lower branches of shrubs and trees (ladder fuels)

Simplified Figures

Star   Stick   Tooth

Forestry Biometric Measurements

I refer to biometrics as the use of the body for size comparisons and field measurement estimates. It's best to take your own measurements and use them regularly to form more accurate estimates.

Distance & Spacing Measurements

To measure short distances and the spacing between fuel elements, you can count your paces. A pace is equivalent to two natural steps. Most people start with the right foot, and when the left foot hits the ground, you count one pace. I'd recommend measuring 100 feet across flat ground and then counting the number of paces it took to cover that distance. Another option is to walk 10 paces (20 steps) and measure the distance you walked, then divide that distance by 10.

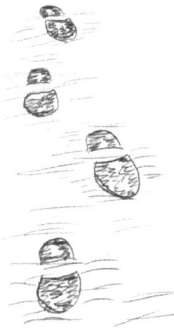

You should practice measuring your pace at least three times and come up with an average. If you don't have time or tools to measure your paces, you can use these general estimates based on the average-sized person: Two steps equal one pace, one pace (2 natural steps) equals five feet, 20 paces equals 100 feet, and 208.1 feet x 208.1 feet equals one acre.

Tree Measurements & Descriptions

You can use some common forestry and fire lingo to estimate tree size based on the diameter of the tree trunk. Tree diameters are measured at 4.5 feet above the ground, which is called the diameter at breast height or DBH. Young sapling-sized trees are often described as pole-sized. Small-sized trees have trunks under 12 inches in diameter. Medium-sized tree trunks are between 12-24 inches in diameter, and large-sized tree trunks are over 24 inches in diameter. There are many other tree measurements, including height, but for our journaling purposes, I would recommend focusing on the distance between the bottom of the tree canopy and the top of the surface vegetation below, as well as the distance between tree canopies.

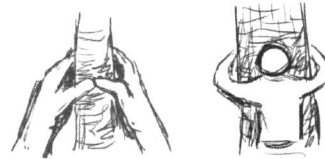

Saplings and pole-sized trees may be one to two hands wrapped around a tree trunk.

Small to medium-sized tree trunks may be one to two arms wrapped around a tree trunk.

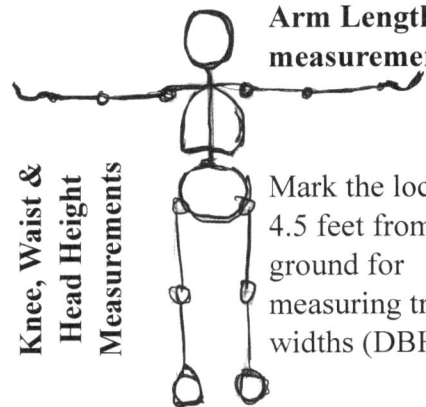

Arm Length measurements

Knee, Waist & Head Height Measurements

Mark the location 4.5 feet from the ground for measuring tree widths (DBH)

Shrub & Grass Measurements

You can use different biometric measurements from the ground to your ankle, knee, and hip to help estimate and describe the heights of shrubs and grasses. Short grasses may be ankle to knee height, while tall grasses may be above your knees or up to your chest.

Tree Canopy Cover

Another observation tied to trees and fire behavior is the arrangement and concentration of the tree canopies, or what is called canopy cover. For this observation, you need to look straight up between a group of trees that best represents the overall canopy cover in the area. In a tall forest, you may be able to use an empty toilet paper or paper towel roll to help focus your perspective. You could also create a stencil cutout from a piece of paper or put a circle on a clear piece of plastic.

Percent Canopy Cover

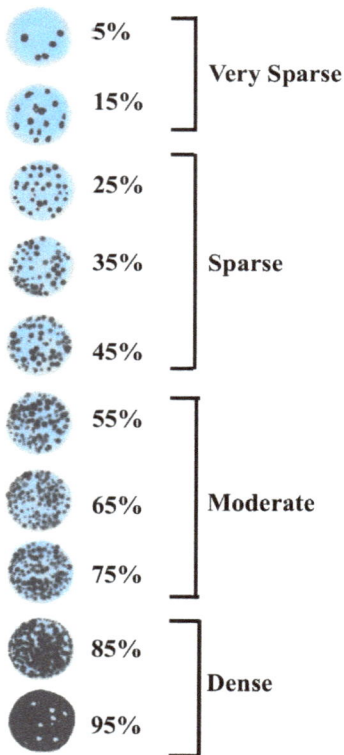

5%		Very Sparse
15%		
25%		Sparse
35%		
45%		
55%		Moderate
65%		
75%		
85%		Dense
95%		

Ideally, take several measurements and obtain an average for the area. Use the canopy cover percentage or associated descriptive term from the graphic.

Sketch a small circle in your journal and use dots to represent the concentration of canopy cover.

You can also sketch the canopy cover by filling in the leaves, branches, and tree trunks if you'd like something more detailed. Don't forget to add the percentage and descriptive term on or next to your diagram or sketch.

Add additional notes and measurements about the distance between tree canopies to build a sense of how a fire could move from one tree to another.

Sketching Canopy Cover Tips

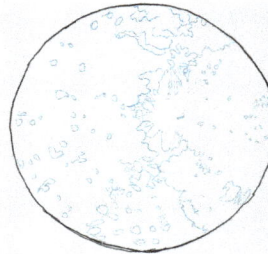

Draw in the outlines of the patches of sky between the trees.

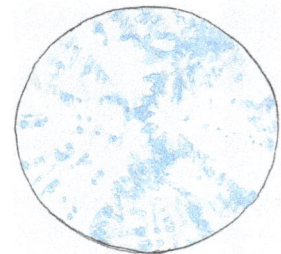

Use blue pencil or water color to fill in the sky area observed.

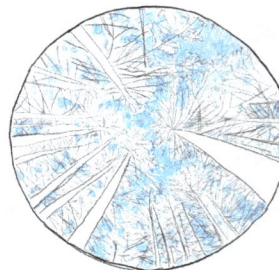

Fill in the colors and shadows for the leaves, branches and tree trunks.

Draw in the outlines for the bunches of leaves, branches and tree trunks

Fuel Beds

Fuel bed is a term used to describe and measure the mix of live and dead surface vegetation within the different fuel groups. Measurements are taken on the size and amount, or loading, of surface vegetation and debris. This can be done with a horizontal or vertical diagram or a sketch. I like to journal the fuel bed with more of a close-up observation, with sketches of individual elements that make up the fuel bed. I'll include more about the fuel bed elements as we move through the chapter.

Weather data is also used in fuel bed measurements, as well as the influences of slope aspect, such as those discussed in Chapter 3: Topography and with the Campbell Prediction System. We'll discuss fuel moisture in more detail further in this chapter.

Sketching the Fuel Bed, Sunlight & Shadows

One great approach for journaling a forest fuel bed is to observe and sketch the shaded and sunlit areas; the inverse of canopy cover. This observation can help you gain a sense of how the fuel bed continuity, sunlight, and winds can influence fire behavior. I like to do this observation in small forest openings. Try to take notes on the percentage of ground area covered in shade using a range of 0 to 10%, 10 to 50%, and over 50%. The shade measurements should be compared to the canopy cover observations.

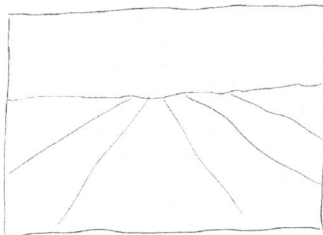

Step 1: Pencil in a light horizon line and any slope lines from the front to the back. These are mostly guides and can be erased as you go or just covered with darker sketch elements.

Step 2: Pencil in the trees and natural slope around the base of trees. Add some close fuel bed elements in the foreground.

Step 3: Lightly sketch the shadows of more distant trees and use darker pencil or paint for shadows closer to the foreground. Erase some penciled areas to create sunlit areas on the fuel bed and between trees.

Step 4: Add black and white pencil, paint, or pen squiggle lines to the thicker or fluffy fuel bed layers in the mid-ground, and flat lines for bare ground or short vertical marks for grass.

Fine Fuels

Fine fuels describe the small (less than 1/4 inch in diameter), fast-drying dead and live vegetation in the fuel bed that has a relatively large surface area-to-volume ratio. These fuels typically include grasses, leaves, and needles. They are the tinder in the landscape and are easily ignited and consumed by fire. We'll use fine fuel observations in our fuel moisture observations in the next section. Here are a few ideas for sketching fine fuels, which should be added elements for your fuel bed observations.

You can sketch simple shapes for individual plants and/or plant parts, like a single leaf, or create fuel bed scenes similar to the examples shared. I usually start with pencil or pen sketch and then add a little color over to help indicate whether they are living or dead. I have several examples from my journal showing grasses, leaves, seeds, and shrubs. You can also draw a horizontal diagram of the fine fuels in the fuel bed.

If you don't want to sketch the fine fuels, you can hold leaves down on your page and trace around them using pencil, pen, or watercolors. You can also dip your fine fuels into a pool of watercolors and dab them onto the page, leaving an imprint and showing the negative space.

Form & Arrangement

Shape & Size

Pieces & Parts

Grassy Fuel Beds

Leafy Fuel Beds

Seedy Fuel Beds

Shrub & Grass Fuel Beds

Dead Fuel Moisture

Fuel moisture is the probable moisture content of various fuels and is measured as a percentage. Fuel moisture estimates are separated by dead and live vegetation categories. Dead fuel moisture is measured by the time it takes for them to equalize within 63% of the relative humidity (RH) level based on the diameter of the fuels. This is called a time lag. Dead fuel moisture levels typically range from 1-30%. The small fine fuels, less than 1/4 inch in diameter or smaller than a pencil eraser, have a time lag of about an hour. The rounded woody debris with a diameter of 1/4 to 1 inch or about the size of a dime or quarter has a time lag of 10 hours. Fallen tree branches and trees, with a diameter about the size of a golf ball or baseball, have a time lag of about 100 hours. Larger logs, with a diameter larger than eight inches, have a time lag of 1000 hours. For journaling purposes, I focus mostly on 1-hour fine fuel moisture, since they are helpful in developing awareness of quickly changing conditions and fire risk.

The bottom visual includes the time lag by fuel size. I have overlaid them on a symbolized fire triangle to help convey the fact that the smaller the fuel size, the less heat is needed to ignite and burn. The fine fuel flames will also be smaller and produce less heat.

In low RH conditions, moisture is passively drawn from the cured vegetation into the air.

In high RH conditions, moisture is passively drawn from the air into the cured vegetation.

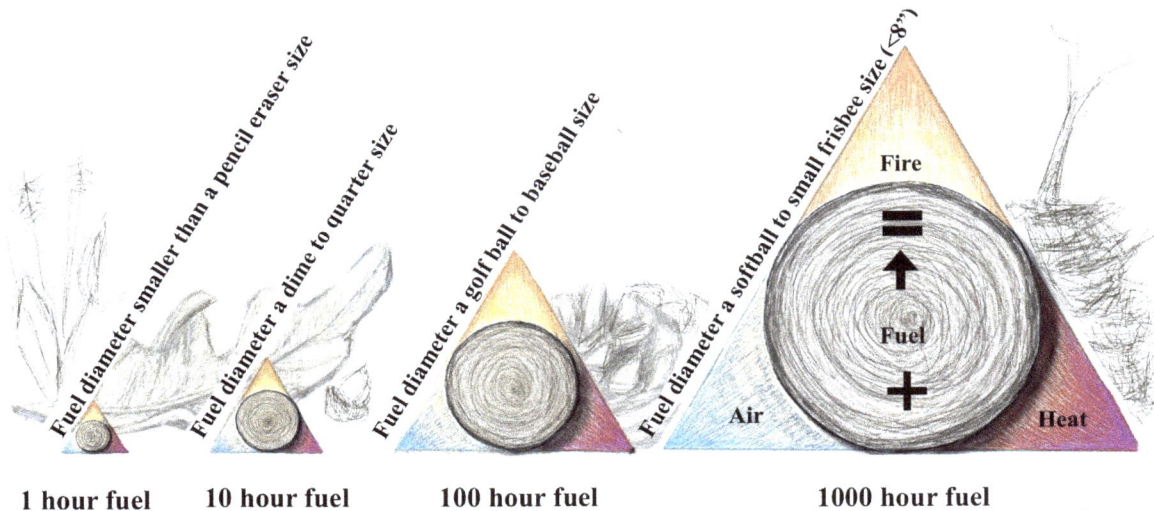

Fuel diameter smaller than a pencil eraser size

Fuel diameter a dime to quarter size

Fuel diameter a golf ball to baseball size

Fuel diameter a softball to small frisbee size (<8")

Fire

Fuel

Air

Heat

1 hour fuel   **10 hour fuel**   **100 hour fuel**   **1000 hour fuel**

Estimating Dead Fuel Moisture

Temperature, winds, RH, elevation, percent slope, and aspect all influence dead fuel moisture. In the graphic below, I've adapted the 1-hour dead fuel moisture table from the 2017 NWCG *Fire Behavior Field Reference Guide* to illustrate the subtle changes in fuel moisture at different temperature and RH levels. Winds are not included in the table, but generally, increased wind speeds reduce dead fuel moisture levels. On the following page, there are graphics displaying adjustments (additions) to the fuel moisture number based on slope and aspect. I've simplified, summarized, and visualized the original fuel moisture table to better observe these changes.

I also combined some of the RH categories from the original table into broader groupings. Narrow RH differences can make observations challenging. As noted in Chapter 2: Fire Weather, many fuel groups reach red flag fire weather conditions when RH is below 15%, but some fuel groups reach critical conditions at 30% RH, while others do so at 50% RH.

These serve as good prompts for observing higher-risk conditions. I like to compare these RH and fuel moisture levels with prescribed burn parameters to develop a broader awareness of when a fire can burn and when it can become extreme. In general, prescribed burns are conducted when RH levels are above 25%, 30%, or 40%, and temperatures are between 60°F and 90°F, depending on the season and burning objectives (USDA 2012 and Fast et al.). These prescriptions are tailored to fuel groups, seasons, and burn objectives.

In the Natural Resource Network's *Common Prescribed Burning Parameters in Northeastern Fuels*, you can find examples of median temperature, RH, and fuel moisture levels for prescribed burning by fuel groups in that area:

- **Grass Fuel Group:** Temperatures between 35-90°F, RH between 26-65%, 1-hour fuel moisture between 6-12%

- **Shrub Fuel Group:** Temperatures 35-90°F, RH 35-65%, 1-hour fuel moisture 6-15.5%

- **Timber Understory Fuel Group:** Temperatures 35-87°F, RH 30-65%, 1-hour fuel moisture 6-13%

NWCG fuels training materials offer one way to estimate 1-hour fine fuel moisture by dividing the RH by 5. This isn't highly accurate but serves as an easy option for journaling.

1 Hour Fine Fuel Moisture Based on Temperature & Relative Humidity

Relative Humidity

Temperature	<15%	15-29%	30-44%	45-59%	60-74%	75-89%	>90%
	1-2%	2-4%	4-6 %	7-8%	8-9%	10-11%	12 %
>109° F							12-13
90-109° F			5-6				
70-89° F							
50-69° F		3-5				10-12	
30-49° F			5-7		9-10		13
10-29° F				8		11-12	13-14

Use this table to find the 1-hour fuel percent moisture using temperature and relative humidity for the observation period.

The 10-hour fuel moisture can be estimated by adding 1-2 percent to the 1-hour fuel moisture, and 2-4 percent for 100-hour fuel moisture.

Fuel Moisture Adjustments For Slope & Aspect

I like to focus my fuel moisture observations between late spring and early summer to notice the changes transitioning into fire season. Add the adjustment number (percent) from one of the graphics to refine the fuel moisture number based on the spring/summer month, percent slope, aspect, percent shade and time of day. Note that the yellow colors over the fuel moisture blocks indicate the slope and time of day with the strongest sunlight exposure. If you want to make fuel moisture adjustments for other months, go online and find the *NWCG Fire Behavior Field Reference Guide*. Use the 1-hour fuel moisture table.

February-April Solar Exposure Adjustment for 1 Hour Fuel Moistures

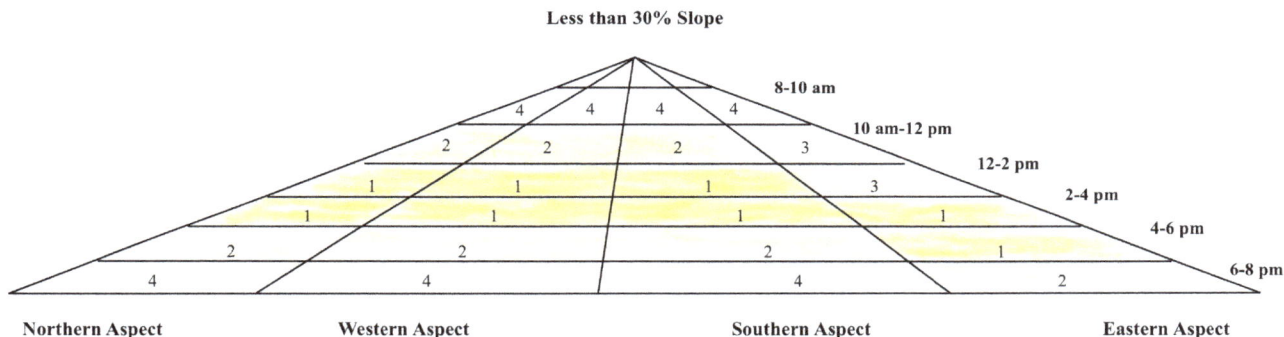

Less than 30% Slope

| | 8-10 am | 10 am-12 pm | 12-2 pm | 2-4 pm | 4-6 pm | 6-8 pm |

Northern Aspect — Western Aspect — Southern Aspect — Eastern Aspect

Over 50% Shade

When the fuel bed is shaded over 50% from canopy cover or clouds, add an additional 1-2 % for observations between 8am and 12pm, and 4-8pm. Add 1-3% for observations between 12-4pm.

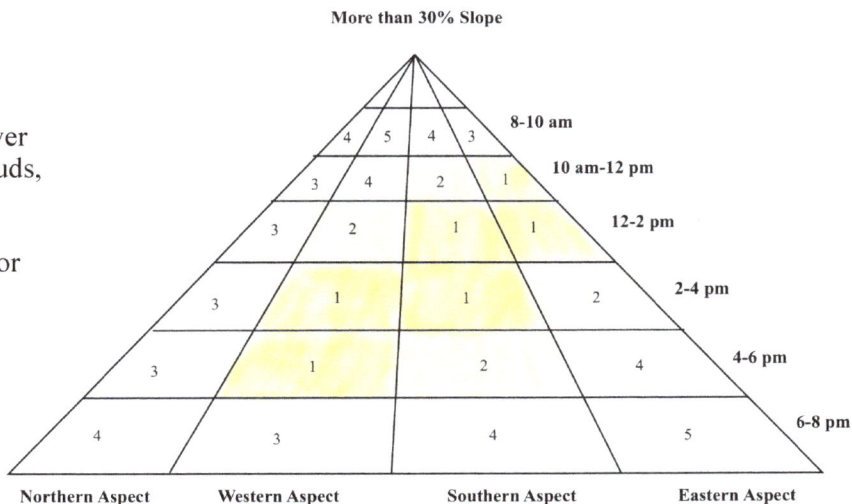

More than 30% Slope

Northern Aspect — Western Aspect — Southern Aspect — Eastern Aspect

85

May-July Solar Exposure Adjustment for 1 Hour Fine Fuel Moisture

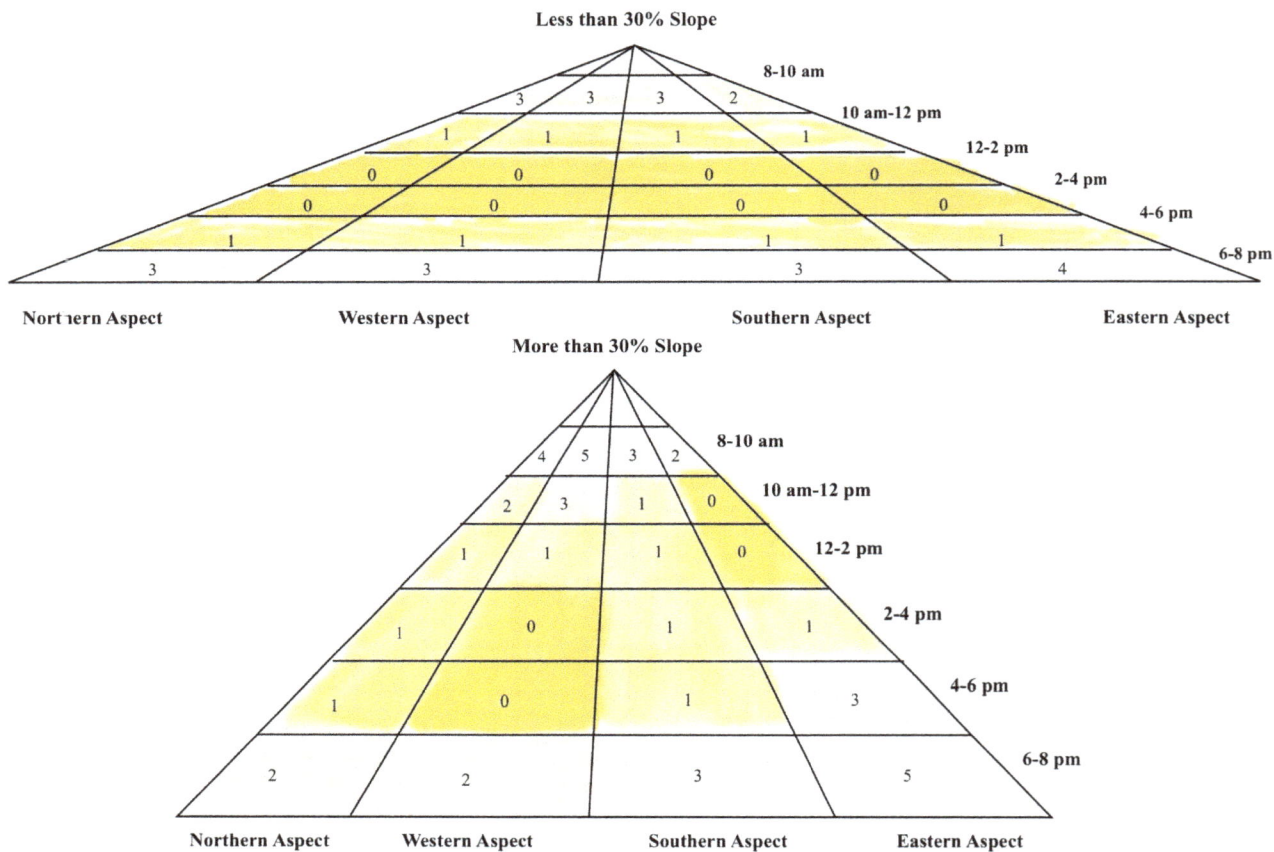

Less than 30% Slope

8-10 am
10 am-12 pm
12-2 pm
2-4 pm
4-6 pm
6-8 pm

3	3	3	2
1	1	1	1
0	0	0	0
0	0	0	0
1	1	1	1
3	3	3	4

Northern Aspect · Western Aspect · Southern Aspect · Eastern Aspect

More than 30% Slope

8-10 am
10 am-12 pm
12-2 pm
2-4 pm
4-6 pm
6-8 pm

4	5	3	2
2	3	1	0
1	1	1	0
1	0	1	1
1	0	1	3
2	2	3	5

Northern Aspect · Western Aspect · Southern Aspect · Eastern Aspect

Over 50% Shade

When the fuel bed is shaded over 50% from canopy cover or clouds, add an additional 1-2 % for observations between 8am and 12pm, and 4-8pm. Add 1-3% for observations between 12-4pm.

Dead Fuel Moisture Snap Test

Let's take a break from the more technical methods of estimating fuel moisture and explore how we can assess fine fuel moisture with our hands. The Southern Fire Exchange provides a fact sheet on prescribed burning, which offers a useful example of how prescribed fire practitioners can use the snap test to evaluate fine fuel moisture. The test is conducted on cured pine needles from the fuel bed, in both sunlit and shaded areas. Slowly and gently bend a single pine needle into a loop, pulling the two ends toward each other.

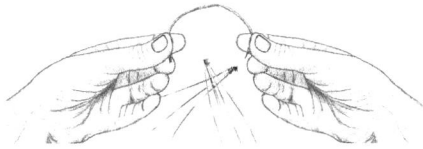

• If the needle doesn't break, the fine fuels are too moist, and a fire is unlikely to spread.

• If the needle breaks when each end reaches about 1/4 to 1/2 inches from each other, a fire could carry.

• If the needle breaks into multiple pieces early in the bend, the fuels are very dry, and more intense fire behavior could be expected.

Hardwood leaves can also be used to test fuel moisture. Gently hold a cured leaf from the fuel bed and slowly bend it at a right angle.

• If the leaf folds instead of breaking, the fine fuels are too moist, and a fire is unlikely to spread.

• If the leaf cracks and breaks but the veins hold their structure, a fire could spread.

• If the entire leaf crumbles, the fuel moisture is extremely low, and more intense fire behavior could be expected.

Fallen Pine Cone Indicators

Pine cones are not fine fuel, but they are part of the fuel bed and can help prompt observations related to humidity levels. When humidity levels are high, pine cone scales close, and when humidity levels are low, they open. This is a mechanical feature of pine cone scales that helps protect seeds from excessive moisture and opens when conditions are favorable for dispersal. Better results are observed when pine cones are located in the open and are not too old or decayed.

Sketching Wet & Dry Pine Cones

There are a couple of easy ways to sketch pine cones. Start with an outline of the pine cone shape. You can hold or position the pine cone vertically, viewing it from the top down. Create contoured horizontal lines around the side of the pine cone sketch. Place these lines below the extended scales or what appears to be a deep shadow and crevice line. Some scales may appear spread at different distances, but don't worry

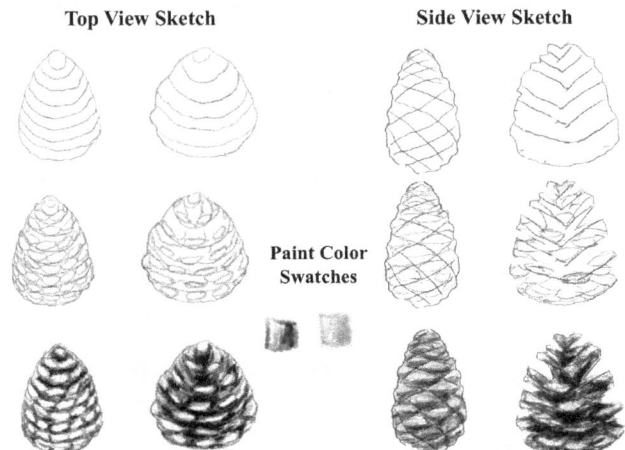

Top View Sketch

Side View Sketch

Paint Color Swatches

about that. Create small oval shapes within the rings and add shadows between them. If you are viewing the pine cone as it lays on its side, create contoured zig-zag lines and then add details and shadows.

Leaf Shape & Fuel Bed Flammability

Fuel bed flammability is influenced by more than just slope, aspect, and fuel moisture. The shape of leaves and how they lie in the fuel bed can significantly affect flammability. A study on the *Patterns of Flammability of California Oaks: The Role of Leaf Traits* (Engber and Varner, 2012) provides excellent examples to focus on in journaling observations. For instance, small, thick, flat leaves have less surface area and less oxygen available for a fire, making them less flammable. Conversely, large, curly leaves arranged in airy layers are more flammable. Fuel beds composed of small, flat leaves typically create shallower fuel beds, while those with large, curly leaves create deeper ones.

A simple approach to journaling leaf and fuel bed flammability is to measure and sketch comparisons of leaf shapes and sizes with their associated fuel bed depths and arrangements (compact or airy). It's also helpful to compare fuel bed elements in sunny and shaded areas to assess fuel moisture for each leaf shape. To visualize these observations, you can use a symbolic color scheme to differentiate moist and dry conditions and relative humidity levels. For instance, I prefer to use gray-brown colors for moist leaves and light brown and yellow colors for dry leaves when comparing shaded versus sunny areas, without using air moisture measurements.

Fuel Moisture Perpetual Journaling

An effective approach to developing sensitivity and awareness around fuel moisture is to make consistent observations over time. On the next page, I share an example inspired by Lara Gastinger's botanical perpetual journals. A perpetual journal captures one observation on a page, with additional sketches added over time, along with associated data and weather metadata. I've adapted the perpetual journal concept for dead fine fuels and included the blue RH color code from Chapter 2: Fire Weather. I find the contrast between the yellow and brown dead fine fuels with the blue background visually striking. Next to each sketch, include a blue color wash or small blue patch corresponding to the relative humidity at the time of observation, as referenced in the color code. Add notes about how the fuels feel, smell, and sound as you hold and bend them. Over time, you can adjust the blue color code with different color breakdowns to more closely relate the RH conditions to your sky color observations.

Small Flat Leaves & Fuel Bed

Large Lobed Leaves & Fuel Bed

High RH   Low RH   High RH   Low RH

RH Color Codes

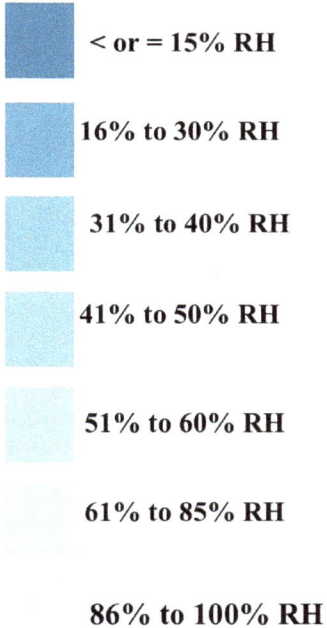

■	< or = 15% RH
■	16% to 30% RH
■	31% to 40% RH
■	41% to 50% RH
■	51% to 60% RH
■	61% to 85% RH
	86% to 100% RH

RH=Relative Humidity

FM=Fuel Moisture

*FM calculated by dividing the RH by 5

July 15
10% RH & 2% FM

June 15
32% RH & 6%FM

Feels crunchy and breaks

Feels dry but bends

May 15
55% RH

Feels soft and bends

Feels brittle but bends

Aug 15
42% RH

April 15
40% RH

Smells like straw

Live Fuel Moisture

Live fuel moisture is significantly influenced by the vapor pressure deficit (VPD) in the atmosphere. The VPD is a critical measurement of plant stress and productivity (Broz et al., 2021). VPD represents the difference between the amount of moisture in the air and the maximum moisture the air can hold at different temperatures. When air moisture levels are low, water vapor is drawn up from the soil, water bodies, and plants due to pressure differences caused by VPD in the air and plants. The interactions between external and internal VPD levels influence the photosynthesis process. I'll delve into VPD changes associated with phenology and seasons in the next chapter. The illustration depicts a single leaf with internal and external water vapor levels at 50% relative humidity, with two different temperatures.

In high temperatures and dry soil conditions, plants can shut down the photosynthesis process, becoming vulnerable to heat stress and death. In extremely hot conditions, leaves wilt and may appear to lean sideways or upside down. Leaves and needles can also appear scorched, exhibiting brown colors similar to those fallen on the ground. Living plants may release volatile organic compounds (VOCs) to protect themselves from heat and water loss, which can lead to interesting scent observations.

Fire practitioners calculate live fuel moisture for different fuel groups using standardized measurements, where fuel bed materials are weighed before and after drying in an oven. Living plant cells can hold up to three times their weight in water. Live fuel moisture levels can range from 30% to 300% depending on the plant, fuel types, and local conditions. Grasses become cured (phenological phase of drying) and more flammable when they reach about 30% fuel moisture level, while shrubs are more flammable when their fuel moisture is between 30% and 90%. The next chapter provides more

information about VPD and fuel curing phases over time.

Cooler temperatures

50% Relative Humidity

◯ Water vapor   ◯ VPD

Multi-Sensory & Descriptive Observations

It's helpful to engage all your senses when comparing live and dead fine fuel moisture levels across different weather conditions and seasons. I typically begin with a comparison table in my journal, with grasses and leaves in one column and my sensory observations in rows. It's intriguing to explore the descriptive words that capture differences in what you see, hear, smell, and feel, and then translate these into visuals that convey the sensory experience. I've provided some examples of my standard sensory visuals for fuel moisture sound, scent, and touch. Additionally, I like to trace leaf shapes onto my page to feel them in my hands while drawing. If it's a colored leaf (not cured), I prefer to smudge the actual leaf color into the traced leaf shape.

Traced Leaf Shape & Smudged Color

Descriptive Words

If you're uncertain how to describe sensory observations, consider consulting terminology and descriptions commonly used for scents and sounds. For instance, scents are often categorized as floral, spicy, citrusy, herbal, sweet, sour, powdery, creamy, mineral, woody, resinous, mossy, smoky, pungent, light, acrid, chemical, or medicinal. It's advisable to smell fine fuels when first picked up, as well as after bending or rubbing them between your fingers. Some descriptive terms for touch can include abrasive, bald, barbed, bendable, angular, blistered, blunt, bristly, bumpy, caked, chapped, coarse, cold, warm, corrugated, cratered, damp, dry, doughy, downy, flaky, smooth, plastic, leathery, slippery, and dusty. For describing sounds associated with touching and listening to dead fine fuels, consider terms like creaking, cracking, leathery squeaks, and rustling paper.

Use verbs to articulate your sensory experiences. Does the scent permeate the air or gently creep into your nose? Is the sound calming or attention-commanding? Employ metaphors and comparisons to elucidate your sensory observations.

There are various visuals you can utilize to represent scent, sound, and touch. I prefer using cartoon-like visuals of a face, nose, or ears, and placing other visuals and notes nearby. I opt for a few simple colors like yellow for dry grasses and leaves, and darker browns and blues for moist fine fuels, but you could employ a mix of colors for better association. Scents are akin to wispy currents in the air, so consider using wavy lines of color for visualization. For touch, sketch fingers or a hand holding something, then add simple visuals, like a flat line for smooth surfaces and a flat line with little hairlines for something hairy or abrasive. Sounds can be visualized as waves, with circular movements and distinct lines. You can also include comic-style flares and accents for sound, such as little marks near a bend in a grass blade to signify breaking instead of bending.

Detailed Fuels Observations

As your knowledge and awareness of fuels and fire behavior grow, or if you already possess training and experience, you can create more intricate journal pages. I like to incorporate a sketch of the fuels group, along with close-up sketches of the fuel bed and fine fuels, then add fuel moisture thresholds and other fire behavior information, as shown in the examples I've shared.

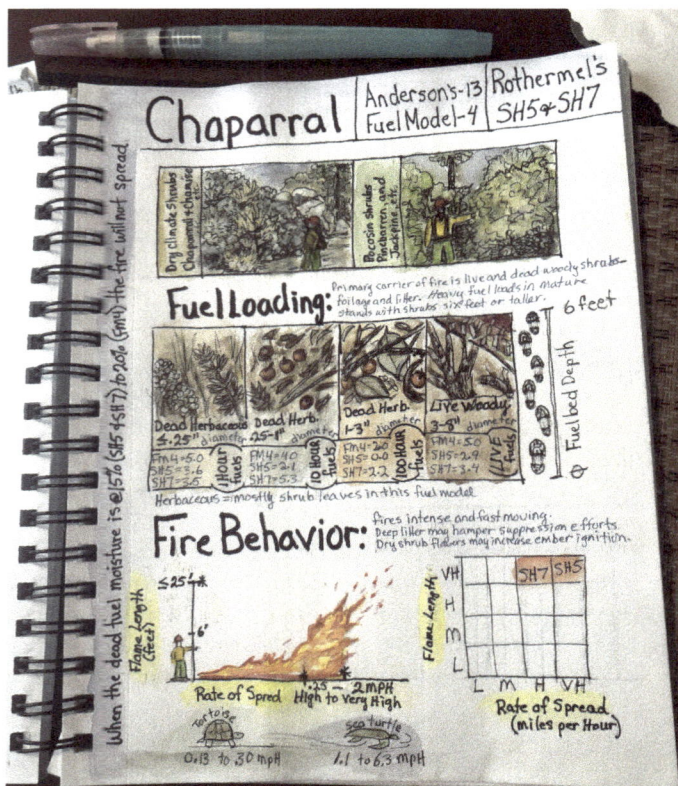

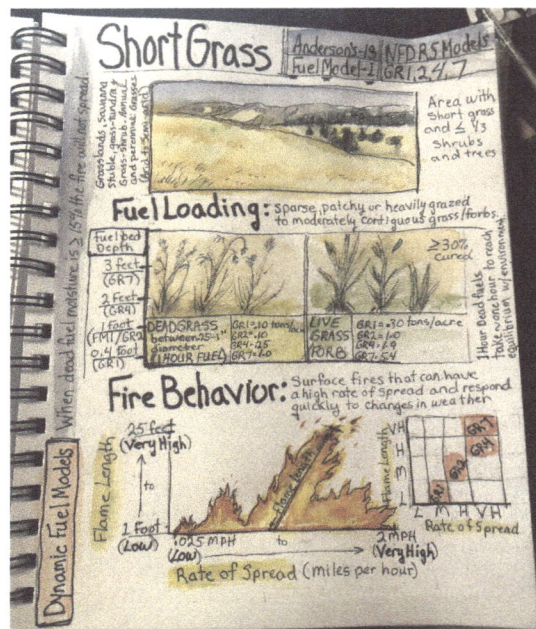

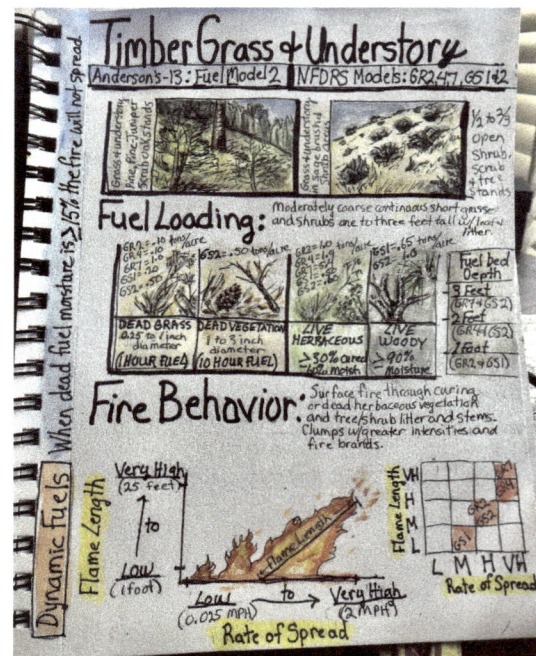

Combining Fire Environment Observations

Here are a few examples of how I integrate weather, topography, and fuels observations into my journal. Note that I don't always emphasize the fire aspects, but can still convey much of the information with a sketch of the landscape (topography), trees, and leaves.

It's more interesting and fun to include insects, animals, and other observations while observing the bigger picture of the fire environment. And over time, you may start to find ways to associate fire with other observations. I'll discuss that further in Chapter 9: Fire Severity and Fire Effects and Chapter 10: Fire Regimes.

Benson Feb. 2022

Benson AZ
Elevation 3,586 ft.
Lat & Long - 110.29 + 31.967
~45 minutes SE of Tuscon AZ
Elevation Range 3000-9,000 ft
Madrean Archipelago Region
Sonoran & mojave Deserts & sky Islands
Low elev. Desert Scrub & semi-desert
Scrubby grasslands, mesquite shrubs
and riparian woodlands.

Mostly flat with nearby rolling hills and distant mountains.

Recent Wildfire
Bighorn Fire - near Tuscon in Mtns
2020 July. 119,987 acres

Fire Regime
- High to Low frequency

Very flammable carrying fuels (grass) but patchy.

Burns within seconds!

char on grass blade

Horizontal Fuels Arrangement
small tree
Bushes
sand/barren

Mostly barren desert with patchy areas of grass and small shrubs

Not sure fire would carry far along the surface or into trees.

Vertical Fuels Arrangement

4-6 ft

No leaves on trees or large shrubs. Minor ladder fuels, but some heavier areas.

Sense of Fire

I Notice...

slightly larger than real-life

Tiny branches & dried flowers on small shrubs

Close to actual size

Brittle

Very narrow grass blades almost like dental floss

Length about elbow to finger tip

Touch: feels like dry hair or twine. Breaks easily.

Smell: Smells like straw.

Listen: Dry scratchy sounding when crumpled.

I Wonder...
What other surface vegetation might fill in and carry fire?
- Dry leaves from shrubs or trees later in the season?

Today's temp & moisture
70°F feels hot in direct sun. feels dry.
Temp: 42°F to 72°F
RH: 27% to 10%
Season: 30°F to 68°F
Climate: 28°F to 97°F

Today's Atmos.
overcast some stretched clouds across the sky

Today's Winds
- Not noticeable while walking
Local / Benson
- 3 mph to 7 mph W
- Region 7 to 36 W/S

Red flag Wx =
- High Temps
- Winds 15+ mph for several hours
- RH ≤ 25%

Area Wind Trends
- Winter winds W to NW
- Summer winds S to SE
- Late summer to fall monsoons

Leaf Flammability Burn Test

An exercise you can use to compare moisture levels and flammability of live and dead fine fuels, or a mix of dead fine fuels in shaded and sunny areas, is to gather several different leaves and conduct a flammability test. Ensure to perform this exercise in an area cleared of all vegetation, on pavement, or in a classroom or laboratory setting. You should also have a bucket or container of water to extinguish the flaming leaves. I recommend using wooden matches rather than a lighter or paper matches to provide a reasonable ignition source and test period. Also, have a stopwatch and consider using a video camera on a tripod to record and observe the flame lengths after you have observed and timed the ignition. The intent of the exercise is not to burn the entire leaf, but to observe the differences between them.

Step 1: Trace or sketch the outline of the leaf shape in your journal, but do not color it in.

Step 2: Start the timer and video camera. Hold a match to the side of the leaf until it ignites or for the duration of the match. Observe how well each leaf ignites and burns.

Step 3: Record the timing it takes to ignite and burn, and add the data next to the leaf outline in your journal. Include any other notes about flames and smoke.

Step 4: Review the video and add any further observations missed during the test.

Step 5: Sketch the approximate flames onto the leaf shape in your journal and color in the remaining leaf with any charred or unburned areas, showing color and texture differences.

There are different fine fuels ignition tests in the prescribed fire section of the Fire & Smoke chapter.

	High Humidity	Low Humidity
Green Leaf		
Dry Leaf		

Chapter 5:
Fire Seasons

United States Fire Seasons

According to the National Wildfire Coordinating Group (NWCG), a fire season is the period when wildfires are likely to occur, spread, and sufficiently affect resource values to warrant organized fire management activities.

The NWCG Fire Season Climatology webpage provides information about regional fire seasons. I highlighted the fire season dates on the map to illustrate how fire seasons start earlier in the south and moves north as daylight hours increase over the seasons. Other seasonal weather systems also influence fire season across different regions, which I'll discuss on the next page.

As an example of the more detailed fire season summaries on the NWCG webpage, I've highlighted some of the California fire season information. In northern California, the fire season typically peaks in summer with increasingly warm and dry conditions, foehn wind events, and infrequent dry cold fronts. There can be a rapid decrease in fire activity in late fall, although dry northeasterly winds can cause significant fire events. The southern California fire season frequently starts in spring as temperatures warm. The Southwest Monsoon system also influences the southern California fire season, bringing increased moisture, wind shifts, and thunderstorms along the Sierra Nevada region. There is an occasional secondary fire season in southern California in fall when there is a shift in the jet stream and the occurrence of foehn wind events.

Regional Fire Seasons

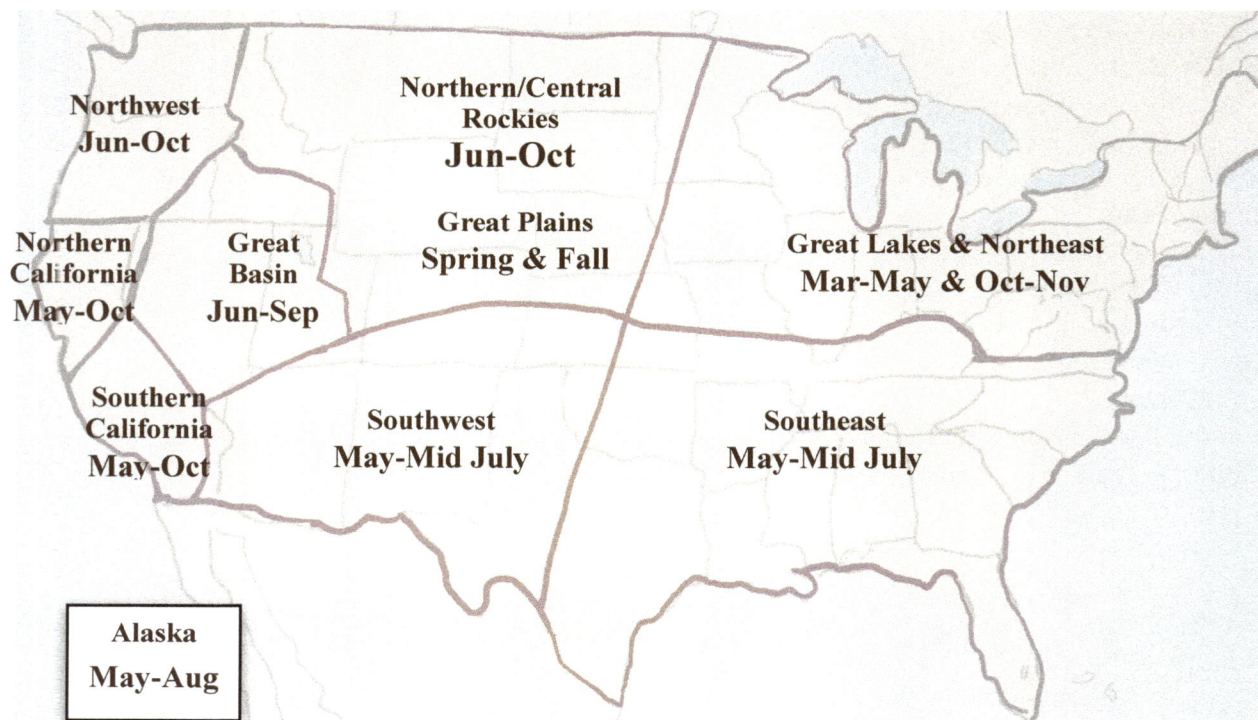

Northwest
Jun-Oct

Northern/Central
Rockies
Jun-Oct

Great Plains
Spring & Fall

Northern
California
May-Oct

Great
Basin
Jun-Sep

Great Lakes & Northeast
Mar-May & Oct-Nov

Southern
California
May-Oct

Southwest
May-Mid July

Southeast
May-Mid July

Alaska
May-Aug

I would recommend you look up your regional fire season information and include as baseline and comparison information for your seasonal journaling. Your local fire season information will have more focused and detailed data, but having information to compare trends is helpful building a deeper sense of seasonal trends.

Fire Season Starting & Ending Conditions

According to the NWCG, all fire seasons begin when fuels are cured. Increasing temperatures, wind events, decreasing precipitation, dry lightning, and low humidity also influence the start of the fire season.

Fire season slowing and ending conditions, or the end of the fire season, typically include increased precipitation and humidity levels, resulting in the vegetation greening up. These conditions are influenced by reduced daytime hours and decreasing temperatures and seasonal weather patterns, like marine layers, onshore flows, Pacific troughs, tropical storms, warm fronts and monsoon bursts. Long periods of smoke can also slow fire activities. I'll share more information and journaling examples on each of these weather elements throughout this chapter.

Seasonal Sunlight

This chapter focuses on fire seasons, yet it's beneficial to explore broader seasonal observations and how they contribute to the narrative of the fire environment. Our understanding of seasons typically revolves around astronomical seasons and the corresponding equinoxes. While calendar dates can serve as prompts for observations, I prefer to consider their manifestation in the landscape. We can contemplate how the sun's angle and the

duration of daylight hours impact seasonal transitions. These solar variations play a role in defining our meteorological seasons, which are determined by annual temperature fluctuations. The interplay of solar hour and angle alterations, along with temperature shifts, influences plant phenology and fire seasons.

As discussed in Chapter 4: Fire Fuels, the angle of the sun also influences vegetation communities and the associated seasons across elevational and slope aspect gradients. The illustration above depicts the path and angle of the sun as it changes between summer and winter. Yellow lines indicate the top of the sun's arc during summer and winter. In summer, the sun follows a wider arc, resulting in stronger warming and drying influences. Additionally, there are more sunlight hours in the day, further increasing heating and drying effects. It's essential to consider how fuel conditions can vary based on slope aspect, time of day, and season.

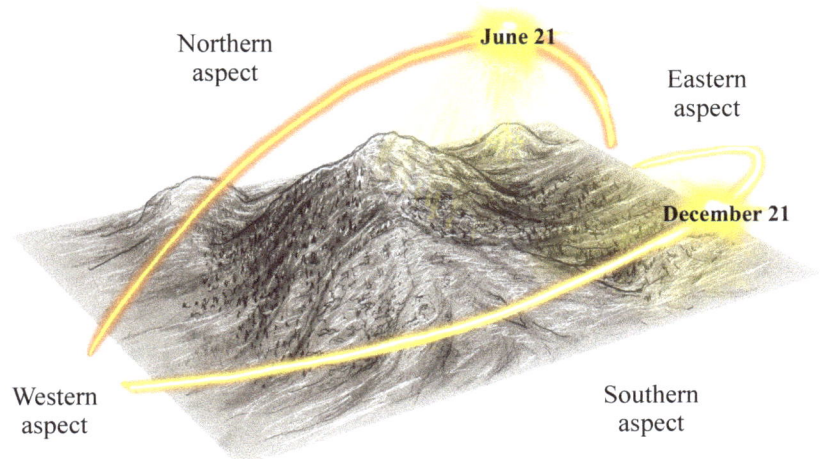

Seasonal Shadows

In addition to the changing sunlight angles across seasons and the landscape, there are also changing shadows. These shadowed areas create microclimates that influence fuel and soil moisture levels. Some prescribed fire practitioners use shadows and sunlit areas to target their ignition patterers. For the illustration, I referenced examples from the Nagwa online learning website (Nagwa, 2023).

The illustration demonstrates how the generalized representation of shadows changes in length and direction throughout the day and across seasons.

To document these observations, choose a scene with trees, shrubs, or buildings exposed to sunlight in different directions. Create a diagram or sketch each month at the same time of day, and measure or estimate the shadow lengths. Spend a few minutes standing between sunlit and shadowed areas to compare skin temperatures and moisture levels and observe fine fuels on the ground. For more information and examples, refer back to Chapter 4: Fire Fuels.

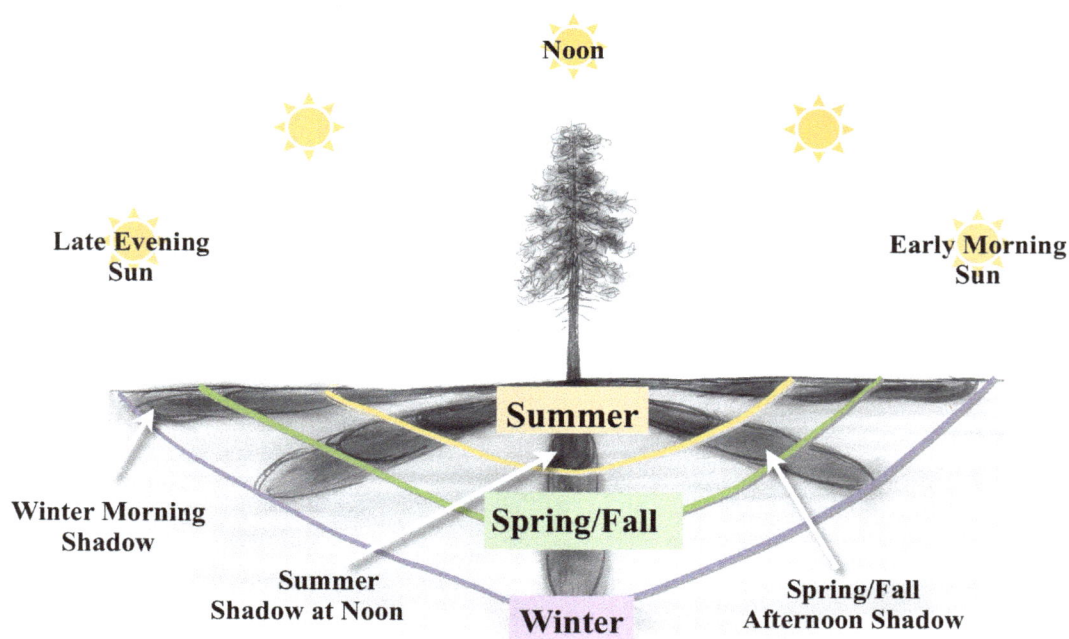

Seasonal Temperatures

The U.S. fire seasons map, on the first page of this chapter, offers a general concept of when fire management agencies define fire seasons and organize staffing to prepare for wildfires. However, you can delve deeper into seasonal weather trends by considering the average temperature trends across meteorological seasons and geographic areas. In the illustrations on this page, I have summarized some of the average seasonal temperatures by state and used my preferred temperature range color codes. My temperature color codes are more broadly spread than the references, and I had to tweak some of the colors to work with this data. Therefore, this example is just intended to give a sense of seasonal temperature differences across the country. What I like about this type of reference is considering how temperatures influence plant and animal phenology. Phenology, as defined by the Oxford dictionary, is the study of cyclic and seasonal natural phenomena, especially related to plants and animals. I also like to compare the weather data in my journal, which includes the daily and monthly averages, highs, and lows, with the live bird migration map on the BirdCast website to look for trends and relationships between weather and migration. Many indigenous fire practitioners use plant and animal phenology to guide their prescribed burn periods.

The U.S. Meteorological Seasons:

- **Spring**: March, April, and May
- **Summer**: June, July, and August
- **Fall**: September, October, November
- **Winter**: December, January, February

Winter Average Temperatures

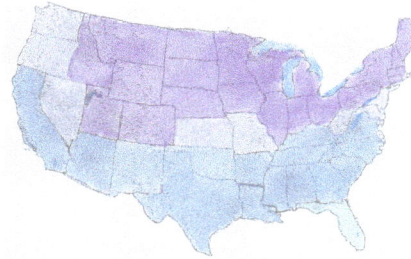

Spring Average Temperatures

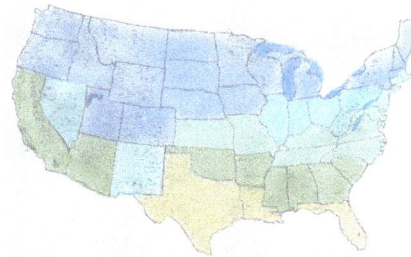

Summer Average Temperatures

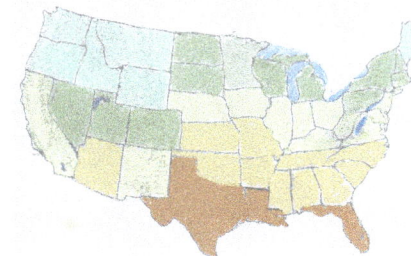

Fall Average Temperatures

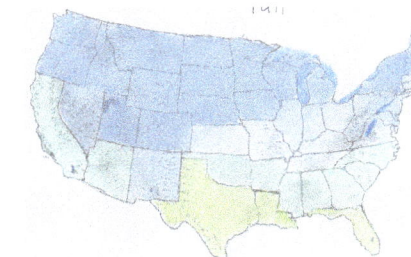

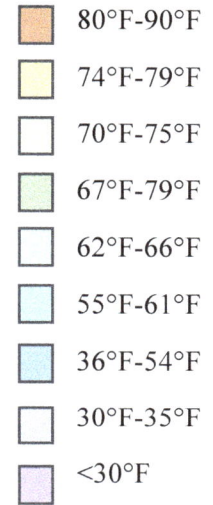

▦	80°F-90°F
▢	74°F-79°F
▢	70°F-75°F
▢	67°F-79°F
▢	62°F-66°F
▢	55°F-61°F
▢	36°F-54°F
▢	30°F-35°F
▢	<30°F

99

In Chapter 2: Fire Weather, I introduced a temperature color code that I attempt to apply consistently in all my temperature journaling. However, there are often subtle color variations depending on my supplies and how I choose to categorize the temperature ranges, as described on the previous page. I prefer to utilize broad temperature categories that are easily perceptible and closely linked to phenology and fire.

Temperature, Phenology, Fuels & Fire Behavior

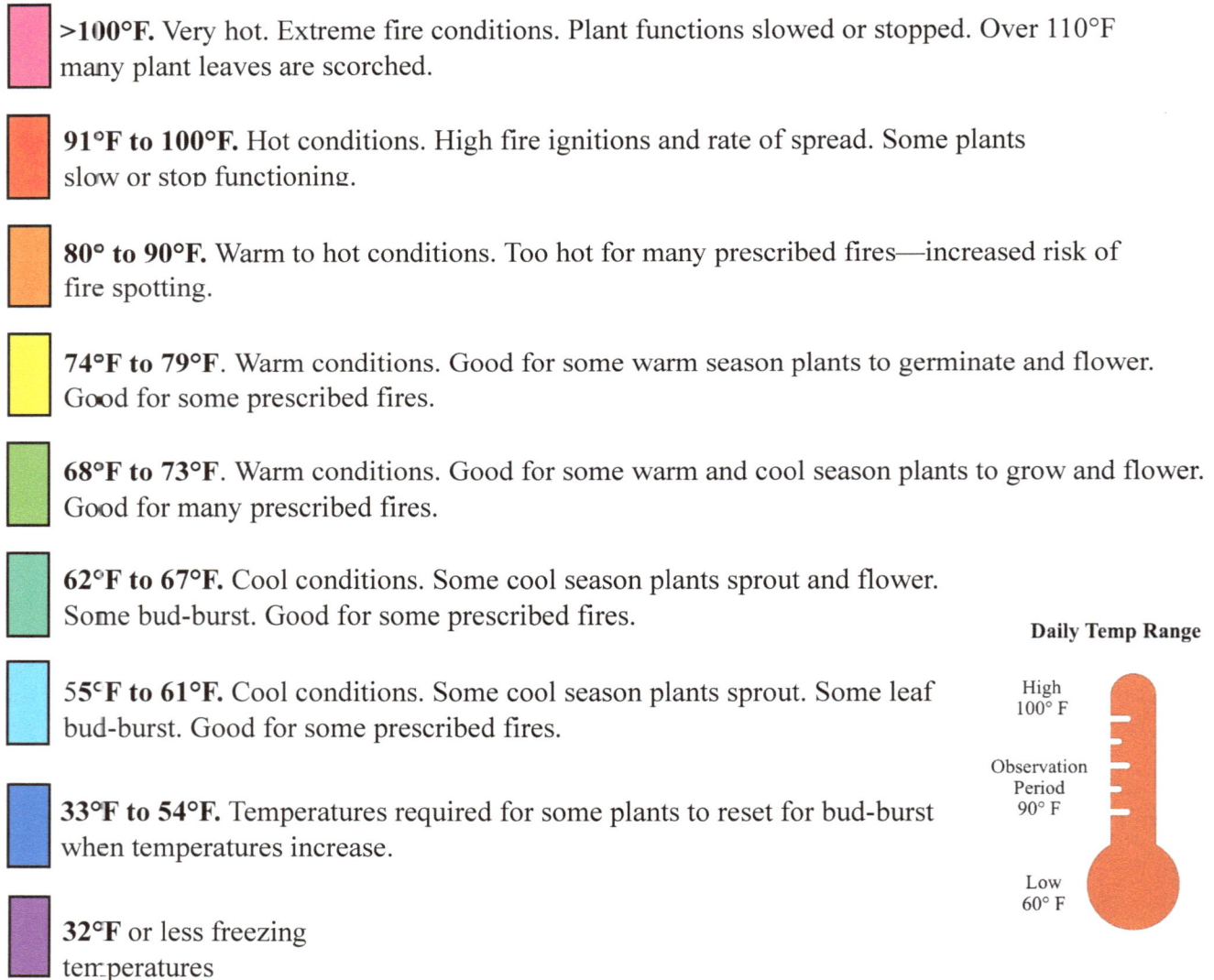

>100°F. Very hot. Extreme fire conditions. Plant functions slowed or stopped. Over 110°F many plant leaves are scorched.

91°F to 100°F. Hot conditions. High fire ignitions and rate of spread. Some plants slow or stop functioning.

80° to 90°F. Warm to hot conditions. Too hot for many prescribed fires—increased risk of fire spotting.

74°F to 79°F. Warm conditions. Good for some warm season plants to germinate and flower. Good for some prescribed fires.

68°F to 73°F. Warm conditions. Good for some warm and cool season plants to grow and flower. Good for many prescribed fires.

62°F to 67°F. Cool conditions. Some cool season plants sprout and flower. Some bud-burst. Good for some prescribed fires.

55°F to 61°F. Cool conditions. Some cool season plants sprout. Some leaf bud-burst. Good for some prescribed fires.

33°F to 54°F. Temperatures required for some plants to reset for bud-burst when temperatures increase.

32°F or less freezing temperatures

Daily Temp Range

High
100° F

Observation
Period
90° F

Low
60° F

Fire Weather Wheel

When I first started exploring temperature and other weather journaling approaches, I experimented with a wide range of data sources and visualizations, finding that too much information was difficult to visualize. I settled on using temperature, relative humidity, and wind data from local websites. One visualization I found useful was a large circle with two rings: an outer daytime weather ring (daily highs) and an inner nighttime weather ring (daily lows). It's essential to differentiate between day and nighttime weather because fire behavior and wildfire updates are typically split between day and night fire-burning periods. Each ring includes a small block for symbolized temperature (colors), moisture (dots), and winds (chevrons) for each day of the month. I've

changed the color codes over time, exploring approaches and redirecting my observation goals.

As my fire weather wheel evolved, I added leaf and stem symbols along the outside of rings or circles to indicate satellite hotspots and wildfires found each day on the National Interagency Fire Center's Fire Situation Map (online). This was an interesting way to visualize how changing weather affected fire ignitions. You could also use the weather wheel concept but apply other phenology observations instead of fire occurrences. I must mention that recreating the circle, rings, and daily data blocks for each month took a lot of time, which would have been easier using a stencil. Since then, I've found bullet journal stencils that work well for monthly weather tracking.

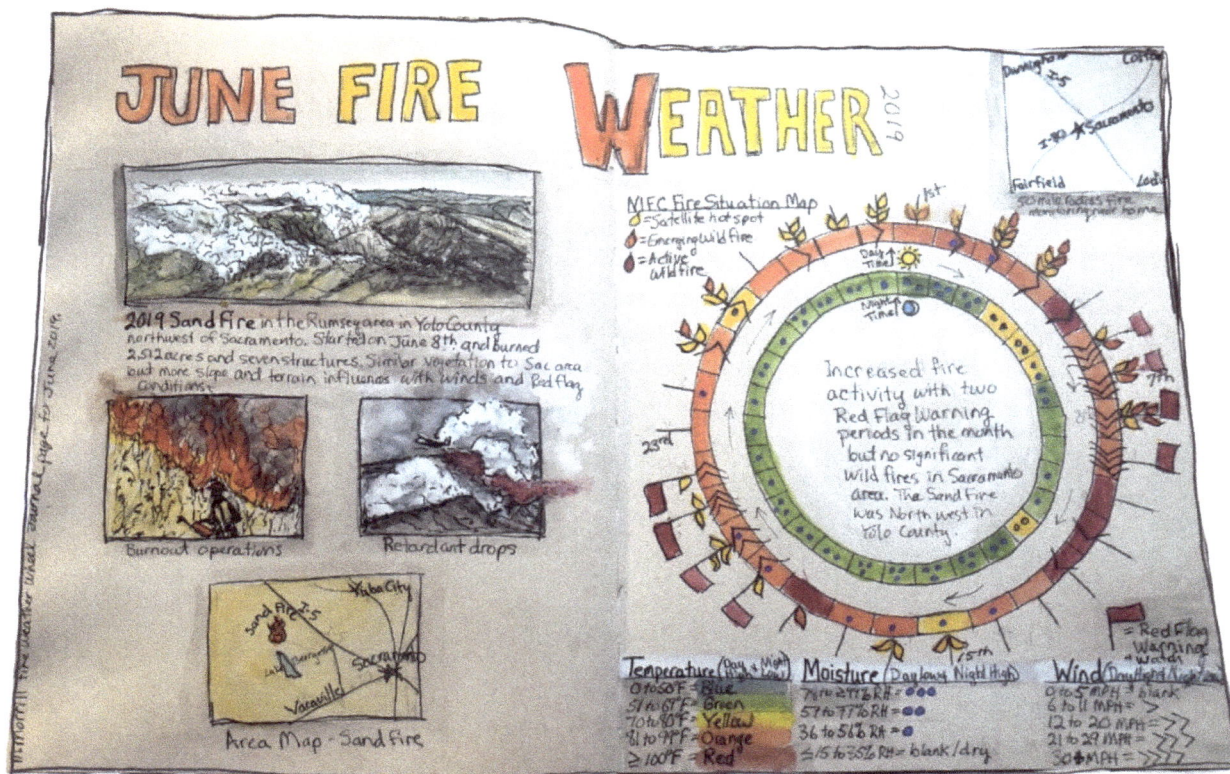

In my fire weather wheel journal pages, I included a location map for satellite fires and hotspot areas of observations, using a 50-mile radius area. I also added a legend for the visualized weather data and one or more small sketches of fuel conditions (curing phase), key weather events like a thunderstorm, and any fire activity that occurred that month, if I could find photos as a reference. You can adjust the legend and weather thresholds for your local area or use my version, which is generalized for low to high fire hazard conditions in a broad range of environments. This makes it less accurate but still helpful for observations and trend analysis.

Temperature & Climate Graph

After a year of exploring fire weather wheel visuals, I opted for a different approach: comparing current temperatures with historic data to observe trends and extreme events. Although more time-consuming, this method offers insightful observations. Many websites provide historic weather data; for my example, I used the Weather Underground website's historic data tab. Note that some data may be from a different weather station, but for general trends, it should suffice for local comparisons. Just select the closest historic weather station location.

Each point on the rising and dropping line is the difference between the historic daily high and low average temperature and current high and low temperatures.

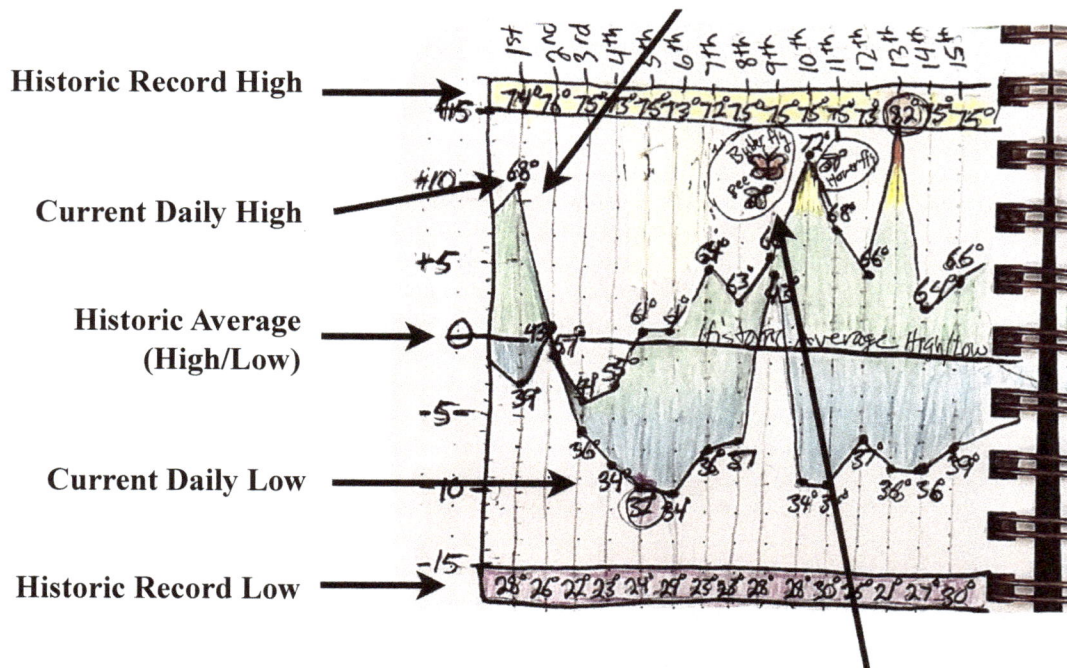

Historic Record High

Current Daily High

Historic Average
(High/Low)

Current Daily Low

Historic Record Low

Nature Observations

The weather and climate comparison graph on these two pages was created on blank pages in a calendar organizer using pencil, pen, and colored pencils. You can update this graph daily or at a later date. I designed a vertical column for each day of the month, with a horizontal line in the middle representing the difference between historic and current daily high and low temperatures.

Along the vertical line of the graph, I included 15 temperature increment marks above and below the historic average center line. If your high and low temperatures vary widely, you may need more temperature increments. I allocated top and bottom rows where I listed the record high and low for each day.

Occasionally, the daily high set a new record, necessitating the crossing out of the old record and adding the new one. I placed a dot/point above and below the center horizon line for each daily column, representing the difference between historic and current high and low temperatures. Next to each point, I included the actual high and low temperature. As more points were added, I connected them with a line. Once the month was complete, I colored in areas between the lines with temperature color codes. I also added tiny sketches along points in the graph where interesting observations were made, such as the first bees and butterflies observed in the season.

Days of the month

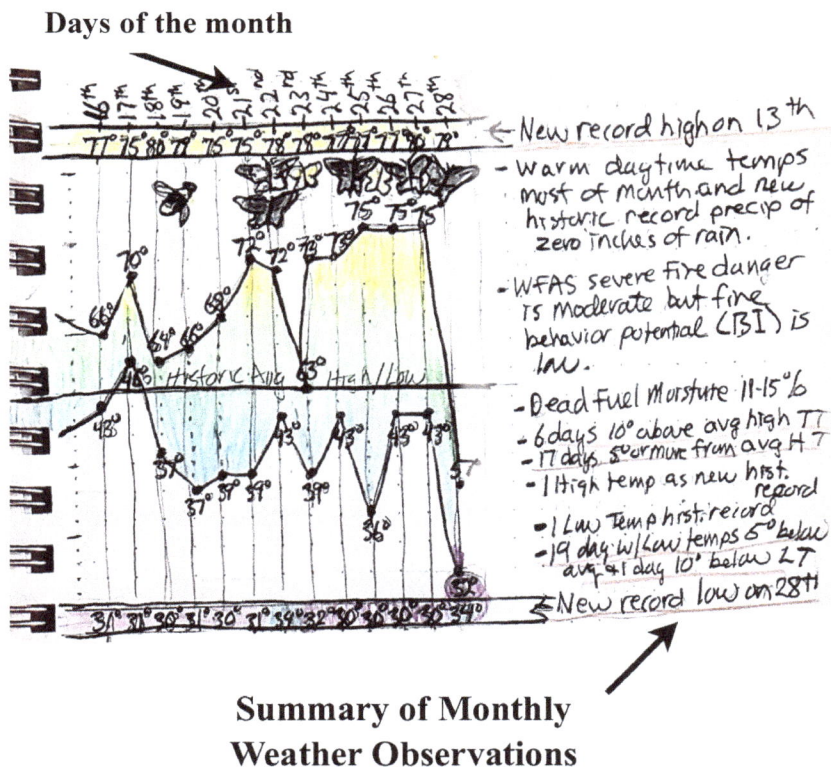

Upon completion of the monthly graph, I circled temperature interest points and added summary notes about the observed trends and how they compared with historic climate trends and overall trends within the season. For instance, I might note that the current month experienced unusually cold temperatures compared to the previous month and historic climate for that season.

I discuss more detailed phenology and fire related observations and journaling approaches later in the chapter, after the following section on seasonal weather patterns.

**Summary of Monthly
Weather Observations**

Phenology & VPD

Journaling seasonal humidity trends can be challenging since most websites only provide precipitation levels for the month and year. In the Chapter 4: Fire Fuels, we learned how the combination of relative humidity and temperature affects the vapor pressure deficit (VPD) in the air and within plants, influencing fuel moisture levels and flammability. Plants in different environments have adapted to different VPD levels and timed their phenology accordingly. I have an RH color code, with associated phenology and fire behaviors graphic, on page 105 that can be used to visualize RH metadata.

The illustration on the next page integrates information from a study on plant responses to rising vapor pressure deficit (Grossiord 2020) and highlights the general stages of plant growth at different seasonal temperatures, humidities, and VPD levels. I have combined live fine fuel moisture levels from the NWCG *Fire Behavior Field Reference Guide* with typical herbaceous and surface fuel phenophases in the relative humidity color codex on the next page to connect fuel moisture levels and changing fire hazards When temperatures are low and moisture levels are high, most plants are in the sprouting or leaf burst phases. Herbaceous and deciduous vegetation typically have a higher moisture content at this phase (Pollet & Brown 2007). Plant cells can hold about three times their weight in water, so live fuel moisture levels can range from 120% to 300%. Fires rarely start or spread in these conditions.

As temperatures rise and with water still available in the soil, plants start to green up and flower, causing fuel moisture to drop, typically reaching 120% to 98% (NWCG 2014). Prescribed fires can be planned for these conditions, but most wildfires will not spread. Plants move from flowering to seed development phases, where live fuel moisture levels can range from 98% to 75%. At this phase, wildfires can ignite and spread with moderate to high rates of spread. When temperatures start to get hot and the moisture in the ground reduces, the VPD in the air pulls more moisture from plants, and the senescence phase begins to cure plants. Live fuel moisture levels drop between 90-60% (shrubs) and 60-30% (grasses), at which point they are measured as dead fuels. Fires during this phase can move at very high to extreme rates of spread. The surface fine fuels in different fuel groups will have somewhat different fuel moisture levels and fire rates of spread, based on differences in leaf types and phenology phases.

Senescence is a complex process for living plants and is the phase when they deteriorate with age (CFA *Grassland Curing Guide*). From an observation perspective, look for the yellowing and browning of grasses and leaves. To integrate humidity observations, you can add notes and thoughts about how humidity and temperature trends influence phenology and fuel conditions. If you use the perpetual journal approach for fuel moisture and humidity levels and the humidity color codex that I created.

Growing Degree Days

An intriguing metric for tracking and assessing seasonal temperature impacts on plants and insects is Growing Degree Days (GDD). Some practitioners of prescribed fire use this data to identify optimal burning dates for specific plant species and to assess the effects of the fire.

While GDD calculations may vary based on the targeted species, many adopt what is known as the GDD base 50. In essence, you calculate the daily average temperature and subtract any temperatures below 50°F, as this is a temperature range in which plants are unlikely to grow. Some calculations also subtract temperatures above 86°F. The GDD for each day is accumulated over the growing season.

Sprouting—Growing—Flowering—Seeding—Curing

Cold Temps with High RH & Low VPD

Warm Temps with Moderate RH & Moderate VPD

Hot Temps with Low RH & High VPD

Cool Temps with Moderate RH & Low VPD

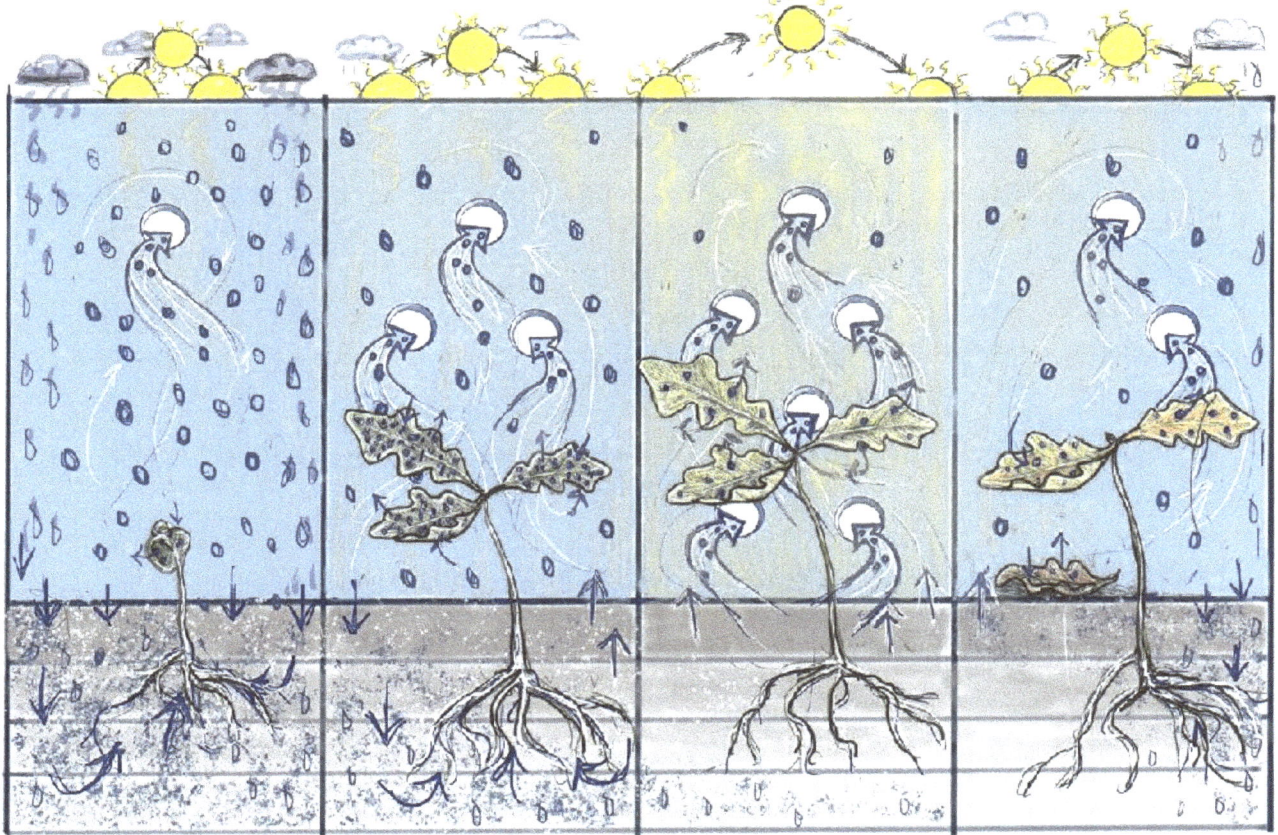

Symbol represents the vapor pressure deficit (VPD) level in the air. The more "holes" in the sky means the higher the moisture deficit level and the lower the relative humidity.

Arrows represent the up and down flow of liquid water droplets between the air and soil.

Circles and drops represent the water vapor and water droplet in the air and soil.

Relative Humidity, Plant Phenology, Fuels & Fire Behavior

< 15% RH. Fire weather condition for many environments. High fire risk. Plants may be stressed or in senescence phase.

16% to 30% RH. Fire weather conditions for some environments. Plants may be in senescence phase.

31% to 40% RH. Low to moderately moist conditions and plants may be in seed or senescence phase. Some prescribed burn prescriptions.

41% to 50% RH. Good conditions for flowering phase of many plants. Good for many prescribed burn prescriptions.

51% to 60% RH. Good conditions for the vegetative growth phase of many plants. Good for many prescribed burn prescriptions.

61% to 85% RH. Good for many tropical plants to grow, with appropriate temperatures. Too moist for many prescribed burn prescriptions.

86% to 100% RH. Good for most plants to germinate, with appropriate temperatures. Too moist for most prescribed burn prescriptions.

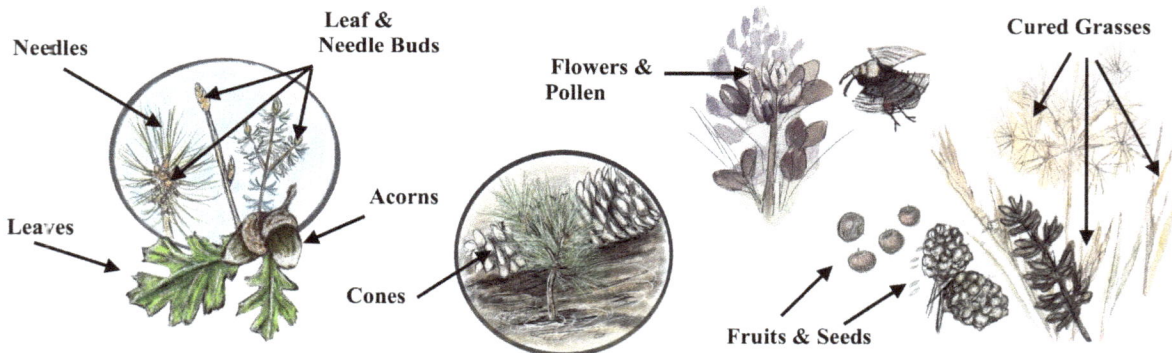

Needles

Leaf & Needle Buds

Leaves

Acorns

Cones

Flowers & Pollen

Fruits & Seeds

Cured Grasses

Journaling Phenology

I like to connect phenology observations to the fire season for more interconnected and systems-scale relationships. There are numerous books on phenology, like the USA National Phenology Network, which can be a helpful reference, but I'll share a few highlights and examples. In this chapter, I focus primarily on how to observe the seasonal changes in vegetation and how that influences fire behavior.

Journaling your phenology and seasonal weather and fuel moisture levels can take many forms. You can use broad or narrow descriptions of the phenophase, with simple symbols, diagrams, and/or sketches along with notes about potential fuel moisture and fire hazard levels for live and dead vegetation. I like to add some detailed phenology observations, along with estimates about the percentage of dominant vegetation within a particular phenophase. For instance, I may observe the majority of trees in their budburst phase and/or 75% of the trees with their leaves grown to full size.

Sometimes I prefer a simple visual like a small diagram, with tree, shrub, and ground-level phenophase observations that can help connect the fuel arrangements, like the example below. I'll combine the graphic with small sketches of a few fun or key observations.

I would also recommend you include seasonal weather (three-month period) and climate data with your phenology observations. The relationships between climate, vegetation changes, and fire can become clearer when weaving together these observations and patterns.

If you decide to track Growing Degree Days (GDD) along with your weather and phenology observations, you might consider modifying my fire weather wheel.

Phenology Observations Diagram

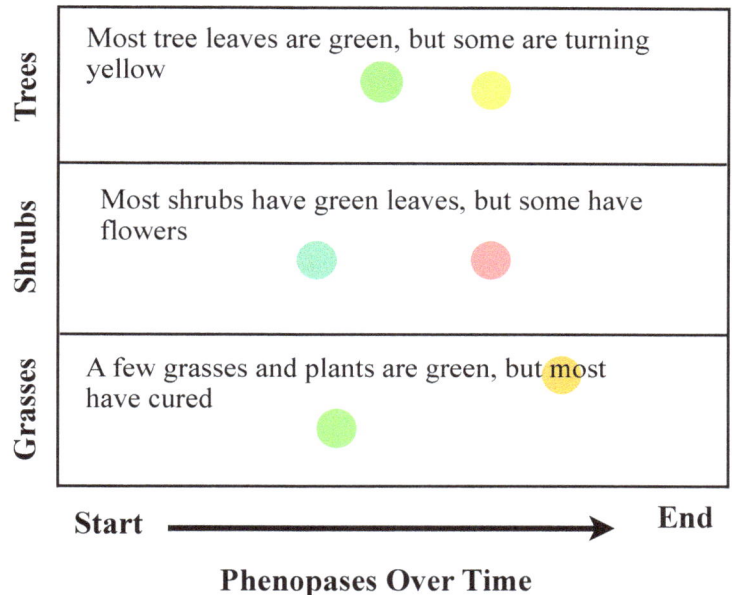

Trees: Most tree leaves are green, but some are turning yellow

Shrubs: Most shrubs have green leaves, but some have flowers

Grasses: A few grasses and plants are green, but most have cured

Start ——————————————→ End

Phenopases Over Time

Plant Phenopase Observations:

- Leaf Budburst
- New Green Grass
- Open Flowers
- Pollen
- Emerging Leaves
- Unfolded Leaves
- 75% of Leaves Full Sized
- 75% Grasses Cured/Dry
- Green Fruit
- Ripe Fruit
- Seeds
- All Leaves Colored
- 50% of Leaves Fallen
- All Leaves Fallen
- Acorns &/or Cones on Trees
- Acorns &/or Cones Fallen

Tree Phenology

Seasonal observations, like tree phenophases, can be a fun to journal and ties in well with fire fuels observations, like accumulating leaves in the fuel bed. This is also a journaling approach that can help build observation skills around climate changes. For example, some plants are initiating their growing phenophases earlier in the spring compared to historical trends. I am not including detailed observations about the phenophases of the many different species of trees, but have included some information and ideas about journaling conifer and broadleaf trees gleaned from the U.S. Phenology Network. I would recommend you try to make these seasonal observations in the spring and fall and over a three-year period.

On the next page, I modified a climate graph generated on WeatherSpark.com by integrating the temperature color codes I use in weather journaling. I feel like the color codes I use for tracking temperatures help me relate to the data and make other connections in my journal. For example, I have color bars for the tree phenophases relating to the seasonal temperatures. I would recommend creating climate-phenophase references for your local area that can be used for comparison with ongoing seasonal observations. One time-saving option is to create a climate (temperature and precipitation) graph for a 10 to 50-year period. You can overlay vellum or tracing paper over your climate reference graph and trace the observed monthly weather, with the dates for phenophase observations.

Pay particular attention to both the individual close-up observations of phenophases as well as the subtle color changes in the vegetation observed from a distance. Keep in mind that the visual appearance of trees, like the color of leaves, can also be altered by stress, disease, and fire effects. Try to get a close look at tree canopies and leaves to better assess seasonal changes. In the last chapter about fire regimes, I have a section with information and observations about tree stress and mortality phases that can assist with differentiating seasonal observations.

Conifer Phenophases

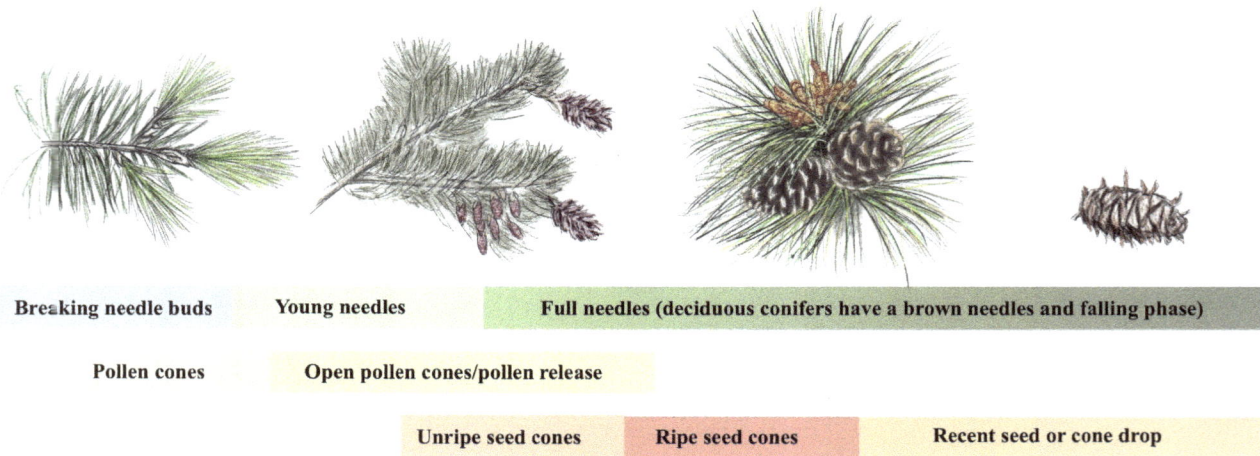

Breaking needle buds   Young needles   Full needles (deciduous conifers have a brown needles and falling phase)

Pollen cones   Open pollen cones/pollen release

Unripe seed cones   Ripe seed cones   Recent seed or cone drop

Mean Monthly High & Low Temperatures, Ashland, Oregon
2015-2023

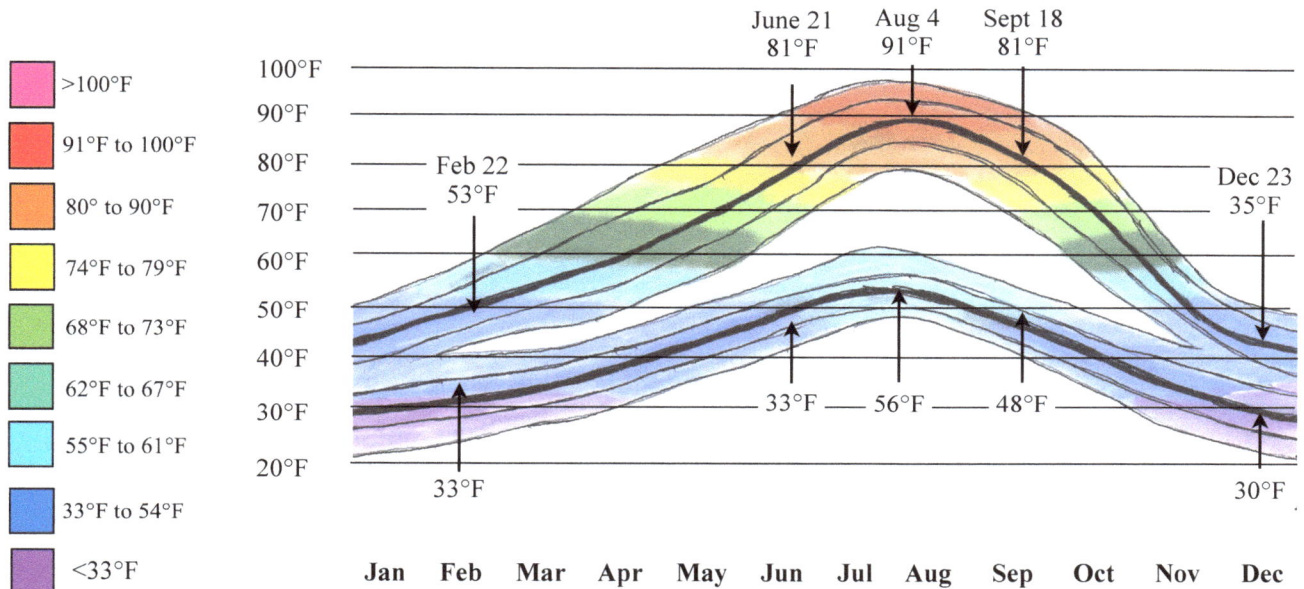

Legend:
- >100°F
- 91°F to 100°F
- 80° to 90°F
- 74°F to 79°F
- 68°F to 73°F
- 62°F to 67°F
- 55°F to 61°F
- 33°F to 54°F
- <33°F

Annotations on chart:
- June 21 81°F
- Aug 4 91°F
- Sept 18 81°F
- Feb 22 53°F
- Dec 23 35°F
- 33°F — 56°F — 48°F
- 33°F
- 30°F

Months: Jan Feb Mar Apr May Jun Jul Aug Sep Oct Nov Dec

Temperature scale: 100°F, 90°F, 80°F, 70°F, 60°F, 50°F, 40°F, 30°F, 20°F

- Top multicolored band—mean monthly high temperatures
- Bottom multicolored band—mean monthly low temperatures
- Thick black center lines—mean monthly high and low temperatures
- Thin black lines adjacent to the thick black lines—75th percentile of the monthly high and low temperatures
- Thin black lines along the outer edge of the color bands—90th percentile of the monthly high and low temperatures

Deciduous Broadleaf Phenophases

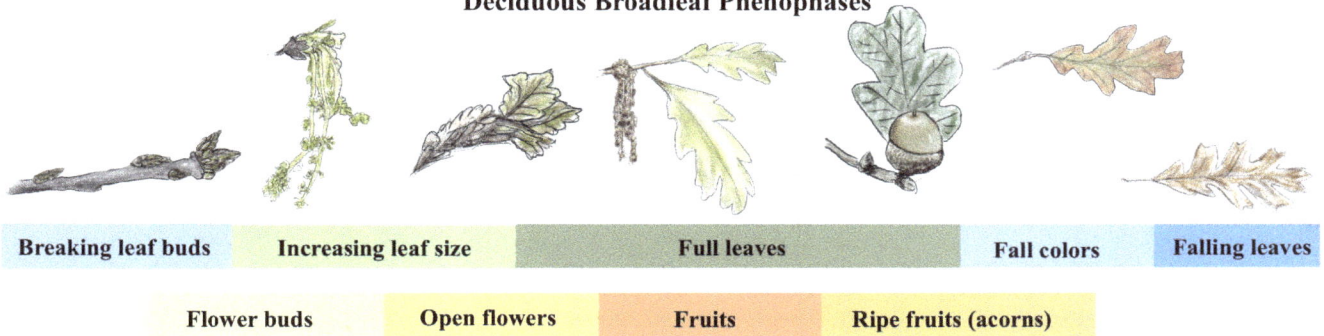

| Breaking leaf buds | Increasing leaf size | Full leaves | Fall colors | Falling leaves |

| Flower buds | Open flowers | Fruits | Ripe fruits (acorns) |

Seasonal Fuels Curing

When journaling about the fire season, it's crucial to closely observe the phenological changes and curing of grasses. According to the Country Fire Authority's (CFA) *Grassland Curing Guide* from Victoria, Australia, grassland curing refers to the process by which grasses dry out, die, or become dormant each year. Curing is quantified as the percentage of cured vegetation within the grassland. This process is intertwined with changing temperatures, relative humidity, vapor pressure deficit, and precipitation trends.

The associated phenological changes also entail fluctuations in live fuel moisture levels, eventually merging with the dead surface fuels that propagate fire. While live and moist vegetation will burn, stronger and longer duration heat sources are required to first dry and then ignite the vegetation.

The CFA *Grassland Curing Guide* serves as a valuable reference for developing observation skills related to seasonal changes and fire behavior. I've summarized some of the information in this section to aid in journaling these observations. I've created simple illustrations depicting grass anatomy and the conditions, appearances, or arrangements that will be used in curing observations. You don't need to know the grass species or the names of all the plant parts, but having a general understanding of what to observe during different phenophases is essential. Primarily, we focus on observing the stems, leaf blades, and inflorescence (seed heads).

Grass stems, leaf blades, and seed heads can vary in shape and size. For journaling purposes, these sketches do not need to be precise but should represent the key elements of the primary or majority of grasses in the curing phase. You don't need to include all other plant species unless desired; we are examining general grassland conditions over time.

Grass Anatomy

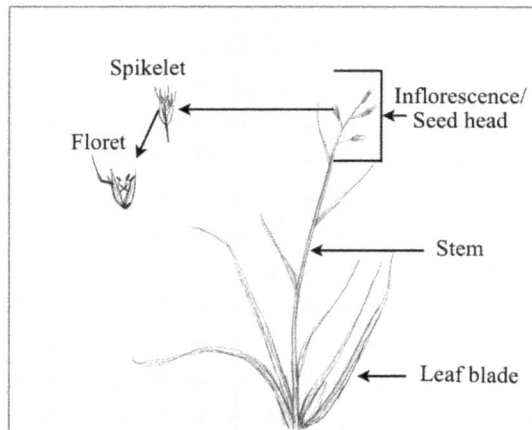

Grass Blade Arrangements

Grass Seed Heads Arrangements

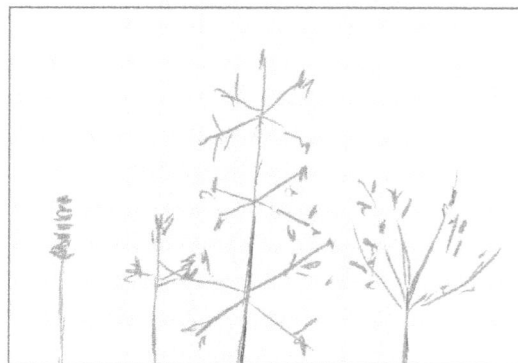

Before delving into grassland curing phase observations, let me share some visualization ideas. The appearance and arrangement of grasses in your area may alter some of your sketches compared to what I'm sharing, but your sketches can be either detailed or simple, depending on your preference. You may have a thick continuous blanket of grass or patches of bunch grass.

You can observe the steps and effort put into the detailed drawing of grass anatomy and arrangements, contrasted with the diagrammatic grassland sketch on the next page. Detailed sketches may complicate key observations, while diagrammed sketches are modified versions of cross-section (vertical fuels) and bird's-eye view (horizontal fuels) diagrams shared in Chapter 4: Fire Fuels.

There are other approaches you could use to visualize curing phases. I've done quick impressionistic watercolor paintings in my journal as well as used graphic visualization. I'd recommend starting with one approach for the first season to make it easier to notice changes between each phase. I like to incorporate some of these visuals and include a mix of fire season observations.

Impressionistic Sketch

Detailed/Realistic Sketch

Grassland Curing Phases

The CFA Grassland Curing Guide breaks down into eleven curing phases, but I find the differences between each a bit too subtle for the time and effort required for journaling. I aim to use the minimum number of observations while still conveying the important changes and conditions. Thus, I've combined the CFA phases into four primary observation phases: Green, Green-Gold, Gold-Green, and Yellow-Gold.

To start your grassland curing observations, choose a location you can visit often, preferably in spring. Whether it's a patch of wild grass in your yard or an open field along a regular route, consistency is key. You don't need to bring your journal each time but make sure to note key changes in each phase. Review the graphic before starting each observation phase. During day-to-day or week-to-week observations,

take a few minutes to examine the grassland scene. You can also incorporate exercises from Chapter 2: Fire Weather to deepen your awareness of temperature and humidity. Assess what percentage of the grass is green, focusing on the most prevalent grass species. Look closely at grass stems, leaf blades, and seed heads, feeling for moisture and noting scents and sounds.

Also, check the base of the grass stems for thatch levels—dead and dry roots, stems, and leaves from previous seasons. If present, add 10-20% to your percent curing estimate and decrease your live fuel moisture levels.

Green Phase (0 to 10% Cured)

Grasses are sprouting and growing, reaching full height with green seed heads beginning to develop. The landscape appears primarily green, emitting strong herbal and astringent smells. Grasses feel and sound like fabric and leave a green smear when squished. Live fuel moisture levels range around 300 to 120%, posing low fire ignition potential unless heavy thatch is present.

Green-Gold Phase (20-30% Cured)

Stems and leaves remain green, while seed heads change color as seeds develop and drop. Some yellowing may occur in leaf blades. The landscape appears mostly green with light, feather-like tops in copper, steel, or gold colors. Smells are similar to the green phase but with subtle grainy scents. Fuel moisture levels average around 98%, with low fire ignition potential and patchy, slow fire rates of spread.

Gold-Green Phase (40 to 60% Cured)

Stems, leaf blades, and seed heads are mostly gold-colored, with some green patches. Most seeds have dropped. The landscape appears mostly gold with some green areas, feeling and sounding like thin, raspy fabric or thick paper. Smells become more straw-like with herbal undertones. Live fuel moisture levels average around 75%, with moderate to high fire ignition potential and rates of spread.

Yellow-Gold Phase (70-100 % Cured)

Stems, leaf blades, and seed heads are mostly to all yellow or light tan, with occasional green spots. Most seeds have dropped, and many grasses are bent or folded to the ground, contributing to thatch buildup. The landscape appears entirely yellow with patches of gold and bleached straw. Live fuel moisture levels average around 60 to 30%, with very high to extreme fire ignition potential and rates of spread.

Journaling Grassland Curing Phases

Green Phase Sketches

Create a two-part box in your journal with the lower rectangle portion as a cross-section of the grasses. It does not need to convey the actual size, shape, arrangement, or concentration of grasses but should visualize differences in the colors of grass stems and leaf blades.

Use the larger square portion of the box to sketch the grass tops or the bird's-eye view. Sketch wavy tops of the grasses in pencil, with more distinct sawtooth or comb-shaped lines for closer grasses, which become smaller with distance. Tops may appear more yellow

Seasonal Grass Curing, Fuel Moisture & Fire Hazard Phases

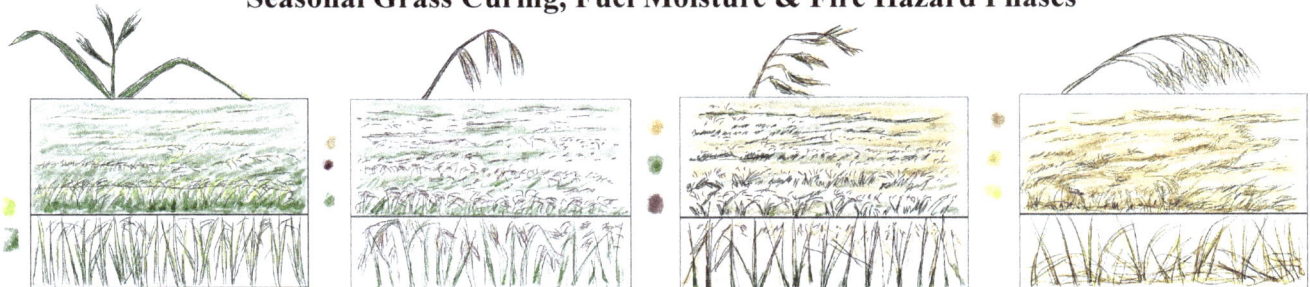

Green Phase
Under 10% of the grasses are cured. Growing green grasses and flowering seed heads. More than 120% fuel moisture levels. No fire ignition or spread.

Green-Gold Phase
25% of the grasses are cured. Seed heads have developed and are changing color. Some leaf blade color changes. Around 98% fuel moisture levels. Limited fire ignition and slow fire rates of spread.

Gold-Green Phase
50% of the grasses are cured. Seeds dropping, grass blades and stems are a mix of gold and green colors. Around 75% fuel moisture levels. Moderate to high fire rates of spread.

Yellow-Gold Phase
Over 75% of the grasses are cured. Most to all seeds have dropped. Little to no green colors. Around 60-30% fuel moisture levels. Very high to extreme fire rates of spread.

in

113

sunlight, but maintain a green tinge for this phase. Apply a yellow-green watercolor wash to sunlit parts and add darker green for the rest.

Sketch key phenophase elements of observation above, below, or on the side of the box, such as green leaves and seeds. It does not need to be accurate; words can suffice. Include narrative descriptions of how the grasses and seed heads feel, smell, and sound when touched. Add estimated fuel moisture levels and thoughts on fire behavior.

Green-Gold Phase Sketches

Follow the same steps as above but with a different color scheme. Tops of grass appear more feathery in the bird's-eye view. Avoid a watercolor wash; instead, use colored pencil for shadows. Add curved dash-lines in colored pencil for changes in seed head colors.

Gold-Green Phase Sketches

Follow similar steps with subtle adaptations. Use pencil for lower shadowed areas of grass and lines for closer grass stems instead of tops. Apply a yellow-gold watercolor wash over blank areas, adding colored pencil or watercolor over sketched shadowed areas.

Yellow-Gold Phase Sketches

Follow similar steps, sketching shadowed and grass stem areas instead of tops. Create more patches and flattened grass areas. Use lighter and darker yellows and golds to accentuate dry grass and shadows. In the vertical diagram, show more bent stems and drooped or fallen leaf blades.

Bringing Together Journal Page Elements

Many of your journal pages about the fire environment will include a combination of weather, fuels, seasonal trends, and fire behavior observations. For the organization of the book, I have separated them for clarity of topic. Blending the topics will offer more flexibility in your journaling practice. Many of the fire season journal pages will be a one-time or annual exercise, except for the grass curing phases. I include those elements in most of my journal pages, even when I'm focused on general nature observations and wildlife. Many of my observations are indirectly tied to seasons, such as listening to seasonal bird calls and insects. Over time, the combination of ongoing observations can build seasonal impressions and trends. See the examples on the next page.

26 June 2021 — Cowlitz Ancestral Lands — R. Morrell — 45.9852 -122.7426 — Ridgefield, WA — Puget Sound Ecoregion

UPLIFTING: The day and rest?

White butterfly flits fast above moist dirt and bark area

sounds "chip chip chip"

I notice a junco call in the bushes and another with a quick dry high-pitched chip call as it hopped down from fence to bounce along the dirt and moss.
It seems so positive and reminds me of a happy-go-lucky youth going about daily routines with a friend.

another junco in bush "tew tew tew"

I wonder if juncos stay in a family unit until breeding season? Do they join in flocks for winter? Are/if flocks are they mixed sex or separated?

I notice red alder trees ~100' to 125' tall with thick understory of broad-leaved bushes, wild rose, blackberry and willow.

TED E. JOHN
15 hrs of daylight — moon waning gibbous

Clear sky
but somewhat smoky or hazy at lower level

Looks like some may be coming from s.w.

Which wildfires are adding to this smoke?

DESIGN 4 FIRE ENVIRO. OBS.

Elev 180 ft
Clark County Fairgrounds

Contiguous dry grasses
Rabbits forage in fields and hide in riparian forest

85% Cured

<20% Slope / Mostly flat and slightly rolling hills.

Native forest areas w/ Doug. fir, western red cedar, western hemlock
Red alder
Big-leaf maple

Scents - Riparian

Soft sweet very pleasant scents of green veg., resins and moisture

200-300 trees waving back & forth

Alder leaves with soft to moderate rattle in wind
Winds >10 mph
Gusts higher
Trailer jostled on occasion of gust.

Some leaves turning red along roads

Thistle purple snow berry

browning some fir trees

Queen Anne's Lace flowering

blackberry
Berries ripening

Phenology & Temp Reactions

- Crows congregating into large flocks to roost at night.
- Robins foraging in flocks
- Ferns browning in open areas w/in forest & conifers w/ heat burns from heat event.

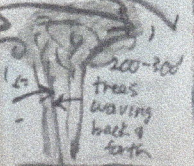

Semipermanent (Seasonal) Air Masses & Pressure Systems

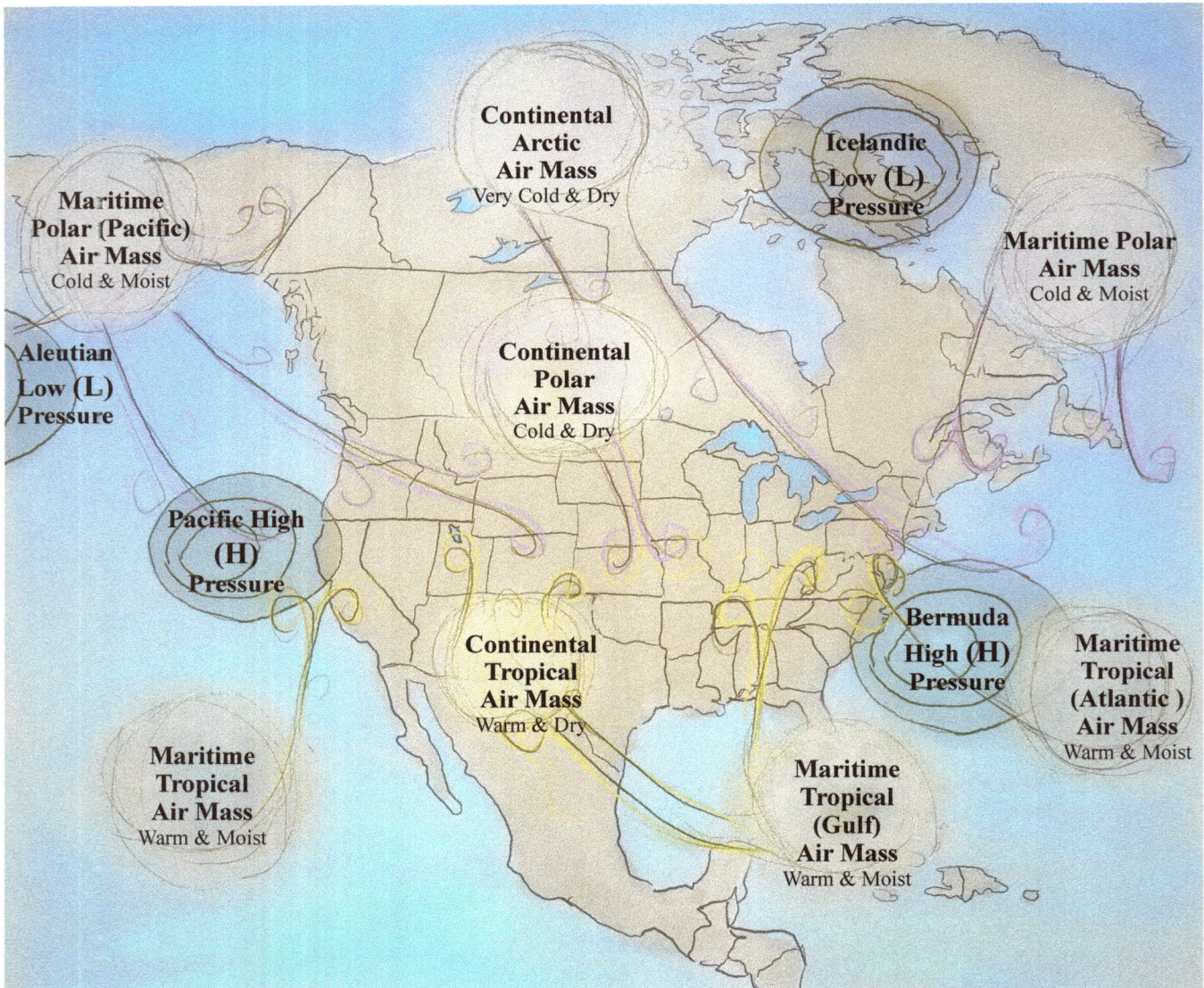

In the graphic, modeled after meteorology101.com, the lighter circular blobs indicate the locations of the different semipermanent air masses, each with associated swirly lines indicating their seasonal movements. The northern, cooler region air masses typically move south in the winter, while the southern, warmer air masses move north in the summer.

Seasonal Weather Patterns

In Chapter 2: Fire Weather, I discussed high and low pressure areas and associated weather systems, such as warm and cold fronts. Additionally, there are semipermanent high and low-pressure systems that persist over areas of the ocean, continents, and regions due to seasonal changes in heating and cooling. These semipermanent systems influence climatic events, atmospheric stability, precipitation levels, and prevailing winds (Ward/NWS, 2020).

In the graphic on the previous page, you'll see various semipermanent air masses and pressure systems that influence much of North America. These air masses and pressure systems expand, contract, and move to some degree in different directions. Generally, colder region systems move southward in the winter and northward in the summer, while warm region systems follow the opposite pattern. Air masses over oceans typically contain more moisture, but they lose moisture as they move over land. I'll provide a couple of examples of semipermanent systems and their relationships with the fire season, but I recommend referencing the map and seeking additional information about the systems influencing your area.

North American (Southwest) Monsoon

Initially, I imagined a monsoon as torrential rains in different regions. However, upon learning more about the North American or Southwest Monsoon, I discovered that not all monsoon systems are the same. According to the National Weather Service, a monsoon is a seasonal prevailing wind that shifts direction from cool ocean air to warm inland air. Monsoon systems exist around the globe, including in Asia, Australia, Africa, and North and South America. The Southwest monsoon resembles a larger-scale seasonal version of the sea and land breeze. Monsoons can bring either very wet or dry conditions, and in the southwest, they are tied to the fire season. This is where our observations of wet and dry thunderstorms from Chapter 2: Fire Weather become relevant.

During spring and early summer, as the land in Mexico heats up, a high-pressure system builds over the area, causing prevailing westerly winds to shift to a southeasterly direction.The winter winds, which were cool and dry by the time they reached the southwest, become warm and moist in the summer

North American (Southwest) Monsoon & Fire Season

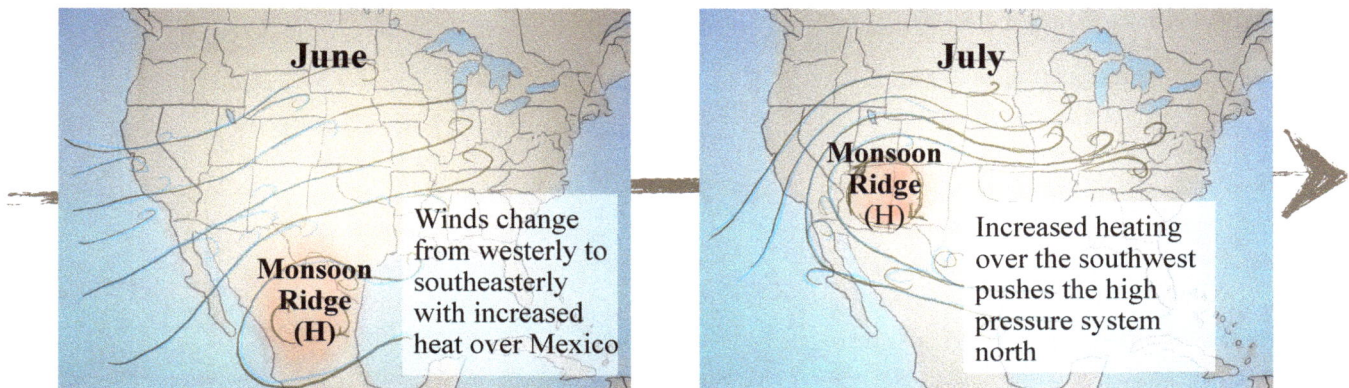

June — Monsoon Ridge (H) — Winds change from westerly to southeasterly with increased heat over Mexico

July — Monsoon Ridge (H) — Increased heating over the southwest pushes the high pressure system north as the high-pressure monsoon system draws air from the Gulf and Pacific coasts. As temperatures increase over the southwest, the monsoon system moves northward, typically in July and August but sometimes lasting until September. These thunderstorms are highly diurnal, and as steep mountain slopes heat up, moisture accumulates into cumulonimbus clouds in the afternoon.

Thunderstorms spread northward from New Mexico into Arizona and southern California, sometimes with bursts and breaks in rainfall. Dry thunderstorms, which pose a risk during the fire season, may exhibit increased wind shear on cumulonimbus clouds, virga, dust storms, and potential for dry lightning. A study by Don Falk, a professor at the School of Natural Resources and the Environment, examined the seasonal monsoon influences on the fire season and large fire activity. By analyzing 400 years of tree-ring samples and fire history data, the study indicated that major wildfires rarely occur when both seasons are wet. Occasional large fires happen when winters are wet and the monsoon is dry. Conversely, increased large wildfires occur when winters are dry and the monsoon is also dry (Arizpe and Falk, 2020).

To understand the monsoon's influence on the fire season, try to observe and journal the timing and location of wet and dry thunderstorms, and take notes on lightning strikes and fire occurrences.

Dry Thunderstorm Observations:

• White and yellow tinged lightning bolts

• Low humidity

• High base of clouds

• Rain evaporates (virga)

• High temperatures

• Dry downbursts, gusty winds, and dust storms

Lightning Observations:

The fire season is defined by more than just fuel conditions and weather trends. Fire ignitions are also a part of the analysis and definition. Chapter 6: Fire Ignitions and Prevention includes information on the human-caused fire ignitions and prevention, which is related to the fire season, but I am focusing on lightning observations in this chapter since they are tied to weather trends.

Journaling lightning strike locations and timing is one approach that can be useful for gaining a sense of the fire season. I shared some information about lightning in Chapter 2: Fire Weather, which will be helpful to refer back to, especially regarding the color of lightning and how it can indicate dry or moist conditions.

There are many websites, such as LightningMaps.org, Blitzortung.org, and My Lightning Tracker, that provide current lightning activity and serve as sources for potential lightning ignitions. Other weather and

Lightning Strike Location Map

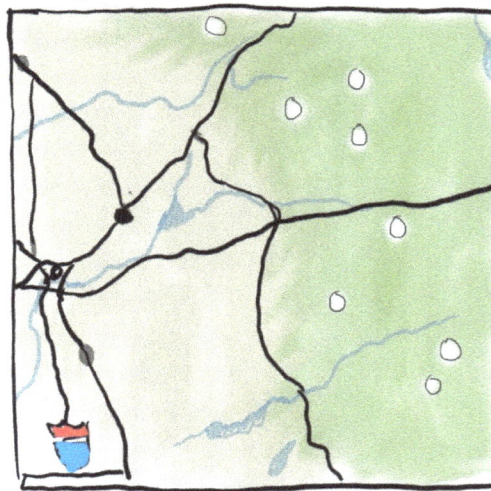

◯   Lightning ground strikes

climate websites may also offer lightning history data, which you could use to evaluate seasonal trends. The NOAA Storm Prediction Center's hourly and daily lightning climatology website features a nice animation of lightning surges across the country, making it an interesting visual for considering seasonal storms.

Journaling Seasonal Lightning Observations:

Take the opportunity when there is active lightning to observe the seasonal timing and location of strikes. I recommend doing this safely indoors or in a vehicle. If observing outdoors, stay away from high places and tall trees. One approach is to create a map with estimated lightning strike locations. Add the date and time of day the lightning was observed, and include notes about how these storms may be related to seasonal weather systems and conditions. You may also want to do a few sketches of cloud and lightning types, noting the color of lightning and signs of dry or wet conditions. Examples in Chapter 2: Fire Weather demonstrate a simple perpetual journaling approach.

Lightning Scars:

If you're fortunate, you may find lightning scars on trees that can be added to your lightning observations. Take time to journal the damage to trees, map their locations, and make assumptions or ask questions about whether the scar was caused by lightning or some other influence, such as cleaving branches from storm winds. Lightning scars often appear as long or spiral stripes from the top to bottom of a tree trunk, but lightning can also blow off the top of a tree and blow out from the roots. Add additional notes about where the observations were taken and incorporate them into your lightning occurrence map.

Blown Tree Top Scar

Strait Vertical Scar

Spiral Vertical Scar

Semipermanent Lows & Highs

The Southwest Monsoon is not the only fire season scenario. Having spent most of my life in northern California, I'd like to use a couple of examples from that region to highlight other semipermanent systems that can influence the fire season.

California Thermal Low

Referencing the definitions and descriptions of these systems from the U.S. Forest Service *Fire Weather Handbook*, the California Thermal Low is a semipermanent weather system occurring in the summer when hot air over California is held closer to the ground and becomes trapped in the area. The semipermanent North Pacific High, located generally between Hawaii and Alaska, directs wind toward the California Low, resulting in onshore winds along the Pacific coast. This system, sometimes called the Pacific monsoon, typically begins in spring and ends in fall, overlaying the sea breeze onto the larger high-pressure system. This seasonal flow pattern occurs both day and night, weakening the nightly land

breeze. The sea breeze, assisted by the high-pressure system, can bring fresh marine air and fog into coastal areas in the morning.

Great Basin High

In a fall and winter fire season scenario, low elevation areas of the Great Basin become warm, creating a high-pressure area. The edge of this pressure system can bring dry, high-speed northeasterly and easterly winds into California. Many significant fire events are caused by this pressure system, including southern California wildfires driven by the Santa Ana winds.

Fall/Winter Fire Season Scenario

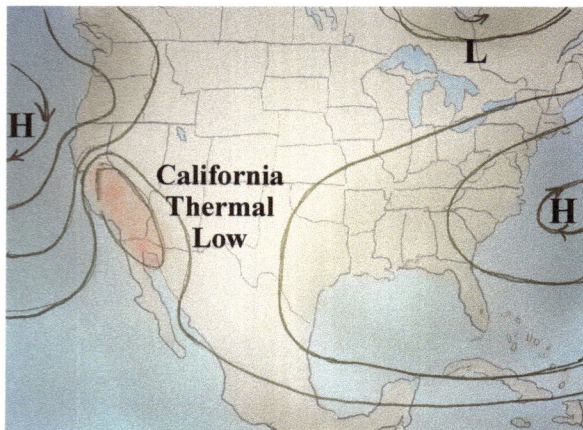

Summer Fire Season Scenario

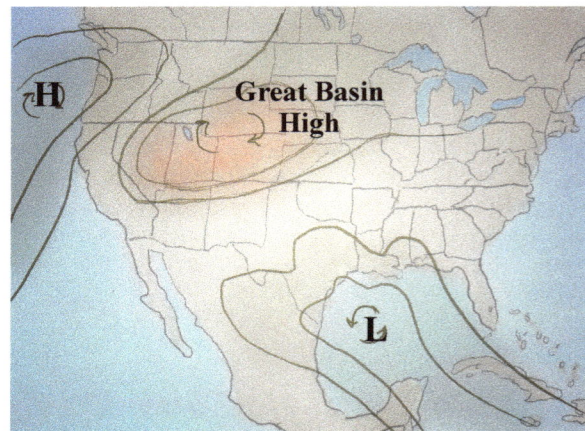

Seasonal Winds

The direction and speed of the wind can offer insight into potential seasonal weather patterns in the area. You may want to reference the Wind Types table in Chapter 2: Fire Seasons, along with the Semipermanent Air & Pressure Systems graphic from earlier in this chapter, to assess potential locations and movements of seasonal winds.

I started by creating four landscape-scale sketches (below) of the area I was observing to get a feel for the terrain influences on wind. I used Google Earth, in the 3D mode, and created screen captures for each direction. From those photos, I created the four sketches.

For the metadata analysis, I used the WeatherSpark website graphs to estimate the percentage of winds in each direction and placed those numbers in the four cardinal directions around the name for each month (next page). I only included the months in the fire season and the months transitioning into and out of the fire season (May-Nov), so I may have missed some weather trend observations.

When I look at my average monthly wind directions on the next page, I can see some subtle trends over the season, but there are more questions than answers.

Where Do the High Winds Blow in Chico, CA?

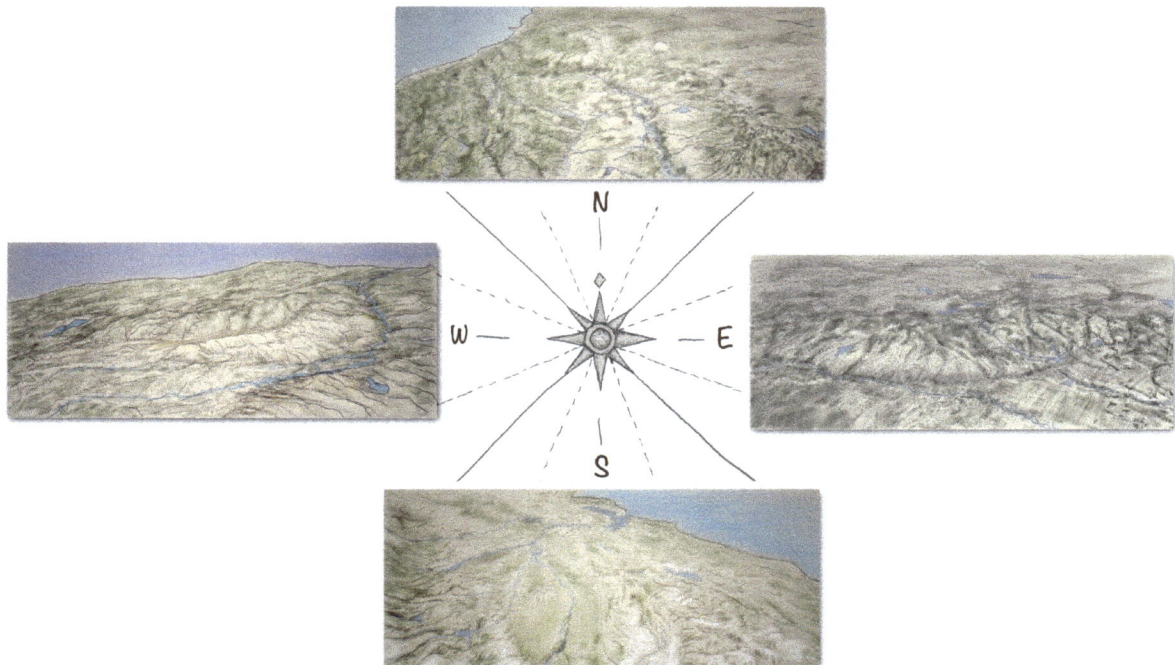

Summary & Review of Monthly Wind Direction

Chico, CA
Average Monthly Wind Directions

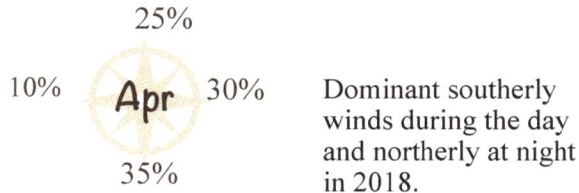

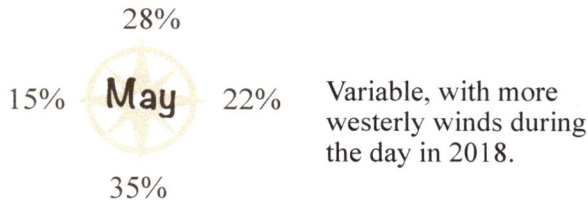

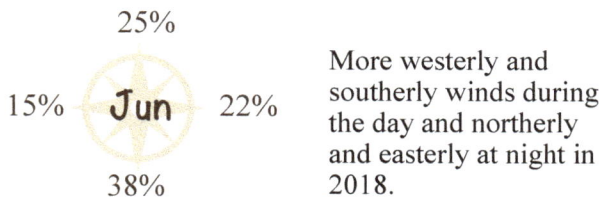

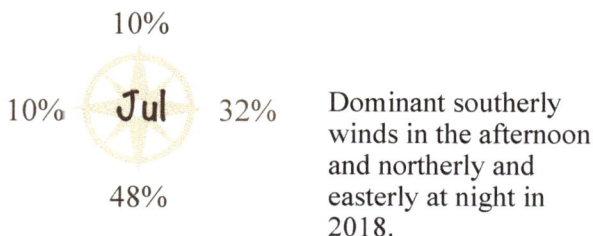

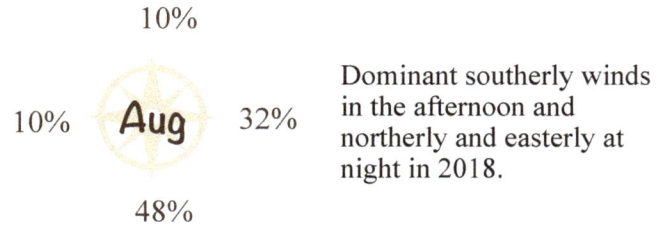

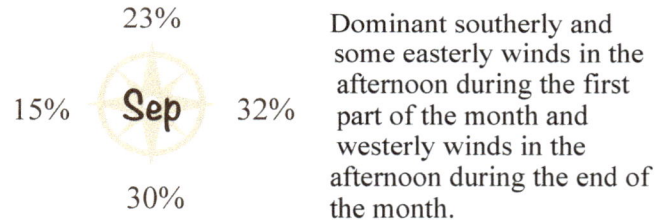

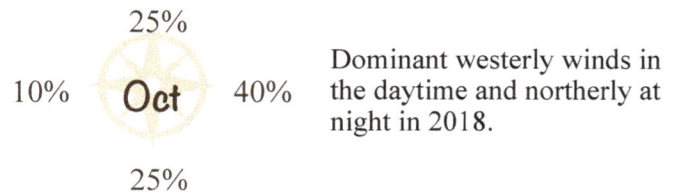

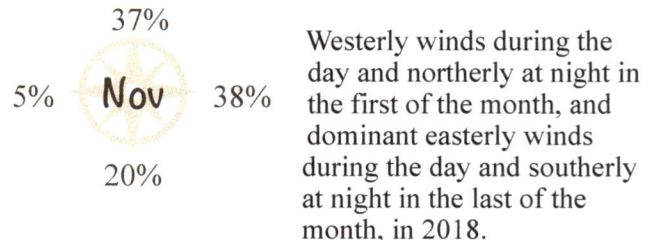

25%

10% **Apr** 30%

35%

Dominant southerly winds during the day and northerly at night in 2018.

28%

15% **May** 22%

35%

Variable, with more westerly winds during the day in 2018.

25%

15% **Jun** 22%

38%

More westerly and southerly winds during the day and northerly and easterly at night in 2018.

10%

10% **Jul** 32%

48%

Dominant southerly winds in the afternoon and northerly and easterly at night in 2018.

Chico, CA
Average Monthly Wind Directions

10%

10% **Aug** 32%

48%

Dominant southerly winds in the afternoon and northerly and easterly at night in 2018.

23%

15% **Sep** 32%

30%

Dominant southerly and some easterly winds in the afternoon during the first part of the month and westerly winds in the afternoon during the end of the month.

25%

10% **Oct** 40%

25%

Dominant westerly winds in the daytime and northerly at night in 2018.

37%

5% **Nov** 38%

20%

Westerly winds during the day and northerly at night in the first of the month, and dominant easterly winds during the day and southerly at night in the last of the month, in 2018.

Seasonal Rain

Many regions have fire seasons defined by seasonal precipitation levels—wet and dry seasons. Precipitation trends influence the typical start and end of the fire season, and precipitation events affect the spread of fires during the season. Some geographic areas split their fire seasons into different periods based on moisture levels. To observe and evaluate the fire season based on precipitation, I visited the WeatherSpark.com website and used the average rainfall data to create an inverted graph.

I thought this visual would help connect the relationship between precipitation and fuel conditions and allow me to add snowfall data, if desired, as a top-facing graph. Since there is little to no snow in Chico, I didn't need that graph. In another area, I could combine snowpack and rainfall graphs for an interesting visual to evaluate moisture changes influencing the fire season. I also used a

WeatherSpark graph for a comparison year (2018) and overlaid (inverted) it with my monthly averages graph for better trend comparison. You could print a similar precipitation graph and paste it into your journal or create a more specialized version like I have. Whichever approach you use, add notes about the general fire season to the graph.

Fire Season Slowing & Ending Rain

Many geographic areas in the United States use precipitation amounts to estimate the slowing and ending of the fire season. The National Wildfire Coordinating Group identifies 0.1 inches of rain within a three-day period as a slowing or stopping event in a grassland ecosystem and 0.5 inches of rain for a forest or shrub ecosystem. When evaluating your precipitation graph, look for these rain levels and consider their influences on the fire season.

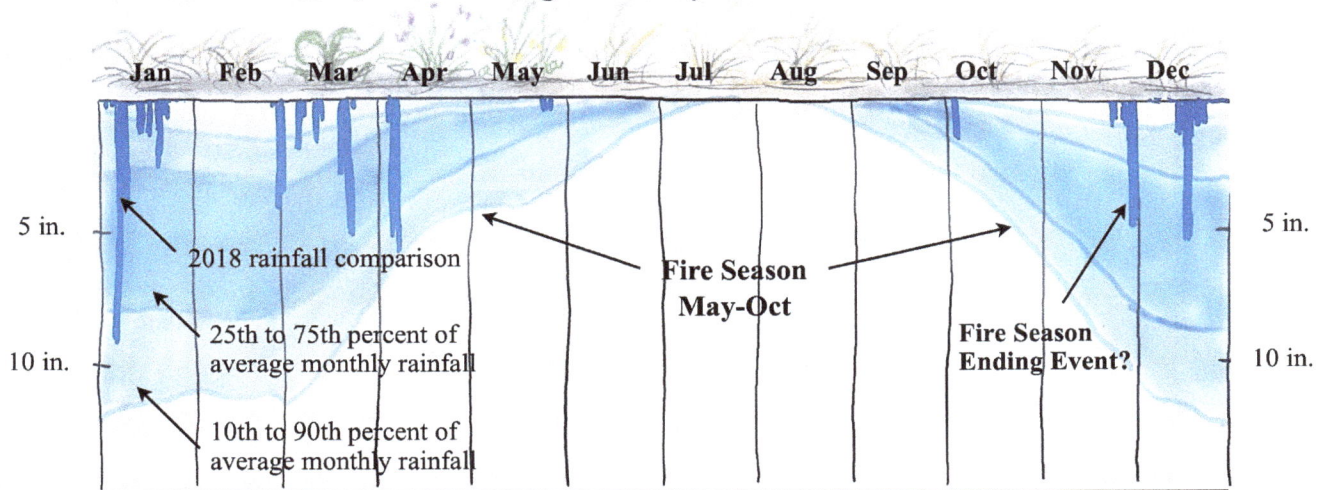

Chico, Calif Average Monthly Rainfall & Fire Season

2018 rainfall comparison

25th to 75th percent of average monthly rainfall

10th to 90th percent of average monthly rainfall

Fire Season May-Oct

Fire Season Ending Event?

Observing Rain for Fire Season Ending Events

Along with journaling about clouds with virga and rain to differentiate wet and dry thunderstorms, you can also use puddles and standing water observations to estimate rain amounts. I found some helpful information on the Weather Insurance Agency's *Rain Amount Guidelines* website and used it to create the illustrations on the next page. They used the National Weather Service definitions of rainfall intensities (light, moderate, and heavy rain) and reframed the data around the observations. For our fire season observations, I would emphasize the 0.10 observations in grasslands and 0.50 observations in forest and shrub area.

Note that soil types will also influence puddling, as well as drought conditions, which make it difficult for water to penetrate dry soil.

You can use weather forecasts as prompts to journal and/or journal puddle observations, adding notes about the forecasted, measured, and/or estimated rain amounts. I would recommend using a perpetual journal approach by making multiple small puddle sketches over time on one to two journal pages for comparisons.

Fire Season Slowing & Ending Rain

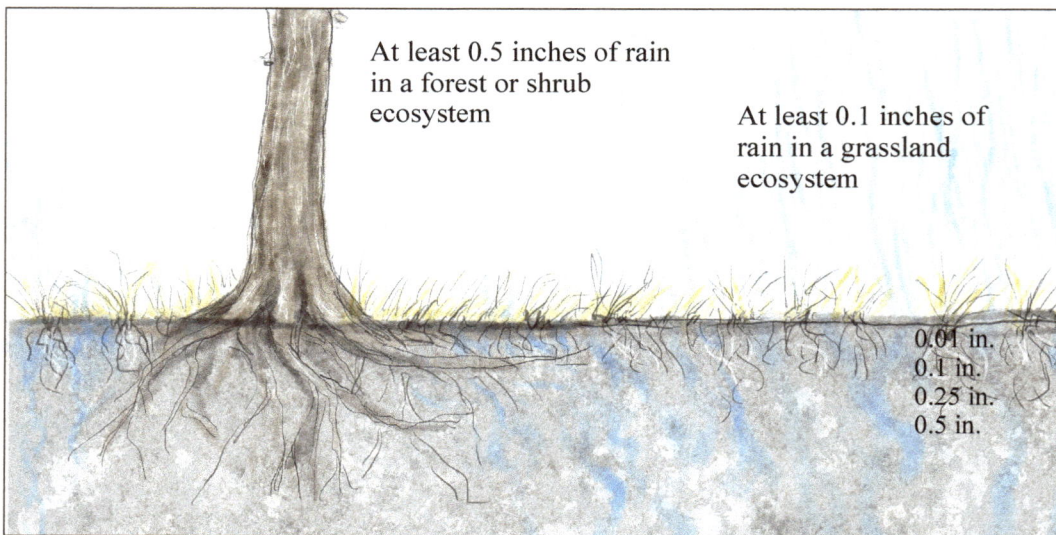

Fire season slowing and or ending can occur when there is at least 0.1 inches of rain in a grassland ecosystem and 0.5 inches of rain in a forest or shrub ecosystem, that occurs within a three day period.

Rain Amount Observations

0.01 inches

A light rain for 2-5 minutes or a drizzle for 2 hours will wet the surface, but leave no puddles.

0.10 inches

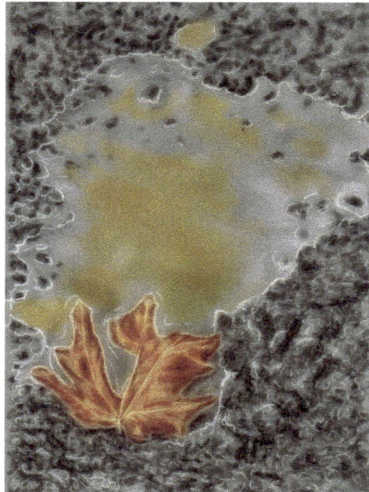

A light rain for 30-45 minutes, a moderate rain for 10 minutes or a heavy rain for 5 minutes will leave small puddles that disappear after a short period.

0.25 inches

A light rain for 2-3 hours, a moderate rain for 30-60 minutes or a heavy rain for 15 minutes will leave many puddles that last for a while.

0.50 inches

A moderate rain for 1-2 hours or a heavy rain for 30-45 minutes will leave deep standing puddles that will last for long periods.

1 inch

A heavy rain for 2-5 hours will leave deep standing puddles that will last for long periods.

Chapter 6:
Fire Ignitions & Prevention

Fire Ignitions
Fire Prevention
Journaling Fire History
Landscape Patches & Patterns
Burn Scars
Origin Area
Lighting Ignition Indicators Human-Caused Ignitions
Campfire Cause Indicators
Fire Cause Consequences
Vehicle & Equipment Cause Indicators Fireworks
Cause Indicators
Cigarette & Match Cause Indicators Journaling When
Ignitions Occur
Fuel Bed Factors
Weather Factors
Journaling Ignition Factors
Journaling Campfire Safety
Journaling Potential Fire Areas Estimating the Fire
Fire Ignition & Prevention Story

Fire Ignitions

Wildfire ignitions come in many forms but are typically categorized as either natural or human-caused. There are only a few natural fire ignition types, including lightning, volcanoes, coal seams, and some bog/peat fires. Coal seam fires are limited to areas where an outcrop of underground coal or some form of heat causes smoldering combustion, which can reach the surface and ignite into flames with oxygen. Bog/peat fires are also limited to specific areas where dry layers of peat can be ignited by lightning or human actions, smoldering deep within the layers long after the upper fire has been extinguished. The smoldering can spread and reappear from the layers several to hundreds of years later.

Human-caused fire ignitions are frequently caused by things such as escaped campfires, burning debris piles, dropped cigarettes, sparks from equipment (like chainsaws), soot particles from vehicle exhausts, hot undercarriages of vehicles or metal pieces/sparks from brakes, dragging chains, misused fireworks and explosives, sparks from power lines, and sparks from shooting ammunition.

Our Fire Imprints

Fire Prevention

When discussing prevention, we typically focus on reducing unwanted, accidental, and illegal human-caused fire ignitions. Depending on your location, human-caused ignitions may account for 70-90% of wildfires. If you feel overwhelmed by wildfire issues, this subject may offer hope for ignition reduction. Historically, fire prevention programs have focused on three areas:

Education emphasizes educating people about activities that can cause fires and safety measures used to reduce the risk of igniting wildfires.

Engineering focuses on scientific and design measures to reduce or contain fire ignitions, such as designing spark arrestors to reduce vehicle exhaust particles or clearing vegetation under power lines.

Enforcement focuses on developing and applying laws and regulations to motivate behavior change that poses high safety risks to people and resources during high-risk periods, such as applying fire restrictions during the fire season.

There is a wealth of fire prevention information available, and it's important to learn and track regulations and recommendations in different areas. Most land management agencies, like the US Forest Service, Bureau of Land Management,

National Park Service, and other federal, state, and local agencies, have websites with specific fire prevention information and also post this information on signs for public access areas like campgrounds. Before venturing into nature, determine the land jurisdiction and information to prepare yourself, especially during fire season and fire weather events. You can explore SmokeyBear.com as a starting point. Some typical fire prevention measures/restrictions include:

- Clearing vegetation and debris at least 3-4 feet around a campfire and having a bucket of water and shovel nearby.

- Using a metal coffee can with sand for disposing of cigarettes or clearing vegetation and debris 3 feet around where you stand when smoking.

- Halting equipment use and target practice during periods of high temperatures and wind events.

- Maintaining vehicles (cleaning, etc.) and carrying fire extinguishers with you, especially during fire season.

When you begin to practice situational awareness, especially during fire weather events, you'll notice when, where, and why fire restrictions have been applied.

Fire History

I like to begin journaling about fire ignitions by examining the fire history in a particular area, including the location of fire areas, their size, shape, and dates. You can find a wide range of fire history maps on the internet, such as the WIFIRE website. When visiting the website, navigate to the Fire Map tool. Once on the Fire Map platform, click on the layers icon and select Historical Fires. Then, zoom into the desired area and adjust the date scroll bar to cover a span of about ten to twenty years, depending on the density of fire areas. You can also capture the maps for at least three different time periods to compare fire locations and sizes over time. Note that various fire history sources may only include wildfires of a certain size category, so not every wildfire ignition area may be visible. You can sketch or print and paste the fire history map into your journal.

I used the WIFIRE map in conjunction with Google Maps to incorporate additional features such as roads, vegetation types (grassland or forest), rivers, and lakes. Remember to indicate the fire history period on your map. Once your map is complete, consider the land jurisdiction areas and whether the fire areas are on private or public land. In my sketch, I only included roads, so I would need to rely on my knowledge of the area to determine the boundaries of private, local, state, and federal lands.

Fire History Map 2000-2020

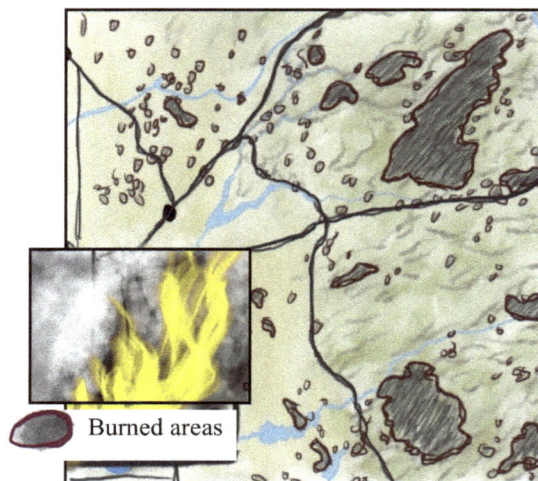

Burned areas

Landscape Patches & Patterns

Another beneficial journaling exercise, complementary to the fire history map, is visiting a lookout point to journal about landscape patches and patterns. These features are caused by various factors and can provide insights into past fire activity or the history of fire exclusion. Fire exclusion, encompassing fire suppression and restricted prescribed and cultural burning practices, often results in vegetation build-up and the dominance of non-diverse forests. Observe and journal about the location, size, and shape of patches in the area.

Additionally, try to discern the openness or concentrations within these patches. What overall patterns do you notice? Observing from a distance may make it challenging to determine whether open or concentrated vegetation patches were caused by

Landscape Patches & Patterns Sketch

Sketch from high view point or web camera to observe potential fire areas.

fire. Consider following up with visits to these areas for closer inspection. You may also want to compare your observations with lightning maps to understand where naturally ignited fires have occurred. Journaling about landscape patches and patterns will involve posing numerous questions, which are vital to include in your journaling practice. Chapter 3: Topography contains an exercise outlining steps for sketching landscapes at this scale, emphasizing land shape and vegetation patches and patterns.

Burn Scars

If you follow your fire history map exercise with a field visit, you may have the opportunity to observe burn scars. In recently burned areas, you'll notice many trees, plants, and rocks stained and charred, along with deep burn scars typically triangular in shape. You may also observe burn scars on tree trunks from fires long ago. Adding these observations to your journal can be visually intriguing, prompting consideration of when and what caused these fires.

You don't need to sketch the entire tree or burn scar; describing the extent of damage and growth around the scar suffices. Older burn scars should show layers of bark-brown around their edges. Look around for other burn scars and note any patterns, observing which side of the tree they appear on. Multiple fires may have occurred, so also record the size of trees burned and different age groups with burn scars, indicating different fire events.

Fire Origin Area

If you have the opportunity to safely visit a burned area, it can be an interesting exercise to estimate the general and specific fire origin area. In Chapter 9: Fire Severity and Effects I'll include many more observations about reading the burned area for clues about the fire behavior. For this exercise, I want to introduce the topic of the fire origin area, so that you might include it in your fire ignitions journaling.

Within the overall burned area, there is what is called a General Origin Area and a Specific Origin Area. Wildland fire investigators define these areas to help focus their search and identify the ignition source and fire cause. The General Origin Area is typically limited to one-half to several acres in size. These areas are often defined by larger scale indicators like the shape of the fire.

The U- or V-shape of a fire is a fire pattern indicator, where the narrow point of the U or V indicates where the General Origin Area is often located. Some larger fires will have many fingers and sprawling shapes that make this challenging to identify. Often these are found at the bottom of a slope or along the edge of a road or trail close to where the fire started. The Specific Origin Area can be as small as a 5 feet by 5 feet space or larger but is always within the larger origin area. The Specific Origin Area is the point at which the initial ignition and flames are influenced by wind, fuel, or slope (fire behavior triangle). Most fires start as a small circular area of creeping flames and become an advancing fire when they spread, grow, and stretch based on those environmental elements.

U-Shaped Pattern/General Fire Origin Area

Advancing fire gaining in severity of effects

Another observation that can be used to narrow down the origin of a fire is to look at the change in fire severity effects. Most fires start in the fine fuels on the ground (grasses and leaves) and then build up energy where it starts burning larger branches, shrubs, and trees. As the fire advances, the amount of charring on tree trunks and drying or burning of leaves increases. You'll want to use binoculars to view the treetops. If you follow those effects backward, you'll come closer to the origin area.

The shape of the fire can also indicate wind speeds. A fairly round-shaped fire likely had light winds, while a long strip or oblong shape will indicate higher wind speeds. A larger fire may have different branches and varied shapes based on wind direction changes. I won't go further into the post-fire pattern indicators in this chapter, but these two observations should help enhance your fire ignition journaling.

Lightning Ignition Indicators

You may also want to include observations of lightning scars in your journal pages. Part of observing ignitions is distinguishing between natural and human-caused wildfires. Refer to examples of lightning scars in Chapter 5: Fire Seasons for review. Some lightning impacts may occur high in the trees, so use binoculars to scan the treetops. Fallen trees in the area should be closely examined, as they may have been burned. Additionally, inspect the base of trees with potential lightning damage. The energy from lightning strikes can create blowholes and fissures in the soil or along the upper roots of the tree. In sandy soils, look for fulgurites, glass-like formations formed when lightning heats sand into crystal-like structures resembling whitened ocean corals.

Human-Caused Ignition Indicators

In this section, I'll share a few observations associated with certain human-caused wildfire ignition types and associated human behaviors from the National Wildfire Coordinating Group's *Guide to Wildland Fire Origin and Cause Determination*. These examples are intended to frame observations and considerations when journaling about fire ignitions and prevention. Consider a variety of ignition causes in your area, such as Chinese lanterns or other unique cultural activities.

Fire Cause Consequences

Certain human behaviors can be used to assess the fire ignition risk and whether they are negligent or deliberate acts. Professional wildfire investigators use these risk behavior observations along with other fire pattern indicators to determine the origin and cause of fires. That information is included in reports submitted to solicitors who work with landowners or managers to recover costs and damages from those responsible for the cause of wildfires. Through legal processes, the responsible party for causing the fire can face imprisonment and be held liable for wildfire damages, fire suppression costs, and land recovery efforts.

Campfire Cause Indicators

Campfire cause categories include fires ignited for warmth, cooking, light, or ceremonial purposes that escape and cause wildfires. Campfires may be located almost anywhere, but the key questions are whether the use of a campfire is approved or authorized by the property owner and whether the behavior was negligent. Indicators of high risk and potential campfire escape/wildfire ignition include:

- **Location:** Campfires in unauthorized areas indicate an increased risk of escape. Authorized areas are evaluated for safe campfire use and often have built-in campfire features, signage, instructions, and postings about fire restriction requirements.

- **Campfire Design**: Placement and setup can indicate the risk of causing a wildfire. Campfires under low-hanging tree branches or next to shrubs and heavy vegetation pose a higher risk of igniting nearby vegetation. Campfires on steep slopes also increase the risk. A scraped-out depression in the soil and a closely arranged circle of large rocks or a metal ring around the depression reduce the risk. Clearance of vegetation and debris around the campfire is essential to prevent potential escape and wildfire ignition.

- **Campfire Management:** Campfires should not be started with accelerants, which can cause unexpected large flames. Leaving accelerants nearby or discarding matches carelessly poses a higher risk. Campfires should never be left unattended, as unexpected wind gusts can spread flames or embers. Even hot coals left unattended pose a risk of reigniting. Removing campfire and cook-stove coals and ash before extinguishing them with water is a high-risk behavior.

- **Fire Extinguishing Tools**: Fire extinguishing tools such as a shovel and a large container of water should be nearby whenever there are active flames. Water should be poured over the fire and hot coals, and the area should be stirred to ensure thorough extinguishing. The back of the hand can be used to check for remaining heat. If heat is detected, more water should be applied and stirred.

A campfire ignition and prevention exercise is further detailed in this chapter.

Vehicle & Equipment Cause Indicators

Several vehicle ignition sources, including hot soot particles from exhaust, sparks from dragging chains, or exposed rims on flat tires. These particles or sparks can ignite nearby vegetation located 10 to 40 feet or more from the vehicle. Leaking fuel and lubricants can also increase the risk of igniting a wildfire, as can the hot undercarriage of a vehicle with dry vegetation underneath. Proper maintenance can prevent many of these ignitions, but other conditions should be considered. Exhaust particles are often emitted when vehicles idle after heavy use. For example, a truck idling after hauling a trailer uphill may have a higher probability of emitting exhaust particles that could cause a wildfire. Similarly, fragments and sparks from brakes may occur when descending a steep hill. These particles and sparks are more likely to spread from the roadside into vegetation when located along steep slopes and during fire weather events.

Motorized equipment, such as chainsaws and lawnmowers, can also cause wildfire ignitions due to soot particles, sparks, and heat from hot areas of the equipment. Similar preventive measures to those for vehicles, such as proper management and use, should be employed. For example, checking for rocks before mowing a grassy field can prevent sparks, and placing hot equipment in a dirt or gravel area after use can reduce the risk of fire ignition.

Developing an understanding of how and where fires may start enables the development of fire prevention measures, fire origin and cause determinations and fire damage and suppression cost recovery.

Fireworks Cause Indicators

Fireworks are typically classified as ground-based (placed on the ground), handheld, aerial, or explosive matierials. Wildfires caused by fireworks can result in significant property damage due to the ignition risk and the timing and locations they are used. Fireworks emit flames and sparks that can reach far into dry vegetation. I recall an incident in Sacramento, California, where a small fire started in my front yard while someone was standing on the sidewalk. Although on a sidewalk and near a road, there was insufficient vegetation clearance around the activity. Proper fireworks locations should be wide and clear, with a large bottle or bucket of water readily available for extinguishing any fires started. Used and malfunctioned fireworks should be soaked in water for at least 24 hours before disposal in the garbage to prevent potential fires.

Cigarette & Match Cause Indicators

Cigarettes and matches are small ignition sources with limited burning times, so environmental conditions are critical to determining them as ignition sources, particularly when used for smoking. They are also used in arson ignitions, although the cigarette is typically not burned down completely, and the entire matchbook is often used. See the graphic and bullets on the next page. The following pages on fuel bed and weather ignition factors addresses the environmental conditions necessary for typical small ignition sources like cigarettes.

Cigarette Ignition Factors

Environmental Ignition Factors:
- Fine fuel bed
- Loose fuel arrangement
- Dead fine fuel moisture less than 14%
- 80° ambient air temperature
- Relative humidity (RH) 22% or less

Probability Of Ignition

Ignition Likely	Ignition Possible	Ignition Unlikely	No Ignition
0% RH	10% RH	18% RH	>18% RH

Ignition Timing Indicators

As you recall from previous chapters, vegetation and weather conditions are vital considerations for determining when a fire can ignite and spread. Fires primarily propagate through smaller surface fuels like grasses and fallen leaves, so our ignition observations mainly focus on the timing of conditions conducive to igniting these fine fuels. Obviously, fire ignitions are less likely during the wet season or when grass is green. However, there are various phases of grass curing where fire ignition and spread may be possible, depending on the intensity and duration of the ignition source. While a cigarette might not ignite a wildfire, fireworks or downed power lines can. Thus, to observe and evaluate fire ignitions, always include observations about fuel and weather conditions.

Fuel Bed Factors

Observing the ignitability and flammability of grass or the fuel bed should concentrate on the arrangement of fine fuels. Refer back to Chapter 4: Fire Fuels for a review if needed. One crucial aspect of small ignition sources, like a cigarette, is the loose arrangement of fine fuels. I like to envision these loosely arranged grasses or leaves as an ember nest—a place where a small spark or ember can grow and emerge into flames. Igniting larger twigs, branches, shrubs, and trees typically occurs after the burning fine fuels have generated enough heat to ignite those larger materials. A more intense heat source could more readily ignite the fine fuels and larger woody materials.

Weather Factors

Another crucial aspect of ignition is dead fuel moisture, including the curing phase and humidity levels. The ambient air temperature also affects the effectiveness of the ignition source. The hotter the air, the less heat is needed from the ignition source to ignite the fuel. Consider the relative humidity and fuel moisture levels throughout the day and seasons when evaluating the ignition source. Also, observe whether the fuels are in direct sunlight or shade. The National Wildfire Coordinating Group's *Guide to Wildland Fire Origin and Cause Determination* provides an example of environmental factors and the probability of ignition from a dropped cigarette. See the visuals below.

Ignition Factor Metadata

Fire ignition factors are key metadata that should be used when journaling about fire ignitors. I recommend you include the date, time of day, weather conditions, slope, aspect, number of daylight hours, fine fuel arrangements, fine fuel moisture conditions, fuel shading, relative humidity, and amount of cloud cover or smoke in the sky. Describe these observations and metadata using a mix of narrative descriptions (words), measurements (numbers), and visuals (pictures). Some general fire ignition factors to estimate the potential for fire ignitions and spread include:

- Increased slope (above 30%) increases ignition and spread potential.

- Increased solar hours (during the fire season period).

- Slope aspect with ignition risk increasing from north, east, west, to south.

- Direct sunlight increases ignition risk, with percentages of area in sunlight affecting risk level.

Over 50% shade lowers risk, while less than 10% shade increases risk.

- Increased percentage of cured grasses (above 20%).

- Lower relative humidity levels (less than 60%, with 30% to 15% reaching more critical levels).

- Lower dead fuel moisture levels (20% or less).

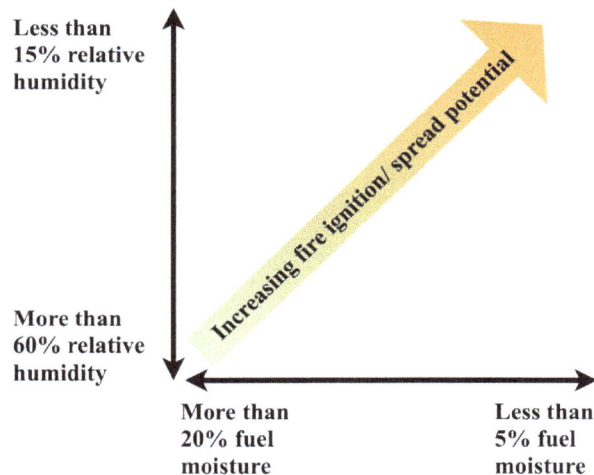

Fire Ignition Areas

Now that you've developed a sense of where past fires have occurred and some of the different cause indicators, let's combine the information and journal about the potential ignition areas and causes. The graphic on the next few pages lists some of the human-caused ignition types that might occur in the observed area. For the purpose of this exercise, don't worry about every ignition type or the official titles and descriptions of ignition causes. The exercise is just to build a sense of where and when potential wildfire ignitions start.

Human-Caused Ignition Areas & Causes Analysis

Human Infrastructure Map

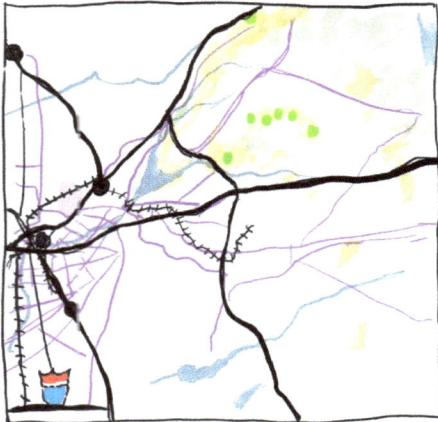

━━━	Roads
╫╫╫	Railroads
────	Power lines
●	Cities
●	Recreation site
	Rivers/lakes
	Federal agency #1 lands
	Federal agency #2 lands
	State agency lands

Fire Ignition Activity/Type	Fire Seasons		
	Spring	Summer	Fall
 (truck)	Year round potential, but more likely in the summer		
(motorcycle)	Year round potential, but more likely in the summer		
(target)	Year round potential, but more likely prior to hunting seasons		
(fireworks)	Mostly in July		
(grill)	Year round, but mostly in the summer		
(campfire)	Mostly in the summer, but also during holiday weekends		
(chainsaw)	Year round, but mostly before winter		
(mower)	Year round, but in the spring and summer		
Fire Weather Events			

Fire Ignition Areas Exercise

Step 1: Create another map with a similar spatial area to your fire history map. Include roads, power lines, railroads, recreation areas, etc. Use different colors for each feature and create a legend.

Step 2: Use your local map as a reference to help you evaluate what potential fire ignition sources may occur and add them to the left column of the graph or table.

Step 3: Create other columns for the months/period within the fire season and transitioning between periods. Add checkmarks or notes to each column that help frame the timing of ignition activities over the season.

Step 4: Consider when fire weather events may occur over the fire season(s) and add colored bands or other visual indicators for the fire weather events within the season and include notes on or next to the column/table.

Step 5: Use your map and table to compare with the fire history map for your area. Do you notice any trends? What thoughts, concerns, and/or questions do you have about potential fire ignitions?

Step 6: Describe how you can use this information. Are there things you would change about your potential fire-ignition activities? Are there fire prevention education, engineering, or enforcement measures in place or that you would recommend?

Step 7: The next step is to travel to some of the areas on your map and journal the fuel conditions using exercises shared in Chapter 4: Fire Fuels. You may want to explore recreation areas and trails and open fields near a neighborhood.

In evaluating the potential fire ignition areas on your map, ask yourself these questions: How much grass covers the landscape, and how much of the grass is cured? How steep are the slopes? Are there signs of wind (past and present), and what directions do those winds come from? What is the temperature and relative humidity? How clear is the sky? Are there trees shading the area? Do you notice areas that are mowed or cleared of grass and other vegetation? How do they relate to the potential fire ignitions? How wide or long are those cleared areas, and how much of the vegetation has changed from the neighboring vegetation?

Fire Ignition & Prevention Story

A journaling approach that can enhance your thinking and analysis of fire ignitions is to craft a story around how a fire may have started and how it could have been prevented. This isn't the same as a fire investigation but should involve some deductive reasoning.

Step 1: I recommend finding a small burned area that is easily accessible and well after all fire suppression and investigations have concluded. If you can't find a burned area nearby, you can simplify the process using a fire from the fire history map.

Step 2: If there's a known fire start date, use that to look up the weather for that day and bring it with you on your field visit. If you have a vague recollection of when the fire started, then choose a date to work with. If not, you can work backward from your observations to estimate a date.

Step 3: Sketch or diagram the burned area, adding surrounding features like roads, rivers, and lakes—you can look those up and add them later. Avoid including the actual name of the wildfire, if there is one, to avoid confusion. Also, refrain from providing official location information; instead, speak generally about the place. This is an imaginary scenario using real observations to frame the ignition and prevention story.

Step 4: Look for a V- or U-shape to the burned area. If found, note it on your map as a potential General Origin Area. Head to that area for closer observations. If there isn't a clear V- or U-shape, look for nearby features that may have been an ignition point, such as proximity to a road, power line, or railroad track.

Step 5: Near the potential General Origin Area, observe any trends in the fire effects. Is there an area with more grass stems remaining compared to others? Do you notice changes in severity of effects across the area? Sketch or write notes about the fire effects you're using to assess the origin area. If you find an area indicating lesser fire effects, mark it on your map as the potential Specific Origin Area.

Step 6: Document the fuels around the outside of the burned area. How much of the grasses and other vegetation burned? How concentrated are the grasses, and what is their curing phase now? Consider the likely fuel conditions during the fire.

Step 7: Review the past weather likely during the fire. If the fire start date is unknown, consider the conditions that allowed the fire to burn based on observed patterns and effects. Note wind direction and speed based on your origin area and severity of effects. Add this information to your journal.

Step 8: Look for signs of fire suppression, such as tire tracks or a cleared strip of dirt as a fire containment line. Document these in your journal.

Step 9: Note potential human access to the area. Consider the types of visitors and fire causes that might have been present. Are there nearby communities, schools, or recreation areas? Are there frequent vehicles or people on nearby trails? Write down these possibilities and your reasoning.

Step 10: Consider potential fire causes and prevention measures that could have reduced the probability of ignition. Document these in your journal.

Journaling Campfire Safety

Let's use a campfire to journal fire ignition prevention activities to avoid the ignition indicators on the previous page. Try to diagram and/or sketch, measure, and add notes about the following campfire safety and wildfire prevention activity. The prevention goal is to reduce the ignition of neighboring materials and to adhere to any fire restriction requirements.

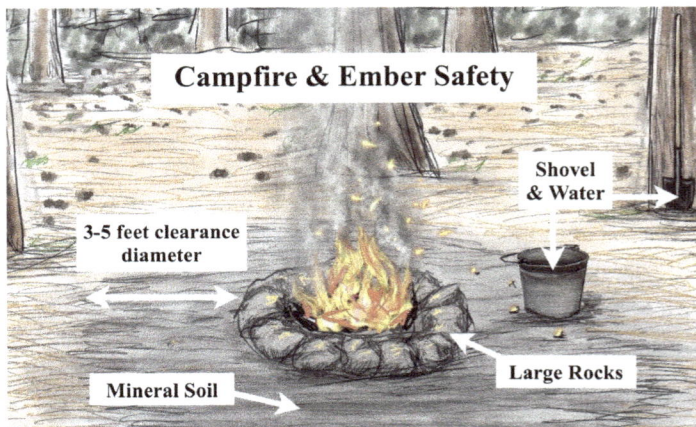

Campfire & Ember Safety
3-5 feet clearance diameter
Shovel & Water
Large Rocks
Mineral Soil

Campfire Set-Up

The engineering approach includes digging a campfire pit about two feet in diameter and clearing away at least a four-foot diameter area of all surface (grasses, leaves, and needles) and ground fuels (duff and roots) down to the mineral soil. The mineral soil layer is where there are no vegetation materials mixed in with the mineral soil. Bring a shovel and a bucket of water and keep them nearby to extinguish the fire when no one will be present to watch the fire. Gather a mix of tinder, kindling, and firewood materials. In many areas, you will be required to use local materials, so keep that in mind before traveling. Tinder materials are tiny fine fuels, the diameter of a matchstick. Kindling materials are smaller sticks and branches, the size of a pencil or your thumb. Firewood includes small to medium logs cut into pieces that will fit into the campfire ring.

There are different arrangements of campfire materials used for different purposes. You can experiment with different campfire wood arrangements and how they burn. This can help convey how different sizes and arrangements of fuels burn.

138

Tepee

The tinder is laid down in a small pile below the kindling, and the larger firewood is arranged in a tepee shape. The fire consumes wood rapidly and requires constant maintenance to keep it burning.

This arrangement is best for a quick warming fire or a small cooking fire.

Log Cabin

The tinder and kindling in the middle and logs stacked across the top. The log cabin arrangement has two to four small to medium-sized firewood logs laid parallel to each other in the fire pit, with two more logs stacked parallel on top of those in the opposite direction.

This arrangement burns more slowly and requires less maintenance.

Lean-To

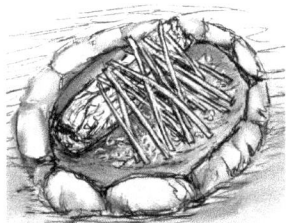

One large log is laid flat on the ground, tinder materials tucked in near the log on the windward side, and kindling sticks laid in a vertical arrangement over the top of the tinder.

This arrangement is good for windy conditions.

Star

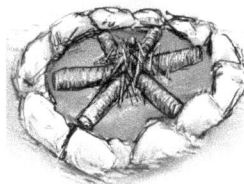

Four or five logs in a circle, with one end of each log pointing into the center. A small tinder and kindling tepee is created in the center between the logs. This arrangement is good when there's less firewood available.

In this arrangement, the fire burns slowly and can be quickly extinguished.

Igniting

To start ignitions, don't use gasoline or other flammable products, use matches or a lighter. Light the tinder and estimate how long it takes to ignite the materials.

Extinguishing

To extinguish, pour water over the fire and drench the coals. Use the shovel to stir and mix the water and moisten the coals throughout the campfire pit. Hold the back of your hand over the coals and slowly bring it closer to check for heat. If the ashes are piled deep and you want to clear out the pit, wait until the coals are completely cool and remove the ash with the shovel, spreading the ash around the outlying area.

Campfire Journaling

Sketch or diagram the campfire pit size and depth, as well as the size and arrangement of the rock ring. Then sketch the campfire wood kindling and tinder arrangements with notes about size and fuel moisture and how long it takes to ignite and burn along with distances embers are carried. Add notes about the sound and smells of the campfire. Also, sketch or add notes about your fire extinguishing tools (shovel and water) and process.

Chapter 7:
Fire Mitigation
& Readiness

Fire Mitigation

The term "mitigation" encompasses various actions, but concerning wildfires, it refers to reducing fire behavior severity through vegetation management. Vegetation management typically targets hazardous fuels, as discussed in Chapter 4: Fire Fuels, where vegetation community and fuel concentration and arrangement affect fire behavior. This chapter examines these elements through the lens of hazards and identifies traits considered hazardous. Mitigation also addresses flammable building materials and emergency access. Some fire prevention engineering activities, like clearing vegetation under power lines, aim to mitigate wildfire ignition risks. This chapter primarily focuses on vegetation management and hazardous fuels reduction, aligning closely with the book's fire environment focus.

international levels, I've adapted to various learning styles and language barriers. To enhance workshops and planning efforts, I've incorporated more visuals. Collaboratively developing notes, visuals, and plans —including printed maps with hand-marked locations, organized flip-chart notes, and large visual storyboards—has proved successful. Graphic facilitation professionals can aid in visualizing group discussions and goals, while nature journaling serves to integrate individual observations, beliefs, and feelings, fostering thoughtful engagement.

In many collaborative sessions, I've used long strips of GIS plotter paper or grouped flip-chart paper to provide presentation and discussion aids, incorporating visuals to frame topics and convey meaning, with space for participants to add notes. Time is allocated for participants to collaborate on their visual storyboards.

Collaborative Planning

Fire mitigation is most effective at a strategic landscape scale, with planning and implementation developed through collaborative processes integrating multiple perspectives. Visit the Fire Adapted Communities' website for collaborative fire planning details. While individual efforts are crucial, collective mitigation involving every individual yields better outcomes. It's essential to establish individual and group values and priorities for collaborative mitigation efforts.

Having worked extensively in collaborative fire planning at local, state, national, and

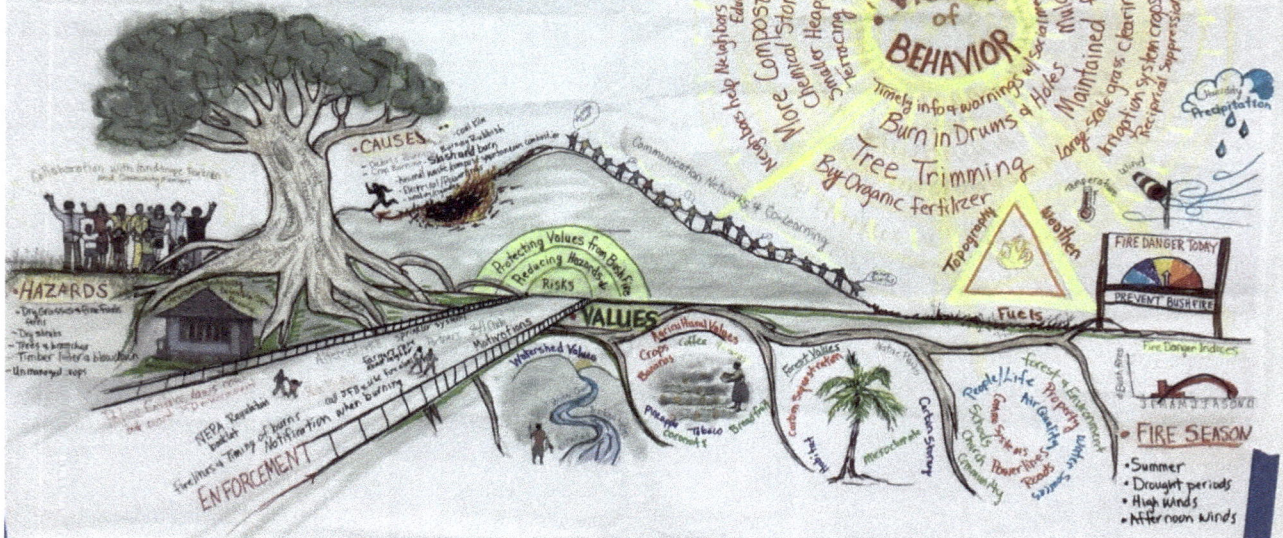

The storyboard on the previous page supported a national fire prevention and mitigation team planning meeting, visualizing discussion topics with space for consensus-driven notes.

The storyboard above was created during a fire prevention and mitigation planning workshop in Jamaica. It captured the vision, issues, and goals of the collaborative group developed during the workshop.

Visual Vocabulary

To create collaborative community storyboards for mitigation or prevention goals, it's helpful to develop a visual vocabulary. This typically includes knowledge or a consensus of basic symbols and simple images that can be used for certain subjects or as a set of defined criteria. For instance, most people recognize that a simple stick figure represents a person, or that a smiley face represents an expression of happiness. If you want to integrate more visual communication styles into your storyboards and journaling, you may want to consider purchasing some reference books that offer examples and techniques to help expand this vocabulary. Here are a few examples:

- Symbols can be used to organize, accentuate, and add context to the text. For example, a temperature gauge or sun can be used with numbers and words to emphasize or organize information about temperatures and heat.

- Spaces between text boxes and visuals are used like commas, and arrows can indicate movements. Arrows are also helpful to accentuate a process.

- Containers like a circular dialog callout and thought bubble can function as paragraphs and add context to the text discussion.

- Arrows and lines between text containers and sketch panels indicate the flow of conversation or scene.

- Titles, labels, and legends can be used to accentuate, organize, and add context to discussions and observations.

- The sun or sunrise can represent a shared vision.

- Roads can symbolize a path, and road signs can represent benchmarks to success. Boulders, cliffs, and washed-out bridges can represent obstacles to the journey. Bridges can represent overcoming an obstacle. Scrolls can represent shared knowledge or tasks.

Simplified Figures

Symbols for Fire

Conversations

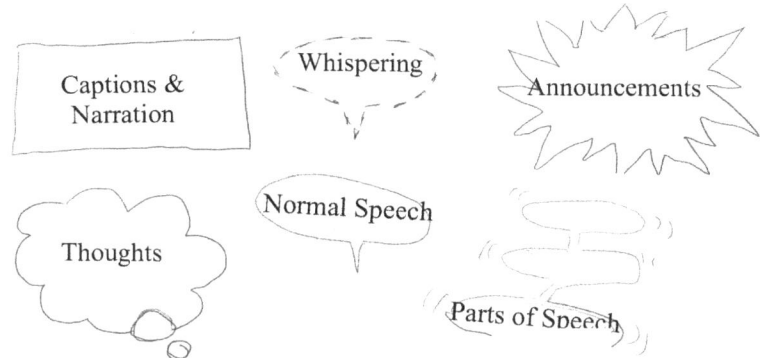

Movements

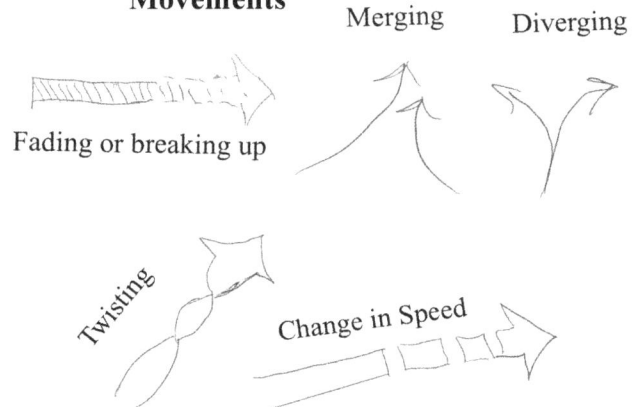

Goals & Objectives

Whether going through a collaborative planning process or considering personal needs and priorities, defining the goals and objectives is a priority. It's easy to get overwhelmed and lose focus, so having identified goals will help maintain focus. Many goals primarily focus on reducing fire hazards around homes and communities, but sometimes they include protecting and enhancing forest health, wildlife habitat, and ecosystem functions. Fire mitigation objectives are often framed around the types and timing of treatments that will be used.

Mitigation projects are often categorized by location (community or natural area) and techniques used in the treatment, such as prescribed fire or mechanical treatments. There is a broader range of objectives that can be met with prescribed fire due to ecological benefits such as habitat enhancement and or indigenous food sources. I will have more prescribed fire journaling information in the next chapter, but the approach to journaling about goals and objectives is the same.

Hazard Mitigation Treatments

When fire mitigation work focuses on communities and infrastructure, it is commonly called a hazardous fuels wildland-urban interface (WUI) treatment. There are many different types of fuel treatments used in these areas, including the use of mechanical equipment or prescribed fire. Both treatment types aim to reduce ignitions and the severity of fire behavior. In this chapter, ignitions are not focused on the cause, but on the ember materials that can become embers. Mechanical treatments often include the use of garden clippers, shovels, chainsaws, and/or larger equipment, like wood chippers and bulldozers. A common objective is to reduce both the horizontal and vertical continuity of vegetation. Other non-fire treatments include the use of animals like goats, sheep, and cattle to reduce the continuity of understory and surface fuels, like shrubs and grass. Weed abatement is also used as an initial treatment and/or for maintenance of desired conditions. Prescribed fire is also used when conditions are right for project objectives and often follows mechanical and/or animal treatments.

Home Defensible Space

Fire mitigation around homes is often called a "defensible space" treatment. When wildland firefighters are responding to a fire moving into a community, they are basically making a stand and defending homes. Creating and maintaining defensible space can not only reduce ember ignitions and the intensity of flames, but it can also improve firefighter safety. Making a home defensible also includes things like building or renovating a home with fire-resistant materials and enhancing driveways and parking access for emergency vehicles.

Fire Embers

Fire embers are the flammable materials that can break free and be lofted by flames and wind. Check the U.S. Fire Administration website "Protecting Structures From Wildfire Embers and Fire Exposure" for more information. Common ember materials include pine cones, fir cones, large seed pods, leaves, pine needles, branches, bark, and wood roofing materials. Another consideration for ember ignitions is where they land. As mentioned in Chapter 6: Fire

Ignitions & Prevention, I like to call these ember nests. These are collections of loosely arranged fine fuels where sparks and embers can ignite into flames and take flight across the landscape. Ember nests can be observed in many places, including vulnerable building locations like awnings, rain gutters, porches, woodpiles, and fences. Whether you're walking in the woods or around your home, it's worthwhile to look for ember sources and nests.

Ember Storm

Ember Sources:
Pine comes, seed pods, leaves, needles, branches, bark and flammable roofing materials

Embers lofted by flames and carried by winds up to a mile away

Ember Nests:
Dry grass and seed heads, dry and loosely arranged leaves, needles, twigs and bark, fallen pine cones and crevices in flammable building materials

Plant Fire Hazard Traits

There are many references for evaluating vegetation fire hazards around your property. Many of these include recommendations for the use of fire-resistant plants around homes, based on your local region. I used the Pac*ific Northwest Extension, Oregon State University "Fire-resistant Plants For Home Landscapes-Selecting plants that may reduce your risk from wildfire"* as a reference to create simplified visuals as a reference in this chapter. Some of these are physical traits like flaking and curling bark, while other plant traits are based on the moisture and chemical content of the plant that can make them more flammable. These hazard traits are not necessarily related to the fire adaptations and fire effects.

Use the reference on the next page to assess fire hazards related to the vegetation you observe within defensible space zones, community fuel break areas, and adjacent lands. I would recommend that you create your own version of higher and lesser hazard traits of the plants around your home and neighborhood as a reference, but my simplified version can be reference.

145

Plant Hazard Trait Observations

Tree & Shrub Hazard Observations

Higher Hazard	Lower Hazard
Close horizontal spacing between trees/shrubs	Wide horizontal spacing between trees/shrubs
Close vertical spacing between trees/shrubs	Wide vertical spacing between trees/shrubs
Leaves or needles yearlong	Leaves seasonally dropped
Concentrated branching	Sparsely branching
Oily and waxy leaves. Strong scented	Watery and supple leaves. Mild scented
Many cones on branches	X No cones on branches
Loose and deeply creviced bark	Smooth bark
Debris generating trees (leaves, needless, bark)	Less debris generated

Ground Cover & Soil Hazard Observations

Higher Hazard	Lower Hazard
Large curling fallen leaves	Small flat fallen leaves
Little horizontal spacing between grasses and plants	Wide space between plants
Tall grass	Short grass
Dry grass	Green grass
Concentrated branching	Sparsely branching
Tall-growing	Low-growing
Full and feathery seedheads	Small and simple seedheads
Debris generating plants (thatch, dead leaves, seeds)	Less debris generated
Thick layers of duff, mulch and or wood chips	Bare mineral soil

Mitigation Measurements

To define and accomplish objectives, we need to have measurable elements for the mitigation treatments. These measurements describe the size of the area (in acres), the dimensions of the treatment (length and width), the percentage of vegetation treated, and the spacing between vegetation elements. There may be slight differences in measurement based on state and local recommendations and regulations. Check the National Fire Protection Association and Fire Adapted Communities websites. I'd recommend looking up your local fire mitigation guidelines. I have used spacing recommendations from California in my graphics.

Defensible Space Measurements

Defensible space measurements are prioritized by zones around the home, starting with the first five feet from the house, then thirty feet from the house, and then all the way out to 100 feet. Depending on the percentage slope of the area, the spacing between trees and shrubs varies. See the graphic below.

Tree Spacing

Slopes Over 40%

20 feet of distance between the tree canopies

Slopes 20-40%

30 feet of distance between the tree canopies

Defensible Space Planning
(Less than a 20% slope)

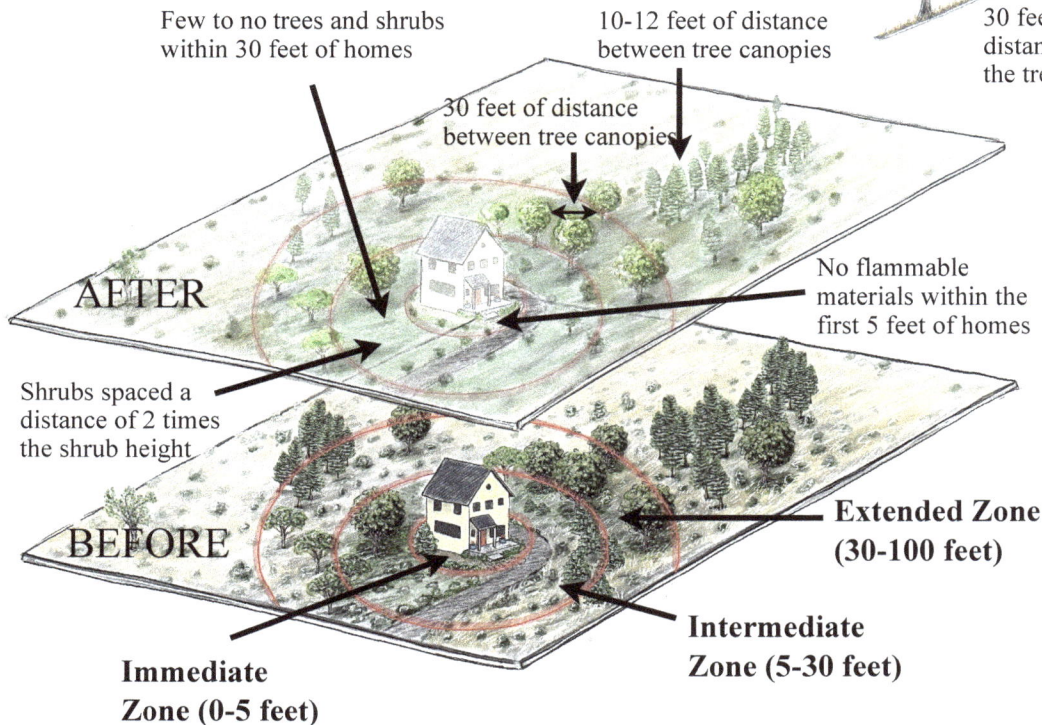

Few to no trees and shrubs within 30 feet of homes

10-12 feet of distance between tree canopies

30 feet of distance between tree canopies

No flammable materials within the first 5 feet of homes

AFTER

Shrubs spaced a distance of 2 times the shrub height

BEFORE

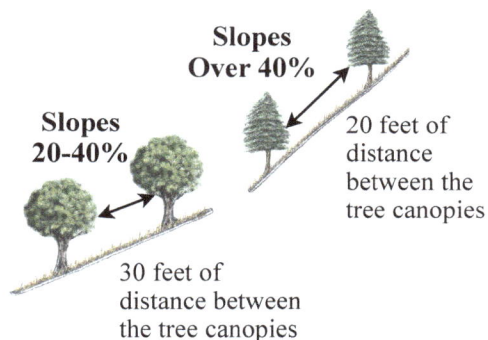

Shrub Spacing

20-40% Slopes: 4 times the shrub heights

>40% Slopes: 6 times the shrub heights

Extended Zone (30-100 feet)

Intermediate Zone (5-30 feet)

Immediate Zone (0-5 feet)

Journaling Defensible Space

Now is a good time to consider a defensible space journaling exercise. Before you start, estimate the slope of the area. You can refer back to Chapter 2: Topography if you'd like to estimate using biometrics (hands). You can also use biometrics for spacing estimates (paces) and refer to Chapter 3: Fire Fuels for examples. If you prefer not to use biometrics, bring a measuring tape. You may also want binoculars to look for ember sources in trees. Have your journal and a pen or pencil ready. If you want to follow the optional step, bring a few colored pencils and/or a small watercolor paint set with a water brush.

Survey Transect Line

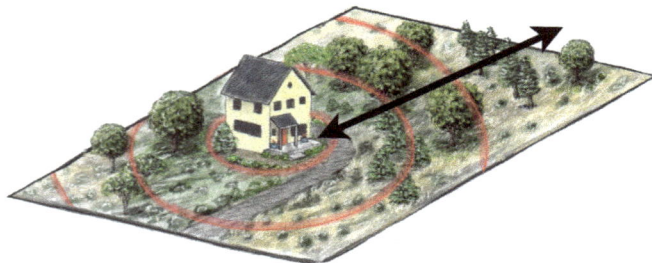

Step 1: Choose a direction to survey. Consider a line leading toward an adjacent forest area where there might be more ember materials. Also, think about a direction with a steep slope below the property, where prevailing strong winds come from or where fire ignitions are likely to start.

Step 2: Estimate the slope of the area using the slope categories for plant spacing on the graphic on the previous page.

Step 3: Use the Defensible Space Planning and Fire Hazard Plant Traits illustrations as a reference for observations within each defensible space zone. Compare current spacing and plant traits with recommended spacing and lower hazard traits. Estimate hazard levels as low, moderate, or high. Add thoughts about possible mitigation treatments to reduce hazards.

Step 4 (Optional): Create a horizontal bird's-eye view diagram of the vegetation for the entire survey area (all zones). Reference Chapter 4: Fire Fuels for examples. Add symbols, color, and/or notes about hazardous elements. Also, create a cross-section diagram of your survey area for vertical elements that pose a hazard, like ladder fuels. Include small sketches of the fuel bed and ember nests. See the example on the next page.

Example Descriptions of Plant Spacing & Fire Hazard Trait Observations (on a slope of less than 20%):

- **Immediate Zone** (5 feet from house): No trees along the transect line, but a few small green plants next to the front porch, with mowed green grass and gravel. Appears to be a low fire hazard vegetation area, unless plants become dry. Keep watered to mitigate the hazard.

- **Intermediate Zone** (5-30 feet from house): Four to five shrubby evergreen trees, 4-6 feet high, growing close together. High fire hazard area. Remove all or leave one or two spaced 8 to 12 feet apart to mitigate the hazard. Mixed green and gold grass mostly tall; need watering and mowing to mitigate hazard.

- **Extended Zone** (30-100 feet from house): Several widely branching deciduous trees, large leaves still on the tree. Spacing between canopies at least 30 feet. No small trees or shrubs underneath, lowest branches 6-8 feet from the ground. Currently low to moderate hazard. Continuous tall mostly dry grasses with green patches near trees. Low to moderate hazard; watering and mowing grasses would mitigate the hazard.

Journaling Ember Sources & Nests

Observe and journal about ember sources and nests around homes and communities. Follow similar instructions to the previous exercise and create a cross-section diagram visualizing ladder fuels, tree spacing, and ember materials. Use lines and arrows to show potential directions embers would fall or blow. Add small sketches of the fuel bed and ember nests, and describe hazards and mitigation actions.

Fuel Bed & Ember Nests Observations

Some live/green grasses and small shrubs near trees

Lots of tree litter with mixed live and dead grass

Survey Transect Line

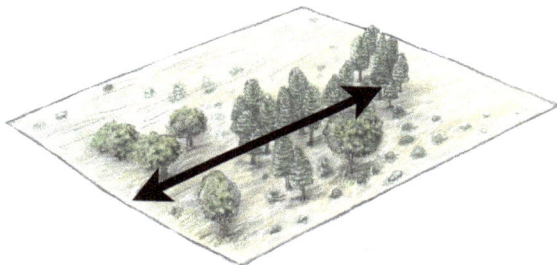

Open areas with some live sagebrush close together with tall concentrated dry grass surrounding them

Some cones, dry leaves and sticks on the ground near trees

Cross-section Diagram of Ladder Fuel & Ember Sources

Possible ember sources that could be lofted and dropped to the fuel bed/ember nests

Ladder fuel could carry surface fire into the trees

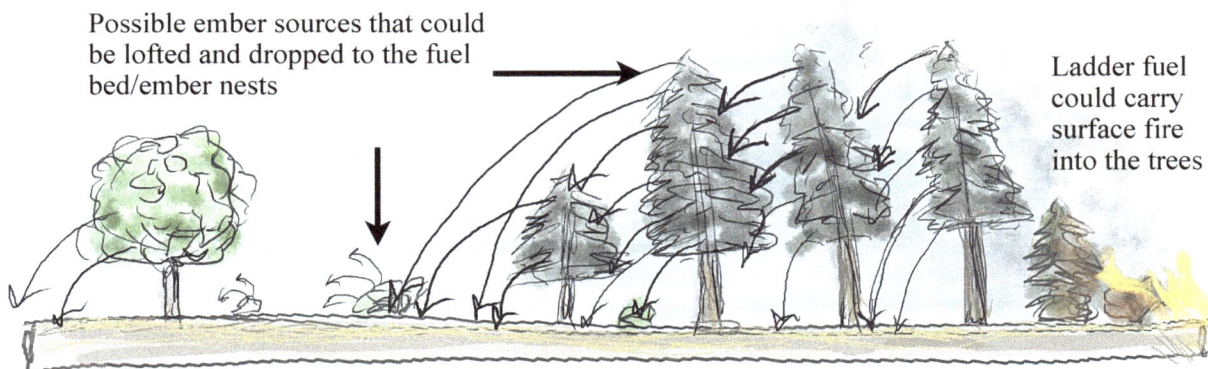

Question Prompts & Example Observations

What are the fire ember source hazards?

There are a number of evergreen trees with a few cones on the branches. These trees are fairly close together and embers could be lofted into nearby trees and on to the ground.

What are the surface fire and ember nest hazards?

There is nearly continuous dry grass in the open areas, with scattered sagebrush. There is less grass under the trees, with a few green patches. Fire could spread across the landscape. There are a few evergreen trees with small trees and bushes next to them creating ladder fuel that could carry fire into the tree canopy. Much of the grass is dry, loosely arranged and tall, and there are fallen leaves and some cones and could be higher hazard ember nests. The sage brush are highly branching with thick and lots of dead leaves which could pose a high ember nest hazard.

What can be done to mitigate some of the fire hazards?

There may not be time and money to do major fire mitigation work in the natural area, after considering the defensible space areas, but could look at reducing the ladder fuels and the risk of crown fires with increased fire embers. Removing a few of the evergreen trees to create enter spacing could also help. Prescribed fire would help reduce the dry grass and clean out dead materials within sagebrush areas.

Fire Mitigation Timing

Planning and implementing fire mitigation treatments can pose challenges due to timing considerations. Balancing goals and objectives while considering values at risk and treatment priorities is essential. Mechanical treatments often offer more flexibility than prescribed fire regarding timing. The following discussion on treatment timing observations aims to integrate fire environment observations into the mitigation process. This is an evolving process due to continual changes in vegetation and weather conditions.

Fire mitigation treatments are scheduled for implementation based on factors such as vegetation community or fuel group types, fire season conditions, and specific goals and objectives. Timing is also influenced by elevation and slope aspect, which affect curing phases differently. Surface fuel treatments in forest and shrub fuel groups may occur late in spring, summer, or fall, while grassland treatments are typically done in spring, just before the fire season, before the fuels cure. Other considerations include plant health, such as tree and shrub trimming in late fall, winter, or early spring when trees are dormant. These seasons are also ideal for trimming to avoid disturbing nesting birds and vulnerable young mammals. Many insects are dormant during fall, winter, and early spring, emerging later when weather conditions warm, providing cues about timing goals. Using animals as indicators for starting and ending fuel treatments can be a natural and effective approach.

Grassland Curing & Treatment Timing

Refer to Chapter 4: Fire Fuels and Chapter 5: Fire Seasons for various observations about fuel conditions. General timing recommendations:

- **Green Phase:** Early in this phase, with increasing temperatures, you may observe more insects, such as ground-nesting bumblebees. While there is minimal fire risk during the green phase of grassland curing, you may begin mowing and weeding the area, considering the plant and wildlife phenology observations to guide timing.

- **Green-Gold Phase:** Grasses pose a lower fire risk during this phase, but as fire season approaches, continue mowing, especially near roads and homes, or in areas where grasses need to be kept short.

- **Gold-Green Phase:** At this stage, ensure areas around homes and roads are mowed. Monitor fire weather conditions, and reduce grassland vegetation to mitigate fire risk. Check for ember nests around buildings and remove flammable materials from porches.

- **Yellow-Gold Phase:** During this high-risk phase, perform work in the morning when temperatures are lower and humidity is higher. Test fuel moisture before mowing and be cautious to prevent sparks that could ignite dry grass. Avoid parking in grassy areas to prevent accidental ignition.

Fire Mitigation Calendar

Create a fire mitigation calendar with visual reminders for timing fire mitigation activities. See an example on the next page. I like to add animal and plant phenology observations along with seasonal weather trend observations as reminders. You could have larger calendars in your version where you add scheduled events, like fuel treatment projects, plantings, and trimming. You could also add other weather data and trends like the growing degree days and associated plant phenology and curing.

Observations for Mitigation Timing

* Use schedule with the grass curing phase observations

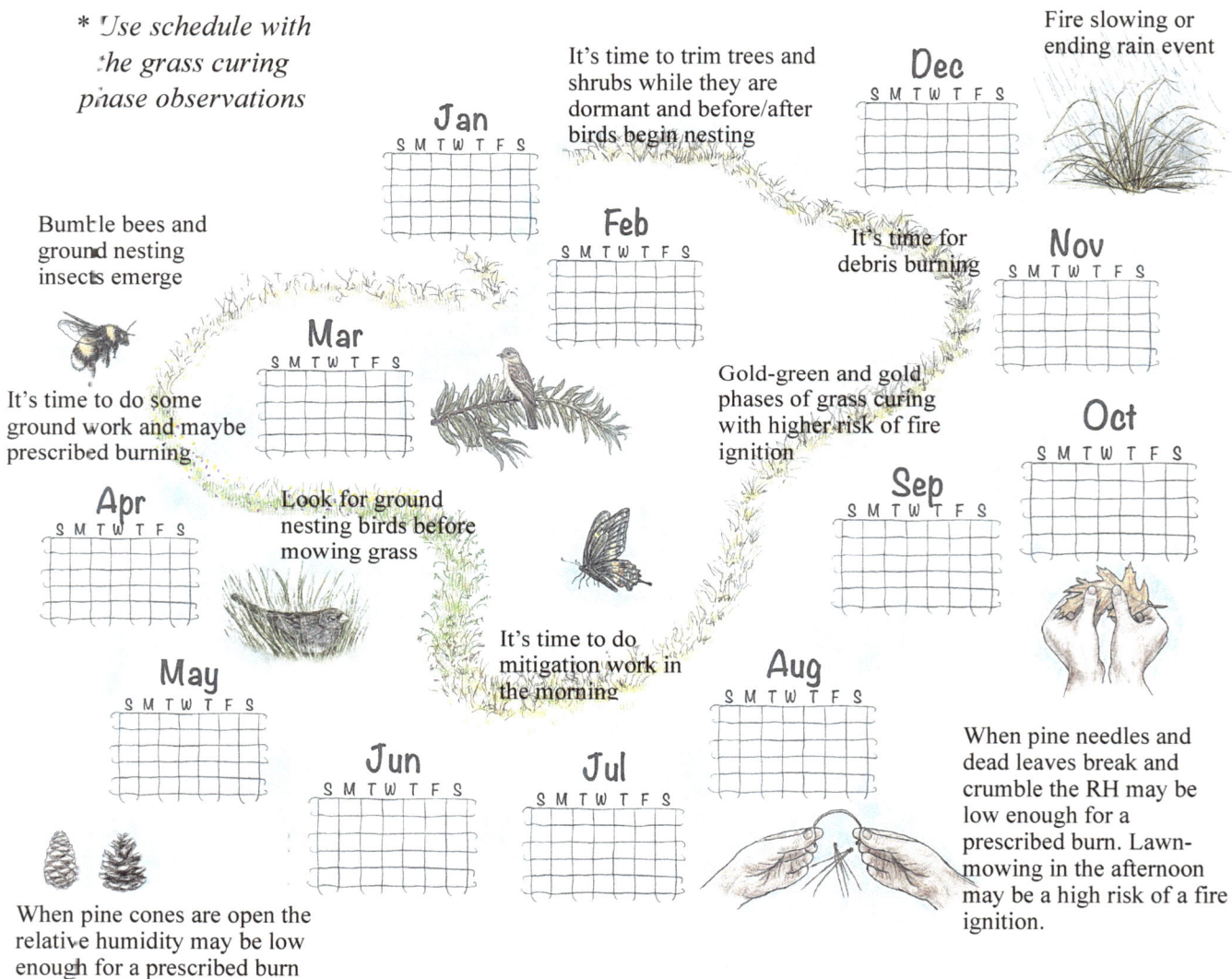

Jan
S M T W T F S

It's time to trim trees and shrubs while they are dormant and before/after birds begin nesting

Dec
S M T W T F S

Fire slowing or ending rain event

Feb
S M T W T F S

It's time for debris burning

Nov
S M T W T F S

Bumble bees and ground nesting insects emerge

Mar
S M T W T F S

Gold-green and gold phases of grass curing with higher risk of fire ignition

Oct
S M T W T F S

It's time to do some ground work and maybe prescribed burning

Apr
S M T W T F S

Look for ground nesting birds before mowing grass

Sep
S M T W T F S

It's time to do mitigation work in the morning

Aug
S M T W T F S

May
S M T W T F S

When pine needles and dead leaves break and crumble the RH may be low enough for a prescribed burn. Lawn-mowing in the afternoon may be a high risk of a fire ignition.

Jun
S M T W T F S

Jul
S M T W T F S

When pine cones are open the relative humidity may be low enough for a prescribed burn

Simplified Mitigation Story

An ideal mitigation story encompasses the fire history, collaborative process goals and objectives, and the phases of treatment: before, during, and after. For our journaling purposes, we will focus on meeting the objectives of a mitigation treatment. This is a stripped-down story that follows a hero's journey format, with characters overcoming challenges to meet objectives. A comic book format or storyboard approach can effectively convey the setting, characters, and activities over the treatment period.

The examples on the following pages are highly simplified, featuring a few sketches and lacking dialogue. You could integrate multiple sketches into a comic book format, with each scene representing a time sequence or panel. Alternatively, you could paste in photos with handwritten notes following the same visual elements.

Journaling the Mitigation Story Exercise:

- **Identify the setting**: Create a map or simple sketch of the setting with key landmark features like roads, homes, water sources, and forest areas. Add a number or icon to denote where the fire mitigation treatments will occur.

- **Identify the characters**: Sketch the people involved in the mitigation work or use symbols to represent them. Include personal notes describing their role and feelings.

- **Outline obstacles and challenges**: List treatment goals and objectives, accompanied by a sketch of pre-treatment fuel conditions, including horizontal and vertical arrangement, ladder fuels, and the fuel bed. Consider topography and weather elements like slope and wind direction.

- **During treatment**: Depict characters or tools in action, focusing on key elements being acted upon. For example, show a rake and shovel scraping and widening a trail.

- **After treatment:** Create a scene showing the landscape after treatment, maintaining the same scale and perspective as the before scene. Include ground, shrubs, low-level tree branches, and possibly full tree height to visualize post-fire conditions.

Throughout the story, include descriptions of fire prevention and mitigation objectives. This could be in text bubbles tied to characters or written nearby with labels and arrows. The goal is to visually convey the accomplishment of treatment objectives.

Landscape Sketch or Map with Treatment Areas

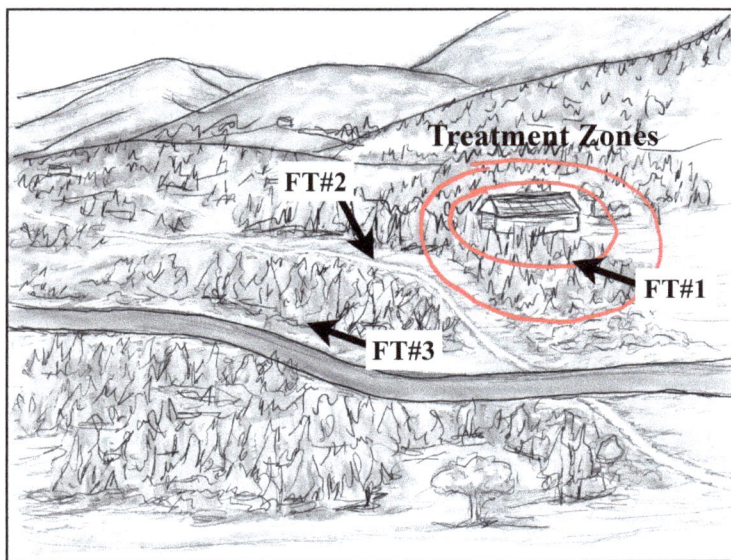

FT=Fuel Treatment

Treatment Elements & Measurements:

- Area Name: county, watershed, community, etc.

- Elevations

- Slope Aspects

- Direction and timing of prevailing winds

- Treatment name(s) or number

- Treatment types (e.g., hand-thinning, chipper, goats)

- Priority and timing of treatments and possible nature cues

- Recommended weather and fuel moisture conditions during treatments

- Range and average percent slope

- Before and after vegetation communities/fuel group conditions

- Before and after fuel bed and ember nest conditions

- Total acres and number of homes treated

- Spacing objectives for different defensible space zones around homes

- Partners with varied goals, interests, and engagement

Fuel Treatment (FT) #1

Fuel Group Sketch- Before

Fuels Sketch- During/After

Fuel Bed Sketch- Before

Grass, leaves, sticks

Fuel Bed Sketch- After

Wood chips

Phased Story Panels

The examples, on this page and the next, illustrate simplified treatment phases. Alongside these before, during, and after panels, you should create a treatment area map and outline the phases of treatments. Additionally, include narrative text below each panel to describe the scene and activities.

Fuel Treatment (FT) #2

Before- Deer Trail

During- Hand Tools

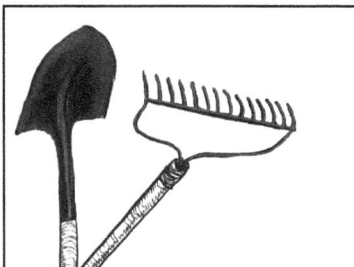

After- Widened Trail

Fuel Treatment (FT) #3A

Before- Thick Understory

During- Goat Grazing

After- Understory Thinned

Fuel Treatment (FT) #3B

Fuel Bed Debris Burned

Drip Torch Ignitions

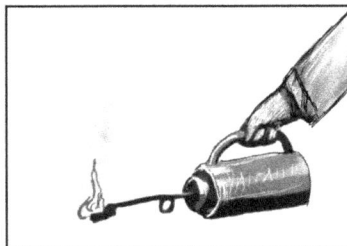

Fuel Bed Consumed

Journaling Goat Grazing

Beyond simply presenting before, during, and after treatment elements, there are more detailed observations to consider regarding how treatments, such as goat grazing, can fulfill our mitigation objectives.

This involves making detailed observations and describing nuances, such as the vegetation consumed by goats and how it affects plant spacing after treatment. Try to sketch a map or outline of the treatment area, including measurements like width, length, or number of acres. Estimate the number of goats in the herd and the duration they will be grazing the area. Additionally, create a few small sketches of goats consuming different plant types and vegetation elements, noting the horizontal and vertical distances of space they create.

Goat Sketching Tips

If drawing goats feels daunting, here are a few quick tips. Remember, capturing observations is not about creating art; the goal is to visually convey the observation.

- Sketch a circle or oblong shape for the body.

- Outline the shape of the legs.

- Sketch shapes for the neck, head, horns, and tail.

- Draw a line for the ground and add some grass.

- Add a touch of color and shadows to the goat, and use a few pencil lines to indicate fur and form.

Horizontal Diagram of a Goat Created Fuel Break Area

Estimate of goat herd size is 350-400 comparing the sample count over the herd area

Sample count of 10 goats

Sources say that a herd of 400 goats can graze 1-2 aces within 24 hours, which can reduce the surface vegetation 25% to 80%, depending on the type of vegetation. This can provide a good fire fuel break, reducing fire intensity and rate of spread.

Question Prompts:

- How much of the grass and leaves will be eaten?

- How long will they graze?

- Will this create a fire fuel break?

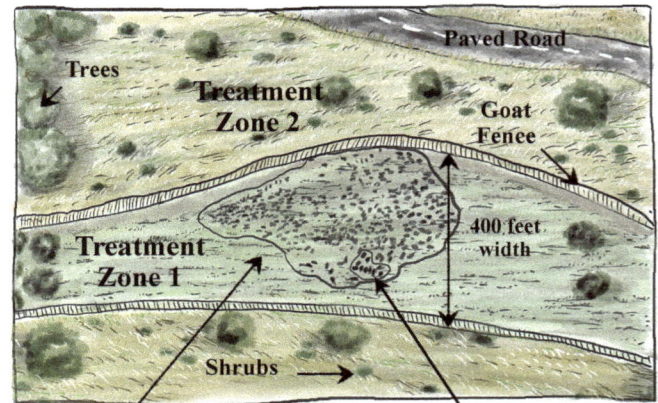

Sketches & Measurements of Goat Grazing

Observed Plant Elements Eaten

3-4 foot high shrub/leaf foraging

6 foot high estimated leaf foraging

1-2 foot high grass before grazing and 3-4 inches after

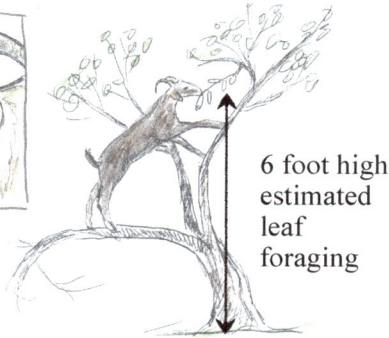

Grass	Leaves	Bark
11	21	0

Wildfire Readiness

I define fire readiness as the awareness and activities that prepare people for wildfires. Traditionally, this includes fire mitigation and prevention activities, as well as evacuation preparations. I would also include the use of nature journaling to enhance observation skills and situational awareness activities, which is the focus of this book. There are many fire readiness programs, like the CAL FIRE Ready, Set, Go guidance, which describe the timing and actions of fire readiness activities. The "ready" aspect typically focuses on conducting fire mitigation treatments, home hardening, and fire evacuation planning before the peak of fire season. The "set" aspect is focused on activities done during the fire season to elevate readiness, such as preparing and updating your evacuation kit and practicing your evacuation plan. The "go" phase means it's time to evacuate your home, animals, and family.

Readiness Calendar

One approach to integrating nature journaling into fire readiness would be to create a calendar similar to the fire mitigation example I shared, but with a broader scope, incorporating observation cues that prompt readiness activities and situational awareness. After you have read Chapter 2: Fire Weather and Chapter 5: Fire Seasons, you should have a good idea of what types of observations are important to be aware of. To create this calendar, I would use the same or a similar visual path for the fuels curing phases as on the fire mitigation calendar, but add more seasonal and fire weather observation cues appropriate to your area. Some observations may be important throughout the season, but you may want to find different cues to keep things interesting. For instance, thunderstorms may be an ongoing observation, but you might want to emphasize lightning during late spring and early summer and wind shear on cumulonimbus clouds in the fall. You can see my example on the next page.

Observations for Wildfire Readiness

Springtime Beaufort wind force observations of wind speeds over 10 mph

Early springtime home defensible space work

It's time to review your evacuation plan and sign up for local fire alerts

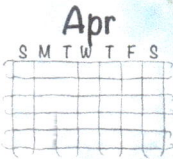

Jan
S M T W T F S

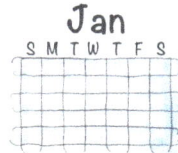

Feb
S M T W T F S

Mar
S M T W T F S

Wind shear effects on cumulonimbus clouds can indicate high wind speeds

Dec
S M T W T F S

Fire slowing or ending rain event

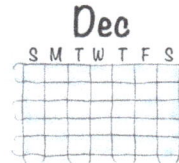

Take a breath

Nov
S M T W T F S

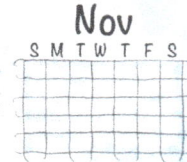

Apr
S M T W T F S

Cumulonimbus clouds with lightning

Pyrocumulonimbus smoke column in the distance indicating extreme fire behavior

Heightened evacuation readiness

Oct
S M T W T F S

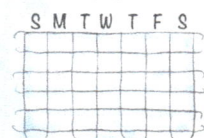

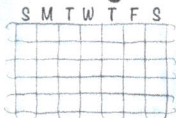

Sep
S M T W T F S

Watch for fire ignitions

Majority of grasses cured. It's time for clearing flammable materials away from the house

May
S M T W T F S

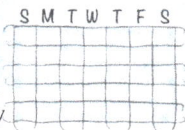

When pine cones are open the RH is fairly low. It's time to check your evacuation kit

Jun
S M T W T F S

Jul
S M T W T F S

Aug
S M T W T F S

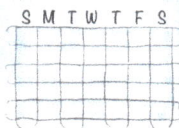

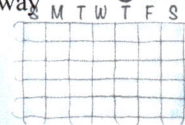

When pine needles and dead leaves break and crumble the relative humidity is low and it is time for heightened readiness

158

Wildfire Evacuation Planning

There are many resources and references to help with wildfire evacuation planning, all with similar elements. A simple checklist is good to print and post somewhere for easy access. You can find one with a quick internet search. A significant part of wildfire evacuation planning is signing up for local emergency alerts and warnings. You can search online for your local area's emergency alerts and find where to sign up. There may also be smartphone apps that can help with this; your local fire or sheriff's department may have recommendations. Official evacuation plans are often developed for cities and towns, so you'll want to search for those and reference them for the upcoming journaling exercise. Personalizing your evacuation plan for yourself, family members, and pets or livestock is crucial. Lastly, you'll want to have an evacuation kit, including important papers and supplies, prepared and accessible during fire season. I won't delve into details about these elements since this book focuses on journaling observations about the fire environment.

Evacuation planning can be stressful and something people don't want to think about until an emergency occurs, but it's crucial for living safely in the fire environment. It's important not only to find or develop evacuation plans but also to practice your evacuation route. I developed a workshop session for a National Fire Learning Network group using the nature journaling approach to help evaluate and practice evacuation plans. If you approach this exercise with slow observations of your surroundings, travel time, and your thoughts and feelings about the route, you can gain insight into how you might respond.

As I developed that session, I went through the journaling practice and learned interesting things about myself and what I would need to consider in my personal evacuation. The process was a little stressful, but the practice of sketching my route and making observations helped alleviate my apprehensions. Workshop participants reported a similar experience, and some included their children in the process, which they wouldn't have done otherwise. Journaling the evacuation route and the landmarks you observe can help familiarize you with a route and provide visual reminders of where you are, especially when visual conditions may be significantly altered, and road signs are difficult to see.

Exercise Preparation

Gather copies of any official evacuation routes and other maps that can be referenced for road and place names, especially if there is fire and evacuation information that should be integrated into your observations (evacuation centers, etc.). Bring a few colored pencils and a notebook or journal to write notes and sketch the route. Bring something to use as a timer and also plan to take mileage measurements.

Be prepared to recognize any stress you may be feeling. Bring snacks and water with you throughout this process. When you start to feel your heart racing, stop what you are doing and take a sip of water. Feel the water on your tongue, sliding down your throat, and imagine the water cooling and calming your body and mind. You can also break up these journaling exercises and finish them when you have more time and feel less stressed. Make time for some fun observations and sketches like something interesting but unrelated to your evacuation route.

Journaling Exercise

There are different ways to approach journaling an evacuation route, but you should plan to walk and/or drive the entire or key portions of the route. I like to start with a metacognitive exercise—thinking about how we think, remember, and respond to stress.

Step 1: Ask yourself these questions: What route do you intuitively want to take when you're in a hurry and why? What is the official evacuation route? Are there differences between your intuitive response and the official or other strategic routes? Are there multiple routes you should consider and why?

Step 2: Sit down at home or at an office with a pencil and paper and draw your evacuation route from memory or based on your assumptions. This is more of a warm-up, so don't worry if you have limited recollections or how nice the map looks. Include roads, intersections, stoplights, and landmarks.

Step 3: After drawing your evacuation route from memory, refer to the official evacuation route map, and/or refer to a printed map or an online map to compare with your map. Make corrections and/or

additions, including estimated mileage between key stops and turns.

Step 4: Take your supplies and write down your starting mileage and time. Drive your route and stop, somewhere safe, when you see key landmarks or come to intersections or turns that you feel anxious about. While stopped, consider how well you can recognize these under poor visibility conditions and add notes about what this landmark tells you about your route, like how long it takes you to get there (mileage and time) and how far until your next turn. Also, consider gas stations and large parking areas as key landmark features. Make note of which ones may be best to access, if needed, during an evacuation. When stopped near intersections or turns, write notes about why this "decision point" makes you anxious. Are you worried the lights may be out and traffic may be too congested? How much would this slow you down versus another route? When I went through this exercise, my husband and I were living full-time in our travel trailer. I realized that getting out of the campgrounds could be a big issue and that I'd need to have evacuation routes for being on foot as well as in the vehicle.

Evacuation map from memory

Step 5: After you've completed your route, consider what additional things you should add to your map and/or personal evacuation plan. For instance, I looked for additional sheltering options along the route (large parking areas). I also noted what I might want to keep in my vehicle, like some type of material to cover the windows and a dry heavyweight pure wool blanket to help protect us from heat and flames.

Step 6: Look over your journaling notes and determine if there are things you should add to your fire readiness phases, like keeping your gas tank full during fire season or moving a horse trailer to a new location for easy access.

Step 7: Consider what fire season and fire weather observations you might use to enhance your situational awareness. You may want to list some important observations and schedule time for these and journaling practices that enhance your situational awareness.

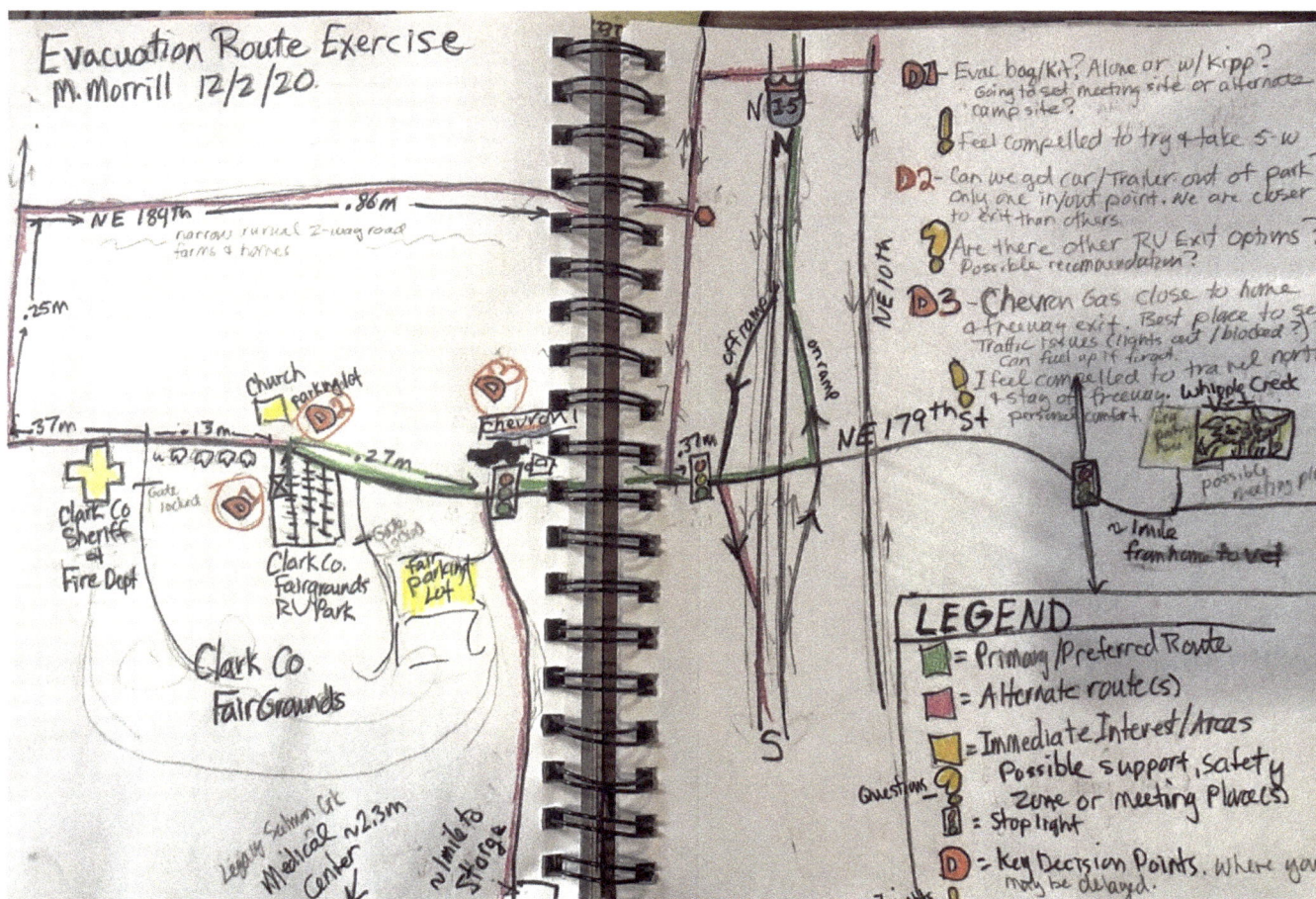

Chapter 8: Fire & Smoke

The Fire Triangle

The fire triangle comprises the ingredients necessary for fire combustion: oxygen, fuel, and heat. The triangle symbol is used in various contexts associated with fire. In mathematics and chemistry, it symbolizes a state of change. In Ancient Greek language, a triangle represented the element of fire and its aspiration to ascend—the top of the triangle pointing upward toward the sky.

We understand that fire is not an element but a process. I don't use the fire triangle extensively in my journaling about fire. Instead, I focus more on observations related to the combustion process and the interactions between the elements of the behavior triangle (weather, topography, and fuels). However, this doesn't diminish the creative inspiration of the triangle in my creative process. Did you know that the term "inspiration," as defined in the Merriam-Webster dictionary, originated in early Latin with the figurative meaning "to breathe into" and in Old English as "the drawing of air into the lungs"? Fire uses heat energy to transform solid carbon material into a gas. In that process, fire inhales oxygen and exhales carbon dioxide. Fire breathes! Photosynthesis is nearly the opposite of fire combustion. Plants absorb carbon dioxide gas and release oxygen to create a solid carbon form. The relationship between plants, air, and fire can offer many inspirational approaches to visualizing and thinking about fire. In the two illustrations on this page, I used the triangle symbol to help convey the fire triangle and fire behavior concepts.

When & Where to Journal Active Fire

Before we delve further into this chapter, I want to emphasize that the majority of observations and journaling activities should occur before any active fire observations, excluding those of a campfire, bonfire, or debris pile burn. There are many awareness-building skills that can prepare you to observe fire on the landscape, and this should be practiced when there is less safety risk.

I have organized this chapter in a way that focuses observations in the safest and most practical manner. I have separated observations of the combustion process to a campfire, which can be done individually or in a small group. Prescribed burn observations should be done in partnership with prescribed fire managers and include a trained fire observer or single resource boss, as defined by the National Wildfire Coordinating Group. Wildfire observations should be conducted at a distance or through virtual information sources. Wildfire smoke can be observed individually or in a group if there is no imminent fire evacuation risk.

Pyrolysis & Combustion

In the natural environment, combustion begins with an ignition source of sufficient heat to ignite fuels. As discussed in Chapter 4: Fire Fuels, the size, surface area, and dryness of fuels make all the difference in the amount and duration of heat needed to ignite fuels of varying sizes. Once the initial ignition has occurred, the pyrolysis and combustion process takes place and continues into neighboring fuels as the fire spreads. Pyrolysis is the thermal breakdown of organic material that occurs without oxygen and prior to the combustion process. The observations listed on this page are from a U.S. Forest Service report on the chemical composition of wildland fire emissions (Urbanski 2009).

The Pyrolysis & Combustion Process

Hot

Hottest

Hotter

(1) Drying & Pyrolysis
Heat removes moisture, evaporates oils and distills plant matter inside the wood (little to no oxygen involved in the process).

Products: water vapor, evaporated plant oils and flammable gases.

(2) Flaming & Cracking
Flammable gases burn and wood cracks to release more gas when reacting with oxygen at very high temperatures (combustion/exothermic reaction).

Products: heat, light, carbon dioxide, and more fully combusted (reduced) gases along with soot particles, char and ash.

(3) Smoldering & Glowing
Once gases are consumed by the flames, a flameless partial combustion occurs with the reaction of the burned wood (char) to oxygen under hot temperatures.

Products: heat, light, partly combusted gases (carbon monoxide, etc.) and highly toxic compounds, like benzene.

Drying & Pyrolysis

Drying and curing of vegetation from sun exposure, along with wind, low relative humidity, and increasing air temperatures, will reduce the level of heat energy needed for the pyrolysis process. The high heat levels from a fire ignition source cause dead and live fuels to lose their moisture, evaporate oils, and distill plant matter. There are no flames in the pyrolysis phase, and little to no oxygen is involved. Pyrolysis occurs inside plant or wood material, where the internal moisture and oils (volatile organic compounds) evaporate and transform into various gases. One observation in the pyrolysis phase is to look for the white steam and smoke lying close to fuels and prior to the flaming phase.

Flaming & Cracking

During the flaming and cracking phase, heat and oxygen interact with the gases from the pyrolysis process and ignite into flames. As the gas from pyrolysis is released and burned, the plant matter and woody materials deeper within crack and release more gas, which continues the combustion and breakdown process. The flaming phase is considered a more complete combustion process and, depending on the fuel type, will be changed into various gases and distilled carbon materials, like carbon dioxide, soot particles, char, and ash. This phase is known as an exothermic reaction, where heat and light become byproducts (radiant heat and light). This is the phase most people associate with fire and is easily observed and journaled by the bright-colored flames and billowing smoke plumes.

Smoldering & Glowing

Smoldering and glowing occur once the flammable gases have been consumed, and the temperatures in the combustion process start to drop. This is considered a partial combustion process, as the char created during the flaming process reacts with oxygen and continues in a flameless combustion and breakdown process. An observation for this phase is the glowing coals. The byproducts of this phase can be highly toxic, with compounds like benzene and carbon monoxide gas.

Plants are made up of water, oils, waxes, and dry matter (lignin, carbohydrates, and minerals), with about 50% of that material as carbon and 41% oxygen. These materials are converted under high temperatures of the pyrolysis and combustion process into gases, char and ash.

Flame Shape, Color & Attachment

Observing flames at a close-up scale can provide valuable insights, such as the size, condition, and chemical compounds within various fuel elements. You can also observe the influence of wind and heat interactions between flames. These observations can be made while looking at a fireplace, campfire, debris burn pile, or prescribed fire. As a fire inhales oxygen, there are pulses within the flames that start at the base (fuel attachment area) and ripple outward toward the tip of the flame (Wu 2012). When there are cool and moist weather and fuel conditions, flames may appear smaller, while warm and dry conditions may result in larger flames. Winds can push flames into stretched and leaning forms. An unstable atmosphere can also cause larger flames to be pulled higher into the air. Flames can lean slightly or strongly in different directions based on the heat interactions between flames and within the larger fire area. Stop and observe the winds, and estimate the speed and direction using the guidance from Chapter 2: Fire Weather.

Fuel size, shape, and arrangement also influence the appearance of flames. A vertically standing grass blade may create a long narrow stream of flames, while a flat or piled stick, log, or pile of leaves may create a billowing flame, as the combustion process works through different fuel sizes and conditions.

Use the following illustrations to help you visualize flame shapes and flow as well as flame colors. Mix these observations in with your pyrolysis and combustion journal pages along with your landscape fire observations.

Flame Form & Flow

Steaming

Streaming flames can be observed in a candle flame, small creeping flames, and sometimes in the larger flame fronts.

Leaning

Leaning flames can be observed when the wind influences the fire, and when flames are drawn toward each other based on heat interactions with the air

Billowing

Billowing flames and fire are caused by the inconsistent pulsing of gases released from wood during the pyrolysis phase and the associated flame pulsing as the gases are burned.

Tips for Black & White Sketches of Flames

On white paper:

Start with a light pencil outline of the ribboning, angular, and stretched and or billowed shapes of the flames, adding a few sketch lines in the darker areas.

Leave areas within and near the bottom of flames for white appearing flames and brighter light emitted.

Smudge the pencils lines to give more of a flowing look, and add darker pencil lines where needed to accentuate darker areas and edges.

Use gray watercolor or create more smudged penciled areas for smoke around the top and sides of the fire.

Erase areas if needed to keep white areas within the base of the flame or use white gouache or gel pen.

On gray or black paper:

Follow the steps above, but add more white to fill the flame areas (watercolor, gouache, pastel, or gel pen).

Use white to highlight smoke around the flames.

Flame Color & Attachment

Flame Attachment

Flames cannot exist if there are no fuels to burn. Drawing/painting flames where they are attached to the fuels (area of combustion) and on or within the fuels is an important observation and element to capture in journaling.

Vertical Attachment

Flames that are attached in a vertical line, like those along grass stems, branches, and tree trunks. The flames stream upwards and sometimes lean out and break-up or merge with other flames below, adjacent, or above the fuels that are burning.

Horizontal Attachment

Flames that merge into a line or front of flames and burn along the surface of the ground through grasses and shrubs. Drawing or painting the horizontal flame movements along the ground can appear as swirling and broken lines, a rounded shape, or even like a snaking yellow-orange dragon. See fire behavior section further in the chapter.

Flame Envelopment

Flames can envelop a single tree (torching) or forested hillside (crown fire). These billowing flames appear more orange-red at a distance and can look like an upside-down waterfall or river currents washing through and around branches.

Color Sketches & Painting Tips

Start with a pencil sketch or apply narrow light yellow colored pencil lines or use watercolor and a paintbrush to create ribbons of yellow color to form the basic shapes of the flames. Add orange around the edges and at the tips of the flames. Add a deep brownish-red (brick red) at the tips of the flames and to accent the edges.

Heat & Light Transfer

We know that the combustion process is an exothermic reaction. Heat is dispersed in different ways through different substances. Heat transfer was discussed in Chapter 2 Fire Weather and Chapter 4: Fire Fuels because the heat transferred between the sun and earth and carried through the air follows the same principles that apply to fire. Conductive heat moves through solids like wood, rocks, and soil. Convective heat moves through fluids like air and is influenced by air turbulence caused by heat and wind. Radiant heat does not need a medium to travel through. It is distributed broadly over an area. Radiant heat can create light, and radiant light can create heat. Both radiant heat and light are released during the combustion and smoldering phases. See the illustration on the next page.

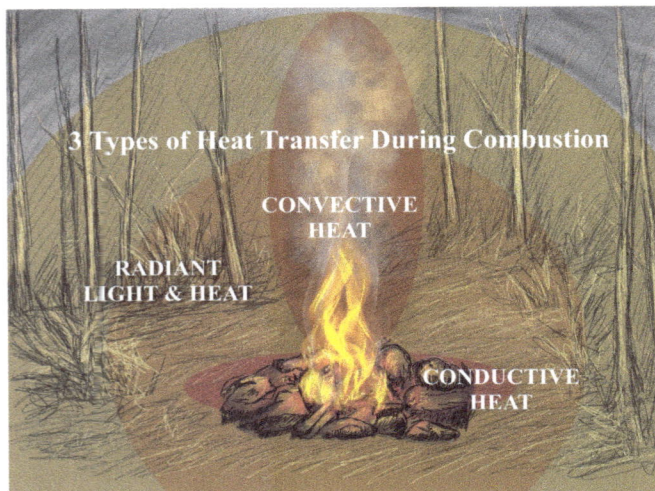

3 Types of Heat Transfer During Combustion

CONVECTIVE HEAT

RADIANT LIGHT & HEAT

CONDUCTIVE HEAT

Other Sensory Observations

Thus far, this chapter has focused on visual observations. The best journaling exercises integrate multi-sensory inputs for more full-bodied and full-brained engagement with the environment. The combustion and heat transfer observations can include the feel of heat on our skin as well as the sounds during the cracking phase. We used the feel, sound, and smell of fine fuels for journaling in Chapter 3: Fire Fuels, and those should be integrated here. You may notice variations in how the different fuels smell when burning. Throughout your journaling observations, integrate as many sensory experiences as you can.

Journaling Campfire Combustion

A great way to journal the pyrolysis and combustion process, heat transfer, and radiant light is to observe a campfire. Please follow the campfire set-up and extinguishing process discussed in Chapter 6: Fire Ignitions & Prevention. If you have the opportunity to observe a prescribed fire or cultural burn, you can

also make these observations. The next couple of pages share information and ideas for visualizing flames. I have used my own descriptive terms to define flame shapes.

In your journal, sketch and write notes about the weather and fuel conditions influencing the campfire pyrolysis and combustion process. Also, journal the different types of heat transfer and light. Start with radiant heat. How far away from the fire can you still feel the heat? As the fire grows, continue assessing the distance the radiant heat has reached. If it's dark outside, you can also look at objects or people around the campfire and visualize and describe how well they are lit at different distances. For convective heat, you do not want to put your hands above the fire! Instead, estimate the flame heights and look for heatwaves and differences in the flame colors and smoke thickness and color to estimate heat differences. For conductive heat, place your hands on the ground just outside the campfire ring. Do you feel any heat? If the fire is not burning too hot, use the back of your hands and move them slowly to the outside of the rock ring. If you are feeling heat before touching, don't go any further. If there is little to no heat detected, touch the back of your hand to one of the rocks and see if you can detect any heat. Use my illustration to inspire ideas for visualizing heat transfer.

Fire Acoustics

The sounds associated with fire can provide very interesting observations. As discussed in other chapters, plants have different levels of moisture and chemicals that can change the scent and sound of fire. Kara M. Yedineck, with the US Forest Service, published a scientific study about fire acoustics. She was able to demonstrate sound differences between different burning tree species and sizes. Yedineck focused on the popping sounds, when the plant's cell walls explode, but you may hear other sounds which can include hissing or roaring as gases are released and consumed. I think the burning of moist, waxy, and/or oily vegetation sounds like the hot grease of bacon in a frying pan. I think the burning of dry grass sounds like the soft rustling of paper. There are a few terms you may want to consider when journaling the sounds of a fire. Timbre is the tone and quality of sound (smooth or rough), amplitude is the loudness or volume of the sound, and pitch is the position of sound within the range of sound frequencies (higher or lower). For example, a bullfrog has a lower pitch than a cricket.

There are a number of different approaches to visualizing sound, including frequency waveforms and sonograms. Sound is transmitted through waves which travel through solids, liquids, and gas. Sound is often measured in megahertz, which is a unit of

alternating current or electromagnetic waves. Sounds can be visualized as transverse wave patterns with peaks and troughs of different distances and heights over time. The closer together the waves, the higher the pitch. The higher the waveform, the louder the sound. Some sounds are also visualized with tiny lines of varying heights over a horizontal timeline.

In my example journal page below, I created a line graph for the fire acoustic frequencies in Yedineck's study mentioned above. I created a different graph for different fuel types and added visuals and notes to further convey sounds. If you journal fire sounds over time, you may come up with your own visuals and descriptions.

Landscape/ Wildland Fire

I am defining the term landscape or wildland fire as those fires that move across a landscape, which can include prescribed fire and wildfire. Not all prescribed fires have low complexity and low-intensity fire behaviors, and not all wildfires have high complexity and high-intensity fire behaviors. Wildfires, forest fires, bushfires, or wildland fires are all terms for unplanned fires. These can start from natural or human-caused ignitions.

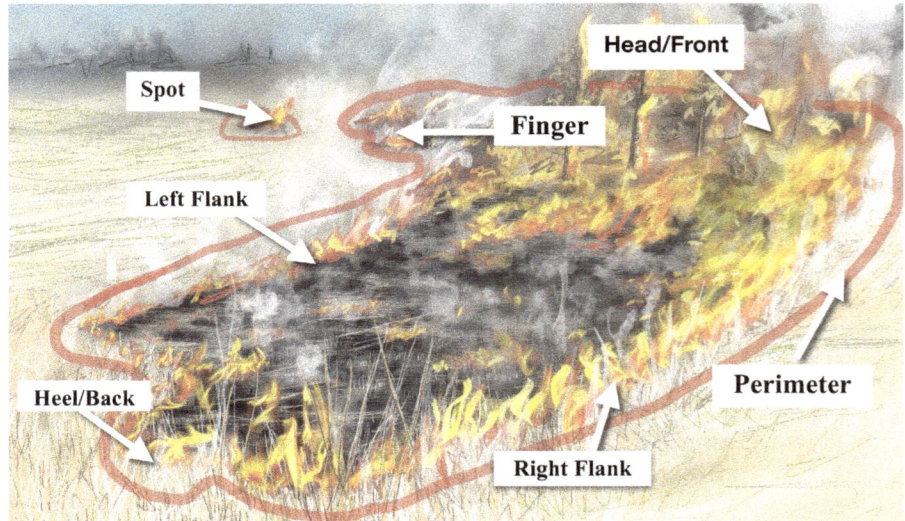

Prescribed burns, cultural burning, and agricultural burning are all types of planned fires. Journaling a fire that is moving across the landscape should include common fire behavior terms and elements. Observing fire behavior also helps clarify observations made in the previous chapters related to weather, topography, and fuels. Further in the chapter, I will share ideas for journaling prescribed fire and wildfire.

Fire Anatomy

A landscape or wildland fire is typically described as a single entity or event, which will have a mix of fire behaviors occurring within the overall perimeter. In the United States, wildfires are typically named by the location they started, and prescribed burns have names and/or numbers associated with a burn treatment unit. Fire activities and behavior are typically defined within elements of fire anatomy.

The National Wildfire Coordinating Group defines fire anatomy as follows:

- **Head:** the portion of the fire with advancing fire behaviors and driven by the wind.

- **Flank:** lateral sides of the fire with mixed fire behavior traits.

- **Heel:** back of the fire with backing fire behaviors.

- **Finger:** an elongated area of fire stretched out from the main fire.

- **Spot:** a separate fire started from embers blown from the main fire.

Fire Behaviors

The National Wildfire Coordinating Group has defined the basic and general fire behaviors based on the location within the head, flank, or heel of a fire. The head of a fire is where you'll observe more intense and faster advancing fire behavior. The flank of the fire has what is called lateral fire behavior, with a combination of advancing and backing fire behaviors. The heel of the fire has what is called backing fire behavior, which is slower moving and has lower heat intensities.

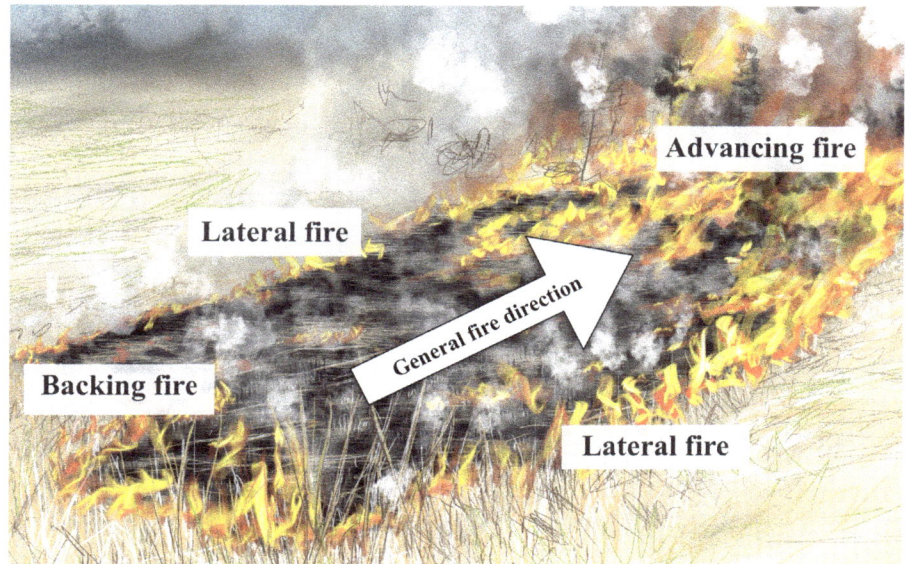

Fire Measurements

There are numerous fire measurements including fire size, flame length, rate of spread, and fire intensity. In the United States, fire size is measured in acres and is based on the burned and active fire area within an overall fire containment perimeter. When you see information about fire size, it does not necessarily indicate the exact number of acres burned. There are often many unburned patches within the fire perimeter. Fire containment is a term used in wildfire management to describe the percentage of active fire that has been contained within the perimeter.

Flame Length

As fires move across the landscape, it can be challenging to calculate flame lengths, but you can estimate for journaling purposes by comparing the flame heights to nearby objects, such as trees, or using biometrics. There are several flame areas that you'll need to know to estimate flame length. There is a flame attachment area, which includes the flame depth into the surface materials. There are intermittent flame attachment areas as the fire progresses in a forward pulsing pattern, and then there is a lifted flame area. At the lifted flame area, you can measure flame height and length, which may be a different number if the flame is leaning. Fire pulsation and flame interactions can have strong influences on fire behavior (Maynard 2013). See the illustration on the next page.

Flame Measurements

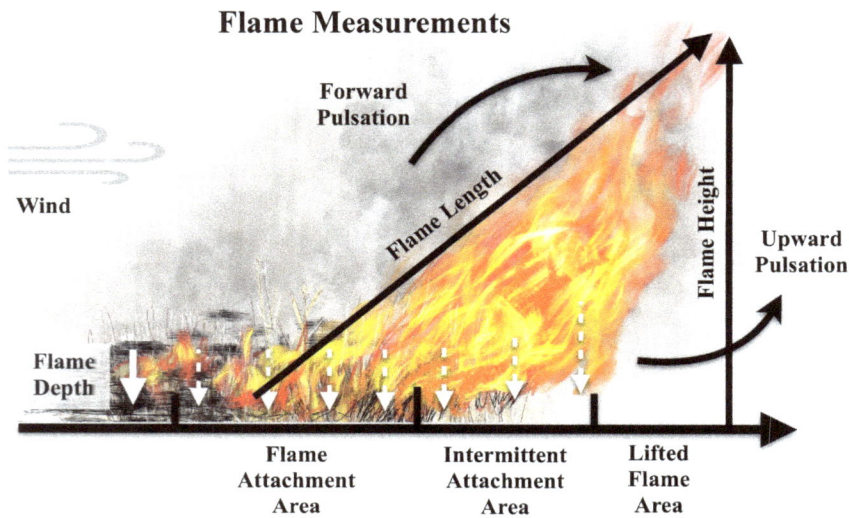

Forward Pulsation

Wind

Flame Length

Flame Height

Upward Pulsation

Flame Depth

Flame Attachment Area

Intermittent Attachment Area

Lifted Flame Area

Fire Intensity

At a generalized scale, we can estimate fire intensity (level of heat) and severity (level of impact) by using surface fire flame length estimates. Flames below 4 feet in height have a lower intensity, flames between 4 and 8 feet have a moderate intensity, and flames above 8 feet in height have a high fire intensity. Crown fire flames are about double the surface flame intensities. I'll talk more about fire types, like crown fire, further in this chapter.

Average Fire Rate of Spread

1.1-6.3 mph

.13-.30 mph

Fire Rate of Spread

A term used to describe and measure the speed at which a fire travels is called the fire rate of spread (ROS). There are mathematical formulas and software programs that can estimate ROS based on the mix of topography, weather, and fuels variables. For our nature journaling purposes, I like to use speed comparisons and metaphors to help give a general sense of fire ROS. I researched different animal speeds to compare with average fire rates of spread, as described by the National Wildfire Coordinating Group.

I found that a slowly ambling tortoise moves at about 0.13 to 0.30 mph, which is comparable to backing and creeping fire patterns. A sea turtle glides through the ocean at a speed of about 1.1 to 6.3 mph, which is comparable to advancing fire behavior patterns.

Fire Shape

Origin Area Shape

When a fire is first ignited, it burns in a circular pattern until the wind or slope stretches it into a different shape. The faster the wind speed, the more stretched the fire becomes.

Fire Shaped by Wind Speed

The illustration below visualizes the change in fire shape for different wind speeds based on the National Wildfire Group's fire behavior training materials. When wind directions change, the fire shape can stretch into different directions, with branching fingers. A similar effect occurs on slopes, but typically spreads in an upside-down triangle shape, starting narrow and spreading wider as the fire moves upslope.

Visualizing Landscape Fire

Before I describe the different fire types and their associated behaviors, let me share some ideas for visualizing fire on the landscape. Once a fire starts to spread over varying topography and fuels, the fire patterns will begin to look different. The fire anatomy illustration should have given you some idea of the shapes transforming with fingers and spot fires. In general, these fire patterns might have an overall circular shape, wavy stringy patterns, or appear as

Note- the size of fires are not to scale. Faster winds would cause larger fires.

Legend

Fire shape: width x length ratio

Fire point of origin

Wind & fire direction

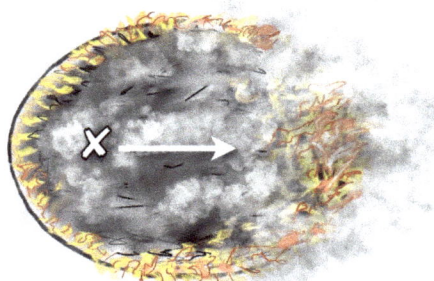

Shape from a 1 mph wind

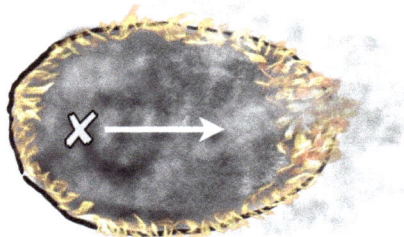

Shape from a 3 mph wind

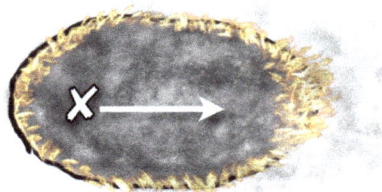

Shape from a 5 mph wind

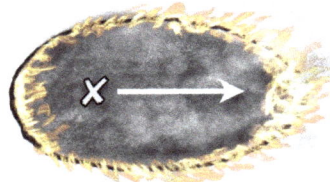

Shape from a 7 mph wind

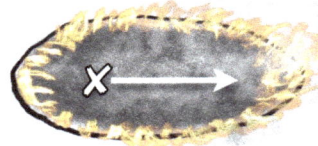

Shape from a 9 mph wind

Shape from an 11 mph wind

Shape from a 13 mph wind

Shape from a 15 mph wind

patches or pockets of fire. Sometimes, the flames are barely discernible from a large glowing area. The glowing fire area may be observed behind trees or in dark conditions. Firelight can also be reflected onto neighboring trees, in the smoke column, and in the sky. In the illustrated examples, I used watercolors and colored pencils to create some of the sketches and a mix of colored pencil, watercolors, and acrylic paints in others. You can explore a mix of art mediums. For visualizing my fire observations in a journal, I use small-sized sketches to reduce the time spent conveying the information. It is more important to describe and visualize important elements of fire behavior, so don't worry about creating art. You should also include some vegetation elements in your sketches so that you can associate the fuel types with the flame heights. Try to leave enough space in your journal to write notes and add measurements about the fire size and behaviors.

Firelight Distance

Another type of fire observation is to look at how far away firelight can be seen under different conditions and landscapes. This will require you to take into account how far you can see by practicing with observations measured at different distances, as outlined in Chapter 3: Topography. The average person on flat ground can see distant mountains from about 100 miles away during clear conditions (Kahn/NASA 1996).

Circular Patterns

Wavy Patterns

Patchy Patterns

Glowing Backgrounds

Glowing Foregrounds

Dark Backgrounds

At night, you can also develop a very general sense of distance to fires using the following observations from Worldbuilding Stack Exchange 2017:

•The light from a wildfire or prescribed fire may be seen shining between trees from 1-2 miles away.

•The light from a wildfire/prescribed fire may be seen on clouds or reflected in smoke from about 3-10 miles away.

•The glowing light from a wildfire/prescribed fire may be seen glowing in the sky and across the landscape from about 10-20 miles away.

Fire Types & Behaviors

There are some basic fire types and associated behaviors defined by the National Wildfire Coordinating Group that we can observe during prescribed burns and wildfires based on where the fire is burning within the landscape. These behaviors are dominated by the fuels.

Ground Fires—Ground fires smolder beneath the ground's surface in the deep layers of duff and roots.

- **Smoldering**—No active flaming and occurs below the surface. Smoldering occurs in ground fires and at the end phase of surface fires, after the flames have passed through the area.

Surface Fires—Surface fires are how most fires spread through the carrying fuels, as discussed in Chapter 4: Fire Fuels. Surface fires can have varying behaviors, including the following:

- **Smoldering**—same as a ground fire.

- **Creeping**—A slow and disorganized surface fire pattern, with slow to no forward rates of spread. Occurs in low or light wind conditions, and flames are not pushed and carried by winds. Flame lengths typically burn at a low intensity and are four feet high or less. The flames are typically lighter yellow and orange in color.

- **Backing**—A slow but organized surface fire pattern, with flames moving slowly against the direction of the wind. This pattern can also be observed at the heel of a fire. Flames are typically one to four feet high and burn with a lower intensity. Flames are typically lighter yellow and orange in color.

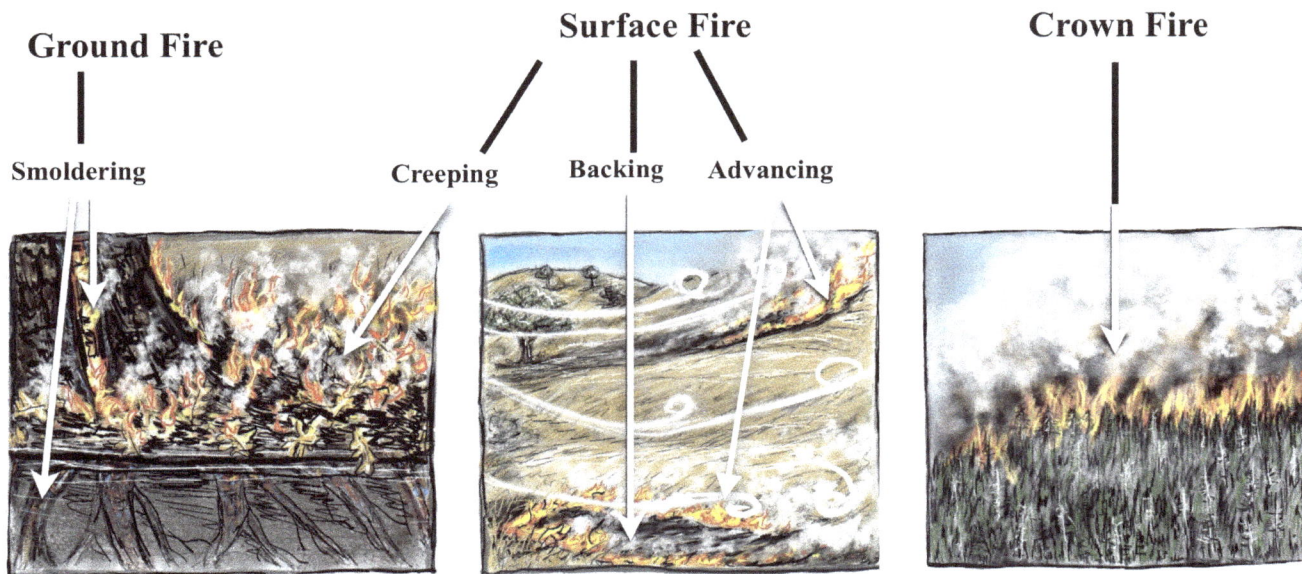

Ground Fire
Smoldering

Surface Fire
Creeping   Backing   Advancing

Crown Fire

- **Advancing**—An organized and moderate to fast-moving surface fire pattern, with flames advancing with the wind. The flames are typically four to eight feet high and burn with a low to high intensity. Flames can be a mix of colors with bright white and yellow areas lower to the attachment area, and orange to red flames depending on the fuel types.

Intensifying Fire Behaviors

Intensifying fire behaviors are defined by the National Wildfire Coordinating Group and are typically driven by a combination of fuel conditions, weather, and topography.

Intensifying Surface Fires

Running—Running fire behavior is a type of advancing fire and occurs when a fire spreads rapidly within a well-defined area of the fire's head.

Torching—Surface fires frequently burn individual or a couple of trees, which is called torching.

Spotting—Spotting occurs when there are ember materials large enough to hold heat but small enough to be lifted and carried in the wind into vegetation outside of the main fire area. These ember materials can be cones, seed pods, leaves, and branches.

Flare-up—Flare-ups often occur in surface fires where there are heavy pockets of vegetation. Large flare-ups and crown fires can create spot fires 15 to 30 miles away.

Crowning

When surface fires burn into ladder fuels, like tall shrubs and low tree branches, the fire can move into the tree crowns. See the illustration on the previous page. When only a few trees burn, it is called a passive crown fire. When the surface fire is intense and/or burning on steep slopes, the surface fire can ignite the tree crowns; this is called an active crown fire. When tree crowns are burning independently from the surface fire, they are called an independent crown fire. Independent tree crowning happens when tree crowns are close together and the fire can move from tree to tree without moving up from the surface. These are more intense fires that can have flame lengths 20 to 30 feet or more above the tree crowns. As surface and/or crown fires burn, ember materials can be blown out away from the main fire front and cause spot fires.

Fire Whirls

Fire whirls are an intensifying fire behavior and phenomena you may observe. These are tall rotating columns of gas, smoke, and flames and flow like water spinning down a drain. Fire whirls are far more common than fire tornadoes, although many news stories may call a large fire whirl a fire tornado. Various sources say that fire whirls commonly

range from 30 to 100 feet high and 1 to 500 feet in diameter. Occasionally, fire whirls can reach 3,000 feet or more in height.

Fire whirls cause spinning and high-speed winds and can pull trees and shrubs out from their roots. Fire whirls are an indicator of atmospheric instability and erratic fire behavior. Fire whirls can occur in different areas within a fire. They can be centered over the burning area, downwind of a burning area, and over open areas adjacent to an asymmetric burning area.

Extreme Fire Behaviors

There are more significant and dangerous fire behaviors that you will not likely observe closely unless you are a firefighter. These typically occur in larger wildfires and are difficult to observe at a distance. There are smoke observations I'll share a little further down that can help identify these fire behaviors. These fire behaviors are driven by a combination of fuels, weather, topography, and fire intensity.

Eruptions

Fire eruptions occur as a fires grows in size and the intensity and interacts with

topographic element cause more extreme fire behaviors. Fire eruptions typically occur on slopes over 20% to 30%, where the convective heat and soot particles in smoke can dry and ignite the vegetation upslope. Whenever there is a significant change and intensifying of fire behavior, it is a watch-out situation for firefighter safety.

Vorticity-Channeled-Lateral Fire

One of the severe and often rare fire behaviors described in Australia is what is called vorticity channeled or lateral fire behavior (Filkov 2019). This fire behavior is somewhat like an eruption but happens when a fire is passing by a steep-sloped canyon. The lateral or flank side of the forward-moving fire hits the steep slope with channeled vorticity (spinning) winds, which causes the flames to spin up and erupt into extreme fire behaviors. In the smoke section, I describe more about the smoke observations associated with this fire behavior.

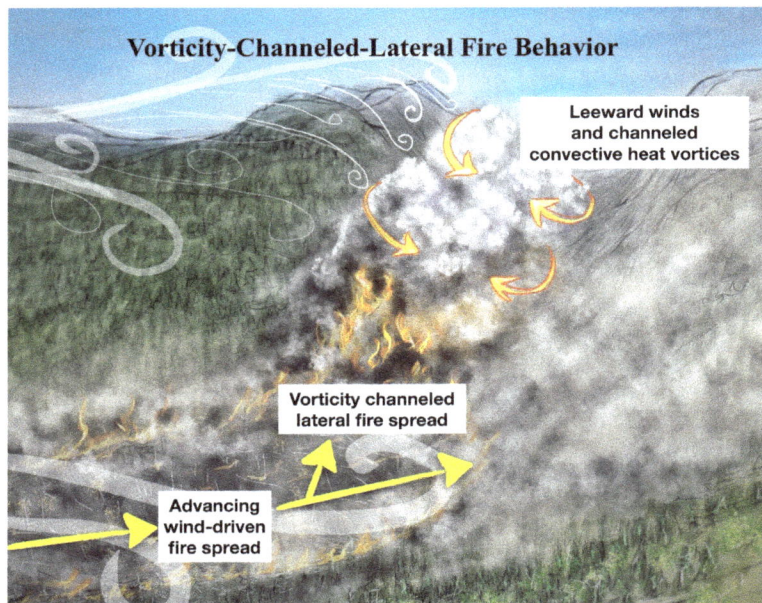

Vorticity-Channeled-Lateral Fire Behavior

Leeward winds and channeled convective heat vortices

Vorticity channeled lateral fire spread

Advancing wind-driven fire spread

Fire Storms

The National Oceanic and Atmospheric Administration defines a firestorm as a condition that occurs when the heat and smoke from a large intense wildfire create its own weather. This fire behavior is driven more by the smoke plume and its self-created weather. As the fire consumes vegetation, the moisture from plants is carried high into the atmosphere with the smoke where the cooler temperatures transform the moisture into a cloud. These are called pyrocumulus clouds, which can become a pyrocumulonimbus cloud that produces lightning and extreme winds. There are additional observations included in the smoke section.

Pyrocumulonimbus

Column collapse

Ember Storms

Any fire can blow embers out into adjacent vegetation and cause a spot fire, but an ember storm occurs when a large smoke plume and winds blow massive amounts of embers miles away from the fire. Ember storms are especially dangerous when a pyrocumulonimbus column collapses and embers are strewn down with strong downdrafting winds.

Conflagrations & Mega Fires

A fire conflagration is commonly defined as a large fire that has significant impacts on humans and natural resources. These are often wildfires occurring in the wildland-urban interface where human infrastructure is intermixed with natural vegetation. A mega fire is defined by the U.S. Interagency Fire Center as a wildfire that burns more than 100,000 acres of land.

Fire Tornadoes

Not all experts agree on the definition of a fire tornado. I have heard meteorologists define them as rare events that dominate fire behavior in a large area. Fire tornadoes, like fire storms, can create their own weather system, which is concentrated over the vortex. They can average 100 to 1,000 feet in diameter.

These can burn vegetation several times faster than non-rotating fire. One study identified several morphologies as indicators of fire-generated tornado-strength vortices (Lareau 2022). This included embedded vortices within entwined smoke columns (a rotating and counter-rotating column) and shedding vortices that detach downwind from the fire, pendant to a leaning smoke column. This study associated wind-flow reversals in weather systems and a number of smoke plume/column indicators as triggers to these fire behaviors. I have additional smoke observations associated with fire tornadoes further into the chapter.

Smoke Observations

I won't delve into the elements that make up smoke, which was discussed somewhat in the fire combustion section. We are focusing on smoke and general air quality observations to support awareness and journaling practices. Smoke comes in many forms and colors. The appearance of smoke changes based on a number of factors, including the size of smoke particles, the concentration of smoke, angle of light, and perspective you have while observing smoke (Junghenn 2020).

The size of smoke particles will change how sunlight refracts and absorbs light. Large carbon particles will give smoke a dark gray, brown, or black color. This happens because large carbon particles absorb more blue and green light waves from the sun, while the red and yellow light waves are refracted outward. Smaller smoke particles have less surface area and absorb and refract less light.

The angle of the sun will also change the appearance of smoke, just as it does with clouds. Smoke may appear white or gray during the day and may look pink or orange at sunrise or sunset. Smoke viewed from above, like in aerial photos, will often appear white as more light waves are reflected compared to the bottom portion of the smoke plume, which can appear gray or black. The radiant light from fire can also reflect and glow within the lower levels of smoke, giving it an orange-colored tinge.

Smoke Color Indicators

White smoke can indicate high moisture levels or steam from drying vegetation and where the initial fire spread is occurring.

White smoke can also indicate where water is being applied during suppression efforts and or lighter fuel types, like grass, are burning.

Tan and light brown smoke can indicate heavier fuels being consumed by the fire and when overall air quality conditions are poor.

Orange smoke can indicate similar conditions as described with tan and brown smoke, but the appearance is also affected by the angle of the sun. In Australia, orange smoke has been associated with vorticity channeled fire behavior at the point where lateral fire is hitting the steep canyon and the flames and smoke have become entrained with the vortex winds (McRae 2009).

Dark brown and black smoke can indicate concentrations of live fuels, especially waxy and oily vegetation and human-made materials.

Dark smoke may indicate a crown fire. Dark smoke is also an indicator of larger carbon particles and higher concentrations of smoke. Smoke plumes often appear darker at the base, where heavier particles are located but also where less sunlight is available to refract.

Smoke Volume & Shape Indicators

The National Wildfire Coordinating Group fire behavior training materials identified the following smoke plume color, consistency, volume, and shape indicators of fire behavior.

- Thin smoke consistency can indicate light fuels and low-intensity fire behavior.

- Dense smoke consistency can indicate heavy fuels and higher intensity fire behavior.

Smoke Shape Indicators

Smoke is often referenced as a smoke plume or a smoke column. Smoke plumes are the gases, smoke, and debris that rise from a fire. A smoke column is the large smoke plume that is entrained with the high-intensity convective heat column from the fire. Drift smoke is another term used to define smoke. It is the lighter smoke that is drifting away from a smoke plume or column. I used the 2009 draft Interpretation of Smoke Plume poster by Rick McRae as a reference to create the illustration on the next page to help with smoke plume journaling. The shape of smoke plumes and columns changes based on fire intensity, wind speed, and atmospheric conditions (stability or instability).

Small & Simple Smoke Plumes

- Rising, billowing, and drifting smoke from a fire.

- Light low-hanging smoke billowing from a fire can indicate light fuels, low-intensity fire behavior, and a stable atmosphere.

- Tall and thin smoke plumes can indicate light fuels, lower intensity fire behavior, and an unstable atmosphere.

Large Smoke Plumes & Columns

- Smoke plumes entrained within the convective heat column.

- Large smoke columns can indicate an unstable atmosphere and high-intensity fire behavior. It can also indicate a dry convective smoke column.

- Large smoke columns, with a cloud forming at the top, or just downwind, can indicate a moist convective column and an active pyrocumulus cloud. This is an early indicator of possible pyrocumulonimbus development and a firestorm.

- A large smoke column with towering clouds at the top indicates a building pyrocumulus cloud and higher potential for pyrocumulonimbus cloud and a firestorm.

- A large smoke column with an anvil-shaped cloud on top indicates a pyrocumulonimbus cloud and extreme plume-driven fire behavior. When a portion of the cloud starts to drop and dissipate, it is a sign of a column collapse and an area of extreme and erratic fire behavior.

- Large smoke columns, leaning dramatically, can indicate strong and or channeled winds.

Weather-Driven Smoke Plumes & Fire Behavior

Light/Simple Plume

Strong Leaning Plume

Strong Dry Plume

Low Drift Smoke/Plume

Convection Column & Smoke Plume-Driven Fire Behavior

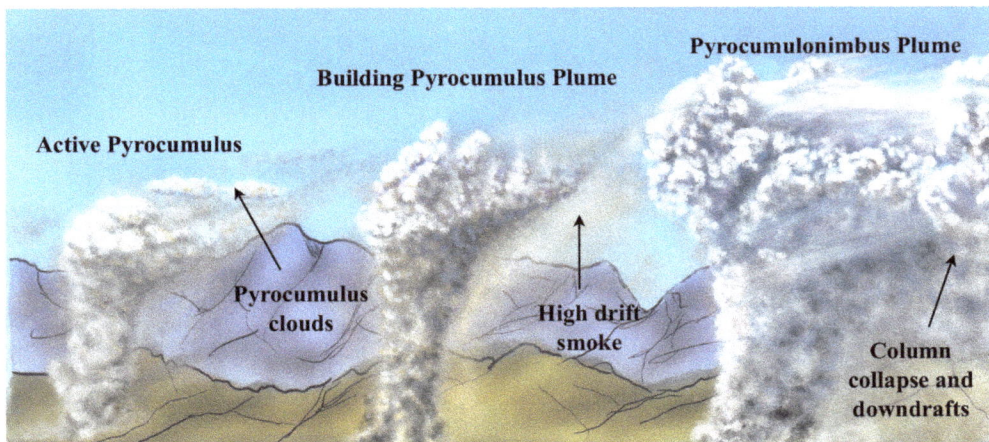

Active Pyrocumulus

Building Pyrocumulus Plume

Pyrocumulonimbus Plume

Pyrocumulus clouds

High drift smoke

Column collapse and downdrafts

Drift Smoke

- Smoke drifting away from a smoke column.

- No drift smoke associated with a smoke column can indicate an initial fire run (spreading) and an unstable atmosphere.

- Drift smoke from the top or side of a smoke column can indicate the direction high winds are blowing.

181

Seasonal Variation in Smoke Height

There are seasonal differences in the smoke mixing height based on changes in atmospheric pressure and seasonal temperatures. The illustration below visualizes these differences.

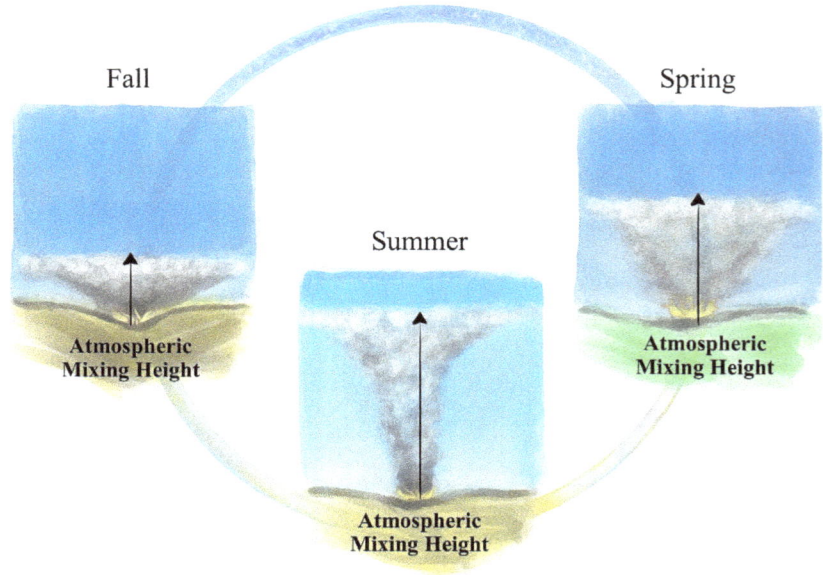

Atmospheric Changes, Smoke Plumes & Fire Intensity

The smoke plume size and shape will vary based on a mix of atmospheric conditions, solar exposure, and wind speeds. There is a big tradeoff with conditions that influence fire behavior and smoke dispersal. The more unstable the atmosphere, the worse the conditions are for fire behavior, but the better the conditions for smoke dispersal and air quality.

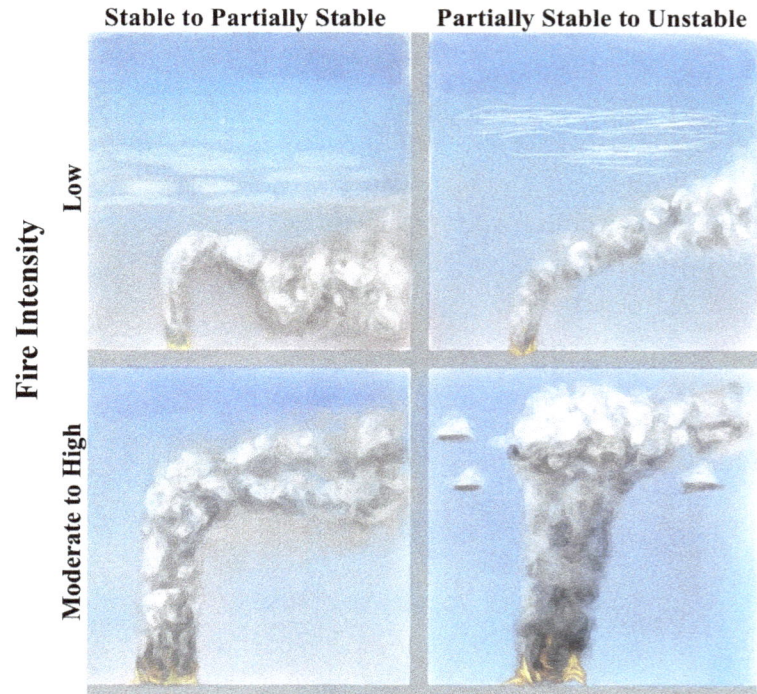

Smoke Plume Shape
Based Atmospheric Stability, Solar Radiation & Wind Speed

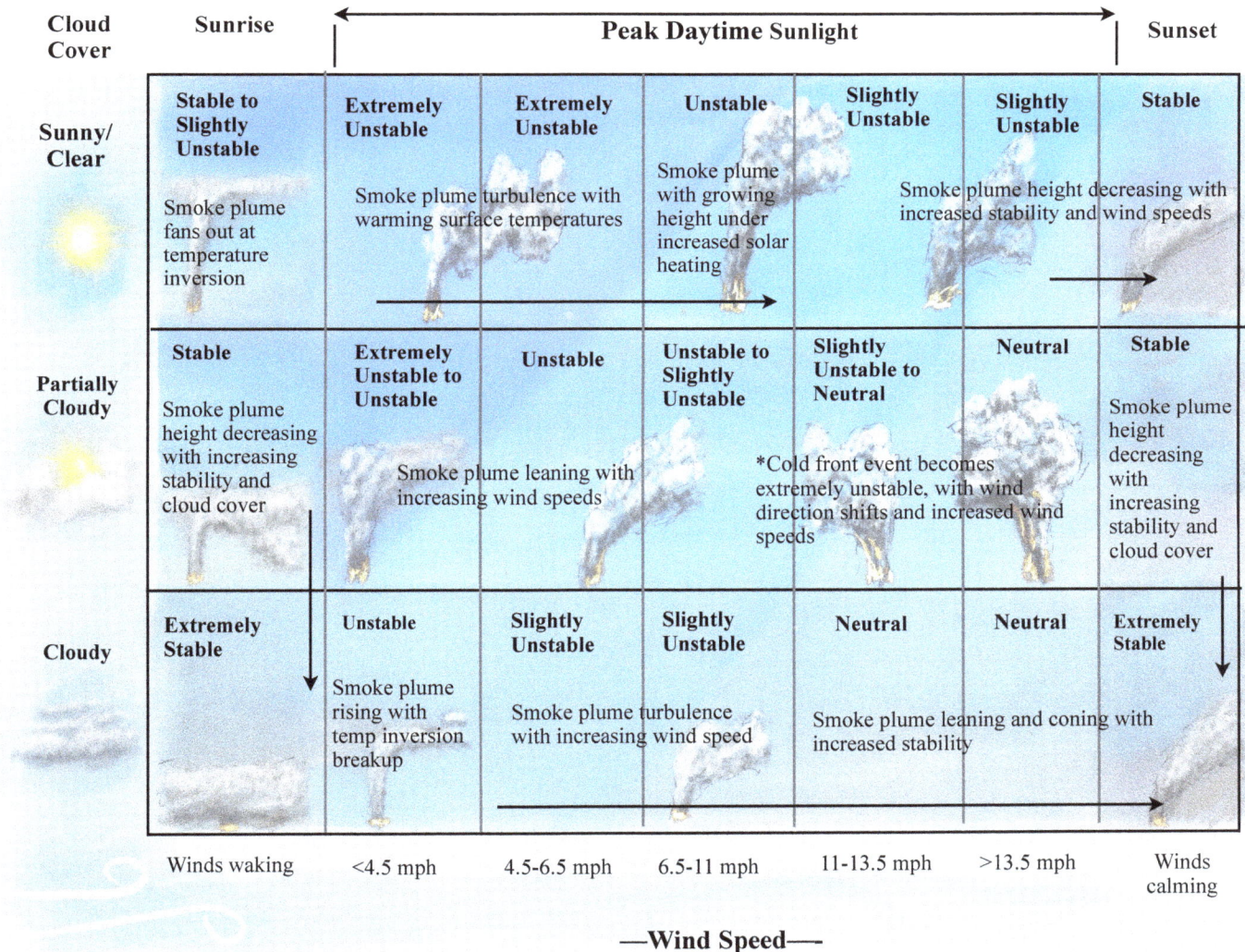

Cloud Cover	Sunrise	Peak Daytime Sunlight					Sunset
Sunny/ Clear	**Stable to Slightly Unstable** Smoke plume fans out at temperature inversion	**Extremely Unstable** Smoke plume turbulence with warming surface temperatures	**Extremely Unstable**	**Unstable** Smoke plume with growing height under increased solar heating	**Slightly Unstable**	**Slightly Unstable** Smoke plume height decreasing with increased stability and wind speeds	**Stable**
Partially Cloudy	**Stable** Smoke plume height decreasing with increasing stability and cloud cover	**Extremely Unstable to Unstable** Smoke plume leaning with increasing wind speeds	**Unstable**	**Unstable to Slightly Unstable** *Cold front event becomes extremely unstable, with wind direction shifts and increased wind speeds	**Slightly Unstable to Neutral**	**Neutral**	**Stable** Smoke plume height decreasing with increasing stability and cloud cover
Cloudy	**Extremely Stable**	**Unstable** Smoke plume rising with temp inversion breakup	**Slightly Unstable** Smoke plume turbulence with increasing wind speed	**Slightly Unstable**	**Neutral** Smoke plume leaning and coning with increased stability	**Neutral**	**Extremely Stable**
	Winds waking	<4.5 mph	4.5-6.5 mph	6.5-11 mph	11-13.5 mph	>13.5 mph	Winds calming

—Wind Speed—

Each square indicates the atmospheric stability rating based on cloudiness, solar radiation (temperature) and wind speed. The smoke plume illustration in each square is one of several potential smoke scenarios based on the aforementioned conditions. The topography, fuels and fire intensity will also influence the smoke plume size and shape.

Journaling Smoke Observations

There are many approaches to journaling about smoke. You can sketch smoke spiraling from a single flame, note differences in attributes between larger smoke plumes, and analyze smoke from satellite images. The illustration below presents one option for visualizing important elements within a complex smoke plume and convection column. The example is from the 2018 Carr Fire tornado. In this case, two large smoke columns were located near each other in steep terrain, and the winds bent and twisted the two columns together into a spinning fire tornado. It was challenging to discern the base of each smoke column, but there was a dark gap area in the middle. Additionally, two different areas in the pyrocumulonimbus cloud top where wind shear was obvious, likely influenced by the spinning columns.

To journal this type of observation, note and sketch the shape of the terrain and the location of the smoke plume and/or column within the landscape. Sketch the

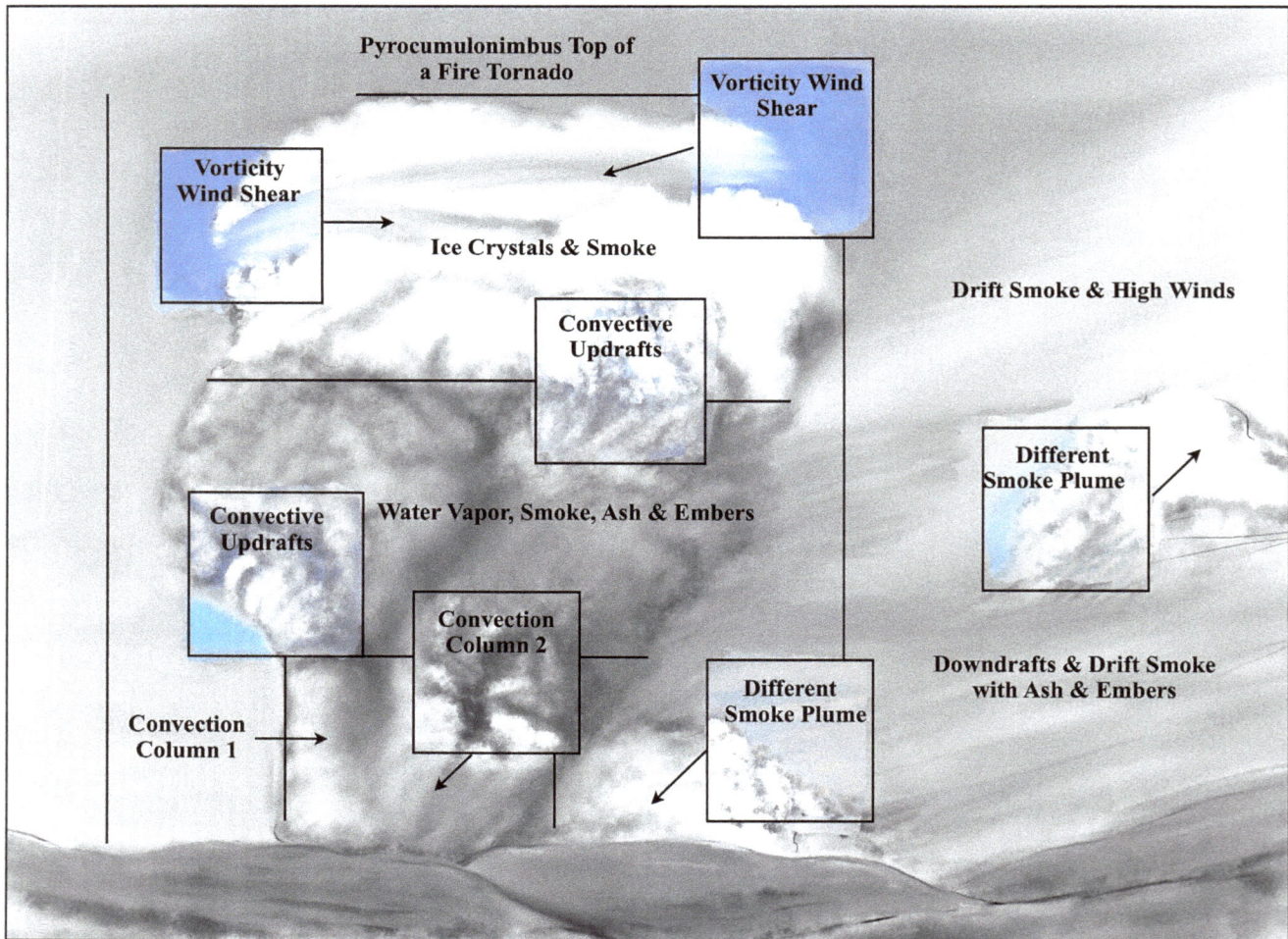

Pyrocumulonimbus Top of a Fire Tornado

Vorticity Wind Shear

Vorticity Wind Shear

Ice Crystals & Smoke

Drift Smoke & High Winds

Convective Updrafts

Different Smoke Plume

Convective Updrafts

Water Vapor, Smoke, Ash & Embers

Convection Column 2

Downdrafts & Drift Smoke with Ash & Embers

Convection Column 1

Different Smoke Plume

shape and size of the smoke, using landscape features to help relate the size and proportions.

Observe interesting areas within the plume that may indicate changes in smoke consistency, color, and shape. Create small boxes over those areas of the smoke plume and use higher levels of detail and color. Add additional lines and arrows to label and accentuate the height and width of different portions of the plume. One thing I noticed while sketching this was the differences in the sky color by the height of the smoke plume/column. The top area is where the smoke plume becomes a pyrocumulonimbus cloud top and punches through the natural mixing height (temperature change). The darker blue sky indicates cooler air conditions. You can use the following tips for sketching a large smoke plume and column.

Smoke Plume Sketch

Step 1: Use a pencil to sketch the overall outline of the landscape and smoke plume. Add cloud-shaped billows or puffs to fill in more of the form. To create the billowy shapes, use a mix of big and small curved lines and half-circles along the top side of the smoke puffs—the smoke is billowing upward.

Step 2: Lightly fill in the sky and darker areas of the smoke with heavier pencil marks. In a pencil or pen drawing, I like to use angled lines to give a more dynamic look to the sky.

Step 3: Continue shading with pencil or pen to accentuate and build up the depth and form. Note that the smoke is typically darker lower in the smoke column and on the shadowed sides of billowy shapes that are opposite the direction of the sun.

Smoke Plume Watercolor Painting

Step 1: Sketch a simple outline of the landscape and smoke plume. Apply a light wash of orange and brown watercolor to most of the smoke plume, but leave white areas along the top portions of billowy smoke forms. For a tall and large smoke plume, like a pyrocumulonimbus, the top will have more cool cloud-like colors, and the lower portions will have more browns and grays.

Step 2: Add more gray, black, and blue or purple watercolor to the darker areas on the undersides of smoke billows, especially along the column area, to give depth to the smoke.

Step 3: Add more black to shadowed areas and near the base of the plume. Add orange and red flames to the base of the smoke column, if visible, and some orange to where the fire is reflecting in the smoke. Add white to the smoke edges and areas receiving direct light from the sun.

I have also utilized diagrams for various spatial and temporal dimensions to illustrate how much and how far smoke is carried over on a large geographic scale. Another approach is to compare the smoke from different types of fires, which can be as simple as symbolic visuals like the smoke jar illustrations in the example below. I encourage you to explore simple and creative methods for visualizing your smoke observations.

Comparative Smoke Journaling

I also enjoy conveying smoke observations over time, which can be achieved by creating a time series of small sketches from on-site and/or online webcams, such as AlterWildfire.

Smoke Over Time Periods

Live Webcam Smoke Sketches

Multiple Smoke Plumes Over Multiple States

Wildfire Smoke

Prescribed Fire Smoke

Smoke & Air Quality

It is important to include observations about air quality when journaling about smoke. To enhance your situational awareness, it is helpful to develop a visual sense of changing air quality conditions over time. One approach is to create a series of small sketches of a landscape with known distances.

There are numerous websites, like AirNow, that provide continuous air quality information and recommendations for human health. By integrating air quality information with your distance observations, you can develop a sense of air quality through visual indicators. In the following journaling examples, I have utilized the Environmental Protection Agency's national air quality guide and a few distance measures to facilitate this approach and is outlined in the graphic on the next page.

Air Quality Observation Tips

• Determine the limits of your visual range within normal air quality conditions and by looking for features at known distances. The visibility range is the point at which even the high-contrast features (buildings and trees) totally disappear.

• Face away from the sun when making your visual range observations.

• During smoke and air quality events, use the visual range indicators on the next page to estimate air quality conditions and follow safety protocols.

Air Quality Sketches

Begin by creating a tall rectangular box for your sketch with small marks along the edge to differentiate high, middle, and low levels of the sky. Add a simple or symbolic landscape at the bottom to provide scale. Start with very light pencil lines to

shade in the sky, starting a little way up from the landscape to allow for a lighter horizon skyline.

Gradually add heavier and thicker pencil lines toward the top of the sky. Use water and a paintbrush or a water-brush to smooth out the pencil lines. Begin at the lower level and work your way up, using the brush to spread the pencil lines around and smooth out the sky shading. You can also add notes about the distance between hills or portions of the landscape to help differentiate stable and unstable atmospheres, which have different visibility levels.

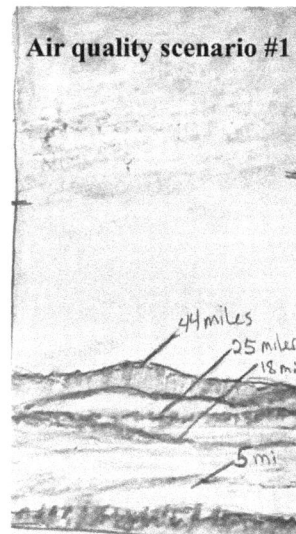

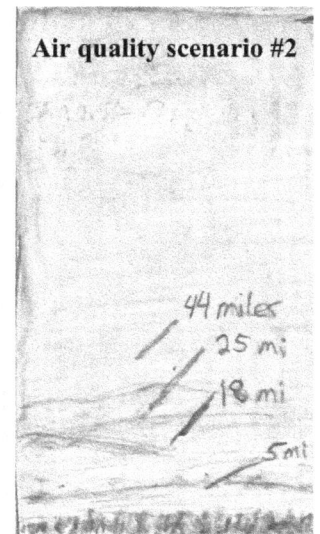

Air quality scenario #1

Air quality scenario #2

Another approach to journaling smoke and air quality includes a sketch using visual range to interpret air quality conditions and to create diagrams and simple sketches for observations of the sky/air color.

Wildfire Smoke & Air Quality Observations In Ridgefield, Washington

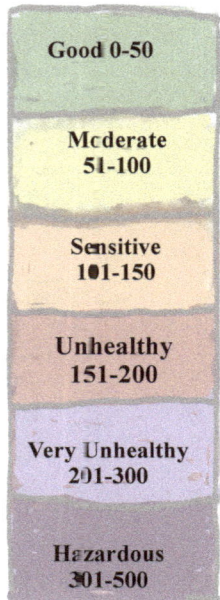

Visual Range Observations
September 12, 2020

Good 0-50

Moderate 51-100

Sensitive 101-150

Unhealthy 151-200

Very Unhealthy 201-300

Hazardous 301-500

2 miles

800 feet

50 feet

300 AQI

4 Day Sky Observations

Day 1: Gray-blue skies, with a smoky haze

Day 2: Gray-blue skies, with a distant fuzzy brown smoke plume

Day 3: Low-lying brown smoke and gray-blue skies

Day 4: Mostly brown skies

Visual Range Indicators of Air Quality

Good: landscape features observable 10 to 100 miles away.

Moderate: landscape features observable within 6 to 9 miles with moderate to minimized outdoor activities.

Unhealthy for Sensitive People: landscape features observable between 3 to 5 miles. Minimize or avoid outdoor activity.

Unhealthy: landscape features observable between 1.5 to 2.75 miles. Minimize outdoor activity and follow air quality guidance.

Very Unhealthy: landscape features observable between 1 to 1.25 miles. Same as above.

Hazardous: landscape features observable .75 miles or less. Same as above.

Prescribed Fire

The terms "prescribed fire" and "controlled burn" are used interchangeably to describe the planned use of fire to reduce hazardous levels of vegetation, manage wildlife habitat, and enhance ecosystem health. "Cultural burning" refers to the indigenous use of fire to achieve various objectives, including the application of traditional ecological knowledge.

While both prescribed fire and cultural burning may employ similar strategies, cultural burning often utilizes more traditional tools, such as tree pitch torches and branches, to ignite fires. Additionally, cultural burning frequently integrates traditional nature-based cues to help form and guide the application of fire, such as the phenology of certain plants and animals. There may also be burn objectives linked to traditional practices, such as managing vegetation for basket-weaving materials. Specific information or tips for journaling cultural burns are not included here, as the traditional ecological knowledge is something that each tribe would need to approve and guide. Many of the fire environment observations in this book are applicable to prescribed and cultural burning.

Burn Prescriptions

Burn prescriptions are developed based on local fuel groups, topography, weather predictions, and burning objectives. Hazard fuels objectives often focus on reducing a percentage of the fuel bed and understory vegetation, while habitat objectives may focus on burning away invasive grasses or creating more open areas with more nutritious vegetation (e.g., young/less woody shrubs and grass). The time of year, time of day, weather conditions, and burning techniques are adapted to meet the burning objectives. A Go/No Go Checklist is one of the planning components in each prescribed burn, reviewed prior to ignitions to determine if the weather and fuel conditions will still meet burning objectives. The weather conditions for each prescribed burn are specific to each location, but around the United States, the weather prescriptions are typically as follows: air temperatures between 68° and 90°F, relative humidity levels of 25% and 80%, and wind speeds below 10 mph (Fast/New Hampshire Cooperative Extension).

Prescribed Fire Anatomy

Prescribed fires are typically planned within burn units of various sizes based on staffing support and management goals for the area. Boundary lines or firebreaks are used to help contain the fire within the planned unit. Roads, bulldozer lines, and trails are often utilized as firebreaks/unit boundaries. Natural barriers like open water and large rock outcroppings are also used as fuel breaks. Fire practitioners sometimes use shovels and other hand tools to clear a "handline" along with the boundary line. This handline is a strip of cleared vegetation down to mineral soil, which can be 1.5 to 3 times as wide as the vegetation height. For grassland conditions, the scraped portion of the handline is generally 1 to 3 feet wide, while forested area handlines may be 20 to 30 feet wide, with a 3 to 4-foot-deep scrape into the soil. A "wet line" is a similar-sized strip of area where the vegetation is sprayed with water from a fire engine hose or other apparatus. A "blackline" is a strip of burned vegetation typically started on one side of the unit, used to create a safe starting point for fire ignitions, which may follow various tactical approaches based on burn objectives. The blackline is often on the lee side of the burn unit, so the fire burns against the wind (backing fire) and can be used as a backfire, which is intended as a starting line for fire spread. A "head fire" is created on the opposite side of the burn unit, where fire ignitions burn with the wind and into the backfire. All of these tactics are employed to keep the prescribed fire within the planned burn area.

Prescribed Fire Anatomy

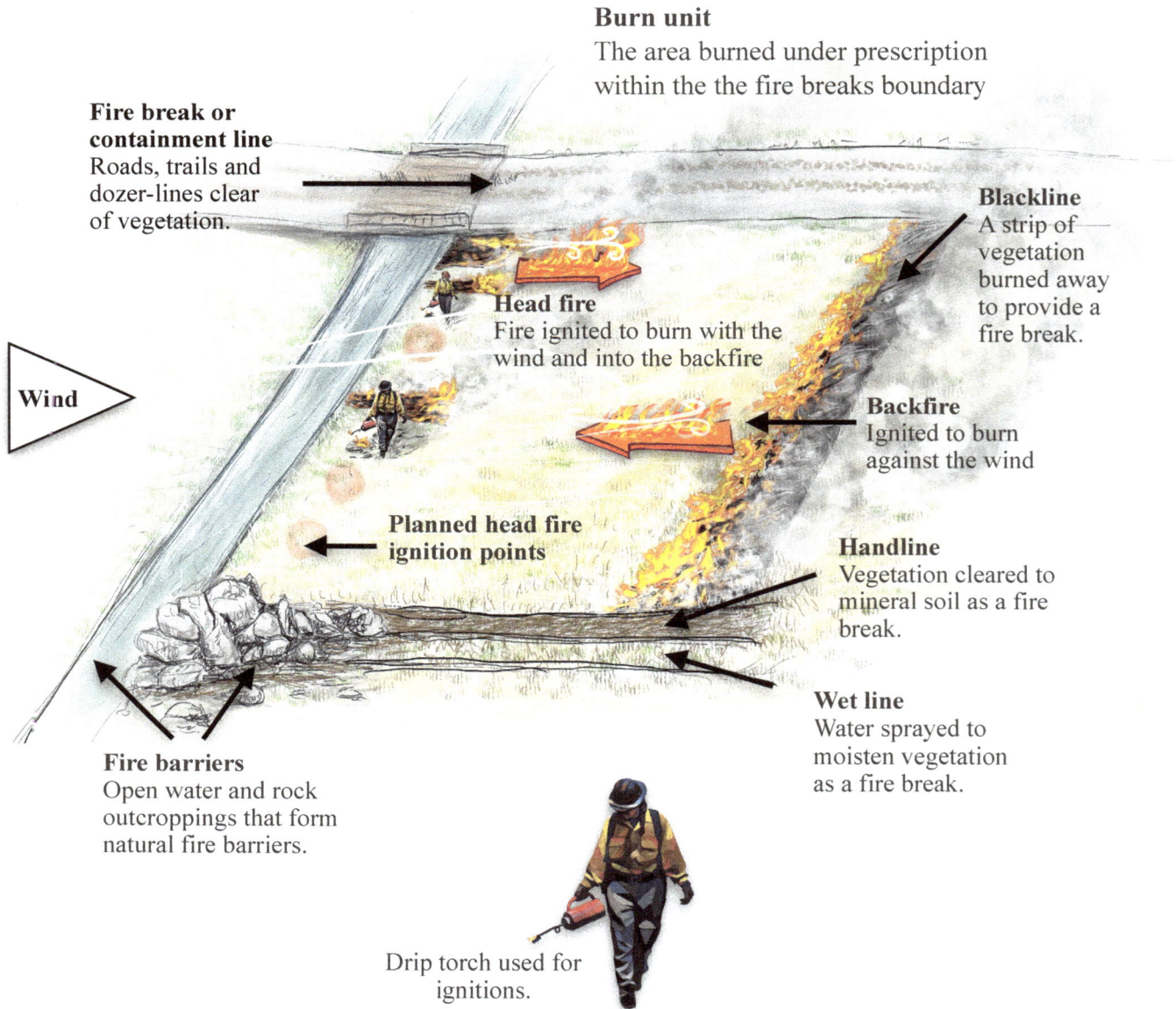

Burn unit
The area burned under prescription within the the fire breaks boundary

Fire break or containment line
Roads, trails and dozer-lines clear of vegetation.

Blackline
A strip of vegetation burned away to provide a fire break.

Wind

Head fire
Fire ignited to burn with the wind and into the backfire

Backfire
Ignited to burn against the wind

Planned head fire ignition points

Handline
Vegetation cleared to mineral soil as a fire break.

Wet line
Water sprayed to moisten vegetation as a fire break.

Fire barriers
Open water and rock outcroppings that form natural fire barriers.

Drip torch used for ignitions.

Fire Ignition Test

The illustration on the right was created from information provided by Dr. Don Hankins of California State University, Chico, the Butte County Fire Safe Council, and Greg Harry of Fire Risk Consultants Pty Ltd in Victoria, Australia. The fire ignition test is a great time to journal about the fuel moisture and flammability of fine fuels.

Hold the leaf upright and ignite it at the tip. If the leaf easy burns from the top down, the fuels may be too dry for some prescriptions and spotting may occur.

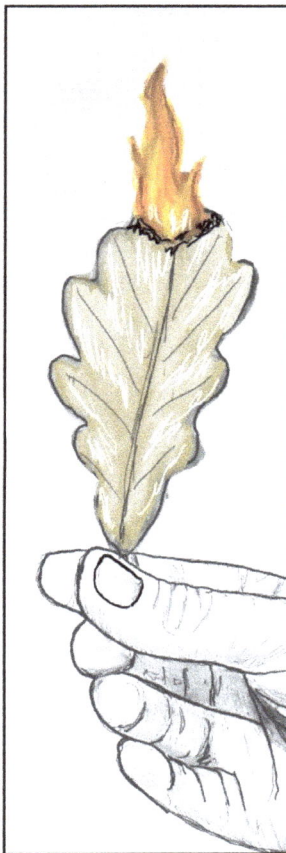

Hold the leaf upright and ignite it at the tip. If the leaf easily burns from the top down, the fuels are dry and the relative humidity is low enough to start the prescribed burn.

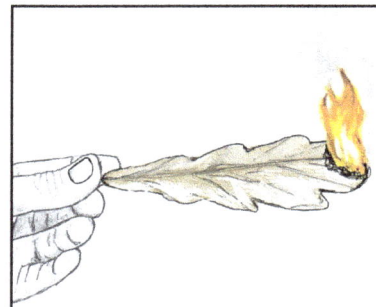

Hold the leaf horizontally and ignite it at the tip. If the leaf easily burns, the fuels are dry, and the relative humidity is low enough to burn.

Hold the leaf upside down and ignite it at the tip. If the leaf does not easily burn from the tip to the base, the fuels are too moist and the relative humidity is to high to ignite and start the prescribed burn.

Prescribed Fire Ignition Tactics

The illustration below depicts some of the ignition and burning tactics used for different burn prescriptions. I will not list the various goals and benefits for each of these ignition patterns but share them to assist with journaling notes and sketches. If possible, obtain the goals and objectives for the fire ignition tactics being used during the prescribed burn. You might visualize these tactics as I have done in the illustration or simply capture the placement of people as dots and use arrows to convey their movements.

Take some time to measure flame lengths and rates of spread during the different phases of prescribed fire. You can use your body biometrics and compare the flame heights with nearby measured objects. For the rate of spread, you might want to use your pace or measure the distance between a few observable elements and track how long it takes for the fire to move between those elements. Speed equals distance divided by time. Alternatively, you can use tortoise and sea turtle speed comparisons to gauge how fast flames appear to be moving.

Fire Ignition Tactics

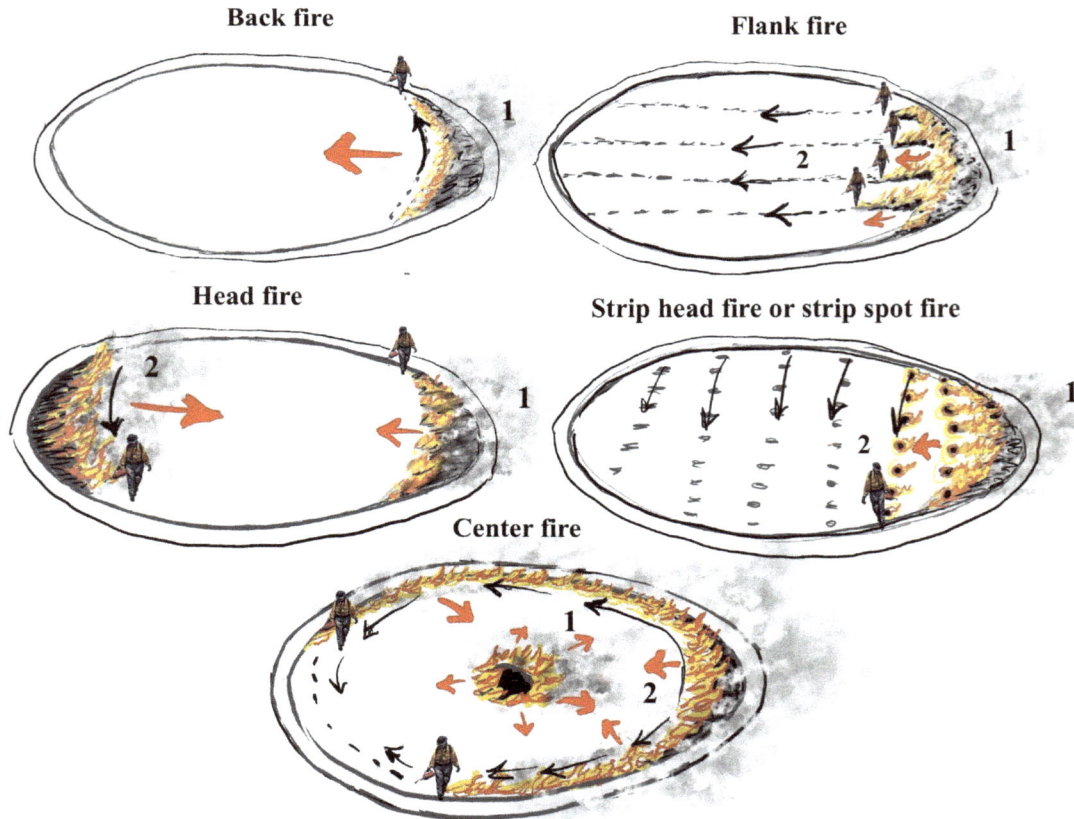

Back fire

Flank fire

Head fire

Strip head fire or strip spot fire

Center fire

Prescribed Fire Journaling

When journaling about prescribed fire, I would gather copies of burn unit maps and location data, the burn plan objectives, and weather parameters for the prescription to summarize in your journal.

I would also include diagrams and sketches of the fuel groups and conditions that best represent the area. Additionally, include notes or visuals about the topography, such as percent slope and aspect. You will want to include a table with the hourly weather data during the burn period. I would include several

Sketching A Silhouette Figure & Fire Scene

Create a pencil or pen outline of the scene and figure.

Use a pencil, pen and or watercolored to the silhouette figure and the large background elements, like trees.

Add light colored pencil or watercolor over the vegetation, flames, and sky.

Add bright yellow color to the flames and light orange color to the flame edges and the edges of the silhouette figure and trees.

Add a bright orange color around the tips and edges of the flames.

Add dark gray, black, and white watercolor and or gouache paint to create smoke.

193

sketches of the fire types and behaviors and smoke, along with some measurements or estimates to assess flame length and fire rate of spread.

I have included some tips in the illustration on the previous page if you want to try the approach of sketching silhouette figures and a fire ignitions scene.

Opportunities for Journaling Prescribed Fire

Currently, there are limited opportunities to journal a prescribed fire, but hopefully, more organizations and partners will come forward to support this amazing tool and reap the benefits of collaborating with nature journalers. During my tenure in a federal fire management program, I partnered with The Nature Conservancy's Prescribed Fire Training (TREX) program to integrate a nature journaling group with a prescribed burn project. Other TREX projects have also integrated nature journaling, including one that provided nature journaling instruction to firefighters. For those seeking opportunities to journal prescribed fire, I recommend reaching out to local prescribed burn associations, nature preserve managers, fire-safe councils, and others engaged in fire mitigation and prescribed fire activities to discuss options. For those planning and coordinating TREX projects that include journalers, I recommend including active fire observations for the journalers to enhance the learning opportunities. It is also advisable to have an experienced fire observer or single resource boss oversee safety for that group.

Wildfire

As mentioned at the beginning of this chapter, wildfires, forest fires, and bushfires are unplanned fires that may be ignited by natural or human causes. I do not recommend journaling an active wildfire near you. There are other priorities to focus on. Instead, I recommend observing and journaling the fire behavior and smoke plumes at a distance using the online tools I have shared in this chapter.

Wildfire Information

Large wildfires are managed by incident command teams and provide one to two fire updates a day. Inciweb is a website where information about many fires around the United States is posted, and state fire management agencies often have websites that post fire information. Many fire updates are also provided on social media, although you'll see a mix of information sources, which can be misleading. Here are a few things to think about as you review fire updates: the name of fires can, on rare occasions, change as other fires start in the same management area or when new incident management teams manage a group of fires as a complex. You'll also see the size in acres change as the fire grows or as more accurate measurements are added. The perimeter of a wildfire may include part or all of what is called a containment line, which is the operational goal line for restricting fire spread. The change in acres is often reported within two timeframes or burn periods (day and night periods).

Fire Data Graphs

Wildfire metadata is an important element to journaling about wildfire, especially daily fire progression. I like to track the fire progression and the potential influences of weather by obtaining the acres burned each day and breaking those into two burn periods (daytime and nighttime). I like to use the morning (nighttime acres) and evening (daytime acres) fire reports from incident management teams and or the National Interagency Fire Center's Situation Report website. I list the acres burned and apply different colors for the evening and morning report data and use that to build a bar graph (see the next page).

I also use a doughnut graph for tracking the percent containment during the period of observation. In the example on this page, I did not track the fire until the end, so I did not create a bar graph for acres burned each day. I also use line graphs to visualize the key weather conditions during the day and nighttime periods. When you visualize the fire data in graphs, you can start to observe and evaluate connections of fire behavior with fire weather conditions. This is a powerful way to make connections to the fire environment. These graphs were created in the Pages app on an iPad. You can also create them in an Excel spreadsheet.

the portion of the graph representing the percentage of fire containment. Create a black outline around each day on the doughnut graph. Eventually, the entire graph will be gray, with black outlines around the percent containment for each day.

- List the fire size (acres burned) each day and add notes about any changes and corrections to reported acres. You can create a bar graph once the wildfire is reported fully contained.

- Track the high and low temperature, relative humidity, and wind speeds and use those to create line graphs, which can be used to help assess weather influences on fire growth and containment.

Fire Progression Maps

A more place-based visual approach to journaling fire progression is to sketch a simple map and add colors indicating the areas burned over different time periods. I use the National Interagency Fire Center's Situation Report website and track the active fire detection points (MODIS/VIIRS layers). I do not like to use the website's hot spot time color codes for my journaling. I prefer to use a yellow-orange for the hot spot detections within the 0-12 hour period, adding gray over those areas when they become 12-24 hour detections and black over the top when over 24 hours. I don't worry about recreating the exact hot spot points from the website, but use dabs or a wash of color over the area. It can be a little challenging to mentally switch from their color code to mind, but if you create a legend it will be easier.

- Create a doughnut graph with an orange color representing the percentage of the wildfire that is not contained. Each day, use a gray color to fill-in

2022 Mosquito Fire Progression

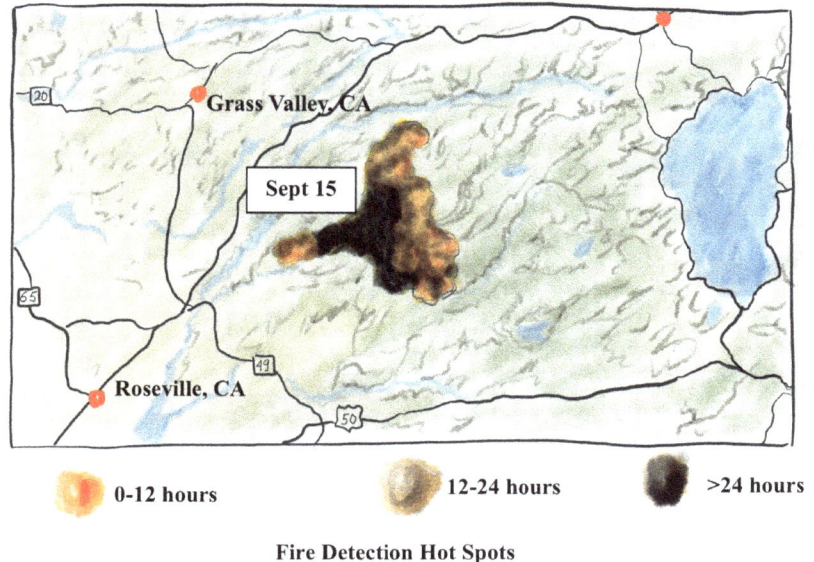

Fire Detection Hot Spots

2018 Campfire Metadata Graphs

38,188 Acres
16% Contained

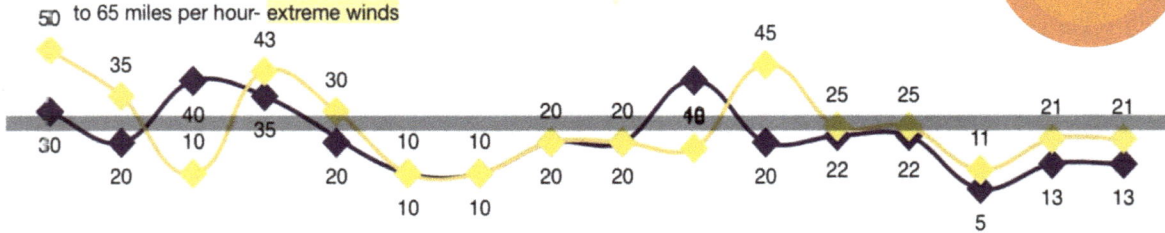

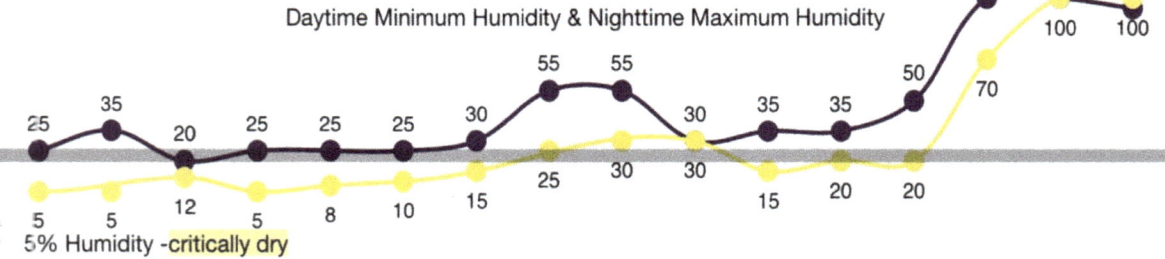

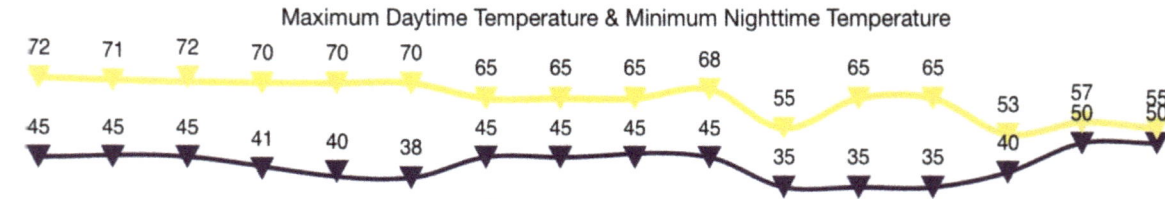

50 to 65 miles per hour- extreme winds

(Wind speed graph values: 50, 35, 43, 30, 45, 25, 25, 21, 21; 30, 40, 35, 20, 20, 40, 22, 22, 11, 13, 13; 20, 10, 35, 10, 10, 20, 20, 20; 10, 10)

Daytime Minimum Humidity & Nighttime Maximum Humidity

(Humidity graph values: 25, 35, 20, 25, 25, 25, 30, 55, 55, 30, 35, 35, 50, 100, 100, 95, 100, 100, 70, 5; 5, 5, 12, 5, 8, 10, 15, 25, 30, 30, 15, 20, 20)

5% Humidity -critically dry

Maximum Daytime Temperature & Minimum Nighttime Temperature

(Temperature graph values: 72, 71, 72, 70, 70, 70, 65, 65, 65, 68, 55, 65, 65, 53, 57, 55, 50, 50; 45, 45, 45, 41, 40, 38, 45, 45, 45, 45, 35, 35, 35, 40)

Acres Burned During Daytime & Nighttime

Date	Acres
11/8	69,021 acres burned
11/9	33,964 acres
11/10	5,619 acres
11/11	16,436 acres
11/12	3,996 acres
11/13	7,848 acres
11/14	5,500 acres
11/15	2,783 acres
11/16	3,180 acres
11/17	2,338 acres
11/18	799 acres
11/19	46 acres
11/20	1.806 acres?
11/21	0 acres
11/22	0 acres
11/23	0 acres

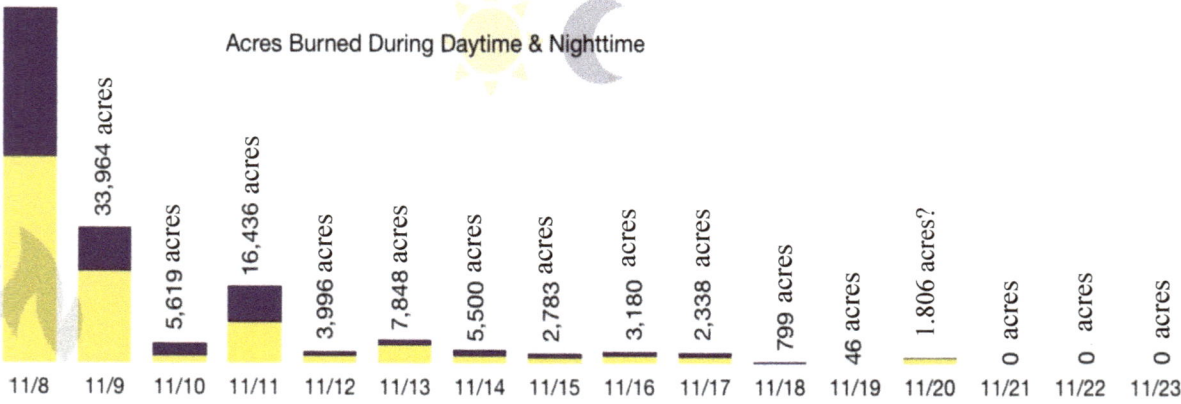

196

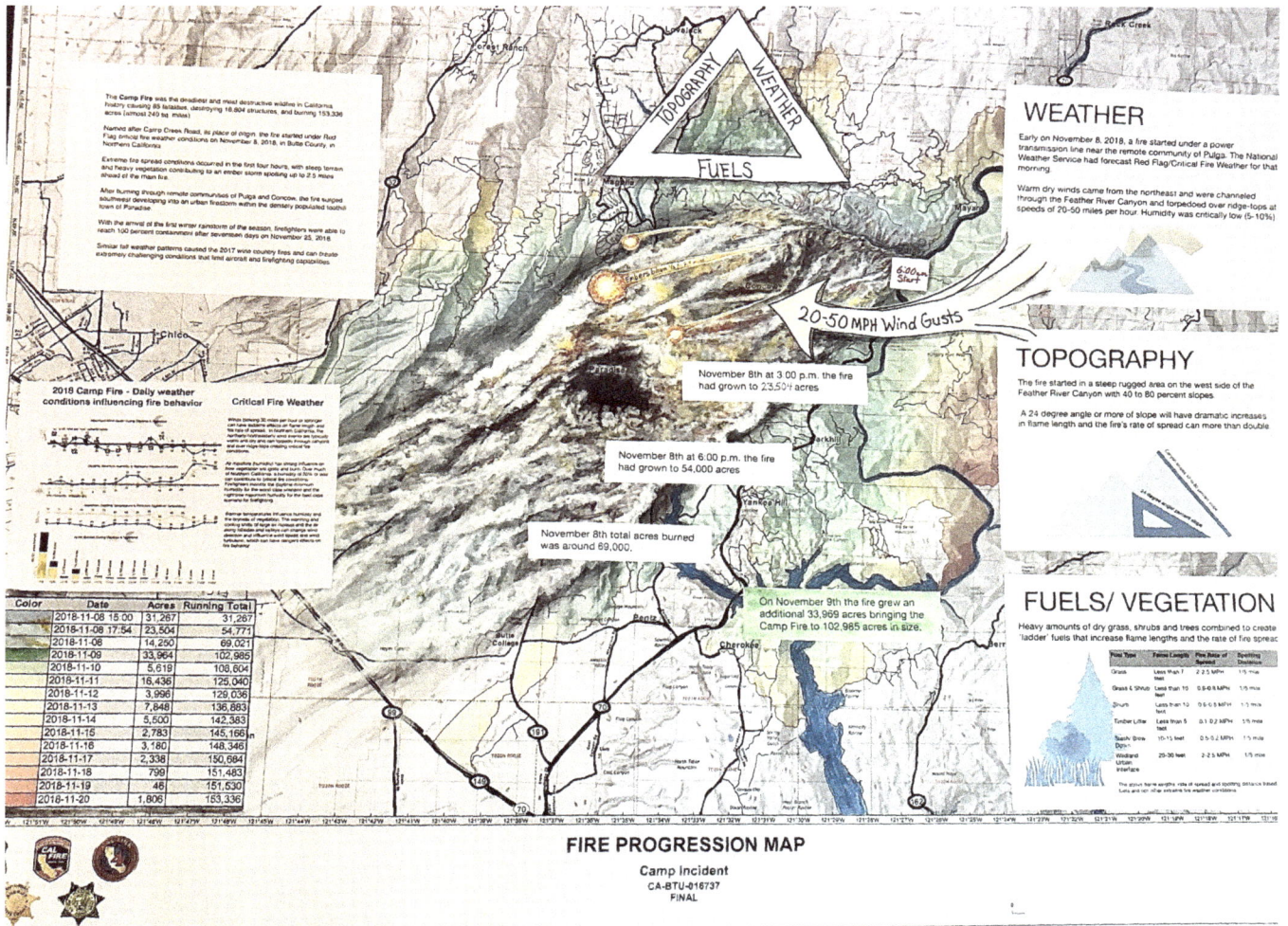

FIRE PROGRESSION MAP

Camp Incident
CA-BTU-016737
FINAL

I have also used the printed fire progression maps from wildfires and added additional fire information and visuals, like this one from the 2018 Camp Fire in northern California. I combined the data graphs of the daily fire and weather data and painted the smoke plume during the first burn period, as captured in satellite images. This was the most intense period of fire behavior and a shocking visual considering the scale and size of the smoke plume. Keep in mind the fire behavior and smoke observations described in this chapter and how those can be added to your journal.

There are other options for journaling about wildfire. You can create sketches and describe wildfires from photos found on the internet and live web cameras, like AlertWildfire. If possible, look for photos or web camera scenes that display a mix of fire behaviors and smoke conditions. This will provide a more accurate representation of a fire. You can also include sketches of various fire suppression activities such as fire crews, fire engines, and aircraft in action.

Journaling Multiple Wildfires

You may also want to journal about multiple wildfires occurring in a larger area. Websites like the National Aeronautics and Space Administration's FIRMS and EOS maps, and social media posts of satellite images of fires and smoke, offer valuable resources. You can use these images to create a large-scale map and then sketch the fire locations and smoke plumes spread over greater distances. I often use stencils of the United States to create these maps, but you can sketch simple outlines, with notes to help define the scale of the area.

Journaling Wildfire Smoke & Air Quality

Nearly all of the smoke and air quality journal pages I shared were from wildfires. Those are critical observations to include when journaling about wildfire smoke and air quality conditions.

Journaling Social & Emotional Observations

In Chapter 1: Pyroskecthology Introduction, I shared some ideas for journaling about feelings and emotions. Wildfires can trigger powerful emotions, which are important to

explore and journal. You can also emphasize powerful images that trigger those emotions. I had a number of friends who were evacuated from the Kincade fire in northern California and felt helpless to support them. I used a news story photo to create a sketch in my journal and tried a creative narrative approach to describe those feelings.

2019 Sand Fire in the Rumsey area in Yolo County northwest of Sacramento. Started on June 8th and burned 2,512 acres and seven structures. Similar vegetation to Sac area but more slope and terrain influences with winds and Red Flag conditions.

Burnout operations

Retardant drops

Area Map - Sand Fire

Chapter 9: Fire Severity & Effects

Fire Severity

Fire or burn severity is a qualitative measure of the degree to which an area has been altered or damaged after a fire. There are three primary severity ratings based on the 2010 U.S. Forest Service *Field Guide for Mapping Post-Fire Soil Severity* (Fire Severity Guide): low, moderate, and high. Other fire severity ratings are used by specialists for fire severity analysis and mapping, including unburned and increased greenness. Fire severity is commonly analyzed within different layers of the environment. For our journaling purposes, I have interpreted and visualized the fire severity categories within the aforementioned guide. These severity categories are organized as: Tall-Intermediate Sized Tree; Small Tree to Tall Bush; Tiny Tree, Shrub & Grass; and Ground (Soil).

Fire Severity Maps

Burn severity maps are developed primarily for land managers and specialists assessing the impacts of large wildfires. These maps are then used to develop post-fire stabilization and rehabilitation treatments. A fire severity map is not required for many of the journaling practices that I will share, but there are some interesting observations. Looking at a fire severity map can also help you decide the best place to make your observations. I like to use the interagency Burn Severity Viewer website to find fire severity maps, which includes a number of wildfires that have been analyzed and mapped across the United States going back to 1984.

I also like to use Google Earth in the 3D mode to view more landscape features, like roads and parking areas, to help me plan more field visits. You'll also want to determine the land ownership before going into the field. I would focus on public lands, like the U.S. Forest Service and Bureau of Land Management, and make contact with the local office to determine the ability to access and any safety recommendations. Note that many burned areas are temporarily closed for public safety, rehabilitation work, and habitat recovery. If access is limited or you don't want to travel to the area, you can still make some observations through photos and online maps.

If you plan to visit a burned area, check the weather and conditions before heading out. These areas can be highly unstable, and moderate wind conditions can increase the risk of falling trees. There may also be risks of mudslides and falling trees after recent rain, where the soil can be destabilized.

Tree & Soil Observations

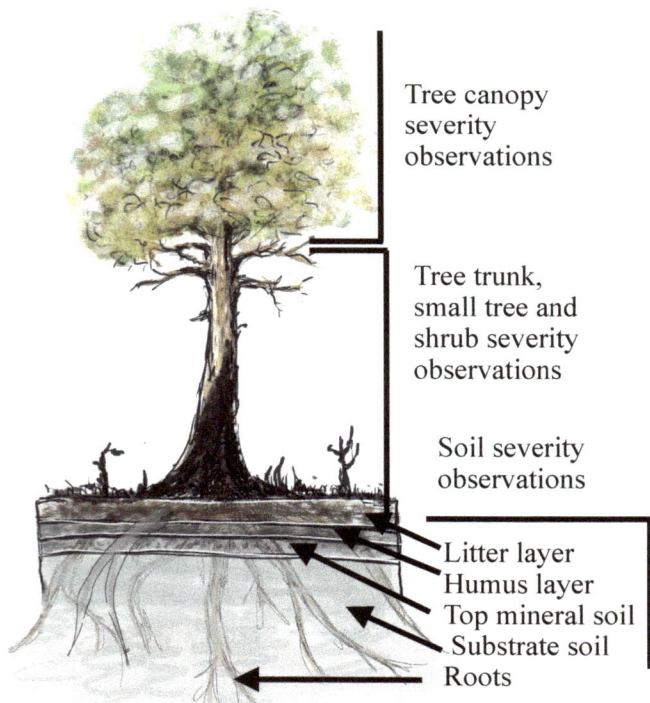

Tree canopy severity observations

Tree trunk, small tree and shrub severity observations

Soil severity observations

Litter layer
Humus layer
Top mineral soil
Substrate soil
Roots

Online Fire Severity Map Viewing Tips

I have several screen capture images and steps for using the burn severity viewer website.

You can use that map to find a location to sketch a burn severity area in the field or create a sketch using a Google Earth image reference.

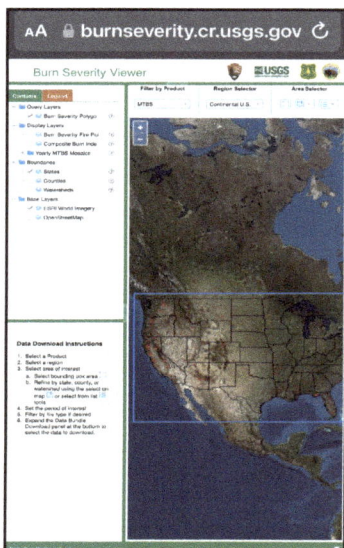

Step 1: Go to the interactive Fire Severity map Viewer and search for fire/burn areas you want to observe.

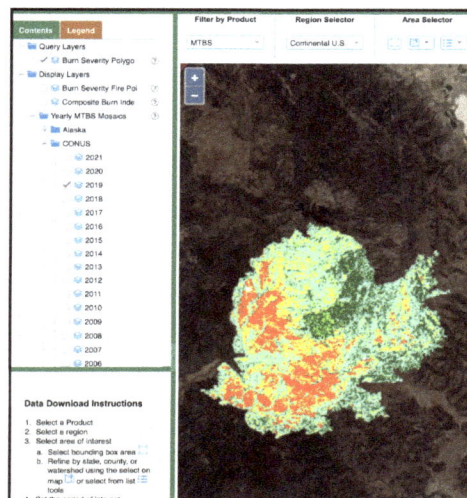

Step 2: Zoom into the fire area and click the Year MTBS Mosaics folder and year of the fire occurred.

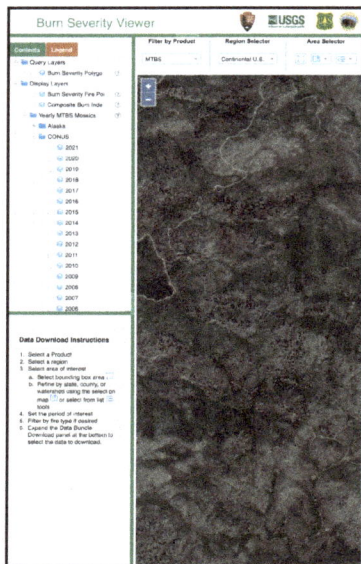

Step 3: Click off the Burn Severity Polygon and Year MTBS Mosaics boxes to view the terrain.

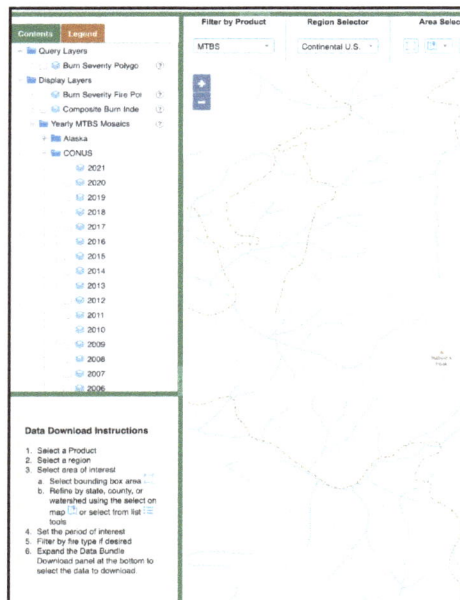

Step 4: Scroll down the legend and click on the Open Street Map to view roads and landscape features. Look for a landscape feature name.

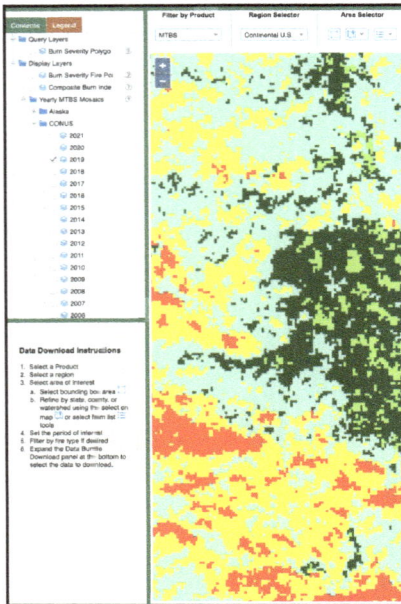

Step 5: Zoom into an area of interest, with mixed fire severity.

Fire Severity Level

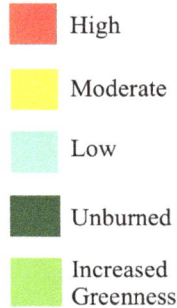

High

Moderate

Low

Unburned

Increased Greenness

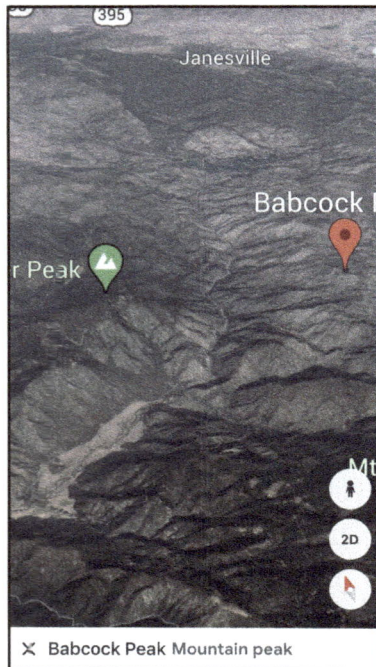

Step 6: Go to Google Earth and search for the name of the landscape feature (Bacbcock Peak). Use the 3-D button and angle the view to show more dimension of the terrain. On a touch screen, use two fingers to make the 3-D adjustments.

Sketching Landscape Burn Severity

I've outlined some steps and examples of how you can sketch the burn severity in a landscape scene. Use the Use the online viewer as described to help you find an area to observe or if you happen upon a burned area in a landscape that you are exploring.

Step 1: Create a small rectangle frame and sketch the outlines of the landscape features, like roads, hilltops, and ridges..

Step 2: Color in light yellow, orange, brown, and green areas. I like to dab in a few darker colors over the lighter colors to accentuate vegetation edges and a few individual shrubs and trees.

Step 3: Use gray or black pencil, pen, or watercolor to add shadows and charred areas across the landscape, especially along landscape lines to keep the shape of the terrain.

202

Step 4: Use a black pencil, pen, or thin-line of watercolor to create the skeletons of completely burned trees.

Estimating Fire Severity

In this section, I have simplified and summarized the Fire Severity Guide for journaling purposes, but the guide is available online if you'd like more detailed information. The majority of these observations are intended for immediate assessments after a fire. If you visit an older burned area, you may still observe some of the fire severity indicators, but conditions will change within the first couple of years.

Vegetation Burn Severity

Vegetation burn severity is focused on the fire effects to vegetation and ecosystem properties, which is measured by the degree of scorch, consumption, mortality, and projected vegetation recovery. The degree of severity is dependent on the fire adaptations of the vegetation community and species, such as bark thickness and sprouting abilities. The concentrations of vegetation, the topography, and climate will also influence the severity of effects. Making observations before the fire and within and adjacent to the burned area after a fire will be helpful in making connections between environmental conditions and fire severity levels.

Tall to Intermediate-Sized Tree Severity

Low Severity

Low severity effects to tall and intermediate-sized trees (subcanopy) may result in up to 15% of the canopies burned in the overall area. Large, dominant, and upper canopy trees may have 5% to 15% of canopies burned in the overall area. Char heights on tree trunks may be up to 3 feet high.

Moderate Severity

Moderate severity effects may result in 10% to 80% of the canopies burned in the overall area, with 3-9 feet high charring on tree trunks.

High Severity

High severity effects may result in 75% to 100% of the canopies burned in the overall area, with char heights over 12 feet.

Low Severity

Moderate Severity

High Severity

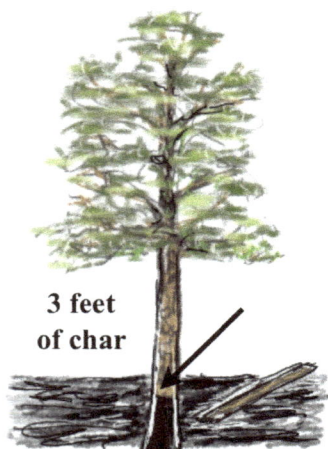

3 feet of char

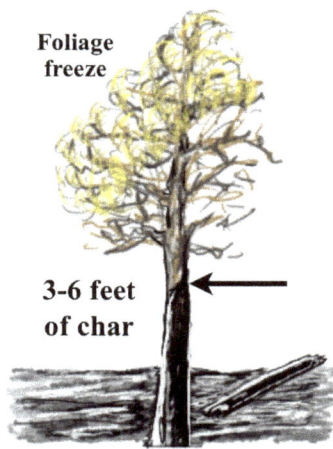

Foliage freeze

3-6 feet of char

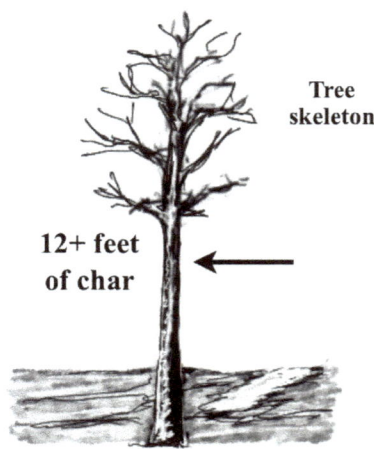

Tree skeleton

12+ feet of char

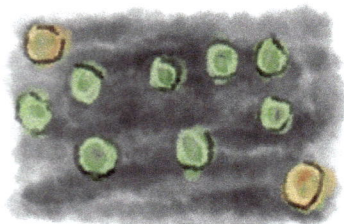

5%-10% of trees burned

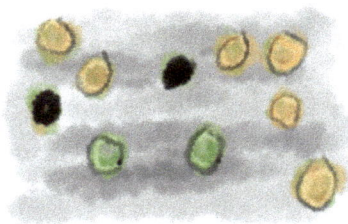

10%-80% of trees burned

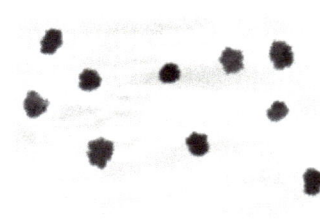

Over 80% of trees burned

To visualize these observations, I have sketch of a single tree, shrub, or plant with the burn severity effects in the vertical dimension and a horizontal diagram with the burn severity for of multiple plants in the observation area.

Small Tree to Tall Bush Severity

Low Severity

Low severity effects to tall bushes, chaparral, and small trees (3-16 feet high) may result in 5% to 30% of the foliage burned in the overall area. There will likely be patches of unburned, scorched, and charred foliage, and much of the leaves and plant structures will still be identifiable.

Moderate Severity

Moderate severity effects may result in 30% to 100% of the foliage burned in the overall area, with most of the foliage consumed on individual plants and a range of shrub and small tree skeletons.

High Severity

High severity effects may result in 90% to 100% of the foliage burned in the overall area, with all of the foliage consumed on individual plants and large stemmed skeletons (little to no small branches remaining).

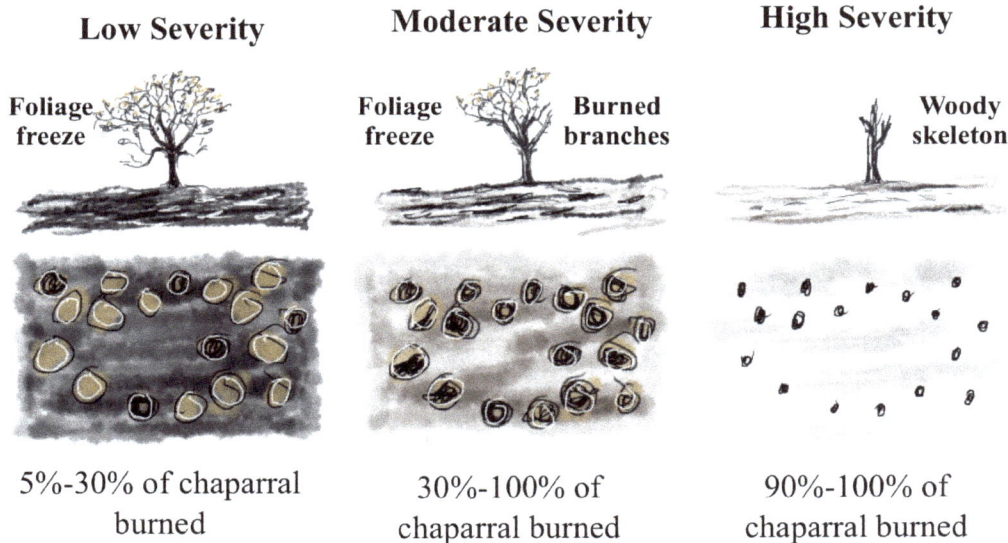

Low Severity

Foliage freeze

5%-30% of chaparral burned

Moderate Severity

Foliage freeze — Burned branches

30%-100% of chaparral burned

High Severity

Woody skeleton

90%-100% of chaparral burned

Tiny Tree, Shrub & Grass Severity

Low Severity

Low severity effects to forbs, grass, shrubs, and tiny trees (less than 3 feet tall) may result in 5% to 30% of the foliage burned in the overall area. The small diameter vegetation, like grass and forbs, may be scorched, charred, or partially consumed. There may be patchy areas on each shrub or tiny tree with scorch, charring, and partially consumed stems, branches, and trunks.

Moderate Severity

Moderate severity effects may have 30% to 90% of the foliage burned in the overall area, with the majority of fine fuels consumed and charred stems to shrub stems.

High Severity

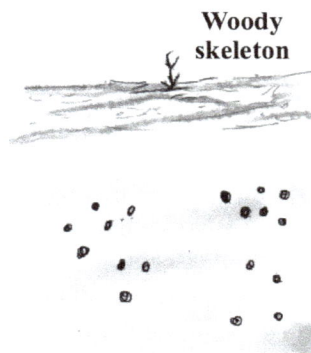

High severity effects may result in 95% to 100% of the foliage burned in the overall area, with full consumption of fine fuels (grass and leaves) and shrub skeletons.

Low Severity

Foliage freeze

5%-30% of shrub/ grass burned

Moderate Severity

Foliage freeze   Burned branches

30%-100% of shrub/ grass burned

High Severity

Woody skeleton

90%-100% of shrub/ grass burned

Ground & Soil Fire Severity

Ground cover, in terms of fire severity, refers to the effective organic materials that influence soil stabilization and the mitigation techniques used to reduce water runoff and soil erosion. Ground cover includes layers of surface woody debris, vegetation litter like needles and leaves, and duff. Duff is the cushy layer of broken-down debris and litter. Ground or soil fire severity is tied to the heat intensity levels directed toward the ground, which are affected by flame heights and flaming duration. Observations include the amount and depth of the black char, where less fire consumption occurred, and the chemical and structural changes to soil. The observations will vary based on the original soil conditions and heat intensity of the fire across the landscape. Effects will include things like reduced litter and duff layers, which influence soil temperatures, nutrients, soil stability, and water infiltration.

Low Severity

Overall low severity areas will appear black, with char covering the remaining materials. Low severity effects include light levels of fire consumption of surface vegetation, ground cover, and soil elements over the area (less than 50% of the overall area). Small-sized branches and plant litter (less than 3 inches in diameter) may have light char and up to 20% consumption on those elements. These plant materials are still mostly intact and recognizable as branches, leaves, and needles. Medium-sized logs and branches (3-8 inches in diameter) may be charred and have up to 20% consumption. Larger logs and branches (larger than 8 inches) may have char and up to 10% consumption. The soil is not typically affected, but areas with larger woody debris (logs, woodpiles) and longer duration fires could have stronger effects. To observe these conditions, you will want to look at the ground surface and dig into the soil to notice any differences in severity levels. The fine network of roots below the surface is still intact in low severity areas.

Low Severity

Less than 50% of the surface litter consumed.

Moderate Severity

50% to 80% of the surface litter consumed.

High Severity

Over 80% of the surface litter consumed.

Moderate Severity

Moderate severity effects include up to 80% consumption of surface vegetation, ground cover, and soil elements over the area. Typically, these materials have partial consumption with branches, leaves, and needles that are still somewhat recognizable. In general, about 100% of the plant litter, 40% of the medium-sized wood, and 25% of large-sized wood elements are consumed. Note that there may still be needles and leaves on the ground when scorched trees drop those over time. The overall surface area will appear black to gray, with patches of lighter ash where the woody debris was heavier and burned longer. The soil typically has slight to no observable effects. Duff layers may experience up to 50% charring but are typically within the first half-inch. In moderate severity areas, the fine roots may have slight to a little charring. Around 40% of the burned area may have soil impacts, such as changes in soil chemistry and water filtration abilities.

High Severity

High severity effects will have 80% or more of the woody debris, litter, and duff consumed over the overall area. There may be a few recognizable materials. Much of the area will have 1-3 inches of light gray or white ash, with potential areas of bare soil. There are not typically leaf casts (fallen leaves and needles) on the surface due to the high severity impacts on trees. Around 98% of the litter is consumed, 60% or more of the small woody debris is charred or lost, 80% or more of the large-woody debris is charred or consumed, and most of the duff layer is consumed. About 80% of the area will have soil effects, with localized areas of red (oxidized) soil beneath the ash layers and some areas with soil impacts down to 6 inches deep. The soil chemistry and structure are altered, and soil stability is reduced or destroyed. Most of the fine roots near the surface are consumed, and large roots (3 inches or larger) are charred.

Soil Hydrophobicity

Ground/soil hydrophobicity or water repellency changes with the severity level and is highly variable across the landscape. Water-repellant soils resist water penetration and filtration into soil layers. This occurs when soil particles are coated with hydrophobic compounds from the burned vegetation and organic materials. These hydrophobic compounds move down in the soil layers where lower temperatures allow them to condense and coat soil particles. The level of soil repellency is also tied to the original ground layers, soil types, and soil particle sizes. You are more likely to observe this effect within the first several years of a fire, but some high severity areas may have longer-lasting effects. There are a mix of observation scales from digging into the soils to see how deep the water is penetrating, to landscape and watershed observations. You may also want to consider soil hydrophobicity observations in a campfire pit.

- **Low severity** effects will have no overall influence on the water infiltrating into the soil.

- **Moderate severity** areas will have mixed water repellency and infiltration levels. Overall, the water filtrates slowly into the soil. You may observe larger-sized water drops sitting on the surface, water pooling in areas, or water runoff downslope.

- **High severity** areas will have strong water repellency down to 6 inches below the soil, with high levels of water runoff that carries ash, debris, and soil downstream. See the illustrations on the next page.

Soil Hydrophobicity

Low Severity

No fire-induced soil water repellency. Water immediately infiltrates.

Moderate Severity

Weak to moderate soil water repellency. Fat water drops may sit on top. Water slowly infiltrates.

High Severity

Strong soil water repellency down to 6 inches deep. Sheets of water, ash, and soil runs off the surface.

Watershed Effects

High severity effects can create strong impacts on the landscape and far downstream. These can be somewhat mild effects, like small water channels between plants. If the channels are not obvious, you might look for strangely-shaped patches of grass that look like a smile. There are more severe effects you may observe, like the carved-out drainage channels along slopes, deep-cut stream banks, and large amounts of woody debris in streams and rivers. See the illustrations on the next page.

Ash and woody debris flows into water channels from high severity fire.

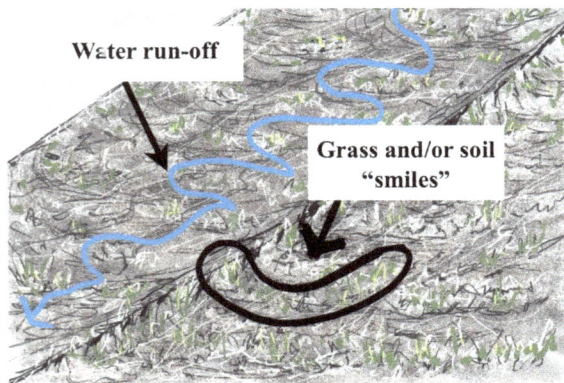

Water run-off

Grass and/or soil
"smiles"

Patchy grass after moderate fire severity can cause runoff and semicircle grass/soil pockets (smiles)

Water Color

The loose ash, debris, and soil materials carried into waterways can change water chemistry, color, and clarity or turbidity—how well you can see through the water. Water colors are often measured by collecting water samples and allowing materials to separate. The resulting water colors are considered true water colors. However, there are a few visual observations of streams, rivers, and lakes that can tell you about water conditions, including the following (California Water Resources Control Board):

- Transparent and blue water can indicate low levels of dissolved organic materials and low biological productivity.

- Higher levels of dissolved organic materials and productive waters (high plant and algal activity) can appear as yellow, brown, and green.

- Some algae can give water a pea-soup appearance, and other algae and dinoflagellates can produce reddish or deep yellow colors in water.

- Soil runoff can give water a yellow, brown, or green coloration.

Journaling Fire Severity Observations

There are different approaches you can take to journaling fire severity observations. I recommend trying to observe a mix of fire severity levels and using sketches, severity measurements, and descriptions. Also, make comparisons between observations along different aspects and slopes, including information about elevation and previous or adjacent vegetation conditions.

Soil Suspended In Water

Ash & Debris In Water

Fire Pattern Indicators

Now that we have a basic understanding of fire severity, let's examine some additional but related observations that can help estimate the fire behaviors that occurred in the area. I have summarized and interpreted this information from the National Wildfire Coordinating Group's *Guide to Wildland Fire Origin and Cause Determination*. If you recall the fire anatomy and associated fire behaviors (backing, lateral, and advancing) from Chapter 8: Fire & Smoke, there are a number of specific observations that can be used to determine those fire behaviors, even without active fire observations. These observations are called Fire Pattern Indicators (FPIs) and were developed to assist wildland fire investigators in determining the fire origin and cause.

FPIs focus on observations that aid in determining the overall fire progression—where the fire was advancing to and from. FPI observations can be more challenging to differentiate on prescribed and cultural burns because they use different ignition patterns over the burn unit. However, FPIs may still be observed in limited and sporadic areas.

I have organized this section by the scale of observation. There are FPIs at the landscape scale, which may be observed from a high viewpoint, aerial photo or fire map; scene-scale observations that consider collective observations; and close-up observations of individual elements.

FPI—Fire Behavior Overview

An FPI can exhibit any one of the three fire behavior patterns (backing, lateral, and advancing), but some indicators are more strongly associated with backing or advancing fire. Several FPIs are just different ways of observing different types of impacts on the same object. The combinations of FPIs on an object, in a given area, will give you a stronger idea of the fire patterns and fire progression. Also, keep in mind that the vegetation community or fuel group may also influence the type of FPI observations you are likely to observe. For example, backing fire behaviors, with low severity effects, may be more prominent in grasslands and open forests, while advancing fire behaviors, with higher severity effects, are likely to occur in heavier concentrations of shrubs, chaparral, and forested areas. Before delving into more FPIs, here are a few reminders of the three fire behaviors we want to associate with these patterns:

Backing Fire

Lower flame lengths moving against the wind, with slower rates of spread and less severe fire effects. These are commonly observed at the heel of a fire and when fires move downslope. This fire behavior does not typically create the stump/shrub cupping, rock spalling, large tree foliage freeze, or large tree angle of scorch FPIs. In fire investigations, backing fire FPIs are flagged and labeled with a blue color.

Lateral Fire

Low to high flame lengths, with varying rates of spread and fire effects. The lateral fire FPIs are commonly observed along the flank of a fire. Lateral FPIs are typically aligned in a 45° to 90° angle from the direction of the advancing fire. Lateral fire FPIs are flagged and labeled with a yellow color.

Advancing Fire

Higher flame lengths moving with the wind, with faster rates of spread and more severe fire effects. Advancing fire behaviors do not typically create distinct grass stem or leaf curing FPIs. Advancing fire FPIs are observed at the head of a fire and when fires are moving upslope. Advancing fire FPIs are flagged and labeled with a red color.

Landscape Pattern Indicators

There are several observations at this scale, including the overall shape and size of a burned area, but there is only one FPI we use in determining fire progression and origin. That FPI is a V- or U-shaped pattern to the fire perimeter.

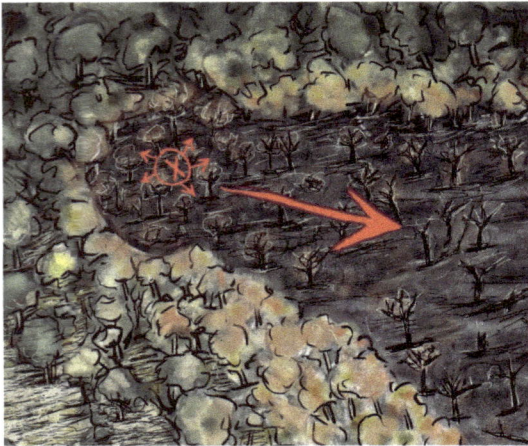

Fire Perimeter Shape

Look for an overall V- or U-shaped pattern to the burned area. This can be challenging to observe on a larger wildfire, with many branching fingers and patchy areas. A U-shape can be an indicator of fire patterns that occur on flat ground or a moderate slope under light wind conditions. A V-shaped fire is primarily an indicator of high winds and/or steep slopes. The bottom of the U or the apex of the V-pattern is often located near the fire origin area. Fires start small and then expand, especially when moving upslope. If you start

your field observations at the narrow apex of the V- or U-shape, you will be able to observe more of the FPIs, where transitional fire behaviors have occurred.

Scene Pattern Indicators

Something to keep in mind when making your scene-scale FPI observations is to look at the amount or level of severity effects across the area. This can be the depth and amount of char on tree trunks or the amount of grass consumed across the area. You will observe a greater variety of FPIs and transitions between them when you are closer to the fire origin. We'll revisit this scale of observation after making close-up observations, but there are two initial observations to look for: a transitional scale of fire severity on trees and the color and patterns of grass stems and ash.

Tree Transitions

When a fire starts, it has lower severity effects, and there will be little to no observable effects on the tree canopy. As the fire progresses and is influenced by winds and/or slope, the advancing fire will intensify, and the severity effects will start to scale up on tree canopies. My illustration shows the overall fire

Advancing fire gaining in severity of effects

progression based on transitional effects on trees. You may not initially observe this transition based on your observation location, so make comparisons throughout your observation period to get an idea of how fire affected the overall vegetation in the area.

Dark & Light Patterns

There is a grass stem FPI we are looking that is a V- or U-shaped pattern with a narrowing and widening between dark and light grass areas that have been clipped, charred, or felled to the ground. Depending on your observation position, you may not see this FPI immediately, so you may need to wait until later or move to another location.

There is also an ash color FPI where white ash indicates more intense fire behavior (advancing) and more complete combustion of materials, giving it a powdered sugar appearance. White ash is easily blown away and may not be observed in older burn areas. It may indicate fuel concentrations but can also suggest an advancing fire. Darker ash indicates less complete combustion and heavier ash particles.

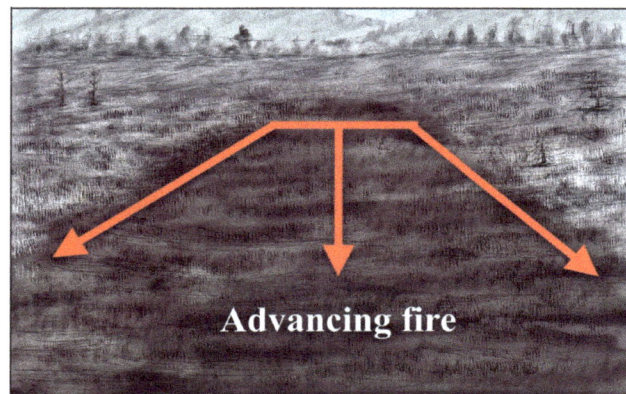

Advancing fire

While making your scene-scale observations, look across the ground. When facing the direction the fire was moving toward, the ground will appear subtly lighter in color due to the white ash blown in that direction from the wind and/or the clipped grass heads facing toward you. When facing the direction the fire came from, the ground will subtly appear darker. My illustration exaggerates this concept for clarity.

Facing the direction the fire was moving toward, the ground will appear lighter.

Facing the direction the fire came from, the ground will appear darker.

Advancing fire direction

213

Close-up Pattern Indicators

Close-up FPI observations require you to move close to different vegetation elements. You may need to bend down or kneel to view things like sticks and grass stems. Ensure you look around the entire plant or rock to see the full extent of individual or multiple FPIs.

Grass Stems

Some grass stem observations may need a closer look, especially near the fire origin area where the grass stems fall into an inward circle. The bent and angled grass stems are also considered an angle of char FPI, which I'll describe more on the next page.

White Ash

As mentioned in the scene-scale FPIs, white ash indicates higher severity advancing fire behaviors. This light and fluffy ash material is often blown onto one side of tree trunks, branches, logs, stumps, and rocks in the direction the fire advanced (deposited).

White ash can also be observed on one side of a tree trunk or branches, where ash was deposited by the wind (deposited) or higher-intensity burning occurred (exposed) in the direction the fire advanced.

White Ash (Small Fallen Branch)

Grass Stem/Fire Origin

Grass Stem/Advancing Fire

Angle of Char

The angle of char forms when fire burns up the sides and around standing fuel, such as a bush, tree, or pole. Char, the black area on plants and trees where pyrolysis, flaming, and smoldering occurred, varies based on the backing, lateral, and advancing fire behavior patterns. On grass stems, you can observe the angle of char on individual grass blades and

Flat Ground Angle of Char

Advancing Fire

Backing Fire

Sloped Ground Angle of Char

Advancing Fire

Backing Fire

Grass Stem/Angle of Char

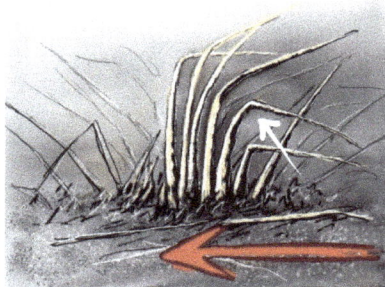

Grass Stem/Angle of Char

bunches. Refer to the illustrations on the right. For trees, the angle of char with a backing fire is parallel to the slope of the land, while an advancing fire creates a steeper angle of char, higher on the side the fire advanced. This steeper angle results from wind eddies and long, leaning flames on the uphill side of the tree. Char can persist on trees for years or even a lifetime, so be cautious not to mistake old fire effects for the burn you are currently observing. Refer to the illustrations below.

Protection

Protection occurs when a non-combustible object or the fuel itself shields the unexposed side from advancing flames and heat damage. Look for differences between the burned and unburned sides of an object. When a log or branch lies flat on the ground, the exposed side typically shows more damage than the other side. When lifted, you may observe more severe charring on the bottom and the side opposite the fire's direction. Protection is evident in backing, lateral, and advancing fires. Compare and contrast both sides of the object, and lift and remove objects to examine the ground underneath. After lifting a rock or branch, you may notice more grass stems or leaves on the side that was previously protected. The grass stem FPI can also indicate protection when the protected side of the grass or grass clump shows less burning than the other side.

Protection (Back Side of Log)

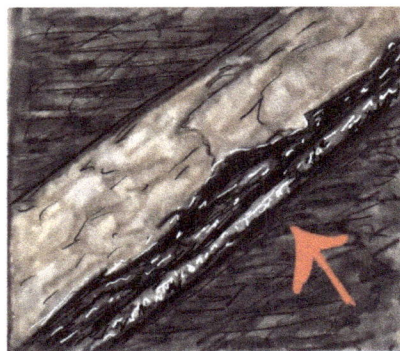

Cupping on Logs & Branches

Cupping manifests as a concave or cup-shaped char pattern on the edges of grass stems, the terminal ends of shrubs, and small stumps. On branches, the smaller limbs and tips are burned away when exposed to the oncoming fire. The opposite side of the shrub or tree retains longer branches, giving it a lopsided checkmark appearance. The cup-shaped char pattern on branches and tree stumps is carved out on the exposed side where the fire originated. In both cases, the shorter or stumpy end faces the direction the fire came from, while the higher angle faces the direction the fire was going. This indicator is more pronounced in advancing fire patterns.

Cupping (Small Tree)

Cupping (Tree Stump)

Foliage Freeze & Angle of Scorch

Foliage freeze occurs when hot winds blow dry the leaves and small branches of living shrubs and trees as the fire passes. The side of the tree with more removed or scorched leaves indicates the direction of fire advancement and serves as an indicator of advancing or lateral fire. The angle of scorch is a demarcation line between the dried leaves versus the green leaves on a single tree, or where all leaves have been removed on one side of the tree and scorched on the other. According to Grey Harry, from Fire Risk Consultants in Victoria, Australia, "scorch height is used as an FPI, associating the height of scorch with the flame lengths associated with different fire behaviors. Scorch heights can also vary by the season the fire occurred" (G. Harry, personal communication, May 24, 2023).

Foliage Freeze

Angle of Scorch

Leaf Curling

In areas with less intense fire behavior, like backing and lateral fire, you may observe the FPI called curling. Curling occurs on taller plants, shrubs, and low branches exposed to heat as the fire passes. Portions of the leaves dry out and shrink on the surface, causing the edges to curl towards the source and direction of heat. The leaf folds in the direction from which the fire originated.

Sooting

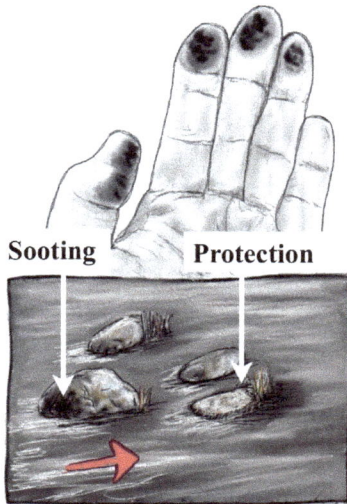

Sooting   Protection

Soot is a powdery black-colored carbon deposit caused by incomplete combustion and the release of volatile organic compounds (oils and resins) from vegetation. Soot is deposited more heavily on the side of an object (rock, log, fencepost, etc.) facing the direction the fire is coming from.

Soot can be observed on objects within backing, lateral, and advancing fires, but is noticeably heavier and more prominent within an advancing fire.

Staining

Staining is caused by the vaporized volatile organic compounds in plants, which condense and disperse in the flames and smoke column. This creates a yellow-orange to brown shiny sticky area on non-combustible objects like rocks, cans, and sticky surfaces.

This effect is most pronounced in advancing fires.

Spalling

Rock spalling occurs when the direct heat from the fire causes a rock to expand and crack or split into slabs or chips.

You may observe a white patch of rock within a darker sooty or orange-colored area where sooting, staining, and spalling occurred. This indicator is more obvious in advancing fire facing the direction the fire came from.

Collective FPIs

Individual FPIs are nearly meaningless in assessing overall fire patterns. You need to combine and compare all of the FPIs for collective trends in fire behavior. The illustrations on the next page summarizes many of the FPIs you would observe on trees and shrubs and across the landscape. The red arrows indicate the direction the fire was moving.I have crowded them together for the many scene and close-up observations into the second illustration, but there should be enough clues to make some assumptions about where the fire started and how it progressed. Test yourself and make notes about how you might change the illustration to be more accurate or for different vegetation conditions.

Collective FPI Observations

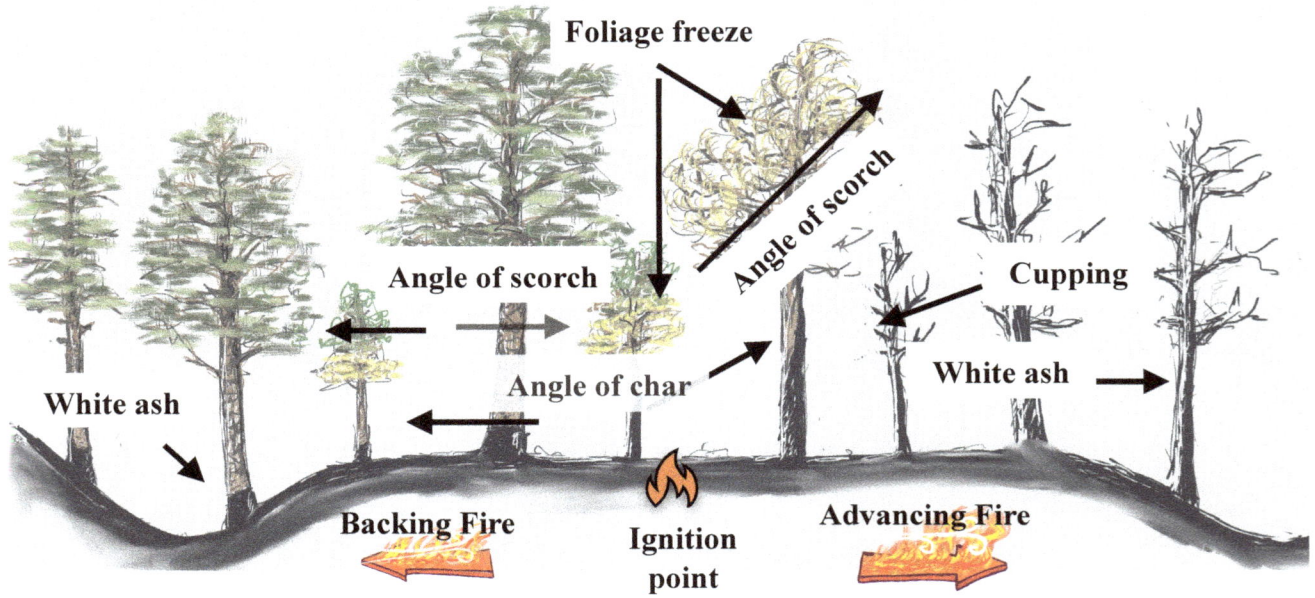

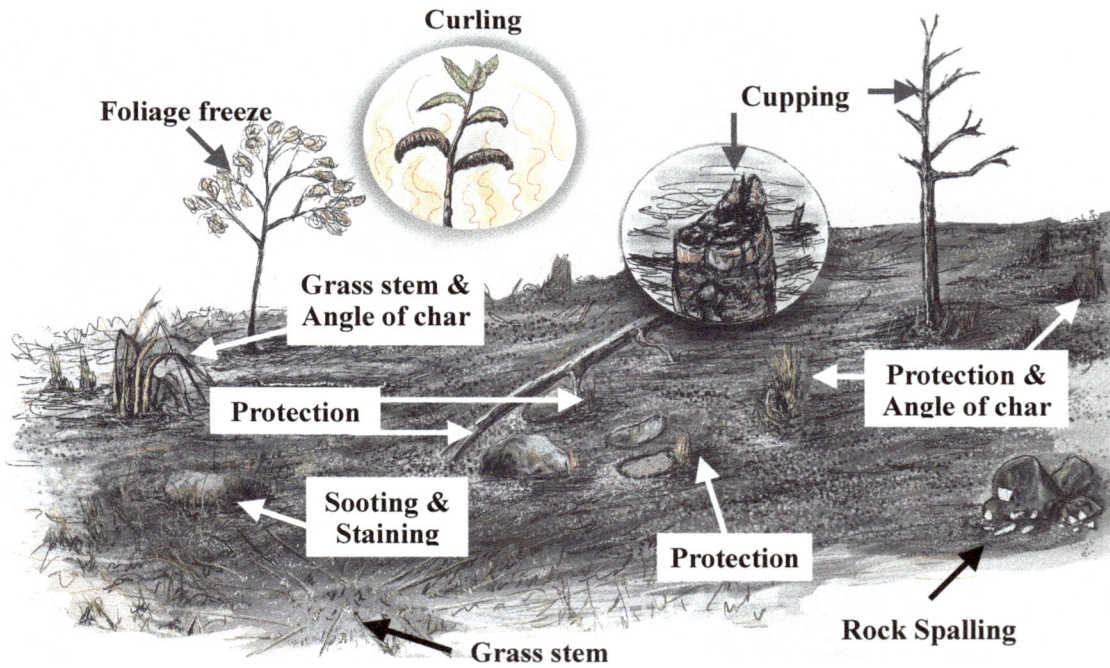

Journaling FPI Observations

I recommend starting your fire pattern indicator (FPI) observations by locating and assessing a fire perimeter or fire severity map to find the best location for both scene and close-scaled observations. If your observation area is an older burned area, you could also use Google Earth to assess the overall shape of the burned area. I have mentioned several online fire map sources in Chapter 8: Fire & Smoke and earlier in this chapter. Make sure this area is accessible to the public or that you have gained permission to access it. Having a map will help you look for roads, parking areas, and trails that may guide your observation route.

Fire Perimeter/Landscape FPI

To journal about your landscape-scale observations, you can create a simple map of the burned area conveying the perimeter shape and the V- or U-shaped pattern that may be the fire origin area. You could also do a small sketch of the area indicating this FPI, including vegetation elements and fire effects, or use the colors associated with backing, lateral, and advancing fire behaviors and associated FPIs. Add questions and assumptions about what may have influenced the landscape-scale fire patterns. Do you see higher severity areas on steeper slopes or southern aspects? Do you know which way the prevailing or storm winds moved through this landscape? This may help support the estimated advancing fire behaviors and fire progression area. You may want to wait until you've made the other FPI observations and then use those FPIs to help guide your decision about journaling this landscape-scale FPI.

Scene & Close-up FPIs

Once you are at the burned site, designate an observation area and route. I'd recommend using the edge of a road or a trail as the edge or center of the observation area. You could grid the area with several or many travel/transect lines. Start your observations by walking back and forth along the edge of the road or trail, looking for a mix of FPIs on the trees and on the ground. If you can see a transition of tree FPIs moving from lesser to greater severity or vice versa, add notes about those scene-scale observations.

Capture these observations using diagrams, sketches, and/or maps. Have a map or simple landscape sketch with your travel/observation route and labels for FPI observation points. Include at least one sketch of each FPI that you observe. Use red arrows in any sketches to indicate the overall direction the fire was progressing. Consider using colored labels or symbols for the backing, lateral, and advancing FPIs on your map or landscape sketch. Also, add any measurements or counts, like the number of backing, lateral, and/or advancing FPIs within an area so that you can make a stronger assumption about the overall fire progression. See my examples on the next page.

Optional FPI Symbols & Codes

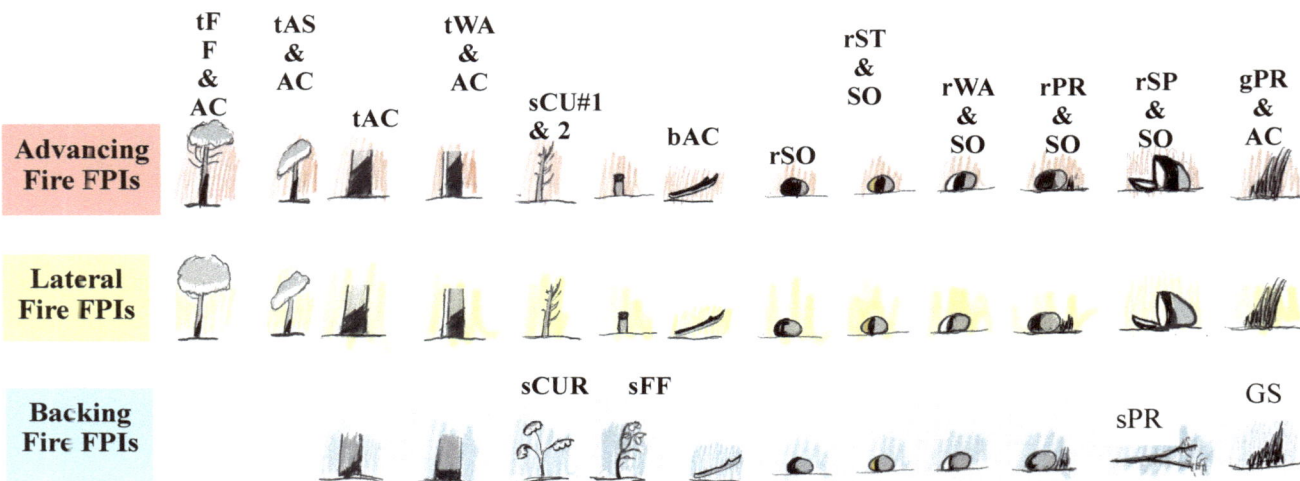

Advancing Fire FPIs — tF F & AC, tAS & AC, tAC, tWA & AC, sCU#1 & 2, bAC, rSO, rST & SO, rWA & SO, rPR & SO, rSP & SO, gPR & AC

Lateral Fire FPIs

Backing Fire FPIs — sCUR, sFF, sPR, GS

FPI Codes
b=branch
g=grass
r=rock
s=woody stem
t=tree
AC=Angle of Char
AS=Angle of Scorch
CU=Cupping
CUR=Curling
FF=Foliage Freeze
GS=Grass Stem
PR=Protection
SO=Sooting
SP=Spalling
ST=Staining
WA=White Ash

FPI Observation Area Map

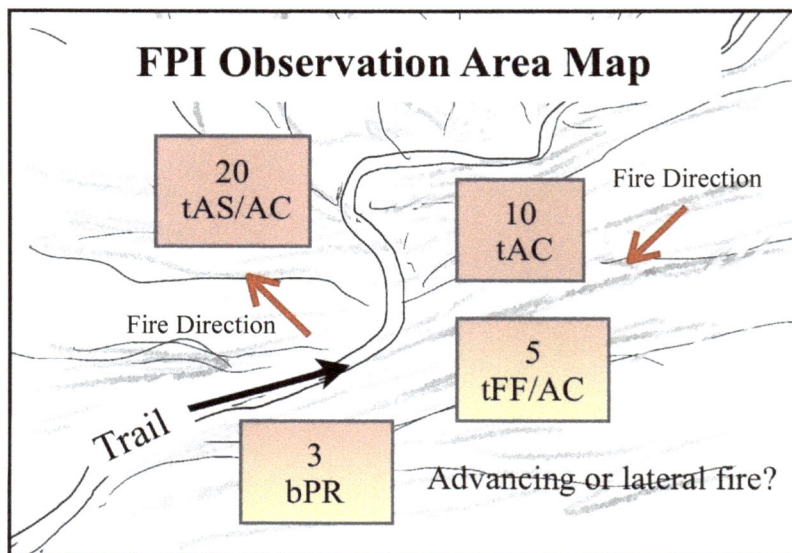

20 tAS/AC

10 tAC

Fire Direction

Fire Direction

5 tFF/AC

Trail

3 bPR

Advancing or lateral fire?

The FPI map is an example of how you could apply FPI codes to a journal page for assessing FPIs and past fire behaviors across the landscape.

Fire Effects

Observing fire effects can feel overwhelming and depressing. I like to frame these observations by considering the potential gains and losses within an ecosystem and reflecting on the time scales at which ecosystems function. While our sense of time can be fleeting, ecosystems often operate within decades and centuries. Additionally, I think about the scale and interactions of plants within an ecosystem.

Many plants are short-lived and have small distributions, while others live for centuries and are widespread. Losing long-lived trees is saddening, but interesting ecosystem changes occur over time, and many forest areas span wide regions. Although witnessing any animal suffer is difficult, I also frame these fire effect observations around populations. Many animal species have adapted to fire as part of the ecosystem, leading to different scales of loss and benefit. It's important to contextualize the scale in your fire effects observations.

Gains

Smoke can help cool air and water temperatures for fish.

Sandhill cranes, hawks, and other predators will hunt the fire's edge for small animals escaping the fire.

Lizards, birds, and mammals bathe in ash to help remove parasites.

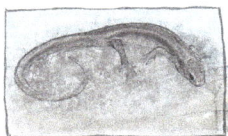

Woodpeckers and other animals come to recently burned areas to feed on new insects also drawn to the burned area.

During Fire

After Fire

Losses

Migrating birds can be stressed or die from heavy smoke.

Voles and small animals can be killed by heat and smoke or hunted by predators while escaping the fire.

Fish and aquatic animals can be killed by ash and debris washed into watersheds.

Some plants are killed, while others plants can seed, sprout and thrive depending on burn severity.

Ecological Transitions & Tradeoffs

First & Second Order Effects

Different terminology is used to describe fire effects. First-order or direct effects often occur during the fire, such as scorching and charring. Fire pattern indicators and fire severity observations are tied to first-order effects. Second-order or indirect fire effects can occur over short or long periods, caused by habitat loss, changes in ecosystem functions, increased predation, and sun exposure.

Habitat Zones & Escape Strategies

When considering the direct (first-order) and indirect (second-order) fire effects on animals, it's helpful to think about their vulnerability. Vulnerability is evaluated by the animal's level of exposure to direct and indirect effects, sensitivity to those effects (younger versus older animals), and adaptive capacity (advantageous traits, like ground-burrowing or flight). The Fire in California's Ecosystems textbook identifies four overarching habitat zones and escape strategies that can help us think about direct and indirect effects on animals: ground-dwelling, subterranean, arboreal, and aquatic. Consider the timing of the fire and the different life and phenology phases of animals in these different habitat zones. Did the fire occur when most bird species completed nesting and fledging their young? If so, there was less exposure to the fire effects for the sensitive chicks and nests. How has food availability been affected, and for how long will it last? How altered is the habitat, and how adaptable are the animals to those changes? Remember that effects are strongly tied to fire severity, so try to integrate those questions and observations with fire effects on animals. Keeping an open mind to observations and considering gains and losses might reveal many overall benefits to animals and ecosystems.

Habitat Zones & Animal Escape Strategies:

1. Ground-dwelling
2. Subterranean
3. Arboreal
4. Aquatic
5. Human/Evacuation

@Pyrosketchology

Journaling Fire Effects

More information and examples on journaling about fire effects to plants and animals, as well as adaptations, will be provided in Chapter 10: Fire Regimes. In this chapter, we focus on immediate fire effects observations. You may observe different animal responses and effects from wildfires or prescribed burns and can journal those observations. Try to add notes about the habitat zones and strategies used. Also, consider how the timing of the fire affects phenology and the level of effects. You might also consider journaling about an assumed fire scenario in an area and evaluate the likely responses of observed animals. Consider using a mix of habitat diagrams (horizontal and vertical) within any of your nature journal pages to convey different fire severity levels and habitat zones. These are observations you'll want to make over time and include with your thoughts about ecosystem gains and losses. I recommend including information about elevation, aspect, climate trends, and weather with these observations. You may also want to consider visual elements in your journal that help indicate spatial elements such as the distance to other habitat elements and water. This could be as simple as a horizontal line or arrow across the top of your journal page, with distances from adjacent habitat areas into the burned area. Or, you may include a vertical bar or column differentiating high canopy trees, understory trees, shrubs, surface cover, and subterranean observations, which can be sketched or tallied along those visual elements.

Cold Canyon Fire Journals, Green Shoots, and Silver Linings

I mentioned at the beginning of this section that fire effect observations can be overwhelming and depressing. They can also be inspiring. Robin Lee Carlson has a website and book (title above) documenting her many years of journal observations after several fires near her home in Northern California. She shared an excerpt with me as a source of inspiration for this chapter. "And so I wondered what it would actually be like after the fire. By forging a personal connection to the habitats at Cold Canyon, I hoped to develop a more nuanced understanding of fire's impact on the canyon and everything that calls it home. I sought a more intimate knowledge of what happens after fire, knowledge that could only be gained by spending considerable time in a place that had burned, visiting regularly over the years. I was moved by the otherworldly landscape I saw when I first visited shortly after the fire and was eager to watch the new face of the landscape emerge. Cold Canyon is not far from my home, and I began hiking there monthly.

A full understanding of fire's role in shaping the natural world cannot just be told but must also be felt in the passage of time and season. I am a biologist by education and early career, and I spent summers hunting spiders and millipedes and learning their ecology. My firsthand participation in fieldwork taught me that experiencing the burned landscape directly was essential to understanding it. To watch annual plants come and go, burned and heat-scorched shrubs and trees resprout, and seeds germinate after being activated by fire and smoke. To watch animals as they returned to burned areas and made use of new resources revealed by fire. To learn all I could about the science of fire and how it has evolved in tight embrace with the species in these habitats. And as a lifelong artist and now science illustrator, I needed to draw what I saw. It would be an act of discovery, a way to ensure that I looked more deeply and more thoroughly—under leaves, into cracks, beneath the surface—over and over again with passing time, to see and feel what is around me with eyes and heart focused on recording both the extraordinary and the mundane. But it would also be an act of consolation, memorializing the fire, marking this point in time with all its simultaneous loss and potential.

My sketchbooks, pens, and paint are my tools for experiencing the world and thinking through all of my discoveries. Translating what I am seeing, hearing, and feeling into images on a page is a way to find correlations and connections between all the different parts of the narrative I am watching unfold over time. It is also a way to share the story. Drawings made in the field are more spontaneous and full of life, and I use this immediacy to connect with other people and share my insights."

Tree Mortality Phases

Journaling vegetation changes over time can be a valuable experience. There may be subtle and significant changes you can observe by picking one area and following it over time. I have an illustration on the next page with some highlighted information and observations.

Observing the phases of tree mortality is one approach to changes over time. According to the Montana State University publication "*After Wildfire —Information for Landowners Coping with the Aftermath of Wildfire*," most trees will survive with 50% of their canopy foliage scorched. There are a few tree species that can survive with 75% to 100% of their canopy scorched. It may take several years for the tree to die, going through phases of partial tree crown foliage browning to all of the foliage appearing brown. It may take more time for some scorched evergreen trees to recover or to drop all of their needles once they've browned. All of this will be variable based on tree adaptations, climate, and topography in those locations.

There are some general tree mortality observations you can make over several years. Using the fire severity effects observations in the previous section will help. Measure the amount of canopy scorch and level of charring to the tree trunk immediately after a fire and over several years and during different

seasons. Look for signs of stress, such as increased tree sap and insect attacks. Observe the amount of needles or leaves that fall from the remaining tree canopy and increased insect or animal activities on the bark and tree trunk. See the illustration on the next page for some of the tree mortality phases and observations after a fire.

Fire Effects & Our Human Stories

Journaling about the fire effects on our human experiences can be challenging, but it can also be cathartic. Your journal is the place where you put your observations, experiences, thoughts, and feelings about fire. In Chapter 1: Pyrosketchology Introduction and Chapter 7: Fire Mitigation & Readiness, I shared some approaches to journaling about your emotions, experiences, and stories.

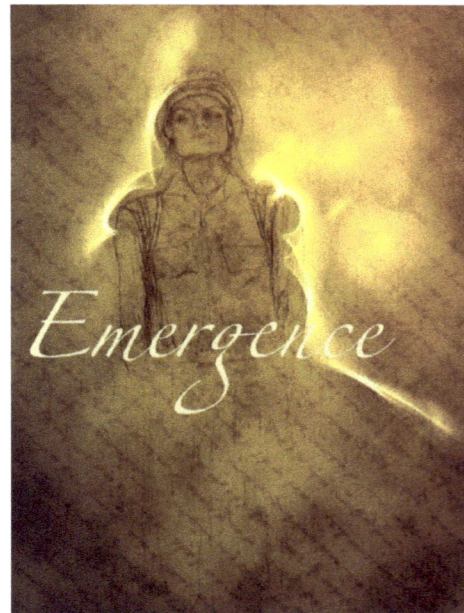

Tree Mortality Phases and Observations After A Fire

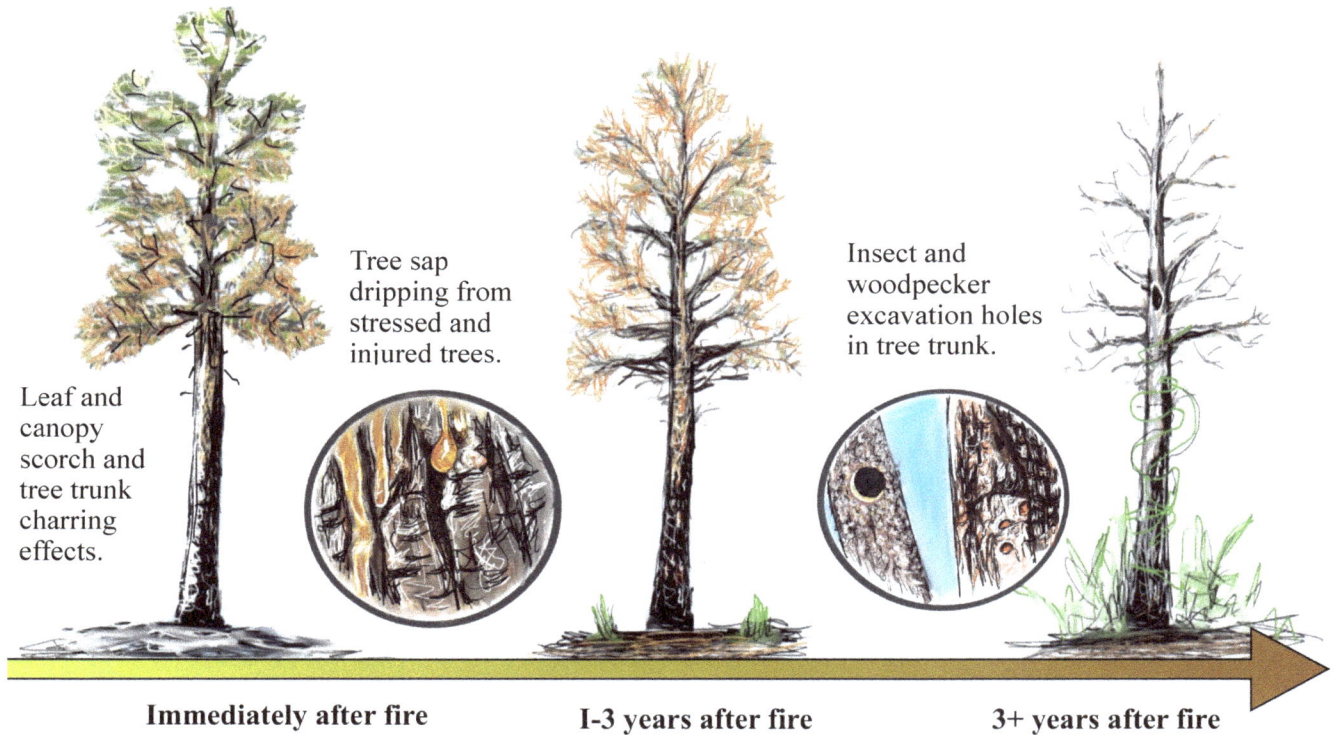

Leaf and canopy scorch and tree trunk charring effects.

Tree sap dripping from stressed and injured trees.

Insect and woodpecker excavation holes in tree trunk.

Immediately after fire

I-3 years after fire

3+ years after fire

Animals in ash

Bringing fire for the benefit of nature

Human-fire imprints

225

Chapter 10:
Fire Regimes

Ecoregions & Fire Regimes
Journaling Ecoregions
Fire Regime Attributes
Fire Size
Journaling Fire Size
Fire Types & Severities
Fire Complexity
Patchiness
Journaling Patchiness
Patch Size
Fire Frequency & Return Intervals
Journaling Fire Frequency & Return Intervals
Tree Rings & Fire Frequency
Fire Synchrony
Fire Seasonality
Climate Trends & Seasonality
Journaling Fire Seasonality
Landscape Patterns
Ecological Succession
Journaling Landscape Patterns
Seasonal Patterns
Observing Tree Stress, Injury & Death
Observing Tree & Forest Recovery
Plant Traits & Fire Regimes
Tree Foliage Traits
Journaling Foliage Flammability Traits
Bark & Branch Traits
Journaling Bark & Branch Traits
Root Structures & Sprouting Traits
Journaling Root & Sprout Traits
Vegetation Communities & Fire Regimes
Multi-Sensory Observations
Fire Followers

Journaling Fire Followers
Animals & Fire Regimes
Ecoacoustics
Journaling Acoustic Observations
Sound Maps
Humans & Fire Regimes
Journaling Human-Fire Relationships

Ecoregions & Fire Regimes

This chapter encompasses broader-scale observations (ecoregions) compared to many of the other observations in the book. It's important to understand how fires influence plants, animals, and ecosystems over time. Many of the journaling exercises will span a range of scaled observations, from large ecoregion maps to detailed sketches of leaves, pine cones, and plant seeds.

An ecoregion is a relatively large area defined by climate, geology, hydrology, and distinct assemblages of plant communities/biomes (U.S. Environmental Protection Agency). There are various sources of information about ecoregions. In the United States, federal fire management agencies use the LandFire.gov website, which combines ecoregion and fire regime information. However, I find the website challenging to use, especially on mobile devices like smartphones.

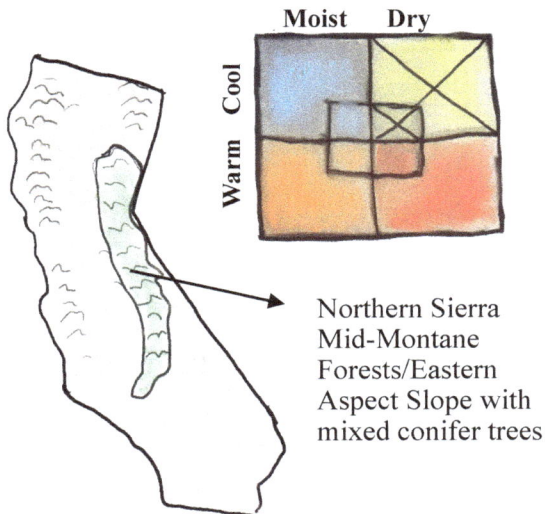

Northern Sierra
Mid-Montane
Forests/Eastern
Aspect Slope with
mixed conifer trees

Instead, I prefer to use the U.S. Environmental Protection Agency (EPA) ecoregions website to view maps and basic information or reference avifauna

regional maps. It is helpful to thick about the scale of an ecoregion and review general climate considerations.

Many biomes and ecoregions are categorized and defined by whether they are located in a dry, moist, or wet climate, as well as by elevational zone. The associated metadata used in journaling should include annual and seasonal mean temperatures and precipitation. Additionally, topography and soil conditions influence vegetation communities and fire regimes.

Many of these biomes and ecoregions are also categorized and defined by dominant vegetation types. For example, the Northern Sierra Mid-Montane Forests ecoregion covers a broad area and includes a mix of dry (pine-dominated) and moist (fir-dominated) conifer forests, mixed conifer forests (fir and pine dominated with other deciduous understory trees), and deciduous forests (aspen, oak, cottonwood). If you are unfamiliar with the term conifer, it refers to tree species that produce cones and have needles or scales that remain on the tree year-round, compared to deciduous trees, which have flowers and leaves that remain on trees during the summer and drop in the fall. Conifers are also called softwoods, while deciduous trees are called broadleaf or hardwood trees.

Journaling Ecoregions

When journaling about ecoregions and biomes, aim for a mix of observation scales and integrate topography (elevation and aspect), climate (dry/moist category, temperature, and precipitation trends), and the dominant vegetation type. Also, include a few key tree or plant species associated with the community. I prefer using simple and small diagrams to convey an ecoregion, similar to the example on the previous page. I use a stencil for the shape of the state and then color in the ecoregion area, adding a box with basic climate considerations where I mark an "X" for the area of observation. This can provide broader context to numerous observations, including fire regimes. Large ecoregions are often broken down into more specific descriptions, which are frequently associated with slope aspect. More detailed examples for journaling about ecoregions can be found further in this chapter.

Fire Regime Attributes

The U.S. interagency Joint Fire Science Program (JFSP) defines a fire regime as the description of fire patterns based on sizes, frequencies, severities, and effects on a given ecosystem. Over the years, various theories and approaches have been proposed to define fire regimes. However, more recent approaches incorporate spatial, magnitude, and temporal elements, including fire size, complexity (patchiness), fire types and related intensities, fire severity, fire frequency/return interval, and seasonality (timing of fire) (Sugihara, 2006).

Fire Size

Fire size is defined by the acres within the fire perimeter area. This does not necessarily mean that all those acres have been burned, as there are often patches and strips of unburned vegetation within the fire perimeter. Fire size and shape are influenced by vegetation (fuels), topography, and weather. In the context of a fire regime, fire size is compared with historic fire sizes within ecoregions. For statistical purposes, the National Wildfire Coordinating Group defines a large fire as one burning 300 acres or more, with an intensity determined by the interactions between the fire's convection column and weather conditions above the surface. The 2006 book "*Fire in California's Ecosystems*" uses fire size definitions associated with ecosystem fire regimes in California (Sugihara, 2006). Some ecosystems have a common fire size of less than 25 acres, while others may commonly burn up to 2,500 acres. Increasing fire size in many U.S. ecoregions is attributed to factors such as vegetation buildup due to fire exclusion and climate change.

Wildfire Sizes & Shapes Over Time (WIFIRE Website)

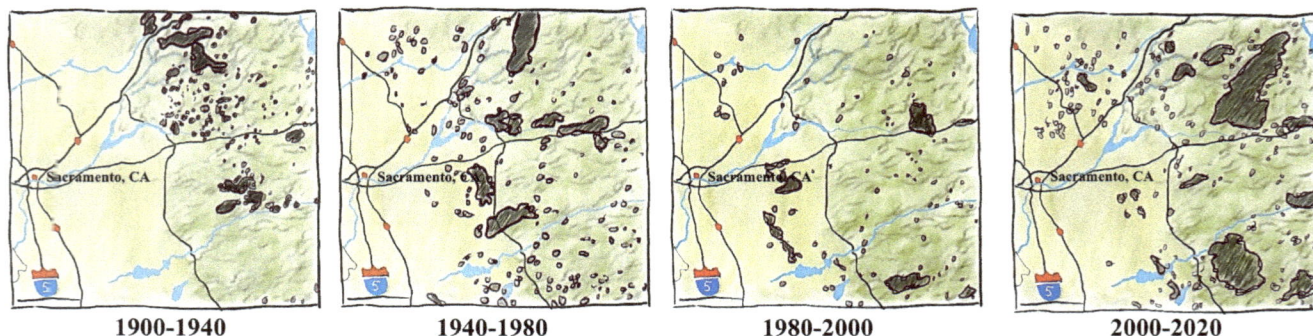

| 1900-1940 | 1940-1980 | 1980-2000 | 2000-2020 |

Journaling Fire Size

When journaling about fire size, it's more practical to focus on relative size and shape rather than exact acreage for every fire across the observation area and time scale. Comparisons with other fires within the ecoregion or large watershed area over different time periods are useful. Utilizing the WIFIRE website's historic wildfire data for the United States, which dates back to the early 1900s, can provide valuable insights. Start by finding the acreage for a couple of reference fires in the area and then make proportional estimates for other fire sizes. I created the illustrations on the following page using the WIFIRE website as a reference for the focus area. By sketching fire locations and sizes onto a simple map with background colors indicating elevational differences, you can gain a better understanding. Explore different time ranges and look for patterns.

Fire Types & Severities

Fire types and severities are often categorized into three levels:

- low severity surface fires

- moderate or mixed severity understory fires

- high severity crown fires

The online fire severity maps I referenced for creating the graphic on the next page includes the following fire severity levels: High, Moderate, Low, Unburned, and Increased Greenness. You can use those maps to envision the fire types and severities that occurred within the area along with site visit photos and sketches in your journal. For further details, refer back to Chapter 9: Fire Severity & Effects and Chapter 8: Fire & Smoke. The upcoming section expands on fire severity as it relates to fire regimes.

Fire Complexity & Patchiness

While general fire size and severity provide insight into fire regimes, they do not capture the complexity of what occurs within the fire area. Fires often exhibit a mix of severities in different scales and patterns, which can be framed in terms of patchiness and pyrodiversity. Patches or mosaics refer to relatively small homogenous areas within the landscape that differ from their surroundings. They contribute to the heterogeneity of vegetation conditions and biodiversity of species, influencing ecosystem effects and biodiversity. Observing fire patchiness can be done using maps and field observations, comparing patches within different fires and where fires overlap.

Patch Size

Journaling about fire severity can feel overwhelming, but it's crucial to maintain perspective on the scale of ecoregions and fire regime patterns. A study by Dominick DellaSala and Chad Hanson examined historic and contemporary high severity fire patches in low to mid-elevation forests across the western states, providing context on patch size. In mixed conifer and pine forests within large ecoregions, high severity patches averaged 1,000 acres, totaling 2-10 million acres burned in each ecoregion.

An important consideration for forest recovery is the proximity of unburned and lower severity areas to high severity patches. These patches typically ranged from 328 to 984 feet from unburned and lower severity areas, allowing for species recruitment and reestablishment. Recovery depends heavily on environmental conditions such as slope, aspect, climate, and distance to unburned areas.(DellaSala and Hanson 2019). Include observations and measurements between severity levels in your journal.

Patchiness & Pyrodiversity

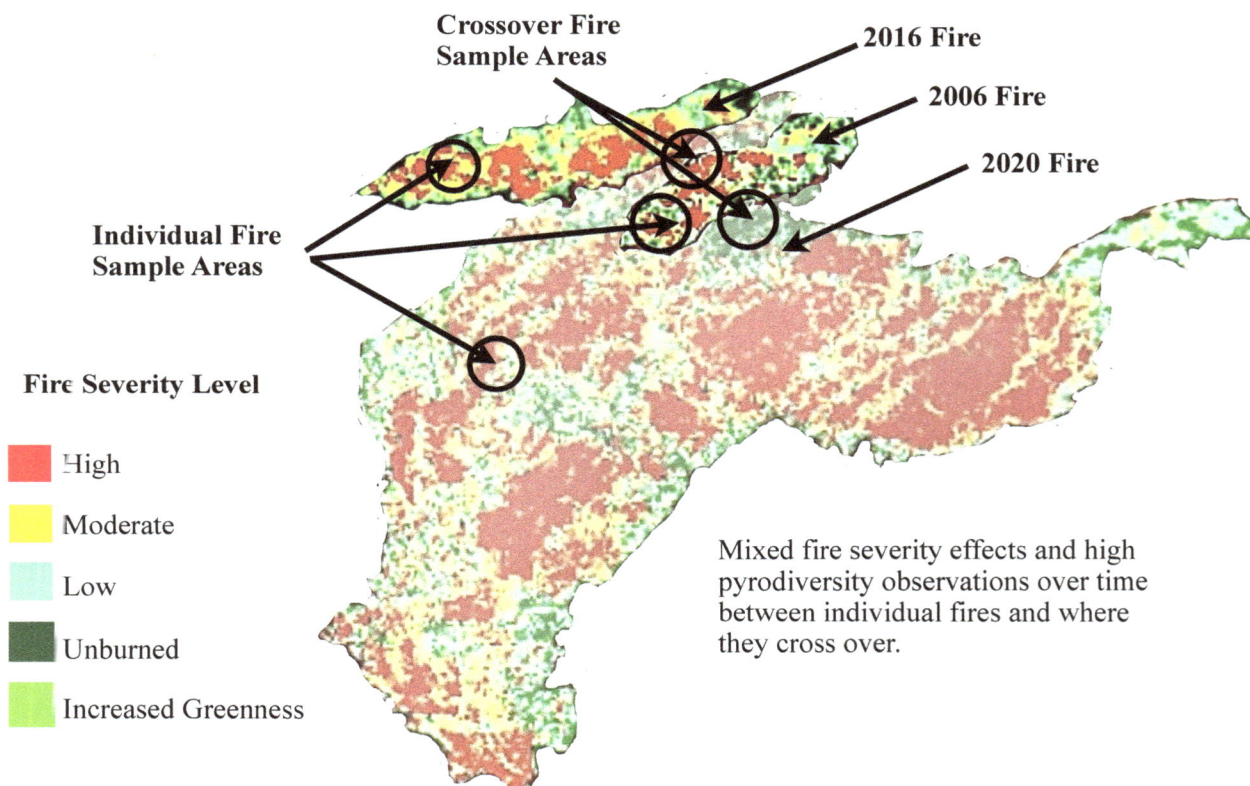

Crossover Fire Sample Areas

2016 Fire

2006 Fire

2020 Fire

Individual Fire Sample Areas

Fire Severity Level

- High
- Moderate
- Low
- Unburned
- Increased Greenness

Mixed fire severity effects and high pyrodiversity observations over time between individual fires and where they cross over.

Common Fire Regime Fire Severity & Complexity (Patchiness) Categories

- Low complexity and low severity typical for grasslands and oak woodlands.

- Moderate complexity and mixed severity of ponderosa pine forests and Douglas fir forests.

- High complexity and mixed severity typical of chaparral communities.

- Low complexity and high severity typical of mixed conifer and giant sequoia forests.

Journaling Complexity & Patchiness

To journal fire severity and patchiness observations, consider sketching the scene or using small diagrams. Use a landscape-scale observation approach, incorporating fire severity map color codes and approximate patterns of complexity and patchiness.

For a simplified approach to capturing field observations immediately after a fire, you can utilize a color scheme representative of changes observed in the field and diagram your observations, like my examples on the next two pages.

Don't forget to use a mix of sample areas within the ecosystem and capture representative areas.

Impressionistic Sketches of Fire Complexity & Patchiness

Realistic Sketches of Fire Complexity & Patchiness

Fire Severity & Fire Regime Complexity Diagram (Online Reference)

Low Complexity & Low Severity	Moderate Complexity & Mixed Severity	Moderate Complexity & Mixed Severity	High Complexity & Mixed Severity	Low Complexity & High Severity

Typical patchiness complexity of grasslands and oak woodlands.

Typical patchiness complexity of ponderosa pine forests.

Typical patchiness complexity of Douglass fir forests.

Typical patchiness complexity of chaparral vegetation communities.

Typical patchiness complexity of mixed conifer and giant sequoia forests.

Fire Severity Levels & Field Observation

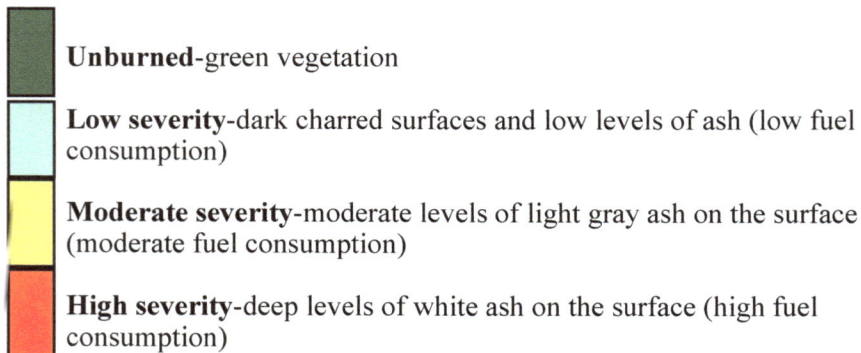

Unburned-green vegetation

Low severity-dark charred surfaces and low levels of ash (low fuel consumption)

Moderate severity-moderate levels of light gray ash on the surface (moderate fuel consumption)

High severity-deep levels of white ash on the surface (high fuel consumption)

Fire Severity & Fire Regime Complexity Diagrams (Field Reference)

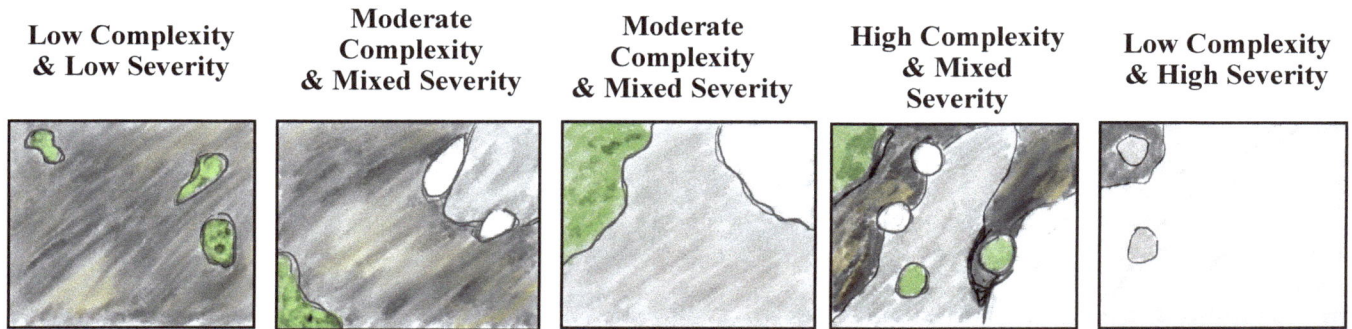

Low Complexity & Low Severity	Moderate Complexity & Mixed Severity	Moderate Complexity & Mixed Severity	High Complexity & Mixed Severity	Low Complexity & High Severity

Fire Severity Levels & Field Observations

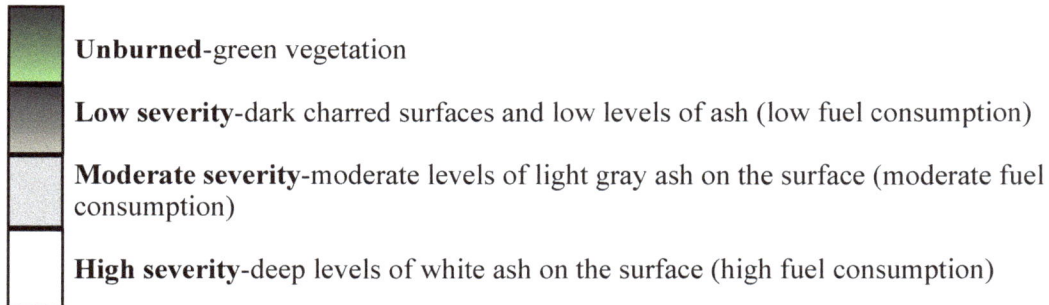

Unburned-green vegetation

Low severity-dark charred surfaces and low levels of ash (low fuel consumption)

Moderate severity-moderate levels of light gray ash on the surface (moderate fuel consumption)

High severity-deep levels of white ash on the surface (high fuel consumption)

Compare your fire regime complexity observations with the typical fire regime complexities for the ecosystem, like those listed on page 231 and the previous page and include notes and questions about why there may be differences.

Fire Frequency & Return Intervals

The U.S. interagency Joint Fire Science Program defines fire frequency as the number of times fires occur within a defined area and time period, while the fire return interval is the time between fires within a defined area. These intervals are associated with ecoregions or vegetation communities. Many sources use the mean fire return interval to quantify the average period between fires under a presumed historical fire regime. Fire regimes vary based on fire types, severities, and sizes over time, affecting vegetation communities, climate, and topography.

Under pre-settlement conditions, fire regimes and associated fire frequency and return intervals can be categorized based on the dominant plant species' response to fire (Sugihara 2006):

- Frequent fire return intervals typically involve surface fires with low severity effects, common in grasslands and savannas.

- Medium fire return intervals have mixed understory crown burned fires with moderate to mixed severity effects, common in mixed conifer forest communities.

- Long fire return intervals typically involve crown fires with mixed to high severity effects, common in north-facing Douglas fir forests and subalpine communities.

Comparing historic/pre-settlement and contemporary fire regimes helps understand environmental conditions, fire hazard levels, and ecosystem health.

Learning about fire regimes associated with different plant species may lead to new field observations. For example, in the gray pine-blue oak vegetation community, a high number of gray pines compared to blue oaks may indicate fire exclusion or suppression.

Similarly, areas with larger concentrations of Douglas fir than expected under historic conditions suggest changes in fire regime. Condition classes are used to compare the current fire regime with historic patterns, highlighting the impact of decreased or increased fire frequencies and return intervals on vegetation communities and ecosystems.

Fire History Maps & Fire Frequency

Earlier in this chapter, I shared the fire history maps from the WIFIRE website that I used for observing fire size. You can also use that site to observe the number of fires occurring in an area over time by using the date scroll bar. This may be a cumbersome exercise, so you might prefer to just use the fire return interval information on the Fire Effects Information System website and add it to your background information for journal observations. There may be limited information for some ecoregions and vegetation communities on different websites, so you may have to generalize or make your own estimates. You may also want to use the observations and notes from Chapter 6: Fire Ignitions & Prevention and consider how human ignition patterns may have changed the fire frequency over time.

Generalized Fire Return Intervals

Moist Mixed Conifer
Less frequent, small-sized, high severity fires

Woodland Savanna
Frequent, large-sized, low severity fires

Dry Mixed Conifer
Mixed frequency, mixed-size, mixed severity fires

30 years

20 years

10 years

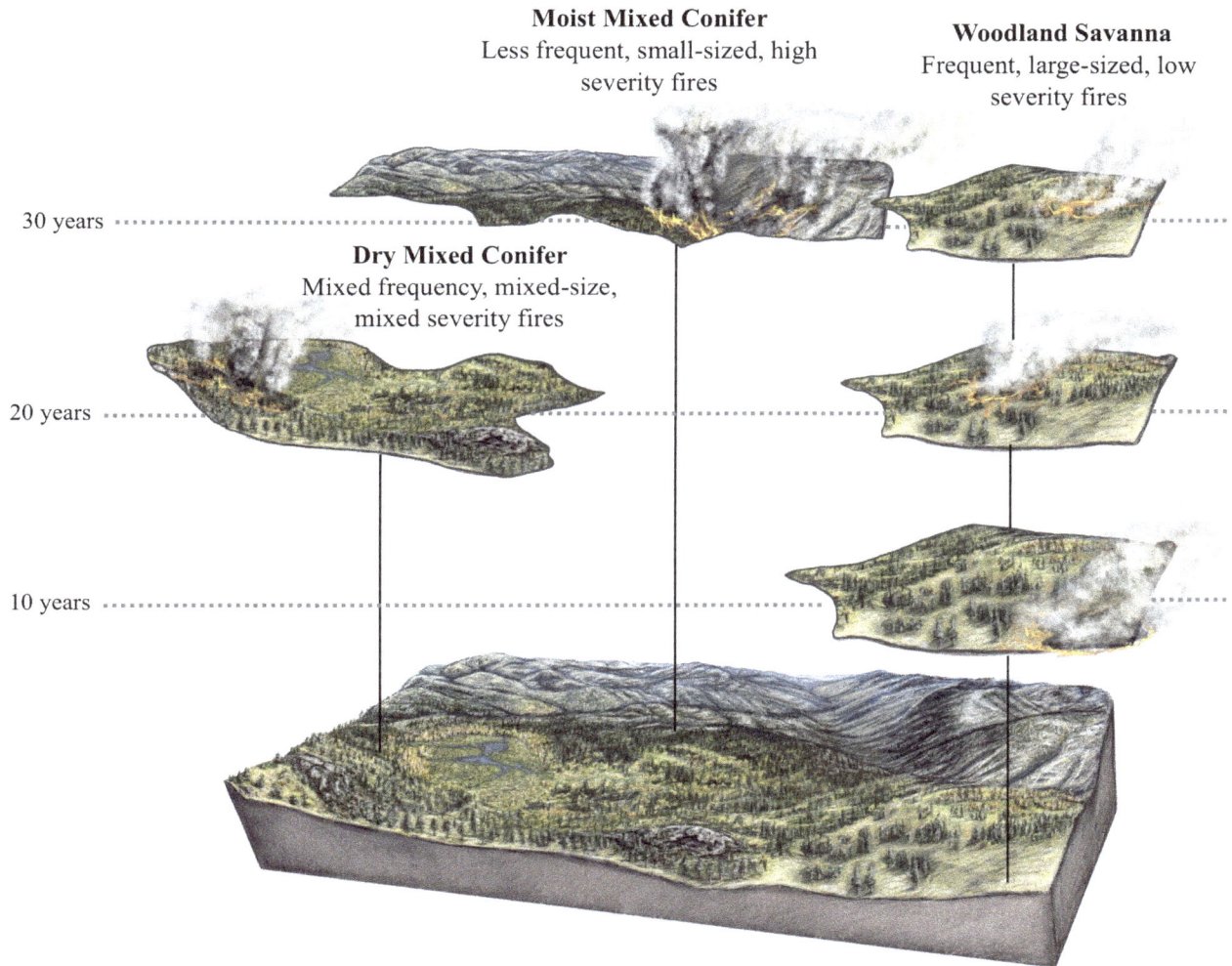

My illustration provides a generalized representation of the fire return intervals for various vegetation communities within a landscape. Each elevated sketch depicts a different fire type and fire frequency associated with that vegetation community. Fire regimes are more accurately represented across larger elevational, ecological, and climatic gradients.

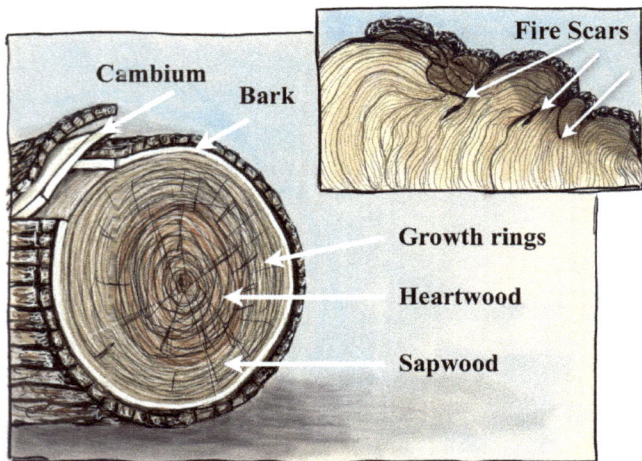

Labels on diagram: Cambium, Bark, Fire Scars, Growth rings, Heartwood, Sapwood

Tree Rings & Fire Frequency

Another option for observing fire frequency or return intervals is to observe tree rings. Trees in temperate climates have distinct dark and light rings, compared to trees in tropical climates. Each year a tree creates a new layer of woody growth. There will be a light layer of wood that forms at the beginning of the season and a dark layer that forms at the end of the growing season, which makes up each annual ring. In areas where the temperatures are more moderate in winter, the darker rings are typically larger than in cold winter climates. The width of both the light and dark lines of tree rings are strongly dependent on tree adaptations and climate interactions, especially temperature, precipitation, and the vapor pressure deficit.

Inside those growth rings, at different time intervals, you'll see black lines and tree deformities that can indicate a fire that occurred that year. These burn or char lines are often more noticeable at the outer edges of the tree where the bark has thickened around the wounds. This can be challenging for those inexperienced with reading tree rings and opportunities to view tree slices (cookies) or fresh cut stumps may be limited. You may be able to observe

tree rings and scars on old tree stumps, but the colors may have faded and woody materials broken down to

where they are less obvious. One option may be to talk with local fire and land managers about forest and timber management projects where you may be able to make observations in recently cut trees. Some parks have tree trunk slices (cookies) displayed in visitor centers, so look for those and add observations to your journal.

Also be aware that insects and other damages to trees can cause discoloration and markings within the tree rings. For example, beetles can attack a tree and leave blue-colored stains across the tree rings. This is caused by fungi that is introduced by beetles to help weaken the tree's defenses. There may also be darker red stains within the tree rings that are caused by tree sap that is distributed to damaged areas to try and fight off insect infestations (North American Tree-Ring Fire Scar Network). Before attempting to read tree rings, review the basic anatomy of a tree trunk. There is the outer layer of bark that provides protection, and the inner bark or phloem is the pipeline for disseminating nutrients. The inner bark dies each year and becomes part of the bark. The cambium layer of cells is the actively growing part of the trunk that also produces new bark. The sapwood is the tree's pipeline for moving water from the soil to the leaves. As newer rings of sapwood are produced, the inner cells lose their function and become heartwood.

In a couple of pages, I have an example using annual temperatures and precipitation to create graphs and compare with tree ring observations that may bring insight to the fire frequency and climate relationships.

Tree Ring & Fire Scar Counting:

- Start at the center of the tree cookie or stump and look for the alternating light- and dark-colored rings in an outward pattern. A magnifying glass may help you see some of the thinner rings.

- Count the number of dark rings from the center out until you reach the bark layer (don't count any rings or markings in the tree bark layer). Add up the number of dark rings to calculate the age of the tree.

- Look for thicker and thinner rings. Thicker rings indicate better growing conditions and more moisture, while narrower rings indicate worse growing conditions, like drought periods.

- Look for black rings and marks within the tree rings where charring and burn scars occurred. These may be more discernible around the outer edges of the tree, but look closely for thinner black lines that are less obvious. You may want to put a question mark by marks you are less certain about. Take notes on whether the darker lines/marks may have been caused by something else like tree sap or fungi.

- Calculate the number of years between the fire-scarred rings/years and consider how this relates to the fire return interval for that forest community fire regime.

Broadleaf & Conifer Tree Ring Examples in California

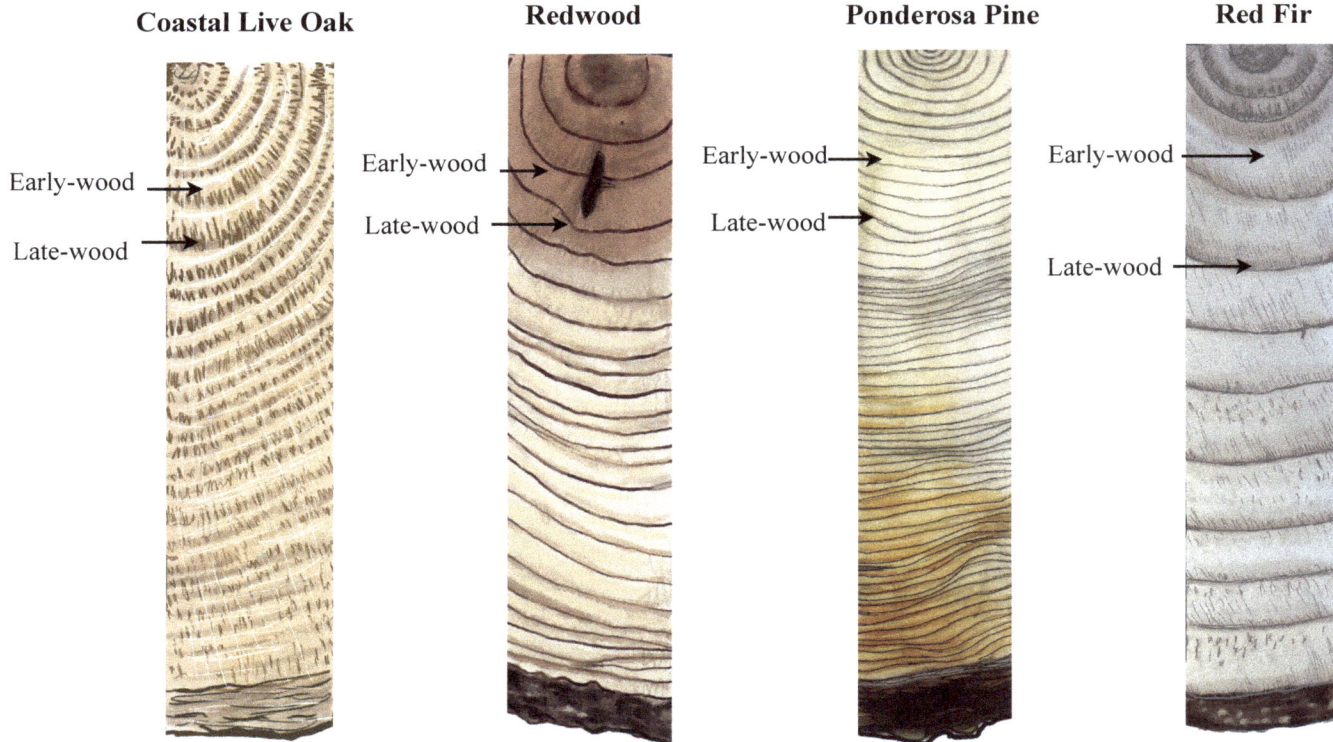

Coastal Live Oak

Early-wood

Late-wood

Redwood

Early-wood

Late-wood

Ponderosa Pine

Early-wood

Late-wood

Red Fir

Early-wood

Late-wood

50-Year Mean Annual Temperature & Precipitation for El Dorado County, California (NOAA Climate at a Glance: County Time Series)

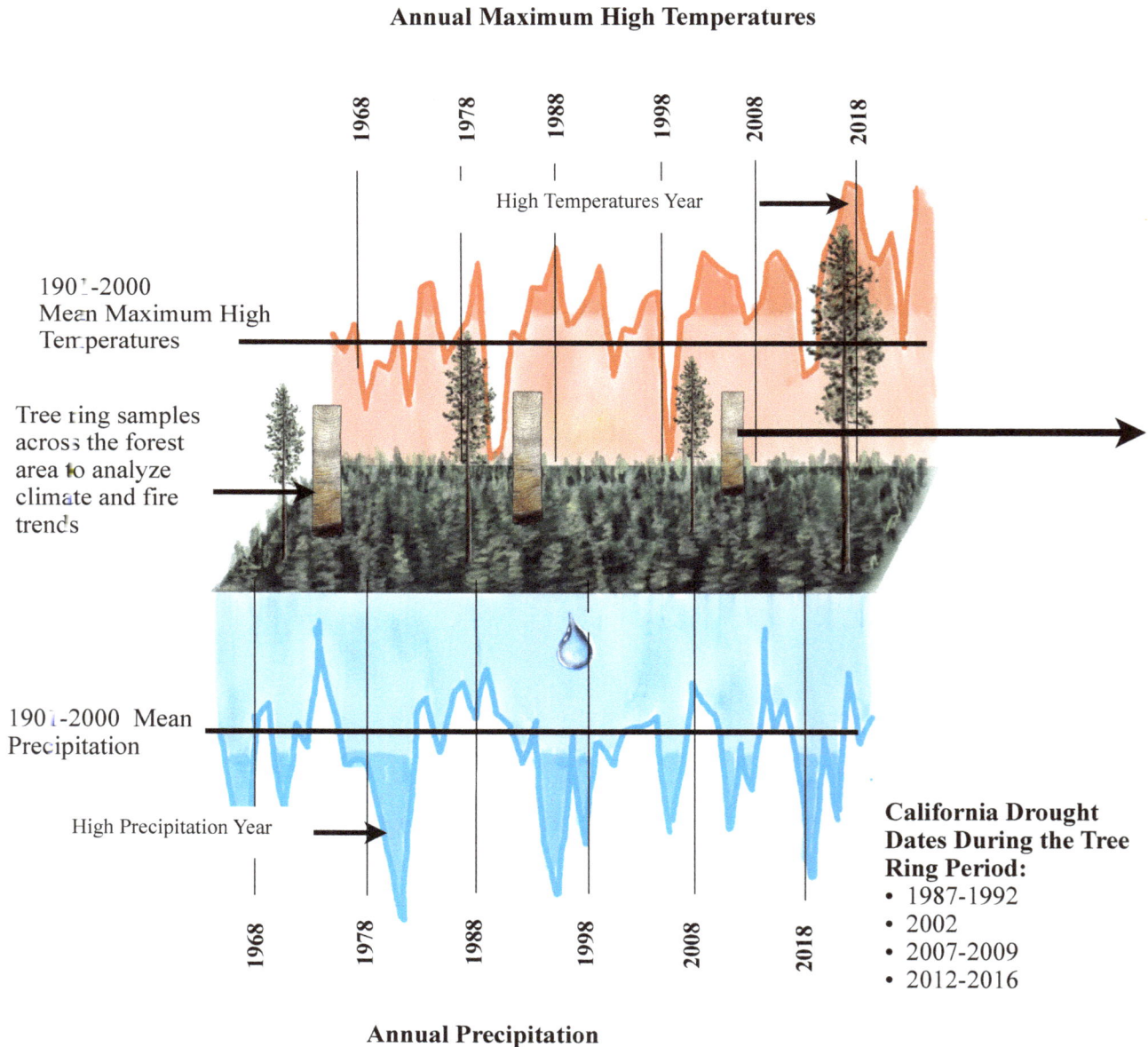

Annual Maximum High Temperatures

1968 1978 1988 1998 2008 2018

High Temperatures Year

1901-2000 Mean Maximum High Temperatures

Tree ring samples across the forest area to analyze climate and fire trends

1901-2000 Mean Precipitation

High Precipitation Year

1968 1978 1988 1998 2008 2018

California Drought Dates During the Tree Ring Period:
- 1987-1992
- 2002
- 2007-2009
- 2012-2016

Annual Precipitation

2019 Ponderosa Pine Tree Ring Observations in El Dorado County, California

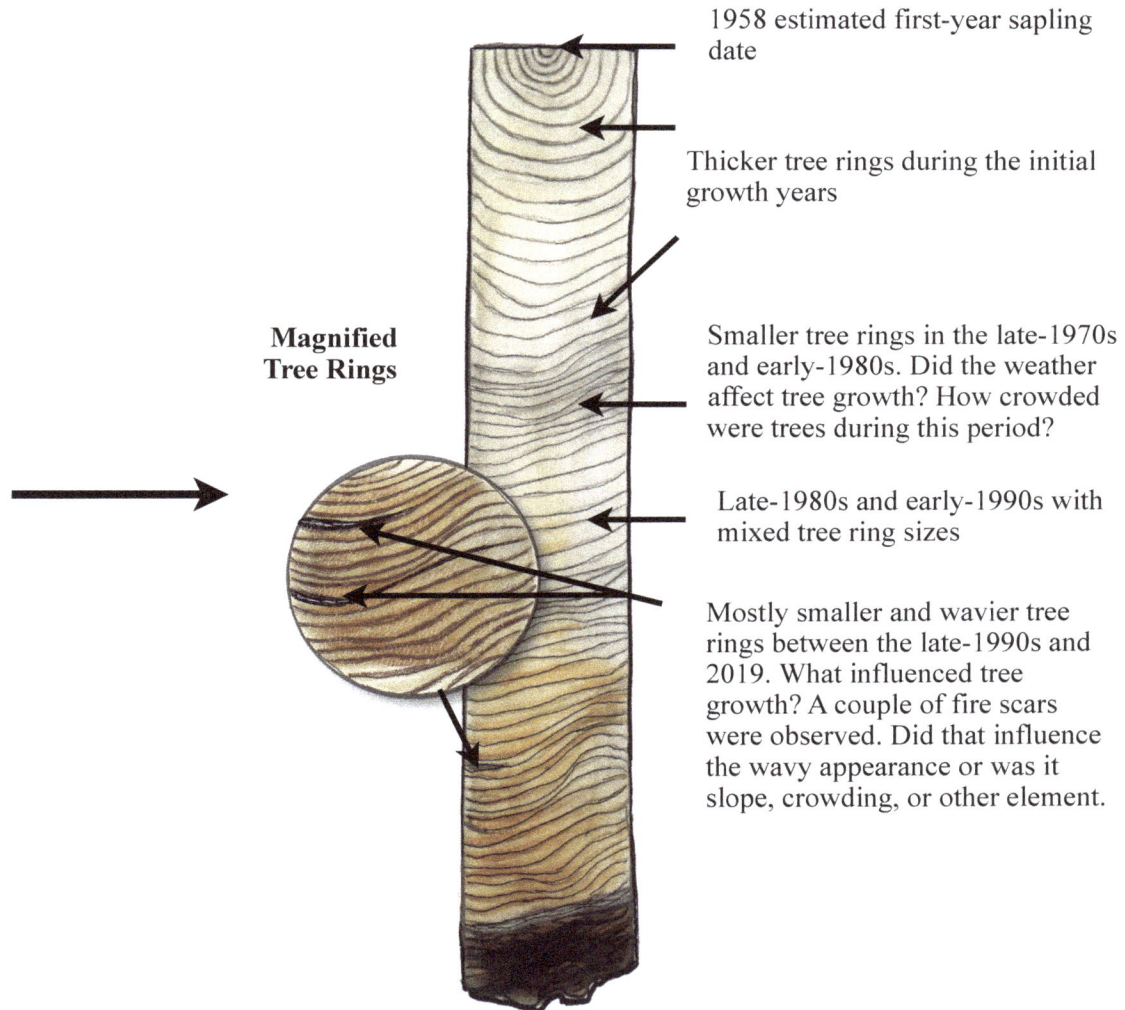

1958 estimated first-year sapling date

Thicker tree rings during the initial growth years

Magnified Tree Rings

Smaller tree rings in the late-1970s and early-1980s. Did the weather affect tree growth? How crowded were trees during this period?

Late-1980s and early-1990s with mixed tree ring sizes

Mostly smaller and wavier tree rings between the late-1990s and 2019. What influenced tree growth? A couple of fire scars were observed. Did that influence the wavy appearance or was it slope, crowding, or other element.

In 2019 the tree was cut down

Fire Seasonality

Fire seasonality relates to the time of year in which fires occur within different vegetation communities and ecoregions. This is strongly related to latitude, longitude, and elevation, which influence the growing season and curing periods of the surface vegetation. In the context of fire regimes, you should also consider how the timing and frequency of fire affect plant and animal phenology. In many areas, the fire seasons are lengthening, and you should consider how that may influence these seasonal cycles of plants and animals.

The illustration below summarizes information from the 2006 book "Fire in California's Ecosystems" by Sugihara, et al. and conveys the seasonality of different ecoregions, elevational zones, and climates within California. You'll notice there are multiple fire occurrence periods indicated as lines or tracks in two of the elevation zones. Those are associated with areas that have moist or dry climates within different elevation zones.

California Fire Seasonality by Elevation

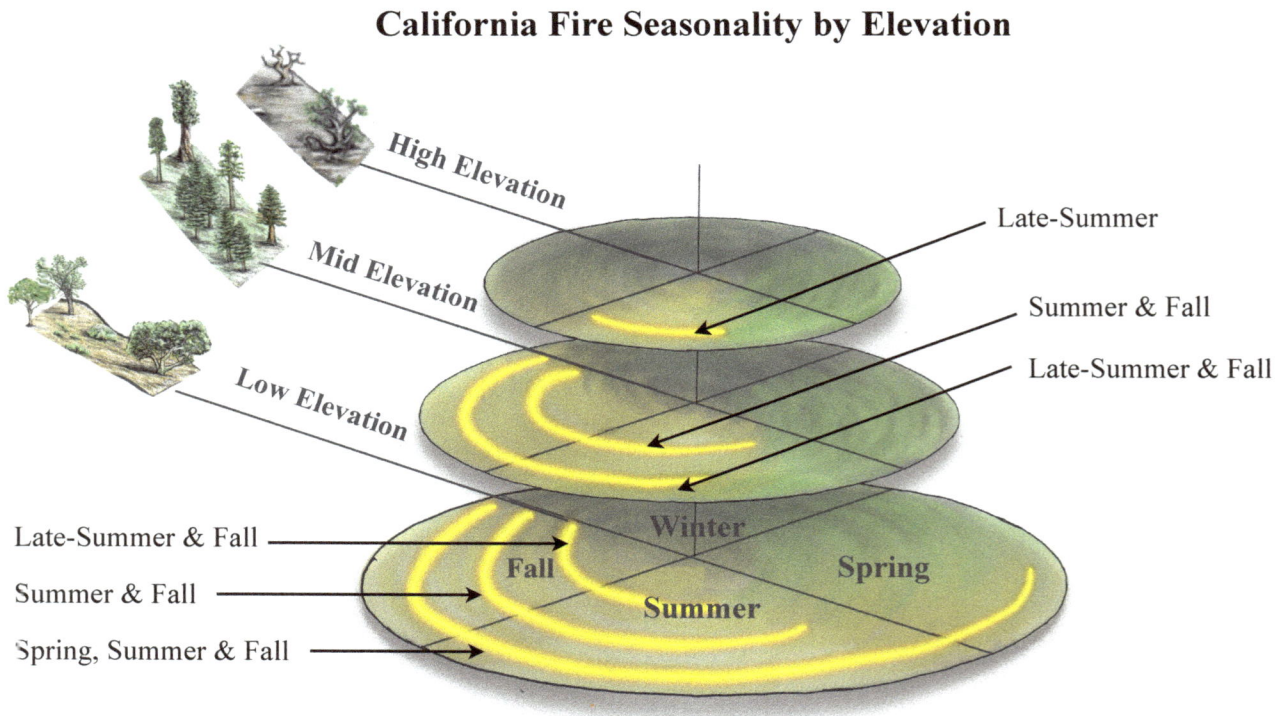

The three circles represent three primary elevational zones in the state. Each elevational circle has four quarters to represent the four seasons. The bright yellow lines represent the periods of potential fire occurrences and fire seasonality within that elevational zone.

I'll describe observations that can be used for journaling about fire seasonality in the next few sections, but finding local references for your area will provide some helpful context that can allow you to make better comparisons of conditions and trends that fit within normal or historical trends versus environments with altered fire regimes and those strongly impacted by climate changes.

Climate Trends & Seasonality

The climate and plant phenology phases (curing) during different seasons will also influence the fire size and severity, so try to integrate that data into your journal. In Chapter 4: Fire Fuels and Chapter 5: Fire Seasons, I shared some information about the vapor pressure deficit (VPD) and how it influences plant conditions and phenophases. Combining VPD data and/or temperature, precipitation, and relative humidity can also be used when journaling about fire seasonality. I would narrow your climate data to the local growing and fire seasons (3-month period). You can include tree ring observations and/or fire occurrences for a more integrated story.

I have used the NOAA National Centers for Environmental Information Climate at a Glance website for the temperature and precipitation graphs on the next page. There are some websites that include VPD and other climate-related maps that could also be used for comparisons with field observations, like those on the PRISM Climate Group, Oregon State University website. See the Average Daily Maximum Vapor Pressure Deficit map below (PRISM).

It can sometimes be challenging to find VPD data for different areas and time periods, as can be the relative humidity data, but you can still make some comparisons from variable data sources, like I have done in the example on page 242.

Temperature and precipitation indirectly influence the size of tree rings, but the VPD is tied to a tree's transpiration and photosynthesis process, which builds the tree rings. The VPD is calculated using the temperature and relative humidity. The higher the air temperature, the more water vapor is held in the atmosphere (higher humidity). If there are high temperatures and less surface water, precipitation, and soil moisture available, the atmosphere pulls moisture from plants. During these periods, trees have trouble retaining water, transpiring, and photosynthesizing. Under repeated hot and dry conditions, with associated low VPD levels, trees slow woody development and can become highly stressed, experience hydraulic failure, and become vulnerable to insect attacks and diseases.

Journaling Fire Seasonality

There are many approaches you could take to journaling about fire seasonality, including the use of fire history maps and climate graphs. Some fire history maps include the date a fire started, which will be important for connecting the seasonality.

I combined the VPD data for the same area and seasonal period from 1980 to 2020 and combined it with a temperature and precipitation graph to try and build a sense of seasonal weather and VPD conditions that might be represented in the tree rings observations. I would combine this data graph, the tree ring and fire scar observations, with a local fire history map that emphasizes the fire occurrence dates to help build a sense of fire seasonality.

I would also recommend including seasonal temperatures, precipitation, and other data such as VPD, EVI, NDVI, drought conditions, wildfire occurrences, and fire severity to develop fire seasonality observations.

The top graph on this page shows nighttime VPD levels between June and September from 1980 to 2020 in the Sierra Nevada region, while the bottom two graphs display the average temperatures and precipitation in El Dorado County, California, for the same period. The county is within the Sierra Nevada region.

Above the middle line in the VPD graph is the level at which plants may struggle with transpiration and photosynthesis. By examining the temperature and precipitation graphs, you can observe trends between temperatures, moisture, and VPD levels.

Many plants prefer a VPD between 0.8 kPa to 1.0 kPa for vegetative development (pulsegrow.com). In my tree ring observation sketch, you may notice differences in tree ring size corresponding to these weather trends in the graphs.

If you were to compare periods of high temperature, low moisture, and high VPD levels with the occurrence of large wildfires, you would observe the relationships between tree rings, fire, and climate.

Comparison of the Average Temperature, Precipitation & VPD

June-September 1980 to 2020

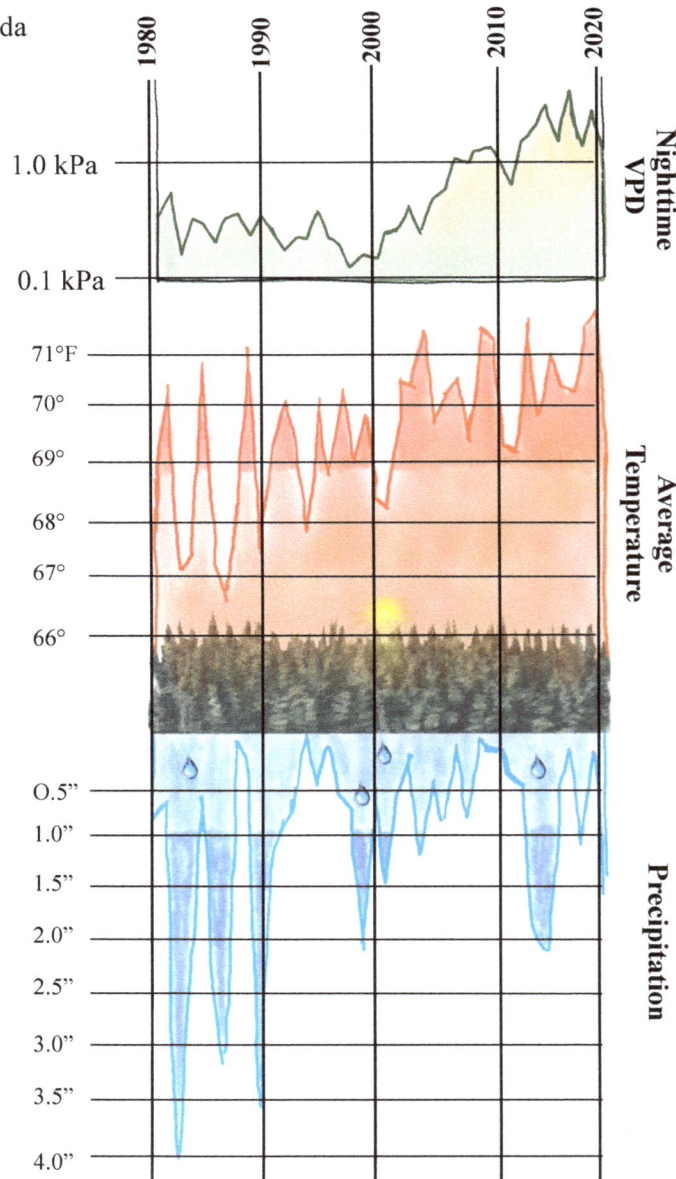

Landscape Patterns

Observing landscape patterns and changes are important for building a sense of fire regimes and pyrodiversity. You can find some fire regime information on the U.S. Forest Service Fire Effects Information System (FEIS) website. Patches in the landscape will change over time—sometimes quickly, sometimes slowly. There are patch dynamics that can also be observed and help convey fire regime elements. These dynamics can result from different influences and factors such as elevation, availability of water, competition between plants, interactions with animals, and the types and severities of impacts, like fire.

In my illustration, I have an example of some key forest types and tree species along an elevational gradient of a western slope in the Sierra Nevada

Dominant Trees & Several Fire Regime Attributes in Western Slope Sierra Nevada Forest Zones

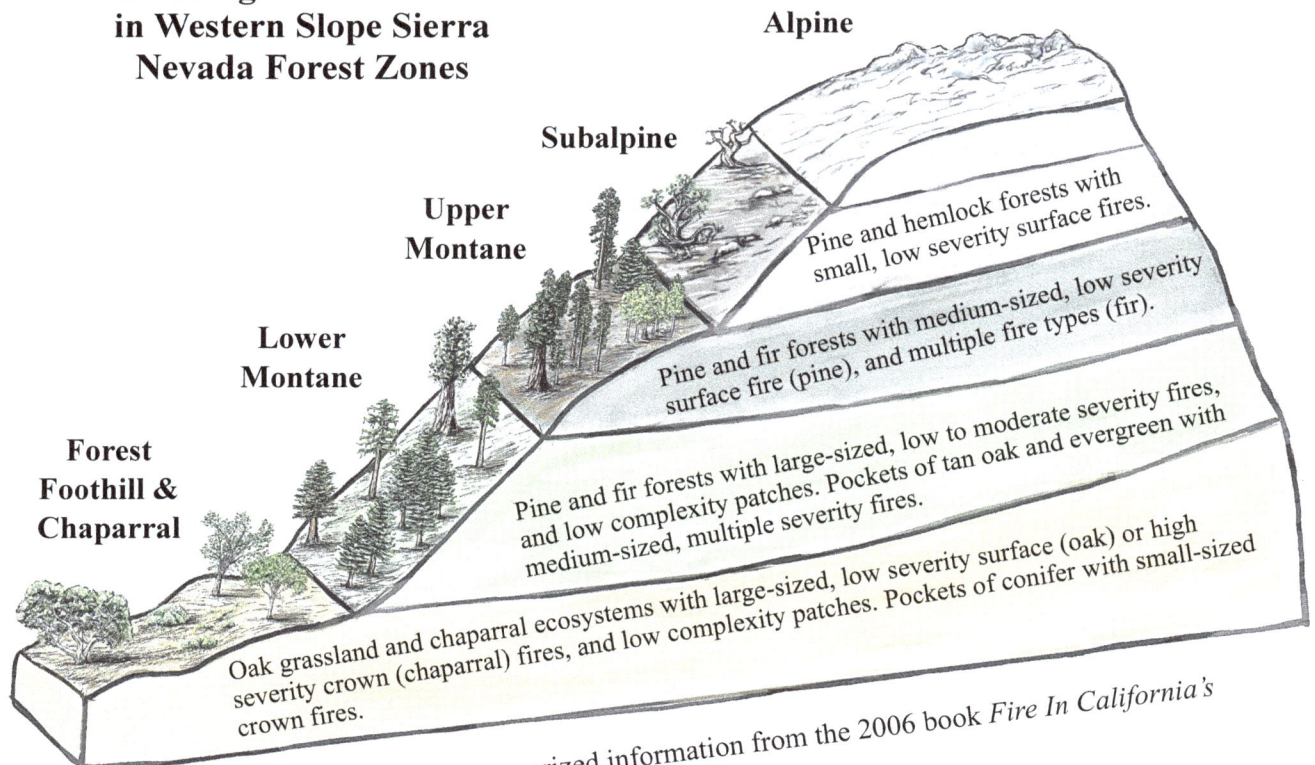

Alpine

Subalpine

Upper Montane

Lower Montane

Forest Foothill & Chaparral

Pine and hemlock forests with small, low severity surface fires.

Pine and fir forests with medium-sized, low severity surface fire (pine), and multiple fire types (fir).

Pine and fir forests with large-sized, low to moderate severity fires, and low complexity patches. Pockets of tan oak and evergreen with medium-sized, multiple severity fires.

Oak grassland and chaparral ecosystems with large-sized, low severity surface (oak) or high severity crown (chaparral) fires, and low complexity patches. Pockets of conifer with small-sized crown fires.

The illustration visualizes summarized information from the 2006 book *Fire In California's Ecosystems* by Sugihara, et.al. 2006.

mountains. By creating this type of visual, you can get some ideas of the tree forms that you may observe in the field and consider the potential patterns and patches that you might observe.

Ecological Succession

Vegetation communities can change slowly over time, with significant changes occurring after disturbances like fire. You can observe the early colonizer and pioneer species that arrive, followed by the climax species and communities. It can take decades to transition into a climax community, but depending on the patch mosaic of the burn, the transition can have variable outcomes. Researching a little about the successional phases and species associated with pioneer or climax communities can help you make connections to these complex changes. There are some species traits you can observe that help identify many of the successional phases. For example, pioneer tree species are commonly those that are quick-growing with frequent and numerous seeds. These seeds often appear smaller in form and lighter-colored in the canopy. They can often be observed along forest edges, like poplars, larches, alders, aspen, and willows. Climax tree species are often the taller and darker appearing trees deep within a forest or dominating the landscape, with slower growth rates and larger reproductive elements, like acorns and

Visual & Systems Thinking

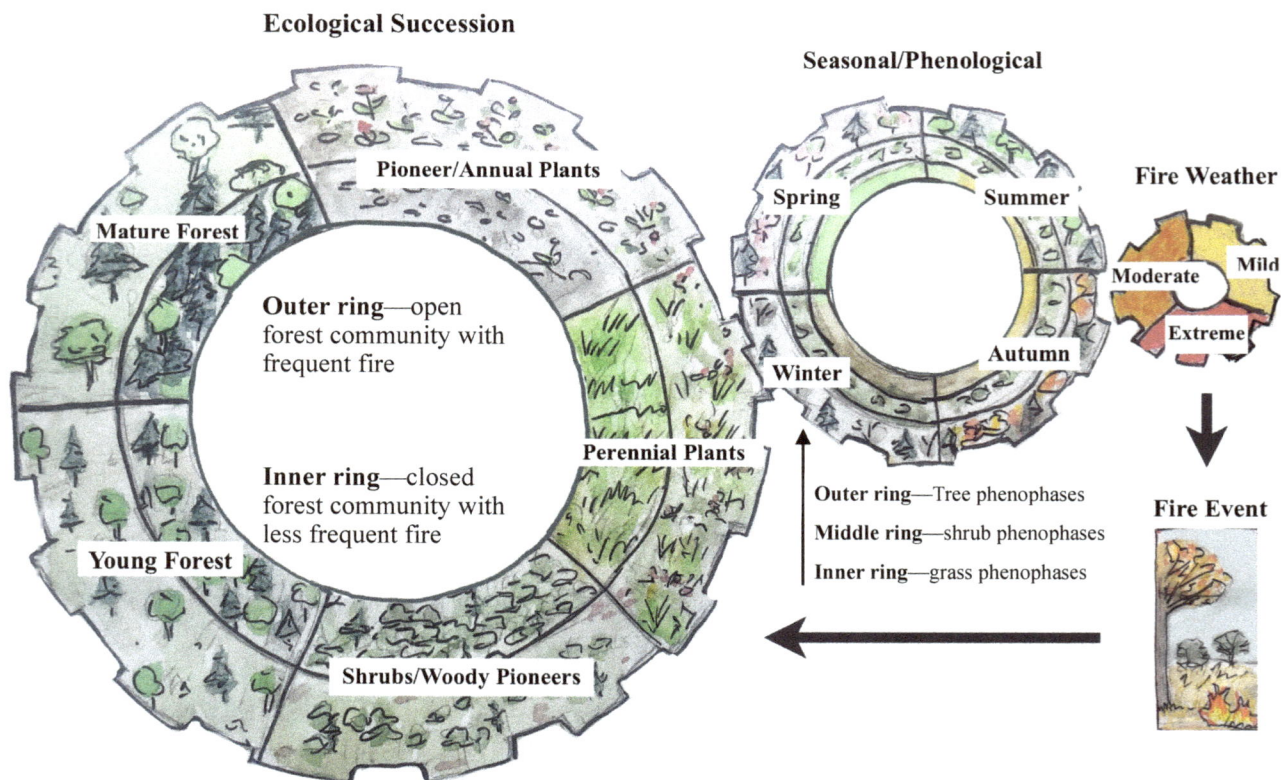

Ecological Succession

Pioneer/Annual Plants

Mature Forest

Outer ring—open forest community with frequent fire

Inner ring—closed forest community with less frequent fire

Young Forest

Perennial Plants

Shrubs/Woody Pioneers

Seasonal/Phenological

Spring   Summer

Winter   Autumn

Outer ring—Tree phenophases

Middle ring—shrub phenophases

Inner ring—grass phenophases

Fire Weather

Moderate   Mild

Extreme

Fire Event

cones. For example, white oaks, Douglas fir, coast redwood, beech, and maple. Even some chaparral communities are considered climax species. I am speaking in a general sense, and there are many species that can be considered climax species depending on the region.

It can be very challenging to journal and visualize this scale of observation. I am providing an example from one of my journals as a lesson learned. This type of visual is more about a visual thinking process, so don't worry about it being completely accurate or pretty. The process of visualizing is a valuable learning tool. In my example, I wanted to use mechanical gears to associate the interactions between succession/seral stages, seasonal phenology, weather, and fire. After completing the visual, I realized that combining the different rings within the ecological succession gear did not accurately portray the time differences in the successional processes between the open forest and closed (crowded) forest communities, which would also have different fire regimes.

Journaling Landscape Patterns

Observing landscape patterns can be done from a high viewpoint, webcams like AlterWildfire, and/or satellite images like Google Earth. I would recommend making observations at different elevations and distances (foreground, mid-ground, background), as explained in Chapter 3: Topography. I like to look at elevational and aspect vegetation patterns when viewing things at a distance (background), vegetation community patterns at a mid-distance, and plant dynamics in the close-up scene. You can also research different vegetation communities and develop a sense of what you might expect to see, such as how tall or short and/or sparse or crowded the dominant trees and shrubs grow at different elevations and slope aspects. If you add fire regime information for those communities, you may also build some insight into observations you might

expect. This information can be included in your journal with visuals like my illustration on the next couple of pages..

I find it helpful to think about the plant and vegetation community appearances at different distances, especially with trees and forests. The angle of the sun, weather, and seasonal changes will alter visibility and how you perceive colors, but when sketching and journaling, you can fall back on some basic color and shape interpretations rather than trying to capture the exact appearance in the field. In the next couple of pages, I have examples of how you could practice sketching different tree species and forest communities as well as capture landscape patterns. Try to include observations that help differentiate between, at least, the overstory, understory, and surface vegetation, and between conifer/evergreen and broadleaf/deciduous trees. A lot of the fire regime and climate weather are often associated with these general forest types and descriptions.

To enhance your skills in differentiating between conifer and broadleaf trees at a distance and between tree species and seasons at the landscape scale, you will also need to get a closer view to clarify or correct assumptions made at a distance. For example, most trees will appear more gray and blue at a distance and could be misidentified. The shapes of trees can also be disguised at a distance. One approach that can help with sketching different tree species is to create tree shapes and color schemes for visualizing different tree categories or species in the scene. When sketching a landscape at different distances, try to find the subtle colors, shapes, and patterns and use that to make your tree identification key. I have some tips for drawing trees in Chapter 4: Fire Fuels if you need more instruction. A tree types/species color scheme example is on the next couple of pages.

Visualizing & Differentiating Trees

Conifer/Evergreen Tree Shapes & Colors

Broadleaf/Deciduous Tree Shapes & Colors

Approximate Tree Canopy Color Codex

Background Tree Shapes & Colors

Conifers visualized with tiny short vertical lines and broadleaf trees as buzzy-blobby areas

Mid Ground Tree Shapes & Colors

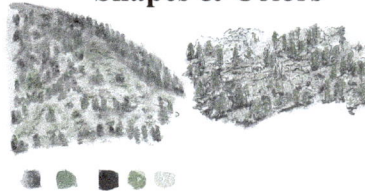

Conifers in conical shapes trees and broadleaf trees in fuzzy rounded blobs

- Tree canopy colors can vary based on the amount and angle of sunlight, weather, and other conditions

- Trees in the distant background areas are typically faint and muted gray-blue in color

- Trees in the mid ground areas are typically muted green colors

- Trees in the foreground and closeup are in full color as in the example color codex

- Stressed, dying and burned trees will change in appearance over time

Cobalt teal blue mixed with burnt Sienna creates a green for fir trees

Cobalt teal blue mixed with sap green creates a green for spruce trees

Sap green mixed with ultramarine to create a green for juniper, cedar and some oak trees

Sap green mixed with burnt Sienna creates a green for pine trees and some oak trees

Sap green mixed with Hanson yellow (Med) creates a green for maple, cottonwood and some oak trees

Sap green mixed with Hanson yellow (Med) creates a green for aspen trees

Feather River Canyon, Butte/Plumas Counties, California
September 2016

Feather River Canyon, Butte/Plumas Counties, California
November 2020

California Mixed Conifer Ecoregion

Steep canyon ridges with scattered strings and small patches of tall trees between thick shrubs or trees along slopes

BACKGROUND
Landscape
Patterns

California Mixed Conifer Ecoregion

2-Years After
the Camp Fire

Southern Slope Yellow Pine & Oak

Conical-shaped tall green trees surrounded by thick patches of short rounded gray-green trees

MID GROUND
Vegetation
Pattens

Skeletal Pine Trees & Sprouting Oaks

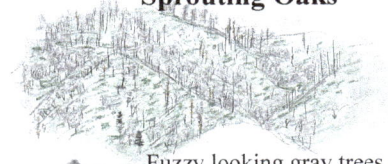

Fuzzy looking gray trees and low-lying green shrubs or trees

Ponderosa Pine, Live Oak & Madrone Trees

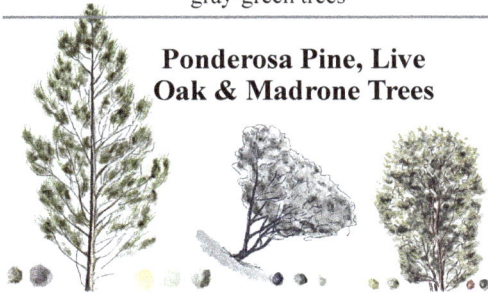

FOREGROUND
Plant Patterns

Tall conical-shaped olive-green tree crowns and yellow- brown bark

Wide-branching trees with gray-green canopy and dark brown/gray bark

Deep yellow-green canopy with red bark

Stressed or Dying Tree Crowns of Pine Trees & Oaks

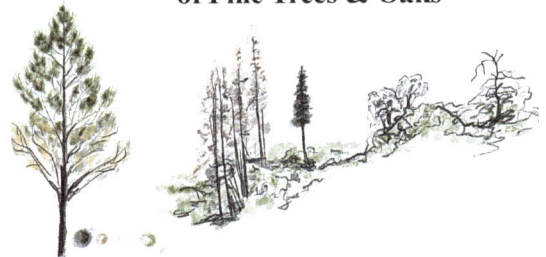

Numerous ponderosa pine trees with partial or full-crowns brown and gray needles. A few oak and or madrone trees with some gray leaves but mostly skeletal with sprouting from near or around the base of trunks.

Tree Stress, Injury & Death

Once you have a good idea of the normal tree phenophase observations (Chapter 4: Fire Seasons) and potential canopy color changes from a distance, you can start to observe things like tree stress, injury, and death from both a distance and up close. Over the next few pages, I have illustrations of some of the potential indicators that can help you observe these changes. I have organized these indicators by location on the tree, starting with some general canopy color phases of stress and either recovery or death. The illustration on the next page references canopy color phases that are often associated with wood-boring and bark beetle attacks and tree fatality phases. Keep in mind that these can be observations in a normal healthy forest, where only a few trees have been killed. But when large forest areas show these signs, there is typically a complex mix of impacts including periods of drought, heatwaves, severe wildfires, and/or exclusion of natural fire regimes. Following that are illustrations of variable foliage and tree canopy indicators of stress and injury, then bark and wood-boring insect indicators that can be observed on the tree trunk and branches. There are a few additional illustrations that cover some other observations and indicators of tree stress or decay, including fungi and frost cracks.

To journal these observations, I would recommend you include both the tree canopy as a whole and the close-up observations. This will build your skills in observing landscape patterns. Try to estimate the percentage of changes and impacts to a tree branch, tree canopy, and tree trunk. In the early phases of stress, there may only be a little thinning and color change to the very top or inner portion of the branches. Track the percentage of impact and change.

Visual Indicators of Tree Stress & Death from Insect Attacks

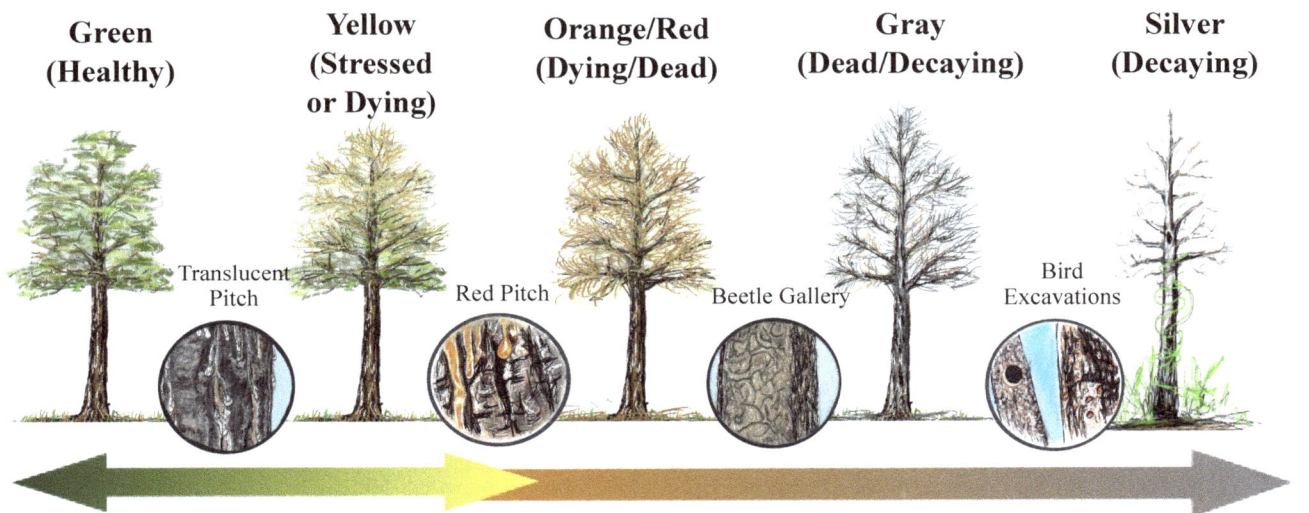

Green (Healthy)   **Yellow (Stressed or Dying)**   **Orange/Red (Dying/Dead)**   **Gray (Dead/Decaying)**   **Silver (Decaying)**

Translucent Pitch

Red Pitch

Beetle Gallery

Bird Excavations

Green phase with healthy living trees

Yellow and red phases, 0 to 4 years after abiotic and/or biotic impacts, with visual indicators of initial stress and/or the early phase of death. Recovery may be possible. Translucent sap/pitch along the stems and trunk is a sign that the tree is still able to fight off the insects. Red pitch, with insect frass that looks like fine sawdust, is a sign that the tree will die.

Gray phase, 5 to 10 years since abiotic and biotic impacts, with most or all needles/leaves fallen, tiny dead and weathered stems, and branches remaining. Branches and trunk have many holes and excavations/ engravings within and under the bark from insects and birds.

Silver phase, over 10 years since abiotic/ biotic impacts, with much of the bark sloughed off and weathered tree trunks. Large excavations and cavities are visible along the trunk.

Foliage Indicators of Tree Stress & Injury

Bottom Up

Dead foliage along the bottom of the canopy

Trees with dead foliage on the lower portion of the canopy may indicate foliage freeze from fire or foliage that has been heat- or cold-scorched by extreme temperatures.

Potential indicator of drought, but could also be normal needle cast

High cone production can indicate drought and or insect attack.

Speckled

Scattered patchy dead foliage throughout the canopy

Trees with above normal or growing scattered patches of dead foliage can indicate drought, disease, insect attacks, and or hail impacts.

Potential indicator of drought, heat scorch, or poor soil conditions

Thinning and dying needles can indicate chemical drift

Flagged

Individual tree branches with dead foliage

Trees with individual branches covered in dead foliage can indicate a localized injury and or insect attack.

Lopsided

Dead foliage dominate on one side of the canopy

Trees with dead foliage more dominant on one side of a tree can indicate heat scorch from high temperatures on the side exposed to the afternoon sun and or heat retaining surfaces (roadside).

Potential indicator of fungal infection (Swiss needle cast)

Thinned/ dead needles and scraped bark can indicate heavy hail

Top Down

Thinning dead foliage starting at the top of the canopy

Trees with dead foliage more dominant starting at the top of the canopy can indicate insect attack.

Potential indicator of tree stress (mistletoe)

Epicormic sprouting can indicate recovery from injury and or stress

Fungi Indicators of Tree Decay

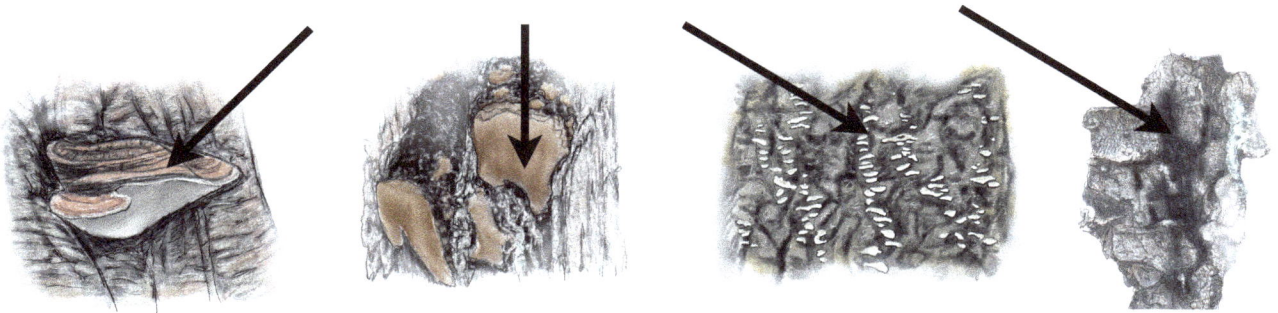

Observations of fungi on trees can indicate tree disease and decay. Look for unusual growths and color changes on tree trunks and compare with foliage conditions to help refine observation skills of tree health.

Sun Scald/Frost Crack Indicators of Tree Sensitivity to Sun Exposure

Summer sun scald

Winter sun scald/frost crack

Winter sun scald/frost crack

Thinned-barked trees with trunks exposed to direct sunlight and in areas with hot and cold temperatures can be vulnerable to sunscald and frost cracks. Look for flaking bark and deep cracks along the bottom of the tree trunk, where the tree is exposed to the afternoon sun. These impacts can make trees more vulnerable to insect attacks.

Bark & Wood-Boring Insect Indicators

Beetle exit holes

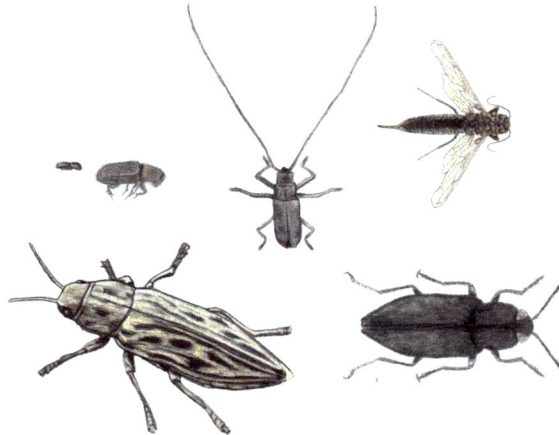

Adult wood-boring insects and bark beetles

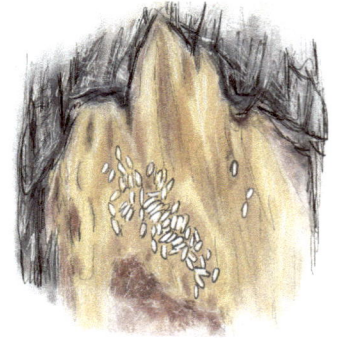

Beetle larvae under the bark and inside the wood

Reddish or white insect frass inside bark crevices and at the base of the tree trunk

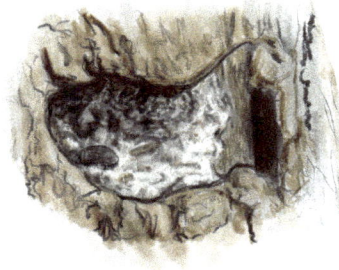

Fungus patches and stains inside the bark and the tree cambium

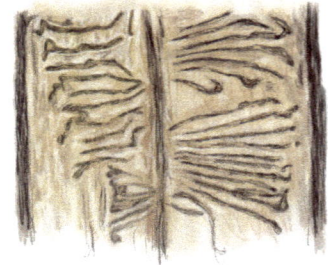

Carved patterns/galleries from beetle larvae in the bark and tree cambium

Bird Indicators of Bark & Wood-Boring Insects

Sapsucker holes

Woodpecker holes and excavations

Animal Indicators

There are a number of animal species that impact the health of trees by creating cavities and deep scrapes, although most of these animals are searching for insects under the tree bark that are likely already under insect attack. Many trees will still survive from a variety of animal impacts. Also keep in mind that many animals have preferred habitats, which can include stressed and burned landscapes. Keep track of the animal observations using different habitat types and conditions. You may start to observe the relationships between animals and habitat conditions.

Tree & Forest Recovery

Tree recovery may look different based on the tree species, adaptations, and type of impacts. It's also helpful to remember that the life of a forest community is more than the individual tree. Observing the different successional stages after a significant impact, like severe wildfire, can be a valuable experience and a representation of the larger ecosystem and environmental changes.

Some trees may recover by sprouting from the trunk or branches, or by reseeding after a fire. Certain tree species need fire to trigger the opening of cones or to sprout, but the fire severity may influence success. Some cones and seeds may survive moderate to high-intensity fire, while others may be strongly charred or consumed. Look closely at the conditions of the tree

Full canopy

Partial canopy and epicormic shoots

Partial canopy

Partial canopy

Basal sprouting/ shoots

Serotinous and fire resilient cones and seeds

Tree saplings

canopy and trunk, at the cones and seeds on the ground or in the trees, and consider whether the tree and forest are recovering from severe climate conditions and/or fire events. Also, include observations about the elevation, aspect, and slope along with recent climate trends that will influence recovery. You may want to tally the number or percent of trees and/or tree species that appear to be recovering or reseeding an area and/or by topographic elements.

Plant Traits & Fire Regimes

The spatial and temporal landscape patterns we observe can also be associated with plant traits and adaptations. Plant relationships with fire are often defined by their structural or physiological traits that determine the level of effects from fire. Some plants and vegetation communities are ranked as more flammable, while others are considered less flammable. However, that does not necessarily correlate with the fire-resilient or adaptive traits that allow a plant to survive, recover, or sprout within their associated fire regime.

I like to think about the flammable plant traits in comparison to the resilient and adaptive traits. In a few pages, I have an illustration that provides some examples of plant morphological structures and sprouting adaptations. I created an illustrated table of flammable plant traits in Chapter 7: Fire Mitigation & Readiness, which can be referenced with this chapter for comparisons of resilient and hazardous traits. We'll delve further into these observations over the next few pages.

Tree Foliage Traits

Plant foliage traits can influence flammability, survival, and recovery. In general, conifer needles are more flammable than deciduous leaves. Some species have small thick leaves with high moisture, which can make them harder to burn. Some pine trees have long needles that can protect buds from the effects of fire, while fir trees have short needles with more vulnerable buds. Other plants have large and/or curling leaves that are highly flammable and, in many ways, invite frequent fire to spread through the area. I used information from A. Engber and J. Morgan's study on *Patterns of Flammability of the California Oaks: the role of leaf traits compared traits* such as leaf size, thickness, surface area to volume ratio, and curling with their associated fire regimes to create the illustration on the following page. Leaf shape and size have a strong influence on the fuel bed conditions, which can be more or less flammable.

Journaling Foliage Flammability Traits

Journaling about tree foliage can be fun, while associating fire regimes can be more challenging. The great thing about journaling is that you don't have to know the answers—you can ask questions. Try to consider the flammability traits in your observations like leaf size, shape, thickness, texture, moisture, and the waxes and oils of leaves and their arrangement in the fuel bed. Use multiple senses like sight, scent, sound, and touch. You can sketch, trace, or diagram the leaf sizes, shapes, and fuel bed levels, and write your thoughts about the foliage traits and fire relationships.Use the example on the next page.

Oak Leaf Flammability & Associated Fire Regimes

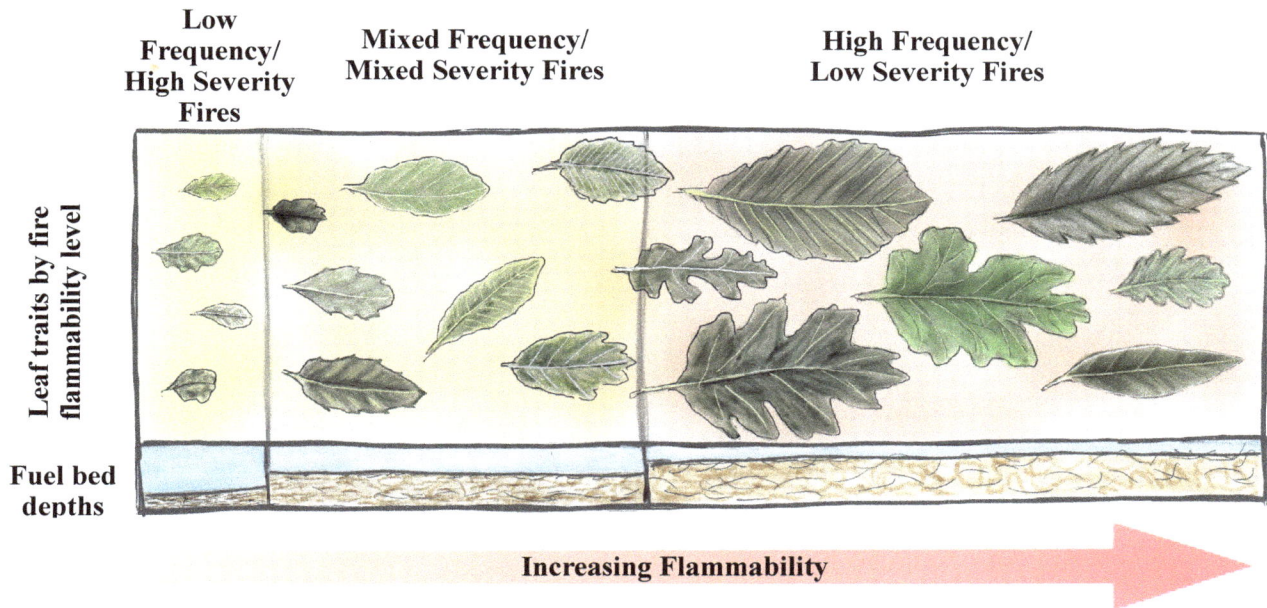

Information interpreted and illustration adapted from *Patterns of Flammability of the California Oaks: the role of leaf traits. Ramon A. Engber and J. Morgan, III*

Low Frequency/ High Severity Fires

- Evergreen oak shrubs
- Small leaf sizes
- Simple to slightly-lobed leaf shapes
- Low fuel depths

Mixed Frequency/ Mixed Severity Fires

- Mixed evergreen and deciduous oak trees and shrubs
- Small to medium leaf sizes
- Simple to slightly-lobed leaves
- Low/moderate fuel bed depths

High Frequency/ Low Severity Fires

- Mixed evergreen and deciduous oak trees and shrubs
- Medium to large leaf sizes
- Simple to highly-lobed leaves
- Thin to thick leaves
- Moderate to high fuel bed depths

Bark & Branch Traits

Bark traits can influence flammability and can insulate and protect the inner cambium of trees from extreme temperatures and the heat of a wildfire. Loose and flaking bark can create more flammable conditions, especially if it builds up on the ground. When making bark observations, look at the tree trunk from the base to as high as possible. Bark thickness can vary along the tree trunk. Some trees develop thicker bark as they age, while others may develop thick bark at an early age. Bark thickness can be a good indicator of more fire-resistant or adapted species. The age at which tree bark thickens and the height of thick bark can be an indicator of fire frequency and fire types. For example, fir trees develop thicker bark with age, which can indicate a longer return interval. Tree branches are another observation that can relate to the fire regime. Some trees self-prune their lower branches, which reduces the likelihood of a surface fire burning into the tree crown.

Journaling Bark & Branch Traits

Bark can be fun to journal about and engage a range of senses. Bark thickness and texture is also an observation that can help you think about fire regimes. Compare the bark of different small and large trees in an area and consider the elevation, climate, and fire regime elements discussed earlier in the chapter. For example, some trees in cool and moist areas may not have thick bark at a young age because the fire regime is less frequent and trees would typically have time to grow and gain bark thickness. Some trees in areas with frequent fires may have thicker bark at a young age. You may also want to tally the number of small and large trees, with thin and thick bark.

The top illustration is an example of how you might visualize different bark observations in an area. You don't need to draw the entire tree, but can create small close-up sketches of different bark types. You could also add your tallies over each section. You can smudge bark on to your page to leave the color and scent of the bark or even paste in a small flat piece of bark, like I included with a drawing in one of my journal pages (bottom image).

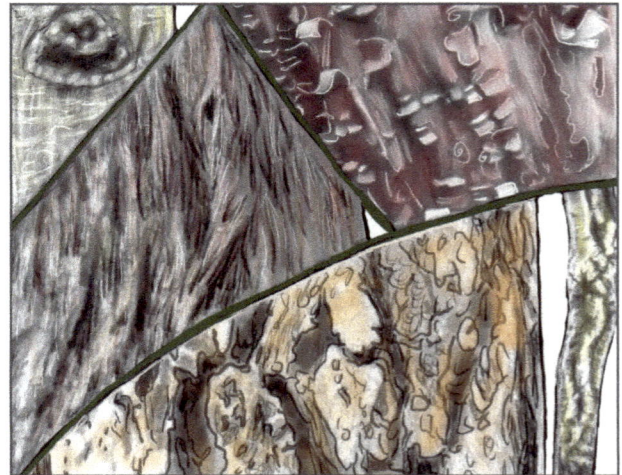

Root Structures & Sprouting Traits

There are various plant structures and sprouting adaptations that are more or less resilient and adaptive to fire (Sugihara 2006). The illustration below visualizes some of these traits. Sprouting of new vegetation comes from the buds along stems or basal burs or features such as a caudex, corm, stolon, rhizome, or bulb, which are located at different depths within the soil. The likelihood of sprouting depends on the adaptations, depth of the rooting system, and the severity of the fire. Some plant species require fire to trigger the release of cones or seeds, or to initiate sprouting, like cypress trees, knobcone pines, and fire lilies. There are other plants that don't need fire, but respond well with increased sprouting or seed release after a fire, like aspen and ponderosa pine. Many other plants will sprout or reseed after a fire based on lower severity effects. These include species like maple and cottonwood, which can sprout, and Douglas fir and sugar pine, which can reseed. There are also plants that are fire-inhibited and less likely to sprout or reseed after a fire. Often, survival, sprouting or reseeding is dependent on the tree trunk width and height, level of impact to the tree canopy, and the depth of roots, which can make them more vulnerable or resilient to fire effects. The fire seasonality is also important to consider with species resilience.

Journaling Root & Sprout Traits

As you make observations, look for and research the plant morphology and potential resistant or adaptive features. You may want to dig up a few different small plants and journal about their root system and look closely for different sprouting locations, like on the tree branches, trunks, and roots after a fire. Add labels and notes about the plant traits and thoughts on how resilient and adaptive they were or could be from fire. Also, try to make observations over the seasons and years. Journaling the different types of sprouting after a fire can be both inspiring and visually stunning, comparing the bright green growth displayed against the charred background or soil. The illustration on the next page is one approach to combining different plant trait observations with fire regime elements.

Various Plant Morphological Structures & Sprouting Adaptations

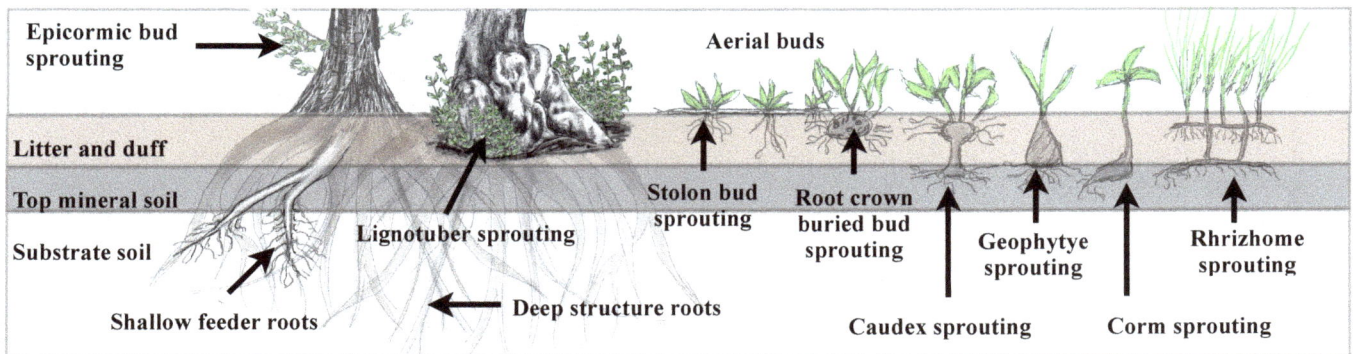

The epicormic and lignotuber sprouting are triggered by fire. The various depths of roots and buds influence sprouting success after a fire. The fire severity effects to the soil will also affect sprouting.

Gray Pine-Blue Oak Foothill Community & Fire Regime

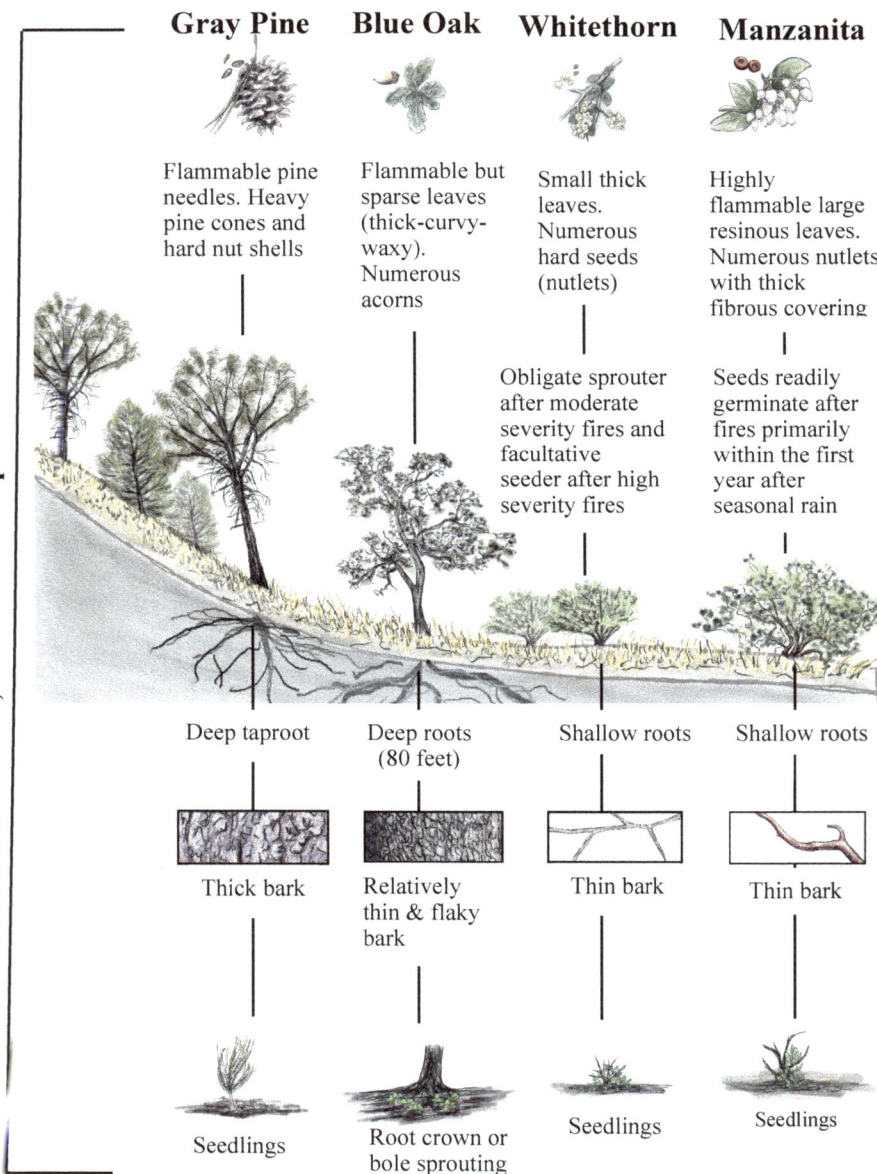

Fire Hazard, Resilience & Adaptation Traits

Gray Pine

Flammable pine needles. Heavy pine cones and hard nut shells

Deep taproot

Thick bark

Seedlings

Blue Oak

Flammable but sparse leaves (thick-curvy-waxy). Numerous acorns

Deep roots (80 feet)

Relatively thin & flaky bark

Root crown or bole sprouting

Whitethorn

Small thick leaves. Numerous hard seeds (nutlets)

Obligate sprouter after moderate severity fires and facultative seeder after high severity fires

Shallow roots

Thin bark

Seedlings

Manzanita

Highly flammable large resinous leaves. Numerous nutlets with thick fibrous covering

Seeds readily germinate after fires primarily within the first year after seasonal rain

Shallow roots

Thin bark

Seedlings

Biophysical/Ecoregion:

• Mediterranean California Dry Mixed Conifer

Other Forest Communities
(within the ecoregion and neighboring observation area)

• Ponderosa pine, Jeffrey pine and or Douglas fir, with madrone and cedar trees

• Canyon live oaks in concentrated patches on some slopes

Pre-settlement Ecoregion Fire Regime:

• 5-50 year fire return interval

• Non-uniform low severity fire, with patches of high severity fire in concentrated fir trees on north-facing slopes

• Fire sizes ranging between 210-1,129 acres

• Fire season typically from summer to fall

Contemporary Ecoregion Fire Regime:

• 7-24 year fire return interval (Gray pine 15-30 year and Blue oak 8-10)

• Low severity fires 43-93% of the time, mixed severity fires 0-48% and high severity fires

- 4-12% (Gray pine moderate severity fires and Blue oak low-moderate severity)
- Fire sizes increasing in areas where fire has been excluded beyond the historic fire regime and vegetation has become concentrated
- The fire season is lengthening based on climate patterns

Vegetation Communities & Fire Regimes

Throughout the previous sections on plant traits and adaptations, I shared some focused observations. The most interesting insights about fire regimes can emerge when you consider the vegetation community and landscape as a whole, integrating individual observations. I had a great time creating the illustration on the previous page, and I think this type of community fire regime profile is something I will attempt for many different habitats and ecoregions. It was enjoyable to include a cross-section diagram of the dominant or characteristic plants and their hazardous and adaptive traits, along with some highlighted fire regime data. I enjoy examining both the hazard traits and adaptive traits and considering how fire plays a role in that ecosystem. What is missing is more climate data and trends, and phenophases. I don't think I'd try to combine climate graphs with this visual, but maybe a few notes about general climate trends.

Multi-Sensory Observations

I have not yet included many of the multi-sensory observations that can be integrated into this chapter. These are potent observations that can bring interesting insights. For example, the observations about tree stress, injury, and death could integrate scent. The smell of trees during high temperatures is often different from cooler temperatures or when comparing high relative humidity or low humidity conditions. There are also strong scents associated with pitch and sap from trees. I'll talk more about sounds a little further in this chapter. A favorite observation for many people is the fire following flowers. Not only are there amazing colors, but delightful scents.

Fire Followers

Fire followers are plant species that positively respond to environmental cues such as charred soil, smoke, and increased sunlight. Fireweed is a beautiful example of a plant that emerges after a fire and can disperse its seeds over long distances. Fire followers emerge from burned areas and may show up on fire severity maps as "increased greenness" areas. There are a number of online citizen science websites, like iNaturalist, that have fire effects monitoring for fire followers. One of the most inspiring examples of journaling the regrowth and renewal in a post-fire area is found in Robin Lee Carlson's book The Cold Canyon Fire Journals-Green Shoots and Silver Linings in the Ashes.

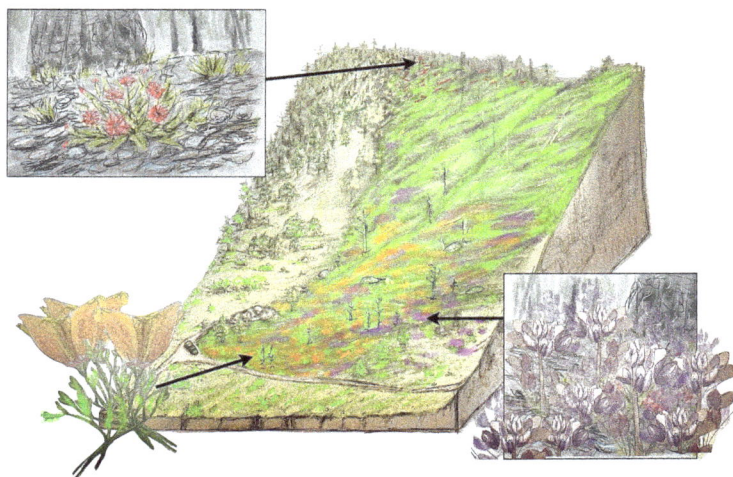

Journaling Fire Followers

Journaling about fire followers can take many forms. You can sketch close-ups of plants and landscape scenes, with flower blooms or simple diagrams with color patches. If you observe burned areas over time, you'll notice different fire-following plant species coming up over time within different microclimate areas. I would recommend you include metadata like elevation, slope aspect, weather, and fire severity, which can show trends over subsequent years. You could also organize your journal pages with large columns for observations on different slope aspects, so that trends may become more obvious. This could also be a new sort of perpetual journal, as described in several of the earlier chapters. My illustration on the previous page is an example of a 3D block landscape with small sketches to highlight some of the individual flower observations. This visual on the previous page can be challenging, but also offers a unique emphasis on the topography. I won't offer additional drawing tips for this 3D landscape since it is not an essential or a basic approach. There are some tips for drawing other 3D illustration types in Chapter 2: Fire Weather and Chapter 3: Topography.

Animals & Fire Regimes

Fires can have mild to extreme modifications to wildlife habitats, enhancing, destroying, and resetting ecosystem dynamics. An ecoacoustic monitoring study in a giant sequoia forest in northern California demonstrated how fire regimes that create more complex vegetation patterns (pyrodiversity) provide more ecosystem resilience and higher biodiversity (Meyer 2022). In our nature journaling practice, we do not need to make associations about the overall ecosystem or habitat impacts from a fire. We can make observations of animal interactions within different ecosystems and fire severity patches, exploring trends that can lead to deeper questions and advanced observations.

You can journal about any and all animal life in an area or focus on animal categories (insects, birds, mammals) or specific species. To make connections to the fire environment and fire regimes, we do need to include targeted metadata and observations, like animal engagement within the different habitat/vegetation zones and fire severity areas. Journaling about animal observations within different habitat zones or niches, like the upper tree canopy, understory vegetation, shrubs, surface vegetation, and subterranean areas, can help make those connections. You could journal about all the animals within those zones or focus on a species that has a strong preference for those habitat elements, like the California spotted owl with a strong preference for high canopy cover. You can also look for relationships to species habitat preferences with fire severity conditions, like observing the black-backed woodpecker with a preference for high fire severity areas.

It would also be interesting to include observations of species considered ecosystem engineers. They can influence habitat and ecosystem functions and sometimes fire behavior. For example, large herbivores require, and can alter, surface vegetation conditions and fire behaviors in grass and shrub communities. Beavers can influence the health of riparian and wetland ecosystems, which can also influence fire behavior and spread. Digging and burrowing insects and animals can help break up the soil and help reestablish some vegetation communities. There are other species that are good indicators of healthy and poor ecosystem conditions. A diversity of aquatic insects, amphibians, and fish can be indicators of ecosystem health, while high numbers of wood-boring beetles and wasps can be indicators of poor forest health. On a basic level, note the diversity and abundance of species.

Don't forget that animal observations will likely vary dramatically by season, so try to make observations over different seasonal periods and integrate them with seasonal climate data.

My journal page below includes observations in an older burned area. Only a few burn scars were slightly observable on trees, but there were obvious patches within the landscape that indicated a fire some 10-20 years previously.

I used a sidebar for listing species observed within different vertical habitat zones. Those zones can be associated with fire types and regimes. I also included a climate graph to associate the hot/cool and moist or dry conditions related to the ecoregion.

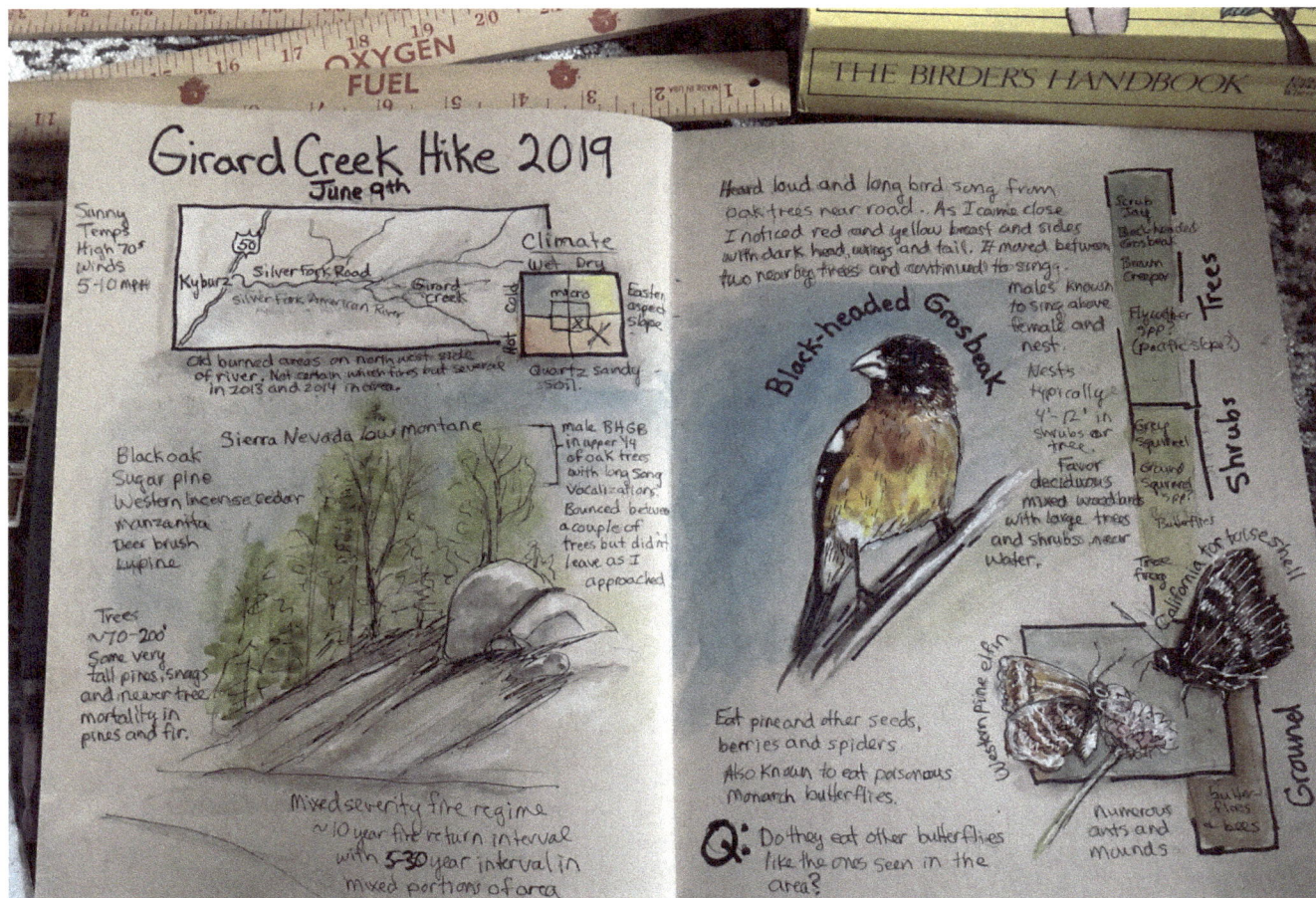

If you can identify the animal species, look up background information about their habitat preferences and potential fire effects (Fire Effects Information System website). In making animal-fire regime observations, try to describe:

- Animal type/species, age, and adaptive traits (flight, burrowing, etc.)
- Animal behaviors (foraging for…)
- Fire severity in the area(s) observed
- Habitat zone(s) observed within different severity areas
- Distance of the observation area to unburned and low severity areas
- Movements between fire severity areas
- Time since the fire and the season and weather conditions during the observation

You can sketch animals or simply use names or other visualizations, such as simple shapes and color codes. Visuals depicting locations and movements within

Tallied Animal Observations by Habitat Zone & Fire Severity Area

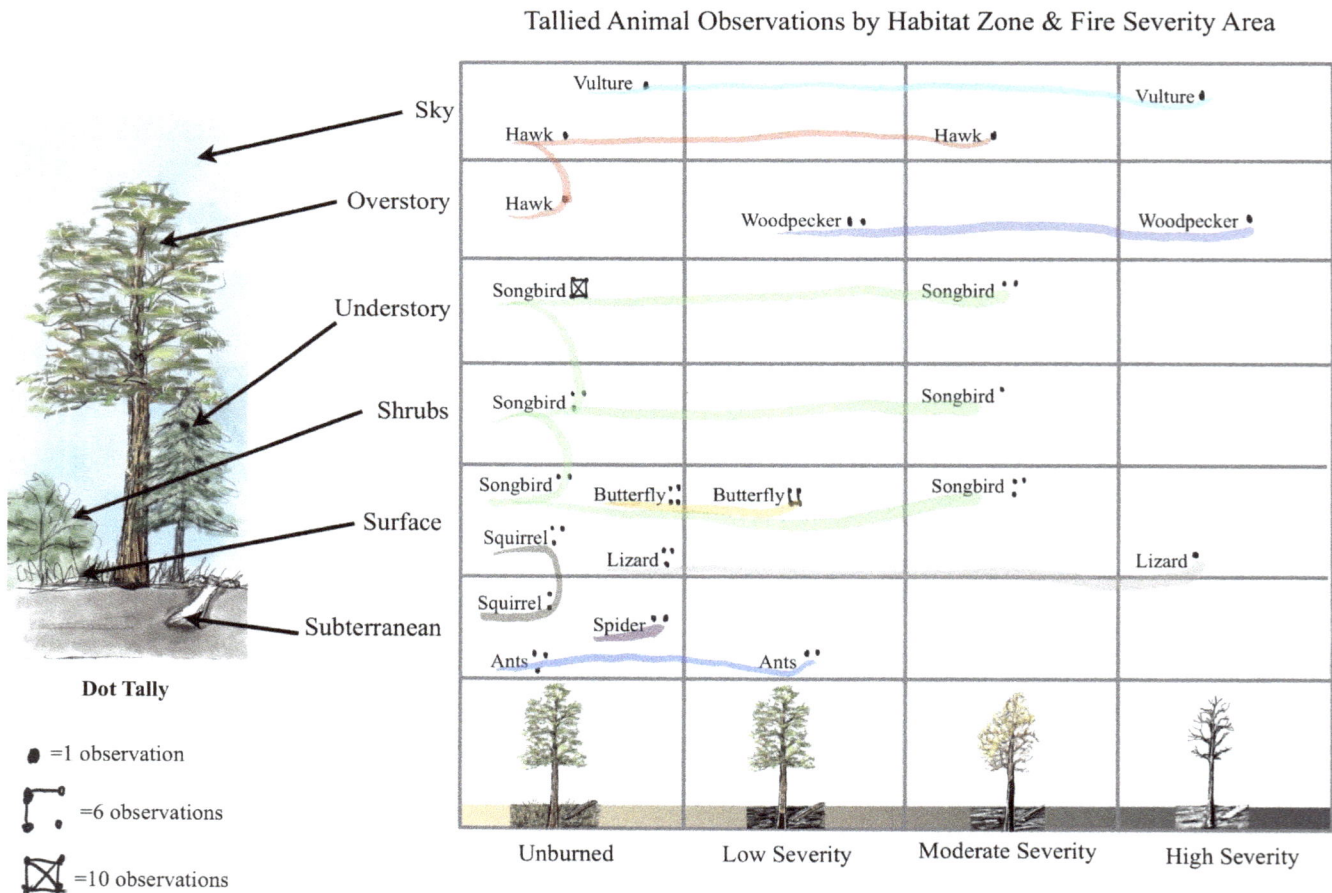

Dot Tally

- = 1 observation
- = 6 observations
- = 10 observations

different fire severity areas could be as simple as a line or bar along the top or bottom of the journal page, with general distance estimates added. A straightforward visualization, like a table, with a few sketched elements, is another approach to journaling observations about animals interacting within different habitat zones and fire severity areas. See my examples.

Ecoacoustics

Ecoacoustics encompass the collective sounds within a given environment and period of time. This is a growing area of study for monitoring the biodiversity of an area. A biophony refers to the collective sounds of vocal non-human animals, while a geophony includes the nonliving sounds. Ecoacoustics encompass all the natural and anthropogenic sounds in the landscape and are termed soundscapes. Most monitoring is conducted with sound recording devices, but we can use our senses to build a sense of biodiversity for an area. We may not hear all the natural sounds in the environment, but that doesn't diminish the value of listening and journaling the things that we can hear. A few things to listen for when considering fire regimes and ecosystem changes:

- Wood-boring insects that can indicate tree stress and fatality (insect calls and chewing sounds)

- Woodpeckers and other birds and animals that feed on wood-boring insects and create tree cavities (e.g., calls and hammer/drumming sounds)

- Ground-burrowing animals/ecosystem engineers (e.g., ground squirrel chips)

- Birds and animals in the overstory, understory, and along the ground (calls and sounds like rustling leaves from feeding activities)

- Tree noises like the gunshot sound from frost cracking or popcorn sound of dehydrated trees struggling to pull water from the ground

- Wind sounds through different vegetation arrangements and conditions

- Wind sounds through different topographic features

- Rain and running water sounds in different ecosystems and conditions

Journaling Acoustic Observations

There may be challenges to differentiating the elements of a soundscape. I would recommend establishing some prompts to help guide you. For instance, you might want to break up what you listen for by location and position. Over the next few pages, I have examples, like showing my position leaning against a tree to listen to sounds around and within a tree, a seated position near a forested area to listen to low-level sounds, and a position in a more open area to listen to higher-level and landscape sounds, like the wind.

There are numerous ways to visualize sound observations, from sketches, sound graphs, and diagrams to music symbols. Add other observations like animal signs (tracks and scat). One approach to visualizing animal sounds that I have experimented with is a simple diagram (angled square) that represents the fire severity type (described earlier in the chapter) and vertical lines for the general location of animals within habitat patches. You can use a color code to differentiate animal types or species. See the example on the next page.

You can also integrate musical notes and compare the soundscape to movie soundtracks and music to describe the energy and mood of the scene. Think about the overall mix and combination of sounds and make comparisons between different landscapes and conditions. I have noticed that some high severity burn areas sound haunting, with groaning trees, scratching and clawing sounds from bare branches, and the strange sound of my footsteps in the ash.

Loud chirps of a ground squirrel

Soft rustling of of fallen dry pine needles and dead grass

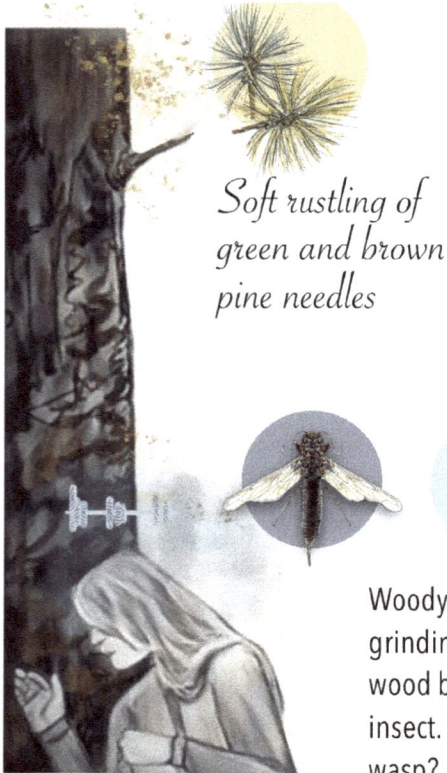

Soft rustling of green and brown pine needles

Woody squeaky grinding sounds of wood boring insect. Beetle or wasp?

Immediately After Fire

Low Complexity & Low Severity

Loud woodpecker drumming on tree trunk

Musical warble from small bird in green trees

Loud woodpecker "pik-pik" calls

Crunching sound of footsteps in charred grass and ash.

Wind rustling of fallen pine needles, dead grass and ash

Sound Maps

One common approach to journaling sound is to create a sound map. This is commonly done with a large circle on the page, with each direction noted at the top, bottom, and sides. The observer is in the center, and each sound is mapped and described within the circle. You can turn this into a 3-dimensional visual by adding sounds in upper and lower habitat zones. I have created 3D sound maps by making two flattened circles and then adding lines along the outer edges of the circles. You can sketch trees and bushes within this 3D diagram or just add marks and estimated vertical and horizontal distances with notes about sound observations.

North

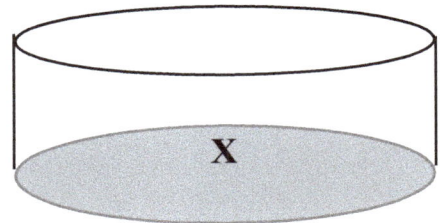

265

Visualizing Sounds of Birds & Bees in Different Fire Severities & Years

Immediately After Fire

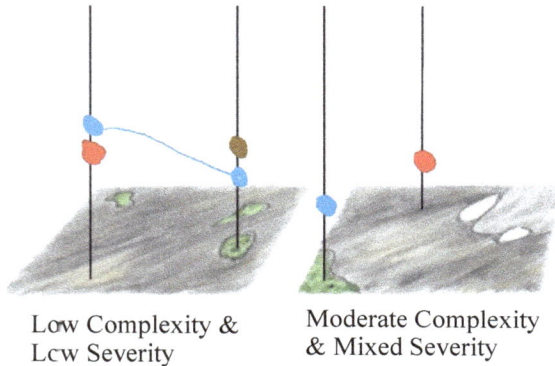

Low Complexity &
Low Severity

Moderate Complexity
& Mixed Severity

- Each vertical line indicates sound observations within a burn severity patch.

- Each colored dot is a sound observation.

- Colored lines link the movement of a bird and sound between observation patches.

Bees
buzzing

Song birds
- Up and down warbles
- rattle-trill
- chip-chip

Woodpeckers
Drumming ……..
pik-pik-pik gribib-gribib

Quail
pi-pit-pit
ka-kah-ko

Hawk
keee-aarr

Dove
Wing whistle

1-Year After Fire

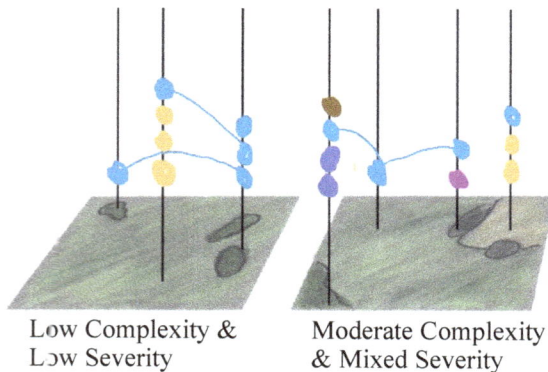

Low Complexity &
Low Severity

Moderate Complexity
& Mixed Severity

Humans & Fire Regimes

The historic and contemporary influences of humans on the landscape are tied to the fire regime. There were historic and indigenous uses of fire, which may offer some insight into the local relationships with fire. There are stories of fire suppression and relationships with fire that have likely influenced the natural (pre-settlement) fire regime and attitudes about fire. Historic land management activities, population growth, and urban expansion also have relationships and stories about your fire regime. Look back at your observations and notes from Chapter 6:

Fire Ignitions & Prevention and Chapter 7: Fire Mitigation & Readiness to help add context to the human relationships with fire in your area.

I was commissioned to create the below illustration for Robert Gray, in Canada, and the FireWriters in the United States, to help communicate the mix of historic and contemporary fire regime changes across a landscape of focus. I used historic and contemporary photos of the landscape to illustrate the changes in vegetation and added small circular sketches to visualize the fire-related stories over time. Adding an arrow for a timeline was one method to integrate time into the visual.

Historic Pyrodiversity

Altered Lands with Limited Pyrodiversity

Managed Lands & Urban Sprawl with Limited Pyrodiveristy

Historic Landscape Relationships

Contemporary Landscape Relationships

There are a wide number of books and reports about indigenous fire practices that may add context to human-fire relationships, and you may find similar reports about the fire history in your area. If you review this information, consider the broader context of human influences on the fire regime elements described in this chapter. Have there been changes in the seasonality, frequency, and severity of fires related to humans?

Consider adding notes and sketches to your journal about the human-fire relationships. You may also want to look at news stories and social media posts about fire and consider how people communicate and relate to fire.

I feel like there is an overwhelming number of news reports that generate fear and uncertainty, which has a strong influence on community and personal relationships with place and fire.

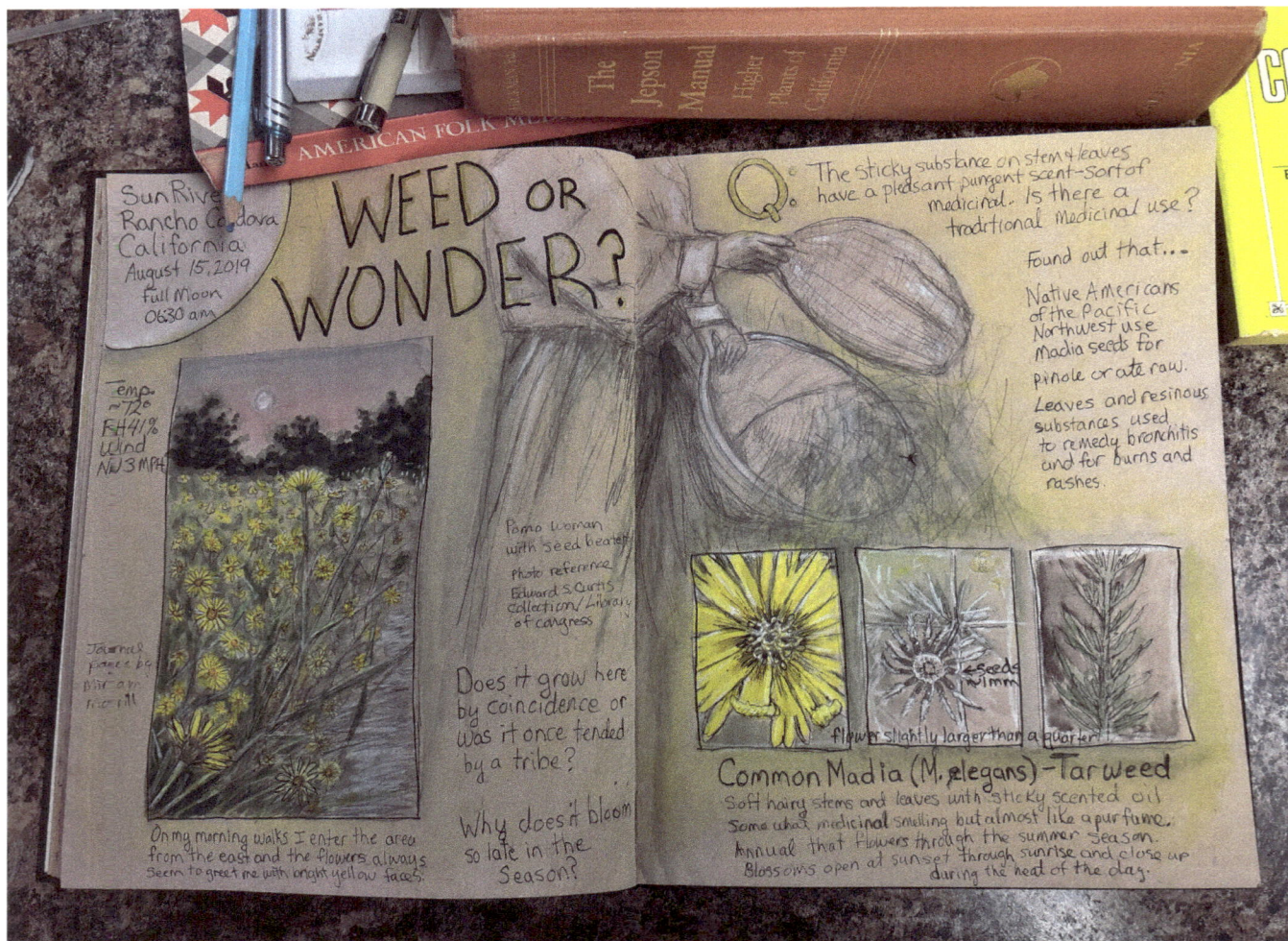

Journaling Human-Fire Relationships

A storytelling approach, like comic book formats, is one visual approach that you could use for journaling human-fire relationships. You may also want to use existing sketches and landscape observations, with additional notes about fire regimes and relationships or create new sketches and diagrams. For example, sketches of landscape patterns and patches may offer observation points where you can include historical, contemporary, and/or personal anecdotes and questions about the human-fire relationships that may have influenced those patterns. A lack of patterns and patches may also be an indicator of human-fire relationships. For example, a thick forest with many single species trees like Douglas fir may be an indication of fire suppression management or lacking prescribed fire use.

Another journaling approach is a bit haphazard but can be fascinating and inspiring when it comes together. This approach is to create some visuals and notes about a plant or animal observed, save some space on your journal page, and then look up information about the species using keywords about fire, fire history, and fire ecology with the species name and add those notes to your journal page.

The journal spread on the previous page was created when I'd first started natural journaling. I walked the same path for many years and had seen the same flowers late in the summer. I had never paid much attention to them but took the time to journal and look up some information. This simple observation helped me find a human-fire story. I learned that Native Americans used these plants (Madia) as a food source, like wheat, and that the women managed them with fire. This patch, of what I thought of as weeds, became a piece of fire history and enhanced my relationship with that place. I added a black and white pencil sketch of a Native American woman and her collecting basket into the blank space on my journal and added notes about the plant and fire.

There are many stories that we can observe and investigate to help frame and define our relationships with fire and the lands around us.

When integrating people into your journal, especially different ethic and cultural groups, consider how to appropriately visualize. I prefer to create silhouette people or just integrate a hand or arm into the scene. This reduces the issues with trying to capture skin color, clothing, and other features.

This illustration was commissioned for the Braiding Indigenous Knowledge and Western Science for Landscape Adaptation to Climate Change Report in 2023. It is one example of weaving the human-plant-animal-fire story into a visual.

Chapter 11:
Getting Started

Getting Started
Observation Prompts
Journaling Observations
Organizing Observations & Page Design
Journaling Supplies & Equipment
Other Resources

Getting Started

This book offers a wide range of background information, examples, and exercises to guide the practice of observing and journaling about the fire environment. I organized the book with the first three chapters emphasizing aspects of the fire behavior triangle (weather, topography, and fuels), which are foundational for observing the fire environment before, during, and after a fire. I highly recommend starting the journaling practices within those chapters, ideally in the order the book was written.

I recommend beginning journaling at locations close to home or work where you can make ongoing observations and enhance your abilities to notice changing conditions, which are key to developing situational awareness. See Chapter 1: Pyrosketchology Introduction for information about situational awareness. I also suggest choosing a few observation goals before heading into the field. By setting your intent, you can reduce some of the anxiety you may feel when surrounded by the many sights, scents, and sounds of the environment that can make it challenging to focus.

In a few pages, I will share some ideas for journaling supplies and equipment, but first, I want to review and summarize the practical pyrosketchology approaches. John Muir Laws outlines a nature journaling framework that enhances the learning process and observation skills. This includes using three foundational prompts to guide observations: I notice… I wonder…? It reminds me of…, and the combination of words, numbers, and pictures to describe observations. In pyrosketchology, we are trying to observe a complex environmental system and ecosystem process, which needs some additional framing to help guide meaningful observations.

Observation Prompts

I Notice…

Frame the "I notice" around the weather, topographic, and fuels elements at different scales, including spatial (landscape/skyscape, scene, and close-up), temporal (decades/years, seasons, days, and hours), and comparative (form and function) or intensity (level of change). Try to focus initial observations on the weather and things that change quickly. You may also want to schedule some of these observations, like an initial weather observation when you arrive and additional weather observations every hour or two.

Different spatial scales of observation include:

- A single object or close-up observation like dead fine fuel moisture or the wind moving through tree leaves (Beaufort Wind Force Scale), etc.

- A scene with some slope and vegetation communities (fire regimes), fuel groups (horizontal carrying fuels), fuel arrangements (ladder fuels), and fuel conditions (grass curing phases), cloud types, and vertical movements within a valley, etc.

- A landscape/skyscape with various topographic elements like elevation, slope, aspect and or cloud types and horizontal movements, etc. This scale of observation can add more context and be used for comparisons of what is occurring at smaller scales.

Different temporal scales of observation include:

- Daily/hourly changes in weather, fuel moisture, etc.

- Seasonal changes in weather, vegetation phenology, and grass curing. It is important to use seasonal observations and metadata to add context to daily observations that may be influenced by ongoing changes.

- Long-term changes in landscape and vegetation patterns, climate trends, etc. This is also important for adding context to ongoing observations, like observing plant stress, which may be caused by a combination of ongoing weather and drought.

Different comparative (form or function) or intensity scales of observation include (see the Fire Behavior Indicators table in Chapter 1: Pyrosketchology Introduction):

- Low, moderate, extreme differences in tree form, leaf shape, bark thickness indicative of fire hazard levels and fire behavior. For example, large curly leaves are more flammable/hazardous than small flat leaves.

- Cloud types and levels, temperatures, moisture levels, and or wind speeds indicative of low, moderate, or extreme fire weather conditions. For example, cumulus clouds indicative of unstable conditions but more moderate fire behavior conditions, whereas cumulonimbus clouds are indicative of more unstable and extreme fire behaviors.

- Topography elements indicative of low, moderate, and extreme fire behaviors. For example, slopes over 20% are more hazardous with more extreme fire behaviors than slopes below 10%.

I Wonder…

Continue to frame observations around the fire behavior elements (weather, topography, and fuels) and review Chapter 1: Pyrosketchology Introduction and the situational awareness information to consider the relationships between those elements and potential fire behaviors.

- What has happened in the fire environment? You might make these observations after an initial field observation and some follow-up research about fire and climate history in the area. Field observations may include things like the Griggs-Putnam wind deformation observations, post-fire pattern indicators about fire behavior, fire severity, landscape patterns, and phase of ecological succession. For example, you may use observations of bark thickness and leaf shapes from Chapter 10: Fire Regimes to frame this question around how frequent fires historically occurred in the area.

- What is happening in the fire environment? Observations may include recent seasonal, monthly, and daily weather conditions, and current fuel groups and fuels curing phases. These may be the observations you start with and then follow up with the observations that can inform you of the past. With both the current and past observations, you can assess and estimate what might happen in the future.

- What may happen in the fire environment? These observations are used for situational awareness as well as enhancing observation skills by comparing what you think might happen with what does happen. For example, you can consider the time of day of your observations and what changes may occur in the weather based on the wind types (morning, afternoon, evening) described in Chapter 2: Fire Weather.

It Reminds Me Of… Observations

Think about how the observations made under the previous prompts relate to each other, to past observations, and to past feelings, responses, and activities. Consider the trends and relationships.

- Under similar climate and weather conditions.

- Within similar topographic elements.

- With similar fuels conditions.

- With similar fire cause, fire prevention, fire mitigation, and or fire readiness activities.

- With similar fire and smoke behaviors.

- With similar fire severity and effects.

Journaling With…

To effectively capture observations in a journal, it is important to utilize a mix of words (narrative descriptions), numbers (measurements and metadata), and pictures (symbols, diagrams, and sketches). Consider the following aspects when employing these attributes within your journaling practice.

Words

Incorporate fire terminology that conveys personal understanding and connection. You may also opt for creative and poetic language to establish deeper personal connections. For instance, use wind types and terminology but describe observations using your own interpretation of the Beaufort Wind Force Scale.

Numbers/Metadata

Include measurements like distance that relate to fire hazards, fire weather, and fire behavior. Ensure these measurements are personally relatable. For instance, I prefer using miles per hour (mph) for measuring winds instead of kilometers per hour. Additionally, provide narrative descriptions or examples that illustrate these measurements in relatable terms. For example, liken fire rates of spread to the speed of a tortoise compared to a sea turtle. When making forestry observations, such as grass height or distance between grass, shrubs, and tree canopies, use biometrics but accompany them with a legend to ensure accurate interpretation.

- Numbers or measurements important for the fire environment may include:

- Directions in which elements are observed, such as looking to the North, or observing elements on different aspects of a slope.

- Distances between elements (miles across a landscape or feet between trees).

- Sizes and shapes of elements, especially when considering fuel moisture and the drying/heating time lags of fine fuels.

- Speed of movement or rates of change, which may be a measurement like wind speed or the number of days or weeks between grass curing phases.

Pictures/Visuals

Visually capture the key aspects of the observation and reduce or eliminate other elements that complicate the information and increase the time needed to visualize. Creating the visuals yourself is a much more valuable approach than using photos, as it engages more of your brain in the process. Helpful visuals include:

- Symbols like cloud types, arrows for wind direction, a triangle for slope angles and elevation, a circle, or mechanical gear for processes.

- Colors for different air temperature or moisture levels or different fire hazard levels.

- Diagrams like a cross-section landscape to convey the slope and vertical arrangement of vegetation (ladder fuels). If you only capture the key elements like the areas where tall grass touches shrubs and shrubs touch tree canopies and leave out the exact number of plants in the scene, you save time and reduce the complexity of what you are observing.

- Sketches that are simple with only the important elements included. For example, you may want to sketch the shape of a leaf with only a few details in one area of the leaf that visualizes the texture or color. Sketches do not need to be artistic and are sometimes more effective when only accenting key elements of the observation.

Comparisons

Use comparisons that combine and organize observations and metadata to better evaluate and describe differences, changes, and trends. You can make individual observations, especially with metadata, and then combine them into a comparison format, like a graph, but I would recommend you add formatted comparison elements, like a comparison table, into your journal prior to making individual observations. You will want to develop several categories for organizing your observations, which may be spatial, temporal, or comparative/intensity-related. For example, you may use the spatial category with a specific location name, elevational zones, and/or slope aspects. Temporal categories may be organized by the time of day, days of the week, seasons, and/or years. Comparative (form or function) or intensity categories may include the shape, size, or phenological phase of a plant or the intensity scale of wind. A few options for organizing or formatting observations include:

- Comparison tables with two or more columns. You can also add symbols, diagrams, and sketches within the table and/or format tables to better relate to the observation element/topic. For example, you may want a large triangle shape with four columns within to add different observation metadata about different elevations or slope aspects. This could be metadata about phenology or grass curing or fuel moisture levels.

- Perpetual journals that include sketches and metadata laid out next to each other or filled on one page using a comparable subject over time. For example, you could journal about the different fine fuels (grasses and fallen leaves) over several consecutive weeks or months or on the same date each year. You could also use a perpetual journal format to observe the differences of dry and wet thunderstorms.

- Time series diagrams or sketches with observations identified within specified and comparable time periods. For example, you may want to journal about smoke columns and/or air quality over a period of weeks or months.

- Data graphs that use metadata like temperature, precipitation, relative humidity, or acres burned to visualize changes in scale over time.

Multi-sensory Observations

Using as many different senses for observations will not only engage different parts of the brain but may also unveil important insights and enhance overall awareness. For example, using scent to help observe fuel moisture and/or plant stress (vapor pressure deficit) may help you cue into changes you might not easily observe visually.

Organization & Page Design

There are no required formats for journaling observations, but it is very helpful to consider how you organize your journal observations, especially for the topics and approaches of this book. I have included several journal page templates, which are basically page design concepts to help organize observations. Consider the following approaches to organizing and tracking observations in your journal:

- Keep several blank pages at the beginning of your journal and use them as an index for key observations. I would consider including the date, location, and key observation categories or topics in your index.

- Label the outside and inside cover pages of your journal with the periods of observation and/or journaling goals and prompts. You can also include a few sketching tips that you want to practice over the year.

- Leave four to twelve blank pages at the back of your journal where you can summarize seasonal and/or monthly observations and trends. You may even want to pre-label or design those pages with something like a weather wheel or temperature graph, filling them in as you go through the year.

- Insert any reference pages that you can reuse in each journal for key reminders, tips, and/or goals for your current journaling practice. This can be something like key metrics and biometrics or the fire behavior indicators that I want to use. For example, you may want to emphasize observations that can be connected and compared with climate and weather by writing the average annual and monthly temperature highs and lows and precipitation. As you enter ongoing journal observations, you can easily refer to your notes on the reference sheet and assess how current temperatures compare to historic climate trends.

- You may also decide that you want to use consistent icons, symbols, and/or shapes for certain information and observations added to your journal, and you can list that as a journaling goal. For example, you may want to use long slender rectangle shapes for your diagrams or sketch outlines about landscape and skyscape observations, rectangle shapes for your scene scale observations (e.g., vegetation community), and circles for framing close-up observations (e.g., single plants).

- Develop a somewhat consistent approach to displaying and organizing your metadata. This can be done with template pages to remind you of what you want to observe and help you sort and find observations and metadata when looking back through previous journal pages. For example, I like to use a two-page spread (two facing pages) and put my location and topographic observations at the top of the left page, my fuels and general nature observations in the center of both pages, and my weather observations on the far right of the right page. I also like to have my temperature

information at the top of the right page, where the color codes that I use are a sort of dog-ear for scanning back through temperature and climate-related observations. You can also leave a wide strip of blank space along the top of the two-page spread for a title, which you may add later. I like to wait until other

Journaling Supplies & Equipment

There are many opinions and attitudes about the equipment and supplies needed for nature journaling. It can be fun to explore and experiment with supplies, but most experienced nature journalers recommend starting simple and cheap. When you're outdoors and trying to journal observations under a range of environmental conditions, it can be challenging to dig through a lot of supplies. Many nature journalers take minimal supplies for capturing field observations and then return home to touch up their sketches and text with other arts and craft supplies. This not only reduces what you carry in the field but allows you to review what you have observed and add some additional thoughts and follow-up information to your journal. This step also helps you learn, organize, and remember what you observed.

The John Muir Laws' website has a lot of tips and recommendations for key nature journaling supplies and brands that can be ordered directly from his website. I'll describe some of the key supplies and tools I use, but journaling is all about personal goals and preferences.

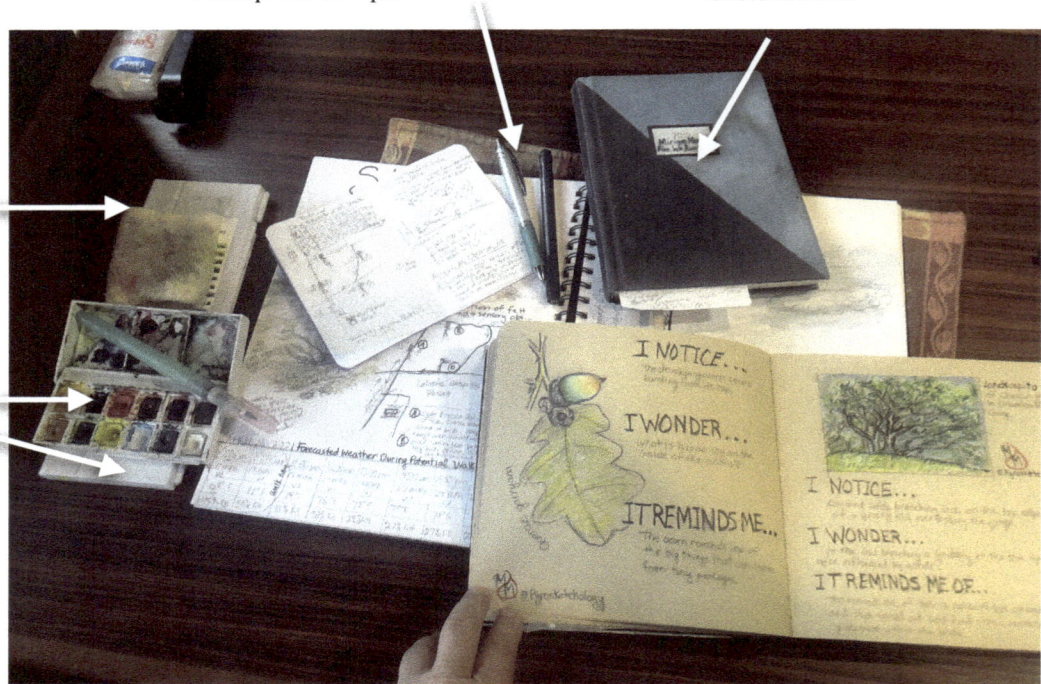

Mechanical pencil and waterproof ink pen

Variable notebooks and sketchbooks

Cotton wristband for cleaning a paintbrush

Small or large watercolor paint set and water brush

My journaling kit includes:

- a small- to medium-sized mixed media sketchbook. I also use daily calendars and organizers for my journaling, but limit the mediums I use on that type of paper. Think about how you expose nature and how much you want to carry. I like to have both a pocket-sized notebook for keeping key observations that enhance situational awareness and a medium or large sketchbook for more detailed and deliberate journaling.

- vellum or tracing paper sheets. I use sheets of vellum paper to add additional data and observations over sketches in my journal. For example, changing wind directions and speeds within the same landscape.

- tape and glue stick. I use tape to adhere vellum paper over pages in my journal and glue sticks to paste in printed maps and other materials into my journal.

- mechanical pencil or standard pencil with an eraser and pencil sharpener. You can eliminate the pencil and just use an ink pen or a few colored pencils.

- a waterproof ink pen. I like to have a small tip and large wedge tip pen for regular text and titles.

- a small watercolor paint set or watercolor pencil set.

- a medium-tip water brush (a paintbrush with water held in the plastic handle).

- a white gel pen or small tube of white gouache paint. I use this to add highlights to illustrations that can cover colored pencil and watercolor mediums.

- a small- or regular-sized ruler.

- a tote bag or backpack. You can use any size tote or backpack that fits your supplies. I like to use a larger one that can include additional things like water, snacks, and a jacket. I like the over-the-shoulder tote because I can access supplies and use it as an arm prop while journaling on the move.

Other Field Equipment:

- a 180-degree protractor for estimating and creating angles.

- stencils of circles, squares, and state, national, and/ or global shapes/boundaries. These are not required but can make it easier to create and organize visuals and text. It can also provide consistent appearances for frequently journaled observations, making it easier for comparisons.

- a measuring tape, magnifying glass, and binoculars.

- a weather meter or kit, but this is not mandatory. I have a Kestrel Wind and Weather Meter.

- a small and light folding chair or stool. I have a small tripod folding stool that I like to carry when planning long periods of journaling.

If you want to participate in active/live fire observations or you want to work with official fire partners to implement fire journaling events, you'll want to have leather boots (without a metal tip or insert), with Vibram soles. In many situations, wearing traditional blue jeans or other cotton pants and a long-sleeved cotton shirt will be sufficient, but Nomex brand pants and shirts, which are fire-resistant, can be ordered and sometimes borrowed from professional fire organizations.

Other Resources

Nature Journaling

John Muir Laws's website also offers many books that can be ordered and free vertical training references. The Roseann Hanson, Exploring Overland, Books and Visual Arts website also provides numerous wonderful resources. Additional books and examples on nature journaling can be found through an internet search for Robin Lee Carlson, Marley Peifer, and Laura Cunningham. I would also highly recommend Dr. Christine Eriksen and Susan Ballard's book "*Alliances in the Anthropocene Fire, Plants, and People,*" which includes examples of art being used to convey experiences with fire in Australia.

Fire Education

The Butte County Fire Safe Council in Northern California offers a number of fire education materials, including the *REDI Jedi Master Program and Guide*, which focuses on fire environment journaling for teachers and students. Many fire education materials are available online, including websites like Living with Fire, which offers a wide range of fire education resources for students. Various fire science consortiums around the United States also provide a diverse mix of fire education resources, many of which include journaling exercises. Try searching the internet for fire education curriculum and materials within your state, region, and/or country. You can also refine your search for different fire-related topics, which will help direct you to more specific resources.

References

Engber, A. and J. Morgan on Patterns of Flammability of the California Oaks: the role of leaf traits compared traits such as leaf size, thickness, surface area to volume ratio, and curling with their associated fire regimes.

AirNow. U.S. Air Quality Index. https://www.airnow.gov/about- airnow/

Almo, Farina. 2021. Ecosemiotic Landscape A Novel Perspective for the Toolbox of Environmental Humanities. Cambridge Elements. University Printing House, Cambridge CB2 8BS, United Kingdom. DOI: 10.1017/9781108872928

ALERTWildfire. Live Webcams. University of Nevada, Reno, University of California San Diego, and the University of Oregon providing fire cameras and tools to help firefighters and first responders. https://www.alertwildfire.org/

Arizpe, Alexis H., Falk, Donald A., et.al. 2020. Widespread fire years in the US–Mexico Sky Islands are contingent on both winter and monsoon precipitation. International Journal of Wildland Fire 29(12) 1072-1087 https://doi.org/10.1071/WF19181.

Baker, B.W., et.al. 2007. *Influence of Slope on Fire Spread Rate*. https://www.fs.usda.gov/rm/pubs/mrs_p04 6/rmrs_p046_082.pdf

Butte County Forest Health Guide. 2021. Fire Ignition Test. https:// buttefiresafe.net/forest-health-guidebook/

Bronz, Adrian, et.al. 2021. A record of vapor pressure deficit preserved in wood and soils across biomes. Sci Rep. 2021 Jan 12;11(1):662.doi:10.1038/ s4198-020-80006-9. PMID: 33436864; PMCID: PMC7804288.

Burn Severity Viewer (United States). https://burnseverity.cr.usgs.gov/viewer/?product=NPS

CAL FIRE. Prepare for Wildfire website. Ready, Set, Go. Accessed April 2023. https://www.readyforwildfire.org/prepare-for-wildfire/go-evacuation-guide/

California Water Resources Control Board. Color of Water Fact Sheet. Clean Water Team. FACT SHEET 3.1.5.9. https:// www.waterboards.ca.gov/ water_issues/programs/swamp/docs/cwt/ guidance/ 3159.pdf

Carlson, Robin Lee. 2022. Cold Canyon Fire Journals, Green Shoots and Silver Linings. Heyday, Berkeley, California. LCCN 2021060772/ ISBN 9781597146029. https://www.heydaybooks.com/ catalog/the-cold-canyon-fire-journals/

Columbia Climate School International Research Institute for Climate and Society ENSO Forecast Navigation website. https:// iri.columbia.edu/our-expertise/climate/forecasts/enso/current/ #:~:text=The continuation of El Niño conditions is forecasted to be,period in Feb-Apr 2024.

Cruz, Miguel G., et.al. 2019. *The 10% Wind Speed Rule of Thumb for Estimating a Wildfire's Forward Rate of Spread in Forests and Shrublands*. Annuls of Forest Science 76, Article Numb. 44.

DellaSala, Dominick. Chad Hanson. 2019. Are Wildland Fires Increasing Large Patches of Complex Early Seral Forest Habitat? Diversity 2019, 11, 157; doi:10.3390/d11090157. https://lpfw.org/ wp-content/ uploads/2020/06/2019_DellaSala-and-Hanson_Are-fires-increasing-large-high-severity-patches.pdf

Engber, Eamon A, Varner, Morgan J. 2012. *Patterns of flammability of the California oaks: The role of leaf traits.* Wildland Fire Laboratory, Department of Forestry & Wildland Resources, Humboldt State University, One Harpts Street, Arcata, CA 95521, USA. www.nrcresearchpress.com/cjfr

Environmental Protection Agency. Wildfire Smoke. 2019. A Guid for Human Health Officials. EPA-452/R-21-901. https:// www.airnow.gov/sites/default/files/2021-09/wildfire-smoke- guide_0.pdf

Farina, Almo. 2021. *Ecosemiotic Landscape A Novel Perspective for theToolbox of Environmental Humanities.* University Printing House, Cambridge CB@ 8BS, United Kingdom. DOI: 10.1017/981108872982

Fast, Andrew J., et.al. Common Prescribed Burning Prescription Parameters in Northeastern Fuels. Natural Resource Network. University of New Hampshire Cooperative Extension. https://extension.unh.edu/sites/default/files/migrated_unmanaged_files/Resource001885_Rep2734.pdf

Filkov, Alexander. et.al. 2019. Frequency of Dynamic Fire Behaviours in Australian Forest Environments. School of Ecosystem and Forest Sciences, Faculty of Science, University of Melbourne, Creswick, Victoria 3363, Australia. Fire 2020, 3(1), 1; https://doi.org/10.3390/fire3010001

Fire Adapted Communities Learning Network. Resources website. Accessed April 2023. https://fireadaptednetwork.org/resources/

Florida Forest Service. Anatomy of a Prescribed Burn. https:// www.fdacs.gov/Forest-Wildfire/Wildland-Fire/Prescribed-Fire/ Anatomy-of-a-Prescribed-Burn

Gooley, Tristin. 2021. *The Secret World of Weather.* The Experiment New York.

Grossiord, Charlotte, et.a. 2020. Plant responses to rising vapor pressure deficit. https://doi.org/10.1111/nph.16485

Grupenhoff, A., Molinar, N. Plant Community Response to Fuel Break Construction and Goat Grazing in a Southern California Scrubland. Fire Ecol 17, 28 (2021). Https://doi.org/10.1186/s42408-021-00114-3

Hewson, E.W., et.al. 1979. *A Handbook on the Use of Trees as an Indicator of Wind Power Potential Final Report.* Department of Atmosphere Sciences, Oregon State University & the US Department of Energy.

Hood, Sharon, et.al. 2021. Bark Beetle and Fire Interactions in Western Coniferous Forests: Research Findings. U.S. Forest Service. https://www.fs.usda.gov/psw/publications/fettig/psw_2021_fettig006.pdf

iNaturalist website. California Fire Followers. California Academy of Sciences and the National Geographic Society. https:// www.inaturalist.org/projects/california-fire-followers-2021

Inciweb, The Incident Information System. Wildfire Information. https://inciweb.nwcg.gov/

Joint Fire Science Program. Fire Regime and Fire Frequency. https://www.firescience.gov/projects/09-2-01-9/supdocs/09-2-01-9_Chapter_3_Fire_Regimes.pdf

Junghenn Noyes, Katherine. et.al. 2020. Wildfire Smoke Particle Properties and Evolution, From Space-Based Mulit-Angle Imaging II: The Williams Flat Fire during the FIREX-AQ Campaign. Remote Sense. 202, 12(22), 3823: https://doi.org/10.3390/rs12223823

Kenna, D., et.al. 2021. *Thermal Flight Performance Reveals Impacts of Warming on Bumblebee Foraging.* Functional Ecology, 35, 2508-2522.

Kearn, Faith. 2021. *Getting to the Heart of Science Communication: A Guide to Effective Engagement.* Island Press. Library of Congress Control Number: 2020944650.

Lareau, Nicholus P. et.al. 2022 Fire-Generated Tornado Vortices. American Meteorological Society. DOI: https://doi.org/10.1175/ BAMS-D-21-0199.1. Page(s): E1296–E1320

Mattila, Anniina L.K. 2015. *Thermal Biology of Flight in a Butterfly: Genotype, Flight Metabolism, and Environmental Conditions.* Ecology and Evolution/ Volume 5, Issue 23/ p. 5539-5551. https://doi.org/10.1002/ ece3.1758

Maynard, Trevor. 2013. Fire Interactions and Pulsation - Theoretical and Physical Modeling. University of California, Riverside. https://escholarship.org/uc/item/851832j6

McRae, Rick. 2009. Interpretation of Smoke Plumes poster. ACT Emergency Services Agency. NSW. http://www.highfirerisk.com.au/ tools/smoke.pdf

Meyer, Erik, et.al. 2022. *Exploring Ecoacoustic Trajectories in a Giant Sequoia Forest After Wildfire.* Frontiers. Remote Sens., Sec. Acoustic Remote Sensing. Volume 3. https://www.frontiersin.org/articles/10.3389/frsen.2022.837866/full

Montana State University. *After Wildfire Information, for Landowners Coping with the Aftermath of Wildfire.* Extension Agriculture and Natural Resources Program Bozeman, Montana. https://ucanr.edu/sites/fire/files/284912.pdf

Nagwa. 2023. *Lesson Worksheet: Shadows.* Website sourced March 2023. https://www.nagwa.com/en/workseets/980140349017/

Nummenmaa, Lauri, et.al. 2014. *Bodily Maps of Emotions.* Proc Natl Acad Sci USA. 111(2):646-51. DOI:10.1073/pnas. 1321664111. Epub 2013 Dec 30. PMID: 24379370; PMCID: PMC3896150.

National Aeronautics and Space Administration. *Fire Information for Resource Management (FIRMS)* https:// firms.modaps.eosdis.nasa.gov/map/ #d:24hrs;@0.0,0.0,3z and EOS Data Analytics Space Solutions for Earth Problems. https://eos.com/

National Fire Protection Association. *Preparing Homes for Wildfire* website. Accessed April 2023. https://www.nfpa.org/Public- Education/Fire-causes-and-risks/Wildfire/Preparing-homes-for- wildfire

National Oceanic and Atmospheric Administration. *What is a Fire Storm? SciJinks It's All About Weather.* Website sourced 2023. https://scijinks.gov/firestorm/

National Weather Service, National Aeronautics and Space Administration. *Air Pressure* website sourced 2022. Https//www.weather.gov/source/zhu/ZHU_Training_Page/winds/pressure_winds/Pressure.htm

National Weather Service, National Aeronautics and Space Administration. *Cloud Classification and Characteristics* website sourced 2021. https://www.weather.gov/lmk/cloud_classification

National Weather Service, National Aeronautics and Space Administration. *NASA's Globe Program—Sky Color and Sky Visibility Field Guide* sourced 2021. http://www.globe.gov/web/s-cool/home/observation-and-reporting/ sky-color

National Weather Service. National Oceanic and Atmospheric Administration. *Fire Weather Topics: "Dry" Thunderstorms* sourced 2023. https://www.weather.gov/abq/clifeature2021drythunderstorms

National Weather Service. National Oceanic and Atmospheric Administration. *Fire Weather* website sourced 2021. http:// www.weather.gov/fire/

National Weather Service. *North American Monsoon* website. Sourced April 2023. https://weather.gov/abq/northamericanmonsoon- intro.

National Weather Service. National Oceanic and Atmospheric Administration. *The Positive and Negative Side of Lightning* website sourced 2023. https://www.weather.gov/jetstream/positive

National Wildfire Coordinating Group. *Fire Behavior Field Reference Guide, Estimating Winds for Fire Behavior*. PMS 437 sourced 2021. https://www.nwcg.gov/publications/pms437

National Wildfire Coordinating Group. 2014. Fire Behavior Field Reference Guide PMS 437. Sourced March 2023. https:// www.nwcg.gov/publications/pms437

National Wildfire Coordinating Group. 2022. *Critical Fire Weather* (P.40) and *Important Winds for Interpreting Forecasts* (P.41) in the *Incident Response Pocket Guid*e (IRPG) PMS 461. NFES 001077. https:// www.nwcg.gov/sites/default/files/publications/pms461.pdf

National Wildfire Coordinating Group. NWCG *National Fire Situational Awareness map*. https://maps.nwcg.gov/sa/#/?/?/ 39.8212/-94.558/6

National Wildfire Coordinating Group. 2016. *Guide to Wildland Fire Origin and Cause Determination.*

PMS 412 NFES 1874. https:// www.nwcg.gov/sites/default/files/publications/pms412.pdf

National Wildfire Coordinating Group. *Fire Season Climatology* webpage. Sourced March 2023. https://www.nwcg.gov/publications/ pms437/weather/fire-season-climatology

NOAA National Centers for Environmental Information Climate at a Glance. https://www.ncei.noaa.gov/access/monitoring/climate-at- a-glance/

NOAA JSTAR Mapper. Landsat Enhanced Vegetation Index (EVI) and Normalized Difference Vegetation Index (NDVI). https:// www.star.nesdis.noaa.gov/jpss/mapper/#zoom=4/date=2023Jul06/ lat=39.5/lon=-98.4/tcon=true/granon=false/bordon=true/view=asc/ l1on=false/satval1=N20/sensval1=Land/prodval1=frpi/ levval1=null/op1=1/l2on=false/satval2=N20/sensval2=Land/ prodval2=frpi/levval2=null/op2=1/l3on=false/satval3=N20/sensval3=Land/prodval3=frpi/levval3=null/op3=1

North American Tree-Ring Fire Scar Network. U.S. Geological Survey website. https://www.usgs.gov/programs/climate-research- and-development-program/news/north-american-tree-ring-fire-scar-network

Pacific Northwest Extension, Oregon State University. 2006. *Fire- resistant Plants For Home Landscapes-Selecting plants that may reduce your risk from wildfire.* PNW 590. August 2006. https://catalog.extension.oregonstate.edu/pnw590

Pollet, Jolie and Brown, Annie. 2007. Fuel Moisture Sampling Guide. Bureau of Land Management Utah State Office. https:// www.wfas.net/nfmd/references/fmg.pdf

PRISM Climate Group, Oregon State University. https:// prism.oregonstate.edu

Pretor-Piney, Gavin. 2006. *The Cloud Spotter's Guide*. Perigee Books. Hodder & Stoughton/Scepter edition / April 2006. ISBN: 978-1-101-20331-6

Scott, Jon H, Burgan, Robert E. 2005. *Standard Fire Behavior Fuel Models: A Comprehensive Set for Use With Rothermel's Surface Fire Spread Mode*. USDA Forest Service, Rocky Mountain Research Station General Technical Report RMRS-GTR-153. https://www.fs.usda.gov/rm/pubs_series/rmrs/gtr/rmrs_gtr153.pdf

SmokeyBear.com. *Now More Than Ever We Need to Prevent Wildfires*. https://www.smokeybear.com/

Sunwoo, Yujin, et.al. 2006. *Physiological and Subjective Responses to Low Relative Humidity*. Journal of Physiology Anthropology Online ISSN: 1880-6805. https://doi.org/10.2114/jpa2.25.7

Sugihara, et.al. 2006. *Fire in California Ecosystems*. University of California Press, Oakland, California. The Regents of the University of California. ISBN-13 948-0-520-24605-8

Tardist, L., et.al. 2018. *Foliage Motion Under Wind, from Leaf Flutter to Branch Buffering*. J.R. Soc. Interface 15: 20180010. http://dx.doi.org/ 10.1098/rsif.2018.0010

The Central Intelligence Agency's (CIA) *Psychology of Intelligence Analysis* (Heuer 1999)

United States Environmental Protection Agency. *Ecoregions* website. https://www.epa.gov/eco-research/ ecoregions#:~:text=Ecoregions are identified by analyzing,use, wildlife, and hydrology.

USDA Prescribed Fire. 2020. *Cooperative Extension Prescribed Fire Prescriptions* website sourced 2022. http://prescribed-fire.extenstion.org/ fire/prescriptions/

U.S. Fire Administration. *Protecting Structures From Wildfire Embers and Fire Exposures*. Article posted Sept. 1, 2022. https:// www.usfa.fema.gov/blog/ci-090122.html

US Forest Service *Fire Weather Handbook* 360. 2019. U.S. Department of Agriculture—Forest Service.

U.S. Forest Service. 2010. *Field Guide For Mapping Post-Fire Soil Severity*. United States Department of Agriculture. Rocky Mountain Research Station. General Technical Report RMRS-GTR-243. https://www.fs.usda.gov/rm/pubs/rmrs_gtr243.pdf

U.S. Forest Service, U.S. Department of Agriculture. *Fire Effects Information System (FEIS)* website. https://www.fs.usda.gov/ research/rmrs/products/dataandtools/tools/fire-effects-information- system-feis

U.S. Penology Network and *Nature's Notebook* website. https:// www.usanpn.org/natures_notebook

Urbanski, Shawn P. et.al. 2009. *Chemical Composition of Wildland Fire Emissions*. Forest Service, U.S. Department of Agriculture, Pacific Southwest Research Station. https://www.fs.usda.gov/research/treesearch/34249

Victoria Australia's Country Fire Authority (CFA) *Grassland Curing Guide*. https://www.cfa.vic.gov.au/ArticleDocuments/1481/grassland- curing-guide.pdf

Walker, Jeffrey. April 2009. *When Air is the Same as our Body, Why Do We Feel Hot?* Scientific America.

Ward, Gary and the National Weather Service. 2020. Meteorology101.com. *Types of Pressure Systems & Semi-Permanent Highs and Lows*. Sourced March 2023. https://meteorology101.com/ pressure-systems/

Weather Insurance Agency. *Rain Amount Guidelines* website. Sourced March 2023. https:// weatherins.com/rain-guidelines/

Weather Underground *Historical Weather* website. Sourced March 2023. https:// www.wunderground.com/history

Weather Spark— *The Weather Year Round Anywhere on Earth Climate Reports* with the weather by month, day, even hour. Great for event and trip planning! Sourced March 2020. https:// weatherspark.com/

Weather Spark website. *City Climate and Weather Data. Full Year.* https://weatherspark.com/

WIFIRE Fire Map—*Historical Fires* webpage. San Diego Supercomputer Center. UC San Diego Commons. https:// firemap.sdsc.edu/

Worldbuilding Stack Exchange. *How Far Can You See A Bonfire?* Website sourced 2022. https:// worldbuilding.stackexchange.com/ questions/206553/ how-far-away-can-you-see-a-bonfire

Wu, Yingchun.2012. *Novel Methods for Flame Pulsation Frequency Measurement with Image Analysis.* Fire Technology 48(2) DOI:10.1007/ s10694-011-0227-8. https://www.researchgate.net/ publication241040656_Novel_Methods_for_Flame_P ulsation_Frequency_Meas urement_with_Image_Analysis

Yedineck, Kara M. et.al. 2017. *Vegetation Effects on Impulsive Events in the Acoustic Signature of Fires.* Acoust Soc Am 141, 557– 562 (2017). https://doi.org/ 10.1121/1.4974199

Yocom LL, Fulé PZ, Brown PM, Cerano J, Villanueva-Díaz J, Falk DA, Cornejo-Oviedo E. *El Niño-southern oscillation effect on a fire regime in northeastern Mexico has changed over time.* Ecology. 2010 Jun;91(6):1660-71. doi: 10.1890/09-0845.1. PMID: 20583708

Acknowledgements

I owe much to my parents who rooted me in the forest soils of Northern California, where my dirty feet and fingers found deep meaning and purpose in nature. Without that grounding, I might never have pursued my career path as an environmental biologist and fire management specialist, finding passion in the challenging and dirty work that comes with fighting fires.

Credit is due to my mother for instilling in me the strong bones and brushes that have guided my skills and interests in art. Art has been my saving grace, the green shoots and colorful flowers that emerge when my heart and mind are darkened and scorched. Creating and admiring art is a profound and personal way to communicate and connect with the world.

I am grateful to the federal agencies—the U.S. Forest Service, U.S. Fish and Wildlife Service, and the Bureau of Land Management—for providing decades of training and experience in natural resource and fire management. Their cross-program training eventually led me into fire education.

Later in my career, I discovered nature journaling through the inspirational books and workshops of John Muir Laws. It began as a personal endeavor to reconnect with nature. After years of working in state and regional fire management positions, I felt adrift in a sea of shifting bureaucracies and landscapes. The enormity of fire management issues and the losses to communities shook my footing and focus. Exploring approaches and opportunities to journal about the fire environment, I became convinced that this approach could enhance our socioecological relationships and awareness of the fire environment.

I am also thankful for the many fire management specialists and education partners who have helped shape the pyrosketchology approach and guide. The first fire journaling workshop with the Klamath Prescribed Fire Training Exchange program in Northern California was pivotal in fostering intergenerational learning and integrating indigenous knowledge into fire journaling. Special thanks to Robin Lee Carlson (Author, Artist, and Nature Journaler), John Muir Laws (Author, Artist, and Nature Journaler), Laura Cunningham (Author, Artist and Nature Journaler) Jeremy Bailey (The Nature Conservancy), Bill Tripp (Karuk Tribe), Margo Robbins (Cultural Fire Management Council, Yurok Tribe), Frank Lake (US Forest Service, Yurok and Karuk Tribes), and Erika Terence and Will Harling (Mid Klamath Watershed Council). Virtual fire journaling workshops with the National Fire Learning Network, National Fire Adapted Communities Network, the International Association of Wildland Fire, and the Confluence Lab, with the University of Idaho, helped me refine information and approaches to pyrosketchology for both broad and specialized audiences.

Julie Tennis (Pacific Education Institute) and Kat Heim (Fire Adapted Methow Valley) have been amazing partners in bringing pyrosketchology approaches to grade school teachers and students in North-Central Washington. Calli-Jane West (Butte County Fire Safe Council) has been one of my strongest supporters and partners in creating trauma-informed fire journaling and prescribed fire

journaling workshops, and student/teacher curriculum, in Butte County, California, and coordinating local reviews of the pyrosketchology guide.

I want to extend a special thank you to Coleen Haskell for her meteorological expertise and review of my fire weather and fire seasons chapters and to Joy Colangelo (Author, Artist, and Nature Journaler) for self-publishing advice and editing support for this guide.

Lastly, but certainly not least, I am forever grateful to my Aunt Marian Kile for editing the many drafts of the pyrosketchology guide, and to my husband, Kipp Morrill, for giving me the gift of time and support to work full-time on writing and illustrating this guide.

I apologize if I have forgotten to mention some of the many supporters of pyrosketchology. This has been a four-year process, and I have been fortunate to receive input from people all around the world..

This illustration was commissioned for the Braiding Indigenous Knowledge and Western Science for Landscape Adaptation to Climate Change Report in 2023.

About the Author

Miriam Morrill is a consultant specializing in fire communication, education, nature journaling, and illustration. In 2020, she retired from her federal position as a State Fire Prevention, Mitigation, and Education Specialist in California. Throughout her career, she held various field, state, and regional positions across the western United States, including Forestry Technician/Firefighter, Wildlife Biologist, Soil, Water, and Air Specialist, Climate Change Adaptation Planner, and Public Affairs Specialist.

Miriam has contributed her expertise to numerous national and international fire response and training teams. Notable projects include fire prevention and investigation training in Jamaica and community wildfire protection planning in Micronesia, the Republic of Palau, and Guam. Since 2020, she has provided visual communication support to fire scientists across the United States, Canada, and the Netherlands, as well as the 2023 Global Fire Science Conference. She designed and led fire journaling workshops for the National Fire Learning Network, Fire Adapted Communities, and Fire Safe Councils, the Nature Conservancy's Prescribed Fire Training Exchange Program, and the International Association of Wildland Fire.

Combining her creative talents with 27 years of experience, Miriam has pioneered a new approach to fire education and community fire adaptation through the innovative Pyrosketchology program. For more information, visit her website at pyrosketchology.com.

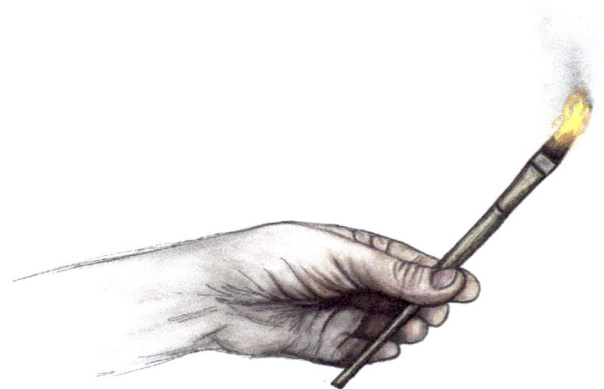

"It is an oft-repeated truth that we must all learn to live with wildfire in this time of climate instability, but how on earth do we start? Miriam Morrill has distilled a lifetime of scientific and artistic exploration into an immersive and practical guide for making fire awareness a part of our daily lives, in easily approachable steps. Based on the wisdom that resilience comes from being rooted deeply in a place, *Pyrosketchology* uses nature journaling to help us know our home places in all of their seasons and conditions and to comprehend when and how fire might impact us. Miriam's beautifully rendered illustrations and graphics are potent communication tools and I am captivated by the images of pages from her own nature journal.

I am thrilled to have this book at my fingertips for reference, but perhaps most importantly, I treasure it as inspiration to understand and find beauty in every aspect of the world around me."

—Robin Lee Carlson, author of *The Cold Canyon Fire Journals*

"I've called on Miriam's exceptional artistic talent time and time again to support the story of wildland fire in our science communication products. She has deep experience and a passionate understanding of the role of fire as a natural, restorative process on the landscape. Her work has played a key role in the excellence and success of story maps, guidebooks, educational presentations and more. I'm always in awe of her capacity as a creative, prolific artist and inspirational teacher."

—Marjie Brown, CEO, www.thefirewriters.com, United States

"This book is an amazing resource for anyone seeking to develop a deep understanding of wildfires. Throughout the pages, full of beautiful illustrations and detailed descriptions, Miriam skillfully introduces the transformative tools of observation and nature journaling. These are so important to enhance our sensemaking and situational awareness around fire. What I admire most about Miriam's work are the ways in which she connects the scientific, artistic, embodied and emotional dimensions of wildfire, thereby helping us build the much-needed holistic approach to wildfires."

—Isabeau Ottolini - Wildfire Social Scientist, Spain

"Miriam's creativity has been enhancing our community's wildfire safety knowledge for over 20 years. Her connection to the forest and wildfire safety sprouted from her upbringing in Concow, a fire-prone landscape which suffered catastrophic burns in 2008 and 2018. Long before these tragedies, Miriam was volunteering as a board member of the Butte County Fire Safe Council and sharing her passion with the community. We are grateful for her artistic skills, heart of a teacher, and deep understanding of the land."

—Calli-Jane West, Executive Advisor, Butte County Fire Safe Council

www.ingramcontent.com/pod-product-compliance
Lightning Source LLC
Chambersburg PA
CBHW042348030426
42335C300031B/3498